A Field Guide to the Classroom Library

A Field Guide to the Classroom Library F

Lucy Calkins

and

*The Teachers College
Reading and Writing
Project Community*

HEINEMANN
Portsmouth, NH

Heinemann

A division of Reed Elsevier Inc.
361 Hanover Street
Portsmouth, NH 03801–3912
www.heinemann.com

Offices and agents throughout the world

© 2002 by Teachers College, Columbia University

Library of Congress Cataloging-in-Publication Data
Calkins, Lucy McCormick.
    A field guide to the classroom library / Lucy Calkins and the Teachers
College Reading and Writing Project community.
        v. cm.
    Includes bibliographical references and index.
    Contents: [v. 6] Library F : grades 4–5
    ISBN 0-325-00500-1
    1. Reading (Elementary)—Handbooks, manuals, etc.   2. Children—Books and
reading—Handbooks, manuals, etc.   3. Children's literature—Study and teaching
(Elementary)—Handbooks, manuals, etc.   4. Classroom libraries—Handbooks,
manuals, etc.   I. Teachers College Reading and Writing Project (Columbia
University).   II. Title.
LB1573 .C183 2002
372.4—dc21   2002038767

Editor: Kate Montgomery
Production: Abigail M. Heim
Interior design: Catherine Hawkes, Cat & Mouse
Cover design: Jenny Jensen Greenleaf Graphic Design & Illustration
Manufacturing: Louise Richardson

Printed in the United States of America on acid-free paper

06   05   04   03   VP   5

This field guide is dedicated to

Kathy Doyle

The Field Guides to the Classroom Library *project is a philanthropic effort. According to the wishes of the scores of contributors, all royalties from the sale of these field guides will be given back entirely to the project in the continued effort to put powerful, beautiful, and thoughtfully chosen literature into the hands of children.*

Contents

Acknowledgments

The entire Teachers College Reading and Writing Project community has joined together in the spirit of a barn-raising to contribute to this gigantic effort to put the best of children's literature into the hands of children.

There are hundreds of people to thank. In these pages, I will only be able to give special thanks to a few of the many who made this work possible.

First, we thank Alan and Gail Levenstein who sponsored this effort with a generous personal gift and who helped us remember and hold tight to our mission. We are grateful to Annemarie Powers who worked tirelessly, launching the entire effort in all its many dimensions. Annemarie's passionate love of good literature shines throughout this project.

Kate Montgomery, now an editor at Heinemann and a long-time friend and coauthor, joined me in writing and revising literally hundreds of the field guides. Kate's deep social consciousness, knowledge of reading, and her commitment to children are evident throughout the work. How lucky we were that she became a full-time editor at Heinemann just when this project reached there, and was, therefore, able to guide the project's final stages.

Tasha Kalista coordinated the effort, bringing grace, humor, and an attention to detail to the project. She's been our home base, helping us all stay on track. Tasha has made sure loose ends were tied up, leads pursued, inquiries conducted, and she's woven a graceful tapestry out of all the thousands of books, guides, and people.

Each library is dedicated to a brilliant, passionate educator who took that particular library and the entire effort under her wing. We are thankful to Lynn Holcomb whose deep understanding of early reading informed our work; to Mary Ann Colbert who gave generously of her wisdom of reading recovery and primary texts; to Kathleen Tolan who championed the little chapter books and made us see them with new eyes; to Gaby Layden for her expertise in the area of nonfiction reading; to Isoke Nia for passionate contributions to our upper grade libraries; and to Kathy Doyle who knows books better than anyone we know.

We thank Pam Allyn for her dedication to this effort, Laurie Pessah for working behind the scenes with me, and Beth Neville for keeping the Project on course when this undertaking threatened to swamp us.

Finally, we are grateful to Mayor Guiliani for putting these libraries into every New York City school. To Judith Rizzo, Deputy Chancellor of Instruction, Adele Schroeter, Director of Office of Research, Development and Dissemination, Peter Heaney, Executive Director of the Division of Instructional Support, and William P. Casey, Chief Executive for Instructional Innovation, we also offer our heartfelt thanks for contributing their wisdom, integrity, and precious time to making this miracle happen.

Contributors

Christina Adams
Lisa Ali Chetram
Pam Allyn
Francine Almash
Janet Angelillo
Liz Arfin
Anna Arrigo
Laura Ascenzi-Moreno
Maureen Bilewich
Melissa Biondi
Pat Bleichman
Christine Bluestein
Ellen Braunstein
Dina Bruno
Theresa Burns
Lucy Calkins
Adele Cammarata
Joanne Capozzoli
Laura Cappadona
Justin Charlebois
Linda Chen
Mary Chiarella
Danielle Cione
Erica Cohen
Mary Ann Colbert
Kerri Conlon
Denise Corichi
Danielle Corrao
Sue Dalba
Linda Darro
Mildred De Stefano
Marisa DeChiara
Erica Denman
Claudia Diamond
Renee Dinnerstein
Kathy Doyle
Lizz Errico
Rosemarie Fabbricante
Gabriel Feldberg
Holly Fisher

Sofia Forgione
Judy Friedman
Elizabeth Fuchs
Jerilyn Ganz
Allison Gentile
Linda Gerstman
Jessica Goff
Iris Goldstein-
    Jackman
Ivy Green
Cathy Grimes
David Hackenburg
Amanda Hartman
Grace Heske
Caren Hinckley
Lynn Holcomb
Michelle Hornof
Anne Illardi
Maria Interlandi
Erin Jackman
Debbie Jaffe
Helen Jurios
Kim Kaiser
Tasha Kalista
Beth Kanner
Michele Kaye
Laurie Kemme
Hue Kha
Tara Krebs
Joan Kuntz Verdino
Kathleen Kurtz
Lamson Lam
Gaby Layden
Karen Liebowitz
Adele Long
Cynthia Lopez
Natalie Louis
Eileen Lynch
Theresa Maldarelli
Lucille Malka

Corinne Maracina
Jennifer Marmo
Paula Marron
Marjorie Martinelli
Esther Martinez
Debbie Matz
Teresa Maura
Leah Mermelstein
Melissa Miller
Kate Montgomery
Jessica Moss
Janice Motloenya
Marie Naples
Marcia Nass
Beth Neville
Silvana Ng
Isoke Nia
Jennie Nolan
    Buonocore
Lynn Norton Manna
Beth Nuremberg
Sharon Nurse
Liz O'Connell
Jacqueline O'Connor
Joanne Onolfi
Suzann Pallai
Shefali Parekh
Karen Perepeluk
Laurie Pessah
Jayne Piccola
Laura Polos
Annemarie Powers
Bethany Pray
Carol Puglisi
Alice Ressner
Marcy Rhatigan
Khrishmati Ridgeway
Lisa Ripperger
Barbara Rosenblum
Jennifer Ruggiero

Liz Rusch
Jennifer Ryan
Karen Salzberg
Elizabeth Sandoval
Carmen Santiago
Karen Scher
Adele Schroeter
Shanna Schwartz
India Scott
Marci Seidman
Rosie Silberman
Jessica Silver
Miles Skorpen
Joann Smith
Chandra Smith
Helene Sokol
Gail Wesson Spivey
Barbara Stavetski
Barbara Stavridis
Jean Stehle
Kathleen Stevens
Emma Suarez Baez
Michelle Sufrin
Jane Sullivan
Evelyn Summer
Eileen Tabasko
Patricia Tanzosh
Lyon Terry
Kathleen Tolan
Christine Topf
Joseph Turzo
Cheryl Tyler
Emily Veronese
Anne Marie Vira
Marilyn Walker
Gillan White
Alison Wolensky
Michelle Wolf
Eileen Wolfring

Introduction: What Is This Field Guide?

Lucy Calkins

When I was pregnant with my first-born son, the Teachers College Reading and Writing Project community organized a giant baby shower for me. Each person came with a carefully chosen book, inscribed with a message for baby Miles. Since then, we have commemorated birthdays, engagements, graduations, and good-byes by searching the world for exactly the right poem or picture book, novel or essay, and writing a letter to accompany it. Inside the letter, it says "This is why I chose this piece of literature precisely for you." In this same way, the book lists and the written guides that accompany them in this field guide have become our gift to you, the teachers of our nation's children. We have chosen, from all the books we have ever read, exactly the ones we think could start best in your classroom, and with these books, we have written notes that explain exactly why and how we think these texts will be so powerful in your children's hands.

The book lists and guides in this field guide are the Teachers College Reading and Writing Project's literacy gift to New York City and to the nation. When, two years ago, patrons Alan and Gail Levenstein came to us asking if there was one thing, above all others, which could further our work with teachers and children, we knew our answer in a heartbeat. We couldn't imagine anything more important than giving children the opportunity to trade, collect, talk over, and live by books. We want children to carry poems in their backpacks, to cry with Jess when he finds out that his friend Leslie has drowned, to explore tropical seas from the deck of a ship, to wonder at the life teeming in a drop of water. We want our children's heroes to include the wise and loving spider Charlotte, spinning her web to save the life of Wilbur, and the brave Atticus Finch.

We told the Levensteins that for teachers, as well as for children, there could be no finer gift than the gift of books for their students. We want teachers to be able to read magnificent stories aloud as the prelude to each school day, and to know the joy of putting exactly the right book in the hands of a child and adding, with a wink, "When you finish this book, there are more like it." We want teachers to create libraries with categories of books that peak their students' interests and match their children's passions, with one shelf for Light Sports Books and another shelf for Cousins of the Harry Potter books, one for Books That Make You Cry and another for You'll-Never-Believe-This Books. With this kind of a library, how much easier it becomes to teach children to read, to teach them what they need to become powerful, knowledgeable, literate people!

Even as we embarked on the effort to design magnificent classroom libraries, we knew that the best classroom library would always be the one assembled by a knowledgeable classroom teacher with his or her own students in mind. But, in so many cities, twenty new teachers may arrive in a school in a single year, having had no opportunity to learn about children's books at all. Even though some teachers have studied children's books, they may not be the ones given the opportunity to purchase books. Or, too often, there is no time to make book selections carefully—funds are discovered ten minutes before they must be spent or be taken from the budget. For these situations, we knew it would be enormously helpful to have lists and arrangements of recommended books for classroom libraries. Even without these worries, we all know the value of receiving book recommendations from friends. And so, our commitment to the project grew.

Our plan became this: We'd rally the entire Project community around a gigantic, two-year-long effort to design state-of-the-art classroom libraries and guides, exactly tailored to the classrooms we know so well. Simultaneously, we'd begin working with political, educational, and philanthropic leaders in hopes that individuals or corporations might adopt a school (or a corridor of classrooms) and create in these schools and classrooms the libraries of our dreams. Sharing our enthusiasm, colleagues at the New York City Board of Education proposed that idea to the mayor. Two years later, that dream has come true—In his January 2001 state of the city address, Mayor Giuliani promised $31.5 million of support to put a lending library in every New York City classroom, kindergarten through eighth grade.

Hearing this pronouncement, educational leaders from around the city joined with us in our philanthropic effort. People from the New York City Board of Education reviewed the lists and added suggestions and revisions. The Robin Hood Foundation, which had already been involved in a parallel effort to develop *school* libraries, contributed their knowledge. Readers from the Teachers Union and from the Office of Multicultural Education and of Early Childhood Education and of Literacy Education all joined in, coordinated by Peter Heaney, Executive Director of the Division of Instructional Support, and Adele Schroeter, Director of the Office of Research, Development and Dissemination. The book selections for the classroom libraries became even more carefully honed, and the written guides became richer still.

Over the past few months, boxes upon boxes of books have arrived across New York City, and in every classroom, children are pulling close to watch, big-eyed, as one exquisite, carefully chosen book after another is brought from the box and set on the shelf. Each teacher will receive between three and four hundred books. With most of these books, there will be a carefully crafted guide which says, "We chose this book because . . ." and "On page . . ." and "You'll notice that . . ." and "If you like this book, these are some others like it. . . . " I cannot promise that in every town and city across the nation the effort to put literature in the hands of students and guidance in the hands of their teachers will proceed so smoothly. But I'm hoping these book lists and these ready-made libraries bearing a stamp of approval will catch the eye of funders, of generous patrons, and of foresighted school leaders. And, every penny that comes to the authors from the sale of these field guides will go directly back into this project, directly back into our efforts to get more books into children's hands.

In the meantime, we needn't be idle. We'll comb through the book sales at libraries, and we'll write requests to publishers and companies. In a letter home to our children's parents, we might say, "Instead of sending in cupcakes to honor your child's birthday, I'm hoping you'll send a book. Enclosed is a list of suggestions." We can and will get books into our children's hands, by hook or by crook. And we can and will get the professional support we need for our reading instruction—our vitality and effectiveness as educators depend on it.

About the Books

When hundreds of teachers pool their knowledge of children's books as we have here, the resulting libraries are far richer than anything any one of us could have imagined on our own. We're proud as peacocks of these selections and of the accompanying literary insights and teaching ideas, and can't wait to share them both with teachers and children across the country. Here is a window into some of the crafting that has gone into the book selections:

- We suggest author studies in which the texts that students will study approximately match those they'll write and will inform their own work as authors.

- In upper-grade libraries, we include books that are relatively easy to read, but we have tried to ensure that they contain issues of concern to older children as well.

- We include books that might inform other books in the same library. For example, one library contains three books about dust storms, another contains a variety of books on spiders.

- We know that comprehension and interpretive thinking must be a part of reading from the very beginning, so we include easy to read books that can support thoughtful responses.

- We try to match character ages with student ages, approximately. For example, we have put the book in which Ramona is five in the library we anticipate will be for kindergartners, and put fourth-grade Ramona in the library we anticipate will be for fourth graders.

- We include complementary stories together when possible. For example, Ringgold's *Tar Beach* and Dorros' *Abuela* appear in the same library, anticipating that readers will recognize these as parallel stories in which the narrator has an imagined trip.

- We have never assumed that books in a series are all of the same level. For example, we have determined that some of the *Frog and Toad* books are more challenging, and this is indicated in our libraries.

- We understand that books in a series cannot always be easily read out of sequence. Because we know the *Magic Treehouse* series is best read in a particular sequence, for example, we have been careful with regard to the books we select out of that series.

- We selected our libraries to reflect multicultural values and bring forth characters of many different backgrounds and lives.

■ We try to steer clear of books that will not meet with general public approval. We do not believe in censorship, but we do believe that books purchased en masse should not bring storms of criticism upon the unsuspecting teacher.

At the same time that we are proud of the work we've done, we also know that there are countless magnificent books we have omitted and countless helpful and obvious teaching moves we have missed. We are certain that there are authors' names we have inadvertently misspelled, opinions expressed with which we don't all agree, levels assigned that perhaps should be different, and so on. We consider this work to be a letter to a friend and a work in progress, and we are rushing it to you, eager for a response. We are hoping that when you come across areas that need more attention, when you get a bright idea about a guide or booklist, that you will write back to us. We have tried to make this as easy as possible for you to do—just go to our website and contact us!

Choosing the Library for Your Class

We have created seven libraries for kindergarten through sixth grade classrooms. The libraries are each assigned a letter name (A–G) rather than a grade-level in recognition of the fact that the teacher of one class of fourth graders might find that Library D is suited to her students, and another fourth grade teacher might opt for Library E or Library F.

In order to determine which classroom library is most appropriate for a particular class in a particular school, teachers need to determine the approximate reading levels of their students in November, after the teachers have had some time to assess their students as readers. Teachers can compare the book the middle-of-the-class reader tends to be reading with the books we note for each level, and choose the library that corresponds to that average text level. More detail follows this general description. In shorthand, however, the following equivalencies apply:

Library **A** is usually Kindergarten
Library **B** is usually K or 1st grade
Library **C** is usually 1st or 2nd grade
Library **D** is usually 2nd or 3rd grade
Library **E** is usually 3rd or 4th grade
Library **F** is usually 4th or 5th grade
Library **G** is usually 5th or 6th grade

The system of saying, "If in November, your children are reading books like these," usually doesn't work for kindergarten children. Instead, we say Library A is suitable if, in November, the average student cannot yet do a rich, story-like, emergent (or pretend) reading of a familiar storybook, nor can this child write using enough initial and final consonants that an adult can "read" the child's writing.

It is important to note that all of the books in any given library are not at the same level of difficulty. Instead, we have created a mix of levels that tend to represent the mixed levels of ability of readers in the classes we have studied. The composition of the libraries, by level, is described on pages xlvii–lvi.

Once you have chosen the library that best corresponds to the average level of your students as readers, you will need to decide which components of the library best suit your curriculum. Each library is divided into components—a core and some modules. The core is the group of books in the library we regard as essential. Each library also contains six modules, each representing a category of books. For example, in each library there is a module of nonfiction books, and in the upper-grade libraries there are modules containing five copies each of ten books we recommend for book clubs. Each module contains approximately fifty titles. The exact quantity from module to module varies slightly because we have tried to keep the cost of each module approximately equal. This means, for example, that the nonfiction module that contains more hardcover books has fewer books overall.

There are a variety of ways to assemble a library. Some teachers will want to purchase the entire library—the core plus the six modules. Sometimes, teachers on the same grade level in a school each purchase the same core but different modules, so a greater variety of books will be available across the hall for their students. In New York City, teachers automatically received the core of their library of choice, 150 books, and then could choose three of the six possible modules.

The Contents of Each Library

Researchers generally agree that a classroom should contain at least twenty books per child. Obviously, the number of books needs to be far greater than this in kindergarten and first grade classrooms, because books for beginning readers often contain fewer than 100 words and can generally only sustain a child's reading for a short while. We would have liked to recommend libraries of 750 titles but decided to select a smaller number of books, trusting that each teacher will have other books of his or her choice to supplement our recommendations.

Because we predict that every teacher will receive or buy the core of a library and only some teachers will receive any particular module, we tried to fill the core of the libraries with great books we couldn't imagine teaching, or living, without. Because we know children will borrow and swap books between classrooms, it is rare for books to be in the core of more than one library, even though some great books could easily belong there.

Usually, these classroom libraries include enough books from a particularly wonderful series to turn that series into a class rage, but the libraries frequently do not contain all the books in a series. Often, more books in the series are included in Modules One and Two, which always contain more books for independent reading, divided into the same levels as those in the core. Our expectation is that once readers have become engrossed in a series, teachers or parents can help them track down sequels in the school or public library.

Within the core of a library, we include about a dozen books of various genres that could be perfect for the teacher to read aloud to the class. These are all tried-and-true read aloud books; each title on the read-aloud list is one that countless teachers have found will create rapt listeners and generate rich conversation.

In every library we have included nonfiction books. They were not chosen to support particular social studies or science units; that would be a different and admirable goal. Instead, our team members have searched for nonfiction texts that captivate readers, and we imagine them being read within the reading workshop. The nonfiction books were chosen either because their topics are generally high-interest ones for children (animals, yo-yo tricks, faraway lands, disgusting animals), or because they represent the best of their genre.

Each library contains about fifteen books that could be splendid mentor texts for young writers. That is, they contain writing that students could emulate and learn from easily since it is somewhat like the writing they are generally able to create themselves.

In each core library, an assortment of other categories is included. These differ somewhat from one library to another. Libraries D and E, for example, contain many early chapter books, but since it is also crucial for children at this level to read the richest picture books imaginable, the core contains a score of carefully chosen picture books. Some cores also contain a set of books perfect for an author study. The categories are indicated on the book lists themselves, and under "Teaching Uses" in the guides.

The vast majority of books in each library are single copies, chosen in hopes that they will be passed eagerly from one reader to another. The challenge was not to find the number of books representing a particular level, but instead to select irresistible books. The chosen books have been field tested in dozens of New York City classrooms, and they've emerged as favorites for teachers and children alike.

The few books that have been selected in duplicate are ones we regard as particularly worthwhile to talk over with a partner. We would have loved to suggest duplicate copies be available for half the books in each library—if libraries had more duplicates, this would allow two readers to move simultaneously through a book, meeting in partnerships to talk and think about the chapters they've read. The duplicate copies would allow readers to have deeper and more text-specific book talks, while growing and researching theories as they read with each other. Duplicates also help books gain social clout in a classroom—allowing the enthusiasm of several readers to urge even more readers to pick the book up. If teachers are looking for ways to supplement these libraries, buying some duplicate copies would be a perfect way to start.

Many of the libraries contain a very small number of multiple (four or five) copies of books intended for use in guided reading and strategy lessons. Once children are reading chapter books, we find teachers are wise to help children into a new series by pulling together a group of four readers, introducing the text, and guiding their early reading. Teachers may also want to offer extra support to children as they read the second book in a series, and so we suggest having a duplicate of this next book as well, so that each child can read it with a partner, meeting to retell and discuss it.

The Levels Within the Libraries

We've leveled many, but purposely not all, of the books in every classroom library. The fact that we have leveled these books doesn't mean that teachers should necessarily convey all of these levels to children. We expect teachers will often make these levels visible on less than half of their books (through the use of colored tabs), giving readers the responsibility of choosing appropriate books for themselves by judging unmarked books against the template of leveled books. "This book looks a lot like the green dot books that have been just-right for me, so I'll give it a try and see if I have a smooth read," a reader might say. It is important that kids learn to navigate different levels of difficulty within a classroom library on their own or with only minimal support from a teacher.

We do not imagine a classroom lending library that is divided into levels as discrete as the levels established by Reading Recovery© or by Gay Su Pinnell and Irene Fountas' book, *Guided Reading: Good First Teaching for All Children* (Heinemann, 1996). These levels were designed for either one-to-one tutorials or intensive, small group guided reading sessions, and in both of these situations a vigilant teacher is present to constantly shepherd children along toward more challenging books. If a classroom lending library is divided into micro-levels and each child's entire independent reading life is slotted into a micro-level, some children might languish at a particular level, and many youngsters might not receive the opportunities to read across a healthy range of somewhat-easier and somewhat-harder books. Most worrisome of all, because we imagine children working often with reading partners who "like to read the same kinds of books as you do," classroom libraries that contain ten micro-levels (instead of say, five more general levels) could inadvertently convey the message that many *children* as well as many *books* were off-limits as partners to particular readers.

There are benefits to micro-levels, however, and therefore within a difficulty level (or a color-dot), some teachers might ascribe a plus sign to certain books, signifying that this book is one of the harder ones at this level. Teachers can then tell a child who is new to a level to steer clear of the books with plus signs, or to be sure that he or she receives a book introduction before tackling a book with this marker.

When assigning books to levels, we have tried to research the difficulty levels that others have given to each text and we have included these levels in our guides. Fairly frequently, however, our close study of a particular text has led us to differ somewhat from the assessments others have made. Of course leveling books is and always will be a subjective and flawed process; and therefore teachers everywhere *should* deviate from assigned levels, ours and others, when confident of their rationale, or when particularly knowledgeable about a reader. You can turn to the tables at the back of this section, on pages xxvii–lx, to learn more about our leveling system.

Building the Libraries

When we started this project two years ago, we initiated some intensive study groups, each designed to investigate a different terrain in children's literature. Soon, a group led by Lynn Holcomb, one of the first Reading Recovery teachers in Connecticut, was working to select books for a K–1 library. Members of this group also learned from Barbara Peterson, author of *Literary Pathways: Selecting Books to Support New Readers* (Heinemann, 2001), who conducted groundbreaking research at Ohio State University, examining how readers actually experience levels of text complexity. The group also learned from Gay Su Pinnell, well-known scholar of literacy education and coauthor with Irene Fountas of many books including *Guided Reading*. Of course, the group learned especially from intensive work with children in classrooms. The group searched for books that:

- Represent a diverse range of shapes, sizes, authors, and language patterns as possible. The committee went to lengths to be sure that when taken as a whole, primary-level libraries looked more like libraries full of real books than like kits full of "teaching materials."

- Use unstilted language. A book that reads, "Come, Spot. Come, Spot, come," generally would not be selected.

- Contain many high frequency words. If one book contained just one word on a page ("Scissors/paste/paper/etc.") and another book contained the reoccurring refrain of "I see the scissors./ I see the paste." we selected the second option.

- Carry meaning and were written to communicate content with a reader. If the book would probably generate a conversation or spark an insight, it was more apt to be included than one that generally left a reader feeling flat and finished with the book.

- Represent the diversity of people in our world and convey valuable messages about the human spirit.

A second group, under the leadership of Kathleen Tolan, an experienced teacher and staff developer, spent thousands of hours studying early chapter books and the children who read them. This group pored over series, asking questions: Is each book in the series equally difficult? Which series act as good precursors for other series? Do the books in the series make up one continuous story, or can each book stand alone? What are the special demands placed on readers of this series?

Yet another group, led by Gaby Layden, staff developer at the Project, studied nonfiction books to determine which might be included in a balanced, independent reading library. The group studied levels of difficulty in nonfiction books, and found authors and texts that deserved special attention. Carefully, they chose books for teachers to demonstrate and for children to practice working through the special challenges of nonfiction reading.

Meanwhile, renowned teacher-educator Isoke Nia, teacher extraordinaire Kathy Doyle, and their team of educators dove into the search for the very best chapter books available for upper-grade readers. Isoke especially helped us select touchstone texts for writing workshops—books to help us teach children to craft their writing with style, care, and power.

Teacher, staff developer, and researcher Annemarie Powers worked full-time to ensure that our effort was informed by the related work of other groups across the city and nation. We pored over bibliographies and met with librarians and literature professors. We searched for particular kinds of books: books featuring Latino children, anthologies of short stories, Level A and B books which looked and sounded like literature. We researched the class-rooms in our region that are especially famous for their classroom libraries, and took note of the most treasured books we found there. All of this infor-mation fed our work.

Reading Instruction and the Classroom Library: An Introduction to Workshop Structures

These classroom libraries have been developed with the expectation that they will be the centerpiece of reading instruction. When I ask teachers what they are really after in the teaching of reading, many answer, as I do, "I want chil-dren to be lifelong readers. I cannot imagine anything more important than helping children grow up able to read and loving to read. I want students to initiate reading in their own lives, for their own purposes."

There is, of course, no one best way to teach reading so that children become lifelong readers. One of the most straightforward ways to do this is to embrace the age-old, widely shared belief that children benefit from daily opportunities to read books they choose for their own purposes and pleasures (Krashen 1993, Atwell 1987, Cambourne 1993, Smith 1985, Meek 1988).

More and more, however, we've come to realize that students benefit not only from opportunities to read, read, read, but also from instruction that responds to what students do when they are given opportunities to read. I have described the reading workshop in my latest publication, *The Art of Teaching Reading* (Calkins 2001). The reading workshop is an instructional format in which children are given long chunks of time in which to read appropriate texts, and also given explicit and direct instruction. Teachers who come from a writing workshop background may find it helpful to structure the reading workshop in ways that parallel the writing workshop so that chil-dren learn simultaneously to work productively inside each of the two con-gruent structures. Whatever a teacher decides, it is important that the structures of a reading workshop are clear and predictable so that children know how to carry on with some independence, and so that teachers are able to assess and coach individuals as well as partnerships and small groups.

Many teachers begin a reading workshop by pulling students together for a minilesson lasting about eight minutes (unless the read aloud is, for that day, incorporated into the minilesson, which then adds at least twenty min-utes). Children then bring their reading bins, holding the books they are currently reading, to their assigned "reading nooks." As children read inde-pendently, a teacher moves among them, conferring individually with a child or bringing a small group of readers together for a ten- to fifteen-minute guided reading or strategy lesson. After children have read independently for about half an hour, teachers ask them to meet with their partners to talk about their books and their reading. After the partners meet, teachers often call all the readers in a class together for a brief "share session" (Calkins 2001). The following table shows some general guidelines for the length of both inde-pendent reading and the partnership talks based on the approximate level of the texts students are reading in the class.

How Long Might a Class Have Independent Reading and Partnership Talk?		
Class Reading Level	*Independent Reading Duration*	*Partnership Talk Duration*
Library A	10 minutes	20 minutes
Library B	15 minutes	20 minutes
Library C	20 minutes	20 minutes
Library D	30 minutes	10 minutes
Library E	40 minutes	10 minutes
Library F	40 minutes	10 minutes
Library G	40 minutes	10 minutes

Periodically, the structure of the minilesson, independent reading, partnership, and then share time is replaced by a structure built around book clubs or "junior" book clubs, our own, reading-intensive version of reading centers.

Minilessons

During a minilesson, the class gathers on the carpet to learn a strategy all readers can use not only during the independent reading workshop but also throughout their reading lives. The content of a minilesson comes, in part, from a teacher deciding that for a period of time, usually a month, he needs to focus his teaching on a particular aspect of reading. For example, many teachers begin the year by devoting a month to reading with stamina and understanding (Calkins 2001). During this unit, teachers might give several minilessons designed to help children choose books they can understand, and they might give others designed to help readers sustain their reading over time. Another minilesson might be designed to help readers make more time for reading in their lives or to help them keep a stack of books-in-waiting to minimize the interval between finishing one book and starting another.

The minilesson, then, often directs the work readers do during independent reading. If the minilessons show students how to make sure their ideas are grounded in the details of the text, teachers may establish an interval between independent reading time and partnership conversations when children can prepare for a talk about their text by marking relevant sections that support their ideas.

Sometimes minilessons are self-standing, separate from the interactive read aloud. Other minilessons include and provide a frame for the day's read aloud. For example, the teacher may read aloud a book and direct that day's talk in a way that demonstrates the importance of thinking about a character's motivations. Then children may be asked to think in similar ways about their independent reading books. Perhaps, when they meet with a partner at the end of reading, the teacher will say, "Please talk about the motivations that drive your central characters and show evidence in the text to support your theories."

Conferences

While children read, a teacher confers. Usually this means that the teacher starts by sitting close to a child as he or she continues reading, watching for external behaviors that can help assess the child. After a moment or two, the teacher usually says, "Can I interrupt?" and conducts a few-minute-long conversation while continuing the assessment. A teacher will often ask, "Can you read to me a bit?" and this, too, informs any hunches about a child and his or her strengths and needs as a reader. Finally, teachers intervene to lift the level of what the child is doing. The following table offers some examples of this.

General Examples of the Conferring That Can Help Readers Grow	
If, in reading, the child is . . .	*Teachers might teach by . . .*
able to demonstrate a basic understanding of the text	nudging the child to grow deeper insights, perhaps by asking: ■ Do any pages (parts) go together in a surprising way? ■ Why do you think the author wrote this book? What is he (she) trying to say? ■ If you were to divide the book into different sections, what would they be? ■ How are you changing as a reader? How are you reading this book differently than you've read others? ■ What's the work you are doing as you read this?
talking mostly about the smallest, most recent details read	generalizing what kind of book it is, giving the child a larger sense of the genre. If it is a story, we can ask questions that will work for any story: ■ How is the main character changing? ■ How much time has gone by? ■ What is the setting for the story? If the text is a non-narrative, we could ask: ■ What are the main chunks (or sections) in the text? ■ How would you divide this up? ■ How do the parts of this text go together? ■ What do you think the author is trying to teach you?
clearly enthralled by the story	asking questions to help the reader tap into the best of this experience to use again later. ■ What do you think it is about this story that draws you in? ■ You seem really engaged, so I'm wondering what can you learn about this reading experience that might inform you as you read other books. ■ When I love a book, as you love this one, I sometimes find myself reading faster and faster, as if I'm trying to gulp it down. But a reading teacher once told me this quote. "Some people think a good book is one you can't put down, but me, I think a good book is one you must put down—to muse over, to question, to think about." Could you set some bookmarks throughout this book and use them to pause in those places to really think and even to write about this book? Make one of those places right now, would you?

Partnerships

When many of us imagine reading, we envision a solitary person curled up with a book. The truth is that reading is always social, always embedded in talk with others. If I think about the texts I am reading now in my life and ask myself, "Is there something *social* about my reading of those texts?" I quickly realize that I read texts because people have recommended them. I read anticipating conversations I will soon have with others, and I read noticing things in this one text that I have discussed with others. My reading, as is true for many readers, is multilayered and sharper because of the talk that surrounds it.

There are a lot of reasons to organize reading time so that children have opportunities to talk with a reading partner. Partner conversations can highlight the social elements of reading, making children enjoy reading more. Talking about books also helps children have more internal conversations (thoughts) as they read. Putting thoughts about texts out into the world by speaking them allows other readers to engage in conversation, in interpretations and ideas, and can push children to ground their ideas in the text, to revise their ideas, to lengthen and deepen their ideas.

For young children, talking with a partner usually doubles the actual unit of time a child spends working with books. In many primary classrooms, the whole class reads and then the teacher asks every child to meet with a partner who can read a similar level of book. Each child brings his bin of books, thus doubling the number of appropriate books available to any one child. The child who has already read a book talks about it with the other child, giving one partner a valuable and authentic reason to retell a book and another child an introduction to the book. Then the two readers discuss how they will read together. After the children read aloud together, the one book held between them as they sit hip to hip, there is always time for the partners to discuss the text. Sometimes, teachers offer students guidance in this conversation.

More proficient readers need a different sort of partnership because once a child can read short chapter books, there are few advantages to the child reading aloud often. Then too, by this time children can sustain reading longer. Typically in third grade, for example, individuals read independently for thirty minutes and then meet with partners for ten minutes to talk over the book. Again, the teacher often guides that conversation, sometimes by modeling—by entertaining with the whole-class read-aloud text—the sort of conversations she expects readers will have in their partnerships.

Book Clubs

Teaching children to read well has a great deal to do with teaching children to talk well about books, because the conversations children have in the air between one another become the conversations they have in their own minds as they read. Children who have talked in small groups about the role of the suitcase in Christopher Paul Curtis's book, *Bud, Not Buddy* will be far more apt to pause as they read another book, asking, "Might *this* object play a significant role in this book, like the suitcase did in *Bud, Not Buddy*?"

When we move children from partnership conversations toward small-group book clubs, we need to provide some scaffolding for them to lean on at first. This is because partnerships are generally easier for children to manage than small group conversations. It is also generally easier for students to read for thirty-minute reading sessions with ten-minute book talks than it is to read for a few days in a row and then sustain extended book talks, as they are expected to do in book clubs.

Children need some support as they begin clubs. One way to do this is to begin with small book club conversations about the read aloud book—the one book we know everyone will be prepared to talk about. Another way to get started with book clubs is for the teacher to suggest that children work in small groups to read multiple copies of, say, a mystery book. The teacher will plan to read a mystery book aloud to the class during the weeks they work in their clubs. Meanwhile, each group of approximately four readers will be reading one mystery that is at an appropriate level for them. The whole class works on and talks about the read-aloud mystery, and this work then guides the small group work. On one day, for example, after reading aloud the whole-class mystery, the teacher could immerse the class in talk about what it's like to read "suspiciously," suspecting everything and everyone. For a few days, the class can try that sort of reading as they listen to the read aloud. Meanwhile, when children disperse to their small groups to read their own mysteries, they can read these books "suspiciously."

Eventually the book clubs can become more independent. One small group of children might be reading several books by an author and talking about what they can learn from the vantage point of having read so many. Another group might read books that deal with a particular theme or subject. Either way, in the classrooms I know best, each book club lasts at least a few weeks. Teachers observe, and coach and teach into these talks, equipping kids with ways to write, talk, and think about texts. However, teachers neither dominate the clubs nor steer readers toward a particular preordained interpretation of a text. Instead, teachers steer readers toward ways of learning and thinking that can help them again and again, in reading after reading, throughout their lives.

Library ⒻContents Description

Library F consists of

I.	Independent Reading & Partner Reading			
	Chapter Books (Levels 9–12)	Level 9	54 Titles	63 Texts
		Level 10	77 Titles	90 Texts
		Level 11	66 Titles	80 Texts
		Level 12	46 Titles	50 Texts
	Nonfiction		58 Titles	58 Texts
	Picture Books		35 Titles	35 Texts
	Poetry		21 Titles	21 Texts
	Short Stories		12 Titles	12 Texts
II.	Guided Reading		8 Titles	32 Texts
III.	Book Club/Literature Circle		12 Titles	72 Texts
IV.	Author Study		10 Titles	20 Texts
V.	Read Alouds		9 Titles	9 Texts
VI.	Books to Support the Writing Process		4 Titles	4 Texts
Total Number of Texts in Library F			**412 Titles**	**546 Texts**

(Because of substitutions made in the ordering process, this number may not be precise.)

Group Description	Level	#	Author	Title	ISBN	Publisher	Quantity	Heinemann Write-Up
CORE								
Independent Reading		1	Clifton, Lucille	Three Wishes	440409217	Dell Publishing	1	
		2	Gantos, Jack	Heads or Tails	374429235	Farrar Strauss & Giroux	1	
	8	1	Kline, Suzy	Horrible Harry Series/ in Room 2B	140385525	Penguin Putnam	1	
		2	Kline, Suzy	Horrible Harry Series/the Kickball Wedding	141303166	Penguin Publishing	1	
		3	Turner, Ann	Dust for Dinner	6444225X	Harper Trophy	1	Y
	9	1	Betancourt, Jeanne	Pony Pals Series/The Blind Pony	59086632X	Scholastic Inc.	1	
		2	Bulla, Clyde Robert	Chalk Box Kid, The	590485237	Scholastic Inc.	1	Y
		3	Cameron, Ann	Gloria's Way	374326703	Farrar Strauss & Giroux	1	
		4	Christopher, Matt	Hard Drive to Short (Vol. 8)	316140716	Little Brown & Co	1	
		5	Christopher, Matt	Soccer Cat's Series/Hat Trick	316106690	Little Brown & Co	1	
		6	Clark, Margaret	Freedom Crossing	590445693	Scholastic Inc.	1	Y
		7	Cleary, Beverly	Henry Huggins	380709120	William Morrow & Co	1	Y
		8	Draper, Sharon Mills	Ziggy and the Black Dinosaurs	940975483	Just Us Books	1	
		9	Howe, James	There's a Dragon in my Sleeping Bag	689819226	Simon & Schuster	1	
		10	Kaplan, Howard	Waiting to Sing	789426153	DK Publishing	1	Y
		11	Kilborne, Sarah	Peach & Blue	679890955	Alfred A. Knopf	1	
		12	King-Smith, Dick	Mr. Potter's Pets	786812060	Hyperion Books	1	
		13	Levy, Elizabeth	Something Queer Series/at the Haunted School	440484618	Bantam Doubleday Dell	1	
		14	Marshall, James	Cut-ups, The	140506373	Penguin Putnam	1	
		15	Mead, Alice	Junebug	440412455	Bantam Doubleday Dell	1	
		16	Mead, Alice	Junebug and the Reverend	440415713	Bantam Doubleday Dell	1	Y

Group Description	Level	#	Author	Title	ISBN	Publisher	Quantity	Heinemann Write-Up
		17	Roy, Ron	A to Z Mysteries/Jaguar's Jewel (#10)	679894586	Random House	1	
		18	Sachar, Louis	Marvin Redpost: Super Fast, Out of Control	60618502X	Demco Media	1	
		19	Sachar, Louis	Sideways Stories from Wayside School	380698714	William Morrow & Co	1	
		20	Sinykin, Sheri Cooper	Magic Attic Club Series/Secret of the Attic	1575130017	Magic Attic Press	1	
		21	Walter, Mildred Pits	Justin & the Best Biscuits in the World	679803467	Alfred A. Knopf	1	Y
		22	Whelan, Gloria	Next Spring an Oriole	394891252	Random House	1	
	10	1	Blume, Judy	Fudge-a-Mania	440404908	Bantam Doubleday Dell	1	Y
		2	Brooks, Bruce	Everywhere	60207299	Harper Collins	1	Y
		3	Byars, Betsy	Blossom Promise, A	440401372	Bantam Doubleday Dell	1	Y
		4	Carlson, Natalie Savage	Family Under the Bridge, The	64402509	Harper Collins	1	Y
		5	Christopher, Matt	Basket Counts, The	316140767	Little Brown & Co	1	
		6	Giff, Patricia Reilly	Girl Who Knew it All	440428556	Bantam Doubleday Dell	1	Y
		7	Giff, Patricia Reilly	Poopsie Pomerantz, Pick Up . . .	440402875	Bantam Doubleday Dell	1	Y
		8	Hesse, Karen	Just Juice	590033832	Scholastic Inc.	1	
		9	Howe, James	Bunnicula	689838638	Simon & Schuster	1	Y
		10	Hurwitz, Johanna	Just Desserts Club, The	688162665	William Morrow & Co	1	Y
		11	King-Smith, Dick	Mouse Called Wolf, A	375800662	Alfred A. Knopf	1	
		12	Lewis, Maggie	Morgy Makes His Move	395922844	Houghton Mifflin	1	
		13	Mohr, Nicholasa	Felita	440412951	Bantam Doubleday Dell	1	Y
		14	Mohr, Nicholasa	Magic Shell, The	590471104	Scholastic Inc.	1	Y
		15	Park, Barbara	Skinnybones	394849884	Random House	1	Y
		16	Rockwell, Thomas	How to Eat Fried Worms	440445450	Dell Publishing	1	Y

Group Description	Level	#	Author	Title	ISBN	Publisher	Quantity	Heinemann Write-Up
		17	Sachar, Louis	Dogs Don't Tell Jokes	679833722	Alfred A. Knopf	1	
		18	Schultz, Irene	Good for Nothing Dog, The	780272382	Wright Group	1	
		19	Smith, Doris Buchanan	Taste of Blackberries, A	59033784X	Scholastic Inc.	1	Y
		20	Smith, Robert Kimmel	War with Grandpa, The	440492769	Bantam Doubleday Dell	1	Y
		21	Spinelli, Jerry	School Daze Series/Picklemania	590454471	Scholastic Inc.	1	
		22	Spinelli, Jerry	School Daze Series/Who Ran My Underwear Up the Flagpole?	590462784	Scholastic Inc.	1	
		23	Whelan, Gloria	Silver	394896114	Random House	1	
		24	Wilson, Nancy Hope	Old People, Frogs, and Albert	374456151	Farrar Strauss & Giroux	1	
	11	1	Baglio, Ben	Animal Ark Series/Kittten in the Cold (#13)	439096987	Scholastic Inc.	1	
		2	Bauer, Marion	On My Honor	440466334	Bantam Doubleday Dell	1	
		3	Belton, Sandra	Ernestine and Amanda Series/Summer Camp Ready or Not!	689808461	Simon & Schuster	1	
		4	Belton, Sandra	Ernestine and Amanda Series/Ernestine & Amanda (vol. 1)	68980847X	Simon & Schuster	1	
		5	Belton, Sandra	Ernestine and Amanda Series/Members of the C.L.U.B.	689816111	Simon & Schuster	1	
		6	Boyd, Candy Dawson	Forever Friends	140320776	Penguin Publishing	1	
		7	Bunting, Eve	Coffin on a Case	64404617	Harper Collins	1	
		8	Catling, Patrick Skene	Chocolate Touch, The	440412897	Bantam Doubleday Dell	1	Y
		9	Chocolate, Deborah Newton	Elizabeth's Wish, Vol. 2	940975459	Just Us Books	1	
		10	Conly, Jane Leslie	Crazy Lady!	64405710	Harper Trophy	1	
		11	Dahl, Roald	BFG, The	141301058	Penguin Publishing	1	Y
		12	Dahl, Roald	Matilda	141301066	Penguin Publishing	1	

Group Description	Level	#	Author	Title	ISBN	Publisher	Quantity	Heinemann Write-Up
		13	DiCamillo, Kate	Because of Winn Dixie	763607762	Candlewick Press	1	
		14	Eager, Edward	Half Magic	152020683	Harcourt Brace	1	Y
		15	Eager, Edward	Knight's Castle	15202073X	Harcourt Brace	1	
		16	Ellerbee, Linda	Get Real series/Girl Reporter Blows Lid Off Town	64407551	Harper Collins	1	
		17	Fletcher, Ralph	Flying Solo	395873231	Clarion Books	1	
		18	Gardiner, John Reynolds	Stone Fox	64401324	Harper Trophy	1	Y
		19	Hermes, Patricia	Mama, Let's Dance	316358614	Berkeley	1	
		20	Holt, Kimberly Willis	Mister and Me	698118693	Penguin Publishing	1	
		21	Hughes, Dean	Angel Park #01: Making the Team	679804269	Alfred A. Knopf	1	
		22	James, Mary	Shoebag	590430300	Scholastic Inc.	1	Y
		23	Naidoo, Beverley	Journey to Jo'burg	64402371	Harper Collins	1	Y
		24	Naylor, Phyllis Reynolds	Shiloh	440407524	Bantam Doubleday Dell	1	Y
		25	Paulsen, Gary	World of Adventure/Time Benders	440412145	Bantam Doubleday Dell	1	
		26	Paulsen, Gary	World of Adventure/Captive!	440410428	Bantam Doubleday Dell	1	
		27	Paulsen, Gary	World of Adventure/Thunder Valley	44041220X	Bantam Doubleday Dell	1	
		28	Robinson, Barbara	Best Christmas Pageant Ever, The	64402754	Harper Collins	1	Y
		29	Taylor, Mildred	Mississippi Bridge	141308176	Penguin Publishing	1	
		30	Tillage, Leon	Leon's Story	374343799	Farrar Strauss & Giroux	1	
	12	1	Brooks, Bruce	Wolfbay Wings/Woodsie (#1)	64405974	Harper Collins	1	
		2	Burnett, Frances	Secret Garden, The	590433466	Scholastic Inc.	1	Y
		3	Krumgold, Joseph	And Now Miguel	6440143X	Harper Collins	1	Y
		4	MacLachlan, Patricia	Arthur, for the Very First Time	64402886	Harper Trophy	1	Y
		5	McLean, Susan	Pennies for the Piper	374457549	Sunburst	1	Y
		6	Myers, A.	Red-Dirt Jesse	14038734X	Penguin Putnam	1	

Group Description	Level	#	Author	Title	ISBN	Publisher	Quantity	Heinemann Write-Up
		7	Paulsen, Gary	Boy Who Owned the School, The	440405246	Bantam Doubleday Dell	1	
		8	Paulsen, Gary	Voyage of the Frog, The	440403642	Bantam Doubleday Dell	1	Y
		9	Pinkwater, Jill	Tails of the Bronx	689716710	Simon & Schuster	1	
		10	Robinet, Harriette Gillem	Children of the Fire	689316550	Simon & Schuster	1	Y
		11	Rylant, Cynthia	Missing May	440408652	Bantam Doubleday Dell	1	Y
		12	Slote, Alfred	Finding Buck McHenry	64404692	Harper Collins	1	
		13	Spinelli, Jerry	Maniac Magee	64404242	Harper Trophy	1	Y
		14	Van Draanen, Wendelin	Sammy Keyes/and the Curse of Moustache Mary	375802657	Alfred A. Knopf	1	
		15	Van Draanen, Wendelin	Sammy Keyes/and the Hotel Thief	679892648	Alfred A. Knopf	1	Y
		16	Wilkinson, Brenda Scott	Definitely Cool	590438425	Scholastic Inc.	1	
		17	Wright, Betty	Christina's Ghost	590427091	Scholastic Inc.	1	
		18	Yep, Laurence	Ribbons	698116062	Putnam & Grosset	1	Y
	13	1	Coman, Carolyn	What Jamie Saw	140383352	Viking Penguin	1	Y
		2	Creech, Sharon	Walk Two Moons	64405176	Harper Trophy	1	Y
		3	Lowry, Lois	Number the Stars	440403278	Bantam Doubleday Dell	1	Y
	13; 14; 15	1	Filipovic, Zlata	Zlata's Diary	140242058	Penguin Putnam	1	Y
	14	1	Hautzig, Esther	Endless Steppe, The	6440577X	Harper Trophy	1	Y
		2	Holt, Kimberly Willis	When Zachary Beaver Came to Town	805061169	Henry Holt & Co	1	
		3	Jacques, Brian	Redwall	441005489	Penguin Putnam	1	Y
		4	Nye, Naomi Shihab	Habibi	689825234	Simon & Schuster	1	Y
Anthologies of Short Stories		1	Brooks, Bruce	Boys Will Be, Vol. 1	786810262	Hyperion Books	1	

Group Description	Level	#	Author	Title	ISBN	Publisher	Quantity	Heinemann Write-Up
		2	Davidson, Margaret	Five True Dog Stories	59042017	Scholastic Inc.	1	Y
		3	Davidson, Margaret	Five True Horse Stories	59042009	Scholastic Inc.	1	
		4	Soto, Gary	Baseball In April & Other Stories	152025677	Harcourt Brace	1	Y
Teaching Writing		1	Baylor, Byrd	Other Way to Listen, The	689810539	Simon & Schuster	1	Y
		2	Fox, Mem	Wilfrid Gordon McDonald Partridge	91629126X	Kane/Miller Book Publishers	1	Y
		3	Greenfield, Eloise	Childtimes: A Three-Generation Memoir	64461343	Harper Collins	1	Y
		4	MacLachlan, Patricia	Cassie Binegar	64401952	Harper Collins	1	
Picture Books		1	Aliki	Marianthe's Story: Painted Words & Spoken Memories (Double Book)	688156614	Greenwillow Books	1	Y
		2	Barnwell, Ysaye	No Mirrors in My Nana's House	152018255	Harcourt Brace	1	Y
		3	Blume, Judy	Pain and the Great One, The	440409675	Bantam Doubleday Dell	1	Y
		4	Cannon, Janell	Verdi	152010289	Harcourt Brace	1	Y
		5	Fleischman, Paul	Lost! A Story in String	805055835	Henry Holt & Co	1	Y
		6	Hurwitz, Johanna	New Shoes for Silvia	590487493	Scholastic Inc.	1	Y
		7	Krupp, Edwin	Rainbow and You, The	688156010	Harper Collins	1	Y
		8	McCully, Emily	Mirettte on the High Wire	698114434	Putnam & Grosset	1	Y
		9	Myers, Christopher	Fly!	786806524	Disney Press	1	
		10	Ray, Mary Lyn	Basket Moon	316735213	Little Brown & Co	1	Y
		11	Ringgold, Faith	Dinner at Aunt Connie's House	590137131	Scholastic Inc.	1	Y
		12	Steptoe, John	Daddy Is A Monster Sometimes	64430421	Harper Trophy	1	Y
		13	Wallace, Ian	Duncan's Way	78942679X	DK Publishing	1	Y
		14	Yolen, Jane	Letting Swift River Go	316968609	Little Brown & Co	1	Y
		15	Young, Ed	Lon Po Po	698113829	Penguin Putnam	1	Y
Poetry		1	Feelings, Tom	Soul Looks Back in Wonder	140565019	Penguin Putnam	1	Y

Group Description	Level	#	Author	Title	ISBN	Publisher	Quantity	Heinemann Write-Up
		2	Hopkins, Lee (selected)	Lives/Poems About Famous Americans	6027767X	Harper Collins	1	
		3	Hughes, Langston	Dream Keeper, The	679883479	Random House	1	Y
		4	Reyes, Carlos	Suitcase Full of Crows: Poems, A	1878325124	Bluestem Press/ UKansasEmporia	1	
		5	Westcott, Nadine Bernard, selector & illus.	Never Take a Pig to Lunch and Other Poems About the Fun of Eating	531070980	Orchard Books	1	
		6	Yolen, Jane	Sky Scrape/City Scape	1563971798	Wordsong	1	
Read-Aloud Texts		1	Coles, Robert	Story of Ruby Bridges	590572814	Scholastic Inc.	1	
		2	Curtis, Christopher Paul	Bud, Not Buddy	385323069	Delacorte Press	1	Y
		3	Hesse, Karen	Out of the Dust	590371258	Scholastic Inc.	1	
		4	Holman, Felice	Slake's Limbo	590455885	Scholastic Inc.	1	Y
		5	Lewis, C.S.	Chronicles of Narnia/Lion, the Witch and the Wardrobe	64409422	Harper Trophy	1	Y
		6	MacLachlan, Patricia	Journey	385304277	Bantam Doubleday Dell	1	Y
		7	McGovern, Ann	Secret Soldier, The	590430521	Scholastic Inc.	1	Y
		8	Park, Barbara	Mick Harte was Here	679870881	Alfred A. Knopf	1	Y
		9	Paterson, Katherine	Bridge to Terebithia	64401847	Harper Collins	1	Y
		10	Paterson, Katherine	Great Gilly Hopkins, The	64402010	Harper Trophy	1	Y
		11	Paulsen, Gary	Monument, The	385305184	Delacorte Press	1	Y
		12	Rylant, Cynthia	Appalachia	152016058	Harcourt Brace	1	Y
		13	Speare, Elizabeth George	Witch Of Blackbird Pond, The	440495962	Bantam Doubleday Dell	1	Y

MODULE 1: More Books for Independent Reading: Filling Out the Lower Portion of the Library

Group Description	Level	#	Author	Title	ISBN	Publisher	Quantity	Heinemann Write-Up
	8	1	Kline, Suzy	Horrible Harry Series/the Christmas Surprise	141301457	Penguin Publishing	1	Y

Group Description	Level	#	Author	Title	ISBN	Publisher	Quantity	Heinemann Write-Up
	9	1	Banks, Jacqueline Turner	New One, The	395666104	Houghton Mifflin	1	
		2	Bess, Clayton	Truth About the Moon, The	395643716	Clarion Books	1	
		3	Betancourt, Jeanne	Pony Pals Series/The Saddest Pony	590512951	Scholastic Inc.	1	
		4	Bledsoe, Lucy Jane	Big Bike Race, The	380728303	Avon Books	1	
		5	Bulla, Clyde Robert	My Friend the Monster	64403785	Harper Trophy	1	
		6	Bunting, Eve	Once Upon a Time	187845059X	Richard C. Owen Publishers	1	
		7	Burns, Marilyn	Spaghetti and Meatballs for All!: A Mathematical Story	590944592	Scholastic Inc.	1	
		8	Dahl, Roald	Magic Finger, The	141302291	Penguin Publishing	1	
		9	Dalgliesh, Alice	Courage of Sarah Noble, The	689715404	Simon & Schuster	1	
		10	Danziger, Paula	Amber Brown Series/Wants Extra Credit	590947168	Scholastic Inc.	1	
		11	Draper, Sharon Mills	Lost in the Tunnel of Time /Ziggy Series	940975637	Just Us Books	1	
		12	Draper, Sharon Mills	Shadows of Caesar's Creek /Ziggy Series	940975769	Just Us Books	1	
		13	Giff, Patricia Reilly	Ballet Slippers Series/Not-So-Perfect Rosie	141300604	Penguin Puffin	1	Y
		14	Herman, Charlotte	Max Malone Series/Makes a Million	805023283	Henry Holt & Co	1	
		15	Herman, Charlotte	Max Malone Series/the Great Cereal Ripoff	805018433	Henry Holt & Co	1	
		16	Jones, Rebecca	Matthew & Tilly	140556400	Penguin Publishing	1	
		17	Kim, A.L.	Qwan	1565655524	Lowell House	1	
		18	Kline, Suzy	Herbie Jones and the Class Gift	140327231	Penguin Publishing	1	
		19	Rose Blue	Quiet Place	531017737	Franklin Watts, Grolier	1	
		20	Smith, Janice Lee	Adam Joshua Capers Series/The Monster in the Third Dresser Drawer	64402231	Harper Collins	1	

Group Description	Level	#	Author	Title	ISBN	Publisher	Quantity	Heinemann Write-Up
		21	Smith, Janice Lee	Adam Joshua Capers Series/ The Superkid!	64420051	Harper Collins	1	
		22	Whelan, Gloria	Indian School	64420566	Harper Collins	1	
		23	Wilder, Laura Ingalls	Little House Books/Pioneer Sisters	64420469	Harper Collins	1	
		24	Wilder, Laura Ingalls	Little House Books/School Days	60271469	Harper Collins	1	Y
		25	Yolen, Jane	Piggins & the Royal Wedding	15261687X	Harcourt Brace	1	Y
		26	Yolen, Jane	Piggins Series, Picnic with Piggins	152615350	Harcourt Brace	1	Y
	10	1	Adler, David	Babe and I, The	152013784	Harcourt Brace	1	
		2	Byars, Betsy	Blossoms Meet the Vulture Lady, The	440406773	Bantam Doubleday Dell	1	
		3	Christopher, Matt	Comeback Challenge, The	316141526	Little Brown & Co	1	
		4	Dahl, Roald	Twits, The	141301074	Penguin Puffin	1	Y
		5	De Jong, Meindert & Maurice Sendak	Along Came A Dog	64401146	Harper Collins	1	
		6	Greene, Constance	Al's Blind Date	140341714	Penguin Publishing	1	
		7	Greene, Constance	Girl Called Al, A	140347860	Penguin Publishing	1	
		8	Gutman, Dan	Shortstop Who Knew Too Much	590137603	Scholastic Inc.	1	
		9	Howe, James	Bunnicula Strikes Again!	689814631	Simon & Schuster	1	
		10	Howe, James	Celery Stalks at Midnight, The	380690543	William Morrow & Co	1	
		11	Mathis, Sharon	Teacup Full of Roses	140323287	Penguin Puffin	1	
		12	Moore, Miriam	Koi's Python	786812273	Hyperion Books	1	
		13	Nye, Naomi Shihab	Come with Me	68815946X	Greenwillow Books	1	
		14	Osborne, Mary Pope	Spider Kane/Mystery Under the May-Apple	679808558	Random House	1	
		15	Rylant, Cynthia	Gooseberry Park	59094715X	Scholastic Inc.	1	Y
		16	Schultz, Irene	Fiji Flood, The	780272269	Wright Group	1	

MODULE 2: More Books for Independent Reading: Filling Out the Upper Portion of the Library

Group Description	Level	#	Author	Title	ISBN	Publisher	Quantity	Heinemann Write-Up
		1	Lowry, Lois	Rabble Starkey	440400562	Bantam Doubleday Dell	1	
	11	1	Baglio, Ben	Animal Ark Series/Owl in the Office (#11)	439084164	Scholastic Inc.	1	
		2	Bauer, Marion Dane	Taste of Smoke, A	440410347	Dell Publishing	1	
		3	DeClements, Barthe	Nothing's Fair in Fifth Grade	140344438	Penguin Putnam	1	
		4	Gutman, Dan	Honus and Me	380788780	Avon Books	1	
		5	Gutman, Dan	Kid Who Ran for President, The	590939882	Scholastic Inc.	1	
		6	Hahn, Mary D.	Doll in the Garden, The	380708655	William Morrow & Co	1	
		7	King-Smith, Dick	Three Terrible Trins	679885528	Alfred A. Knopf	1	
		8	Lawrence, Jacob	Harriet and the Promised Land	689809654	Simon & Schuster	1	
		9	Naylor, Phyllis Reynolds	Shiloh Season	689829310	Simon & Schuster	1	
		10	Park, Barbara	Don't Make Me Smile	394847458	Random House	1	
		11	Park, Barbara	Kid in the Red Jacket, The	394805712	Alfred A. Knopf	1	
		12	Park, Barbara	Maxie Rosie & Earl Partners in Grime/Geek Chronicles	679806431	Random House	1	
		13	Paulsen, Gary	Dunc's Doll	440406013	Bantam Doubleday Dell	1	
		14	Paulsen, Gary	Dunc's Halloween	440406595	Bantam Doubleday Dell	1	
		15	Scieszka, Jon	Time Warp Trio Series/2095	59010439X	Scholastic Inc.	1	
		16	Simon, Seymour	Einstein Anderson Series/Science Sleuth	440848490	Scholastic Inc.	1	Y
		17	Skolsky, Mindy	You're the Best, Hannah!	64408469	Harper Trophy	1	
		18	Soto, Gary	Summer Life, A	440210240	Bantam Doubleday Dell	1	
		19	Taylor, Mildred	Song of the Trees	440413966	Penguin Publishing	1	
		20	Taylor, Mildred	Well, The	140386424	Penguin Publishing	1	
		21	Tillage, Leon	Leon's Story	374343799	Farrar Strauss & Giroux	1	

Group Description	Level	#	Author	Title	ISBN	Publisher	Quantity	Heinemann Write-Up
		22	Weeks, Sarah	Regular Guy	64407829	Harper Trophy	1	
		23	White, E.B.	Charlotte's Web	64400557	Harper Collins	1	
		24	Yep, Laurence	Case of the Goblin Pearls, The	64405524	Harper Collins	1	
	12	1	Atwater, Richard	Mr. Popper's Penguins	590477331	Little Brown & Co	1	Y
		2	Byars, Betsy	Burning Questions of Bingo Brown, The	140324798	Penguin Putnam	1	
		3	Byars, Betsy	Summer of the Swans, The	140314202	Penguin Putnam	1	
		4	Collier, James Lincoln	War Comes to Willy Freeman	440495040	Bantam Doubleday Dell	1	
		5	Danziger, Paula	Snail Mail No More	439063361	Scholastic Inc.	1	
		6	Duffey, Betsy	Utterly Yours, Booker Jones	140374965	Viking Penguin	1	
		7	Fenner, Carol	Yolanda's Genius	689813279	Simon & Schuster	1	Y
		8	Garfield, James	Follow My Leader	140364854	Penguin Putnam	1	
		9	George, Jean Craighead	Who Really Killed Cock Robin?	64404056	Harper Trophy	1	Y
		10	Lowry, Lois	Anastasia Again!	440400090	Dell Publishing	1	
		11	McKissack, Patricia	Color Me Dark	590511599	Scholastic Inc.	1	
		12	O'Connor, Barbara	Beethoven in Paradise	374405883	Farrar Strauss & Giroux	1	
		13	Paterson, Katherine	Sign of the Chrysanthemum, The	64402320	Harper Trophy	1	
		14	Peck, Robert	Soup and Me	394931572	Alfred A. Knopf	1	
		15	Skolsky, Mindy	Welcome to the Grand View, Hannah!	64407853	Harper Trophy	1	
		16	Smith, Robert Kimmel	Bobby Baseball	440404177	Bantam Doubleday Dell	1	
		17	Spinelli, Jerry	Knots in My Yo-yo String: The Autobiography of a Kid	439162203	Scholastic Inc.	1	
		18	Van Draanen, Wendelin	Sammy Keyes/and the Runaway Elf	37580255X	Alfred A. Knopf	1	
		19	White, Ruth	Belle Prater's Boy	440413729	Bantam Doubleday Dell	1	

Group Description	Level	#	Author	Title	ISBN	Publisher	Quantity	Heinemann Write-Up
		20	Wilkinson, Brenda Scott	Ludell and Willie	60264888	Harper Collins	1	
		21	Wright, Betty	Dollhouse Murders, The	590434616	Scholastic Inc.	1	
	13	1	de Angeli, Marguerite	Door in the Wall, The	440227798	Bantam Doubleday Dell	1	Y
		2	Freedman, Russell	Indian Winter, An	590480707	Scholastic Inc.	1	

MODULE 3: Multiple Copies of Books for Small Group Work

Group Description	Level	#	Author	Title	ISBN	Publisher	Quantity	Heinemann Write-Up
	9	1	Hesse, Karen	Sable	805057722	Henry Holt & Co	4	
		2	Preller, James	Jigsaw Jones Mystery/Case of Hermie the Missing Hampster	59069252	Scholastic Inc.	4	
	10	1	Spinelli, Jerry	School Daze Series/Report to the Principal's Office	590462776	Scholastic Inc.	4	
		2	Wagner, Jane	J.T.	440442753	Bantam Doubleday Dell	4	Y
	13	1	Avi	Ragweed	380801671	Harper Trophy	4	Y
		2	Clements, Andrew	Landry News, The	689828683	Simon & Schuster	4	
		3	Hinton, S.E.	That was Then, This is Now	140389660	Viking Penguin	4	
	14	1	Avi	True Confessions of Charlotte Doyle, The	380714752	William Morrow & Co	4	
		2	Berry, James	Ajeemah and His Son	64405230	Harper Collins	4	

MODULE 4: Enrichment

Group Description	Level	#	Author	Title	ISBN	Publisher	Quantity	Heinemann Write-Up
Author Studies		1	Bunting, Eve	Butterfly House	590848844	Scholastic Inc.	1	
		2	Bunting, Eve	Going Home	64435091	Harper Collins	1	
		3	Bunting, Eve	I Have an Olive Tree	60275731	Harper Collins	1	
		4	Bunting, Eve	Picnic in October, A	152016562	Harcourt Brace	1	
		5	Bunting, Eve	Wall, The	395629772	Clarion Books	1	
		6	Rylant, Cynthia	All I See	531070484	Orchard Books	1	Y
		7	Rylant, Cynthia	Angel for Solomon Singer, An	531070824	Orchard Books	1	Y

Group Description	Level	#	Author	Title	ISBN	Publisher	Quantity	Heinemann Write-Up
		8	Rylant, Cynthia	Islander, The	789424908	DK Publishing	1	Y
		9	Rylant, Cynthia	Scarecrow	15201084X	Harcourt Brace	1	
		10	Rylant, Cynthia	Tulip Sees America	590847449	Scholastic Inc.	1	Y
Memoir		1	Fritz, Jean	Homesick My Own Story	698117824	Penguin Putnam	1	
		2	Rylant, Cynthia	But I'll Be Back Again	688126537	William Morrow & Co	1	
		3	Rylant, Cynthia	Soda Jerk	688126545	William Morrow & Co	1	
Nonfiction		1	Cummings, Pat	Talking with Artists	395891329	Clarion Books	1	
		2	Lasky, Kathryn	Sugaring Time	68971081X	Simon & Schuster	1	
		3	Mochizuki, Ken	Baseball Saved Us	1880000199	Lee & Low Books	1	Y
		4	Sturges, Philemon	Sacred Places	399233172	G.P. Putnam's Sons	1	
		5	Wick, Walter	Drop of Water, A	590023195	Scholastic Inc.	1	Y
Poetry		1	Carlson, Lori	Cool Salsa: Bilingual Poems on Growing Up Latino in the United States	44970436X	Ballantine Books	1	
		2	Cullinan, Bernice, ed.	Jar of Tiny Stars: Poems by NCTE Award-Winning Poets, A	1563970872	Boyds Mills Press	1	
		3	Gordon, Ruth	Peeling the Onion	60217286	Harper Collins	1	
		4	Kennedy, X.J.	Knock at a Star	316488003	Little Brown & Co	1	
		5	Nye, Naomi Shihab	This Same Sky	689806302	Simon & Schuster	1	
Teaching Writing		1	Lowry, Lois	Autumn Street	440403448	Bantam Doubleday Dell	1	Y
		2	MacLachlan, Patricia	Cassie Binegar	64401952	Harper Collins	1	
		3	Van Allsburg, Chris	Polar Express	395389496	Houghton Mifflin	1	Y
Series Books		1	Banks, Lynne Reid	Indian in the Cupboard Series/ Indian in the Cupboard, The	380600129	William Morrow & Co	1	Y
		2	Banks, Lynne Reid	Indian in the Cupboard Series/ Mystery of the Cupboard, The	380720132	William Morrow & Co	1	
		3	Banks, Lynne Reid	Indian in the Cupboard Series/ Return of the Indian, The	380702843	William Morrow & Co	1	

Group Description	Level	#	Author	Title	ISBN	Publisher	Quantity	Heinemann Write-Up
		4	Banks, Lynne Reid	Indian in the Cupboard Series/Secret of the Indian, The	380600129	William Morrow & Co	1	
		5	LeGuin, Ursula	Catwings Series/Catwings	531071103	Orchard Books	1	
		6	LeGuin, Ursula	Catwings Series/Catwings Return	590428322	Scholastic Inc.	1	
		7	LeGuin, Ursula	Catwings Series/Jane on Her Own	531301338	Orchard Books	1	
		8	LeGuin, Ursula	Catwings Series/Wonderful Alexander and the Catwings	590543369	Scholastic Inc.	1	
		9	Scieszka, Jon	Time Warp Trio Series/Knights of the Kitchen Table	590981293	Scholastic Inc.	1	Y
		10	Scieszka, Jon	Time Warp Trio Series/Summer Reading is Killing Me	439083303	Scholastic Inc.	1	
		11	Scieszka, Jon	Time Warp Trio Series/Tut Tut	140363602	Penguin Puffin	1	
		12	Scieszka, Jon	Time Warp Trio Series/Your Mother was a Neanderthal	590981382	Scholastic Inc.	1	Y
		13	Seldon, G.	Chester Cricket's Pigeon Ride	440413893	Bantam Doubleday Dell	1	
		14	Seldon, G.	Cricket in Times Square	440415632	Bantam Doubleday Dell	1	
		15	Yolen, Jane	Young Merlin Trilogy/Hobby/Find Your Fate/Book Two	590371185	Scholastic Inc.	1	
		16	Yolen, Jane	Young Merlin Trilogy/Merlin	152008144	Harcourt Brace	1	
		17	Yolen, Jane	Young Merlin Trilogy/Passager/Book One	590370731	Scholastic Inc.	1	

MODULE 5: Multiple Copies for Book Clubs

Group Description	Level	#	Author	Title	ISBN	Publisher	Quantity	Heinemann Write-Up
	9	1	Cooney, Caroline	Burning Up	440226872	Bantam Doubleday Dell	4	
		1	Reed, Teresa	Magic Attic Club Series/Keisha Leads the Way	1575130173	Magic Attic Press	4	
	10	1	Mathis, Sharon	Sidewalk Story	140321659	Penguin Puffin	4	
	11	1	Clements, Andrew	Frindle	689818769	Simon & Schuster	4	

Group Description	Level	#	Author	Title	ISBN	Publisher	Quantity	Heinemann Write-Up
		2	George, Jean Craighead	There's an Owl in the Shower	64406822	Harper Trophy	4	Y
		3	Johnson, Angela	Maniac Monkeys on Magnolia Street	375802088	Alfred A. Knopf	4	
		4	Slote, Alfred	Trading Game, The	64404382	Harper Collins	4	
		5	Spinelli, Jerry	Wringer	64405788	Harper Collins	4	
	12	1	Baglio, Ben	Animal Ark Series/Goat in the Garden (#4)	59018752X	Scholastic Inc.	4	
		2	MacLachlan, Patricia	Baby	440411459	Bantam Doubleday Dell	4	Y
		3	Van Draanen, Wendelin	Sammy Keyes/and the Skeleton Man	375800549	Alfred A. Knopf	4	
MODULE 6: Nonfiction								
		1	Bridges, Ruby	Through My Eyes	590189239	Scholastic Inc.	1	Y
		2	Erlbach, Arlene	Kids' Invention Book, The	822598442	Lerner Publishing Group	1	
		3	George, Jean Craighead	How to Talk to Your Cat	60279680	Harper Collins	1	
		4	George, Jean Craighead	How to Talk to Your Dog	60270926	Harper Collins	1	
		5	Govenar, Allen	Osceola: Memories of a Sharecropper's Daughter	786823577	Hyperion Books	1	Y
		6	Schroeder, Alan	Minty, A Story of Young Harriet Tubman	803718888	Penguin Putnam	1	
		7	Tamar, Erika	Garden of Happiness, The	152305823	Harcourt Brace	1	
	8; 9; 10	1	Micucci, Charles	Life and Times of the Peanut	618033149	Houghton Mifflin	1	
	9	1	Barrett, Norman	Coral Reef	531141101	Franklin Watts, Grolier	1	
	9; 10	1	Levine, Ellen	If You Traveled on the Underground Railroad	590451561	Scholastic Inc.	1	Y
	9; 10; 11	1	Berger, Melvin	Do Stars Have Points?	439085705	Scholastic Inc.	1	

Group Description	Level	#	Author	Title	ISBN	Publisher	Quantity	Heinemann Write-Up
		2	Berger, Melvin	Do Tarantulas Have Teeth?	439095786	Scholastic Inc.	1	
		3	Curlee, Lynn	Liberty	689828233	Atheneum	1	
		4	Gibbons, Gail	Wolves	823412024	Holiday House	1	
		5	Mochizuki, Ken	Passage to Freedom: The Sugihara Story	1880000490	Lee & Low Books	1	
		6	Pinkney, Andrea Davis	Alvin Ailey	786810777	Hyperion Books	1	
	10	1	George, Jean Craighead	Animals Who Have Won Our Hearts	60215437	Harper Collins	1	
		2	George, Jean Craighead	One Day in the Alpine Tundra	64420272	Harper Trophy	1	
		3	Scholastic	Magic School Bus Series/Meets the Rot Squad	590400231	Scholastic Inc.	1	Y
		4	Simon, Charnan	Community Builders Series/Bill Gates	516261320	Children's Press	1	
		5	Simon, Charnan	Community Builders Series/Jesse Jackson	516261339	Children's Press	1	
	10; 11	1	Bierman, Carol	Journey to Ellis Island: How My Father Came to America	786803770	Hyperion Books	1	
	10; 11; 12	1	Ash, Russell	Top 10 of Everything 2000	789446324	DK Publishing	1	
		2	Ganeri, Anita	How Would You Survive as an Ancient Roman?	531153053	Franklin Watts, Grolier	1	Y
		3	Grupper, Jonathan	Destination: Rainforest	792270185	National Geographic	1	
		4	Jenkins, Steve	Top of the World: Climbing Mount Everest, The	395942187	Houghton Mifflin	1	Y
		5	Levine, Ellen	If Your Name was Changed on Ellis Island	590438298	Scholastic Inc.	1	
		6	Markle, Sandra	Outside & Inside Sharks	689826834	Aladdin	1	
		7	Parker, Steve	Brain Surgery for Beginners	1562948954	Millbrook Press	1	

Group Description	Level	#	Author	Title	ISBN	Publisher	Quantity	Heinemann Write-Up
		8	Short, Joan	Crocodilians	1572552174	Mondo Publishing	1	Y
		9	Solheim, James	It's Disgusting — and We Ate It!	689806752	Simon & Schuster	1	
		10	Szabo, Corrine	Sky Pioneer, A Photobiography of Amelia Earhart	792237374	National Geographic	1	
		11	Tahta, Sophy	Where Does Rubbish Go?	811105511	EDC Publishing	1	
		12	Wright-Frierson, Virginia	Desert Scrapbook, A	689806787 (hc)	Simon & Schuster	1	
	11	1	Fritz, Jean	Where Was Patrick Henry on the 29th of May	59041206X	Scholastic Inc.	1	Y
	11; 12; 13	1	Burns, Diane	Wildflowers, Blooms & Blossoms	836821483	Gareth Stevens Publishing	1	
		2	Denenberg, Barry	Stealing Home: Story of Jackie Robinson	590425609	Scholastic Inc.	1	Y
		3	Kehret, Peg	Shelter Dogs	807573345	Albert Whitman	1	
		4	Krull, Kathleen	Lives of the Musicians	152480102	Harcourt Brace	1	Y
		5	Llewellyn, Claire	Big Book of Bones, The	872265463	NTC Publishing	1	
		6	McDonough, Yona Zeldis	Sisters in Strength	805061029	Henry Holt & Co	1	Y
		7	Myers, Walter Dean	Malcolm X	60277076	Harper Collins	2	
		8	Segaloff, Nat	Reef Comes to Life, A	531109941 (hc)	Franklin Watts, Grolier	1	
		9	Simon, Charnan	Community Builders Series/ Jane Addams	516262351	Children's Press	1	
	12	1	Burleigh, Robert	Flight	698114256	Penguin Putnam	1	Y
		2	Stanley, Jerry	Children of the Dust Bowl: The True Story of the School at Weedpatch Camp	517880946	Random House	1	Y
	12; 13; 14	1	Angelou, Maya	Journey of the Heart	14038359X	Penguin Publishing	1	
		2	Budiansky, Stephen	World According to Horses, The	805060545	Henry Holt & Co	1	Y
		3	Jackson, Donna	Wildlife Detectives	395869765	Houghton Mifflin	1	Y

Group Description	Level	#	Author	Title	ISBN	Publisher	Quantity	Heinemann Write-Up
		4	McKissack, Fredrick	Black Hoops: History of African Americans in Basketball	590487124	Scholastic Inc.	1	Y
	13; 14; 15	1	Beil, Karen Magnuson	Fire in Their Eyes	152010424	Harcourt Brace	1	
		2	Bird, Bettina & Joan Short	Insects	1572552166	Mondo Publishing	1	Y
		3	Myers, Walter Dean	At Her Majesty's Request	590486691	Scholastic Inc.	1	Y

Benchmark Books for Each Text Level

TC Level	Benchmarks: Books that Represent Each Level
1	*A Birthday Cake* (Cowley) *I Can Write* (Williams) *The Cat on the Mat* (Wildsmith)
2	*Rain* (Kaplan) *Fox on the Box* (Gregorich)
3	*It Looked Like Spilt Milk* (Shaw) *I Like Books* (Browne) *Mrs. Wishy-Washy* (Cowley)
4	*Rosie's Walk* (Hutchins) *The Carrot Seed* (Krauss) *Cookie's Week* (Ward)
5	*George Shrinks* (Joyce) *Goodnight Moon* (Brown) *Hattie and the Fox* (Fox)
6	*Danny and the Dinosaur* (Hoff) *Henry and Mudge* (Rylant)
7	*Nate the Great* (Sharmat) *Meet M&M* (Ross)
8	*Horrible Harry* (Kline) *Pinky and Rex* (Howe) Arthur Series (Marc Brown)
9	*Amber Brown* (Danziger) *Ramona Quimby, Age 8* (Cleary)
10	*James and the Giant Peach* (Dahl) *Fudge-A-Mania* (Blume)
11	*Shiloh* (Naylor) *The Great Gilly Hopkins* (Paterson)
12	*Bridge to Terabithia* (Paterson) *Baby* (MacLachlan)
13	*Missing May* (Rylant) *Where the Red Fern Grows* (Rawls)
14	*A Day No Pigs Would Die* (Peck) *Scorpions* (Myers)
15	*The Golden Compass* (Pullman) *The Dark Is Rising* (Cooper) *A Wizard of Earthsea* (Le Guin)

Descriptions of Text Levels One Through Seven

TEXT LEVEL ONE

This level roughly corresponds to the following levels in other systems:

Reading Recovery© (RR) Levels 1–2
Developmental Reading Assessment (DRA) Levels A–2

Text Characteristics for TC Level One

- The font is large, clear, and is usually printed in black on a white background.

- There is exaggerated spacing between words and letters. (In some books, publishers have enlarged the print but have not adjusted the spacing which can create difficulties for readers.)

- There is usually a single word, phrase, or simple sentence on a page, and the text is patterned and predictable. For example, in the book *I Can Read*, once a child knows the title (which is ideally read to a Level One reader) it is not hard for the child to read "I can read the newspaper," "I can read the cereal box." These readers are regarded as "preconventional" because they rely on the illustrations (that support the meaning) and the sounds of language (or syntax) and not on graphophonics or word/letter cues to read a sentence such as, "I can read the newspaper."

- Usually each page contains two or three sight words. A Level One book *may* contain one illustrated word on a page (such as "Mom," "Dad," "sister," "cat") but it's just as easy for a child to read "I see my mom. I see my Dad. I see my sister. I see my cat." because the sight words give the child a way into the text.

- The words are highly supported by illustrations. No one would expect a Level One reader to solve the word "newspaper." We would, however, expect a child at this level to look at the picture and at the text and to read the word "newspaper."

- Words are consistently placed in the same area of each page, preferably top left or bottom left.

Characteristics of the Reader

Readers in this group will demonstrate most of these behaviors.

- Remember the pattern in a predictable text
- Use picture cues

■ Use left to right directionality to read one or two lines of print

■ Work on matching spoken words with printed words and self-correcting when these don't "come out even"

■ Rely on the spaces between words to signify the end of one word and the beginning of another. These readers read the spaces as well as the words, as the words are at first black blobs on white paper

■ Locate one or two known words on a page

Benchmarks

The following titles are representative of the kinds of books found in this grouping.

A Birthday Cake, Joy Cowley
Cat on the Mat, Brian Wildsmith
The Farm, Literacy 2000/Stage 1
Growing Colors, Bruce McMillan
I Can Write, Rozanne Williams
Time for Dinner, PM Starters

Assessment

The following titles can be used to determine if a reader is ready to move on to the next grouping of books. This type of assessment is most effective if the text is unfamiliar to the reader. If these titles will be used as assessment texts, they should *not* be part of the classroom library.

My Home, Story Box
The Tree Stump, Little Celebrations
DRA Assessments A–2

We move children from Level One to Level Two books when they are consistently able to match one spoken word with one word written on the page. This means that they can point under words in a Level One book as they read and know when they haven't matched a spoken word to a written word by noticing that, at the end of the line, they still have words left on the page or they've run out of words. When children read multisyllabic words and compound words and point to multiple, instead of one, word on the page, we consider this a successful one-to-one match.

TEXT LEVEL TWO

This level roughly corresponds to the following levels in other systems:

Reading Recovery© (RR) Levels 3–4
Developmental Reading Assessment (DRA) Levels 3–4

Text Characteristics of TC Level Two

■ There are usually two lines of print on at least some of the pages in these books, and sometimes there are three. This means readers will become accustomed to making the return sweep to the beginning of a new line.

■ The texts are still patterned and predictable, but now the patterns tend to switch at intervals. Almost always, the pattern changes at the end of the book. The repeating unit may be as long as two sentences in length.

■ The font continues to be large and clear. The letters might not, however, be black against white although this is generally the case.

■ Children still rely on the picture but the pictures tend to give readers more to deal with; children need to search more in the picture to find help in reading the words.

■ High frequency words are still helpful and important. The sentences in Level One books tend to begin with 2 to 3 high frequency words, for example, "I like to run. I like to jump." At this level, the pages are more apt to begin with a single high frequency word and then include words that require picture support and attention to first letters, for example, "A mouse has a long tail. A bear has a short tail."

■ Sentences are more varied, resulting in texts that include a full range of punctuation.

Characteristics of the Reader

Readers in this group will demonstrate most of these behaviors.

■ Get the mouth ready for the initial sound of a word

■ Use left to right directionality as well as a return sweep to another line of print

■ Locate one or two known words on a page

■ Monitor for meaning: check to make sure it makes sense

Benchmarks

The following titles are representative of the kinds of books found in this grouping.

All Fall Down, Brian Wildsmith
I Went Walking, Sue Williams
Rain, Robert Kalan
Shoo, Sunshine

Assessment

The following titles can be used to determine if a reader is ready to move on to the next grouping. This type of assessment is most effective if the text is unfamiliar to a reader. If these titles will be used as assessment texts, they should *not* be part of the classroom library.

The Bus Ride, Little Celebrations, DRA 3
Fox on the Box, School Zone, DRA 4

We generally move children from Level Two to Level Three texts when they know how to use the pictures and the syntax to generate possibilities for the next word, when they attend to the first letters of unknown words. These readers will also read and rely on high frequency words such as *I, the, a, to, me, mom, the child's name, like, love, go,* and *and.*

TEXT LEVEL THREE

This level roughly corresponds to the following levels in other systems:

Reading Recovery© (RR) Levels 5–8
Developmental Reading Assessment (DRA) Levels 6–8

Text Characteristics of TC Level Three

It is important to note that this grouping includes a wide range of levels. This was done deliberately because at this level, readers should be able to select "just right" books for themselves and be able to monitor their own reading.

- Sentences are longer and readers will need to put their words together in order to take in more of the sentence at a time. When they are stuck, it's often helpful to nudge them to reread and try again.

- The pictures are not as supportive as they've been. It's still helpful for children to do picture walks prior to reading an unfamiliar text, but now the goal is less about surmising what words the page contains and more about seeing an overview of the narrative.

- Readers must rely on graphophonics across the whole word. If readers hit a wall at this level, it's often because they're accustomed to predicting words based on a dominant pattern and using the initial letters (only) to confirm their predictions. It takes readers a while to begin checking the print closely enough to adjust their expectations.

- Children will need to use sight words to help with unknown words, using parts of these familiar words as analogies, helping them unlock the unfamiliar words.

- The font size and spacing are less important now.

- Words in the text begin to include contractions. We can help children read these by urging them to look all the way across a word.

Characteristics of the Reader

Readers in this group will demonstrate most of these behaviors.

- Reread and self-correct

- Read with some fluency

- Cross check one cue against another

- Monitor for meaning: check to make sure what has been read makes sense and sounds right

- Recognize common chunks of words

Benchmarks

The following titles are representative of the kinds of books found in this grouping.

Bears in the Night Stan and Jan, Berenstain
The Chick and the Duckling, Ginsburg
It Looked Like Spilt Milk, Charles G. Shaw
Mrs. Wishy-Washy, Joy Cowley

Assessment

The following titles can be used to determine if a reader is ready to move on to the next grouping. This type of assessment is most effective if the text is unfamiliar to a reader. If these titles will be used as assessment texts, they should *not* be part of the classroom library.

Bread, Story Box, DRA 6
Get Lost Becka, School Zone, DRA 8

We move a child to Level Four books if that child can pick up an unfamiliar book like *Bread* or *It Looked Like Spilt Milk* and read it with a little difficulty, but with a lot of independence and with strategies. This reader should know to reread when she is stuck, to use the initial sounds in a word, to chunk word families within a word, and so on.

TEXT LEVEL FOUR

This level roughly corresponds to the following levels in other systems:

Reading Recovery© (RR) Levels 9–12
Developmental Reading Assessment (DRA) Levels 10–12

Text Characteristics of TC Level Four

- In general, the child who is reading Level Four books is able to do more of the same reading work he could do with texts at the previous level. This child reads texts that contain more words, lines, pages, and more challenging vocabulary.

- These texts contain even less picture support than earlier levels.

- Fluency and phrasing are very important for the Level Four reader. If children don't begin to read quickly enough, they won't be able to carry the syntax of the sentence along well enough to comprehend what they are reading.

- These books use brief bits of literary language. That is, in these books the mother may turn to her child and say, "We shall be rich."

- These books are more apt to have a plot (with characters, setting, problem, solution) and they tend to be less patterned than they were at the previous level.

Characteristics of the Reader

Readers in this group will demonstrate most of these behaviors.

- Reread and self-correct

- Read with fluency

- Integrate cues from meaning, structure, and visual sources

- Monitor for meaning: check to make sure what has been read makes sense, sounds right, and looks right

- Make some analogies from known words to figure out unknown words

- Read increasingly difficult chunks within words

Benchmarks

The following titles are representative of the kinds of books found in this grouping.

The Carrot Seed, Ruth Krauss
Cookie's Week, Cindy Ward
Rosie's Walk, Pat Hutchins
Titch, Pat Hutchins

Assessment

The following titles can be used to determine if a reader is ready to move on to the next grouping. This type of assessment is most effective if the text is unfamiliar to a reader. If these titles will be used as assessment texts, they should *not* be part of the classroom library.

Are You There Bear?, Ron Maris, DRA 10
The House in the Tree, Rigby PM Story Books
Nicky Upstairs and Downstairs, Harriet Ziefert
William's Skateboard, Sunshine, DRA 12

We move a child to Level Five books if that reader can independently use a variety of strategies to work through difficult words or parts of a text. The reader must be reading fluently enough to reread quickly, when necessary, so as to keep the flow of the story going. If a reader is reading very slowly, taking too much time to work through the hard parts, then this reader may not be ready to move on to the longer, more challenging texts in Level Five.

TEXT LEVEL FIVE

This level roughly corresponds to the following levels in other systems:

Reading Recovery© (RR) Levels 13–15
Developmental Reading Assessment (DRA) Level 14

Text Characteristics

- Sentences in Level Five books tend to be longer, more varied, and more complex than they were in previous levels.

- Many of the stories are retold folktales or fantasy-like stories that use literary or story language, such as: "Once upon a time, there once lived, a long, long time ago. . . . "

- Many books may be in a cumulative form in which text is added to each page, requiring the reader to read more and more text as the story unfolds, adding a new line with every page turn.

- The illustrations tend to be a representation of just a slice of what is happening in the text. For example, the text may tell of a long journey that a character has taken over time, but the picture may represent just the character reaching his destination.

- There will be more unfamiliar and sometimes complex vocabulary.

Characteristics of the Reader

Readers in this group will demonstrate most of these behaviors.

- Reread and self-correct regularly

- Read with fluency

- Integrate a balance of cues

- Monitor for meaning: check to make sure what has been read makes sense, sounds right, and looks right

- Demonstrate fluent phrasing of longer passages

- Use a repertoire of graphophonic strategies to problem solve through text

Benchmarks

The following titles are representative of the kinds of books found in this grouping.

George Shrinks, William Joyce
Goodnight Moon, Margaret Wise Brown
Hattie and the Fox, Mem Fox
Little Red Hen, Parkes

Assessment

The following titles can be used to determine if a reader is ready to move on to the next grouping. This type of assessment is most effective if the text is unfamiliar to a reader. If these titles will be used as assessment texts, they should *not* be part of the classroom library.

The Old Man's Mitten, Bookshop, Mondo
Who Took the Farmer's Hat?, Joan Nodset, DRA 14

We move children from Level Five to Level Six texts when they are consistently able to use a multitude of strategies to work through challenges quickly and efficiently. These challenges may be brought on by unfamiliar settings, unfamiliar language structures, unfamiliar words, and increased text length. The amount of text on a page and the length of a book should not be a hindrance to the reader who is moving on to Level Six. The reader who is ready to move on is also adept at consistently choosing appropriate books that will make her a stronger reader.

TEXT LEVEL SIX

This level roughly corresponds to the following levels in other systems:

Reading Recovery© (RR) Levels 16–18
Developmental Reading Assessment (DRA) Level 16

Text Characteristics of TC Level Six

- The focus of the book is evident at its start

- Descriptive language is used more frequently than before

- Dialogue often tells a large part of the story

- Texts may include traditional retellings of fairy tales and folktales

- Stories are frequently humorous

- Considerable amount of text is found on each page. A book in this grouping may be a picture book, or a simple chapter book. These books offer extended stretches of text.

- Texts are often simple chapter books, and often have episodic chapters in which each chapter stands as a story on its own

- Texts often center around just two or three main characters who tend to be markedly different from each other (a boy and a girl, a child and a parent)

- There is limited support from the pictures

- Texts includes challenging vocabulary

Characteristics of the Reader

Readers in this group will demonstrate most of these behaviors.

- Reread and self-correct regularly

- Read with fluency

- Integrate a balance of cues

- Demonstrate fluent phrasing of longer passages

- Use a repertoire of graphophonic strategies to problem solve through text

Benchmarks

The following titles are representative of the kinds of books found in this grouping.

Danny and the Dinosaur, Syd Hoff
The Doorbell Rang, Pat Hutchins
Henry and Mudge, Cynthia Rylant
The Very Hungry Caterpillar, Eric Carle

Assessment

The following titles can be used to determine if a reader is ready to move on to the next grouping. This type of assessment is most effective if the text is unfamiliar to a reader. If these titles will be used as assessment texts, they should *not* be part of the classroom library.

Bear Shadow, Frank Asch, DRA 16
Jimmy Lee Did It, Pat Cummings, DRA 18

TEXT LEVEL SEVEN

This level roughly corresponds to the following levels in other systems:

Reading Recovery© (RR) Levels 19–20
Developmental Reading Assessment (DRA) Level 20

Text Characteristics of TC Level Seven

- Dialogue is used frequently to move the story along

- Texts often have 2 to 3 characters. (They tend to have distinctive personalities and usually don't change across a book or series.)

- Texts may include extended description. (The language may set a mood, and may be quite poetic or colorful.)

- Some books have episodic chapters. (In other books, each chapter contributes to the understanding of the entire book and the reader must carry the story line along.)

- There is limited picture support

- Plots are usually linear without large time-gaps

- Texts tend to have larger print and double spacing between lines of print

Characteristics of the Reader

Readers in this group will demonstrate most of these behaviors.

- Reread and self-correct regularly

- Read with fluency, intonation, and phrasing

- Demonstrate the existence of a self-extending (self-improving) system for reading

- Use an increasingly more challenging repertoire of graphophonic strategies to problem solve through text

- Solve unknown words with relative ease

Benchmarks

The following titles are representative of the kinds of books found in this grouping.

A Baby Sister for Frances, Russell Hoban
Meet M&M, Pat Ross
Nate the Great, Marjorie Sharmat
Poppleton, Cynthia Rylant

Asessment

The following titles can be used to determine if a reader is ready to move on to the next grouping. This type of assessment is most effective if the text is unfamiliar to a reader. If these titles will be used as assessment texts, they should *not* be part of the classroom library.

Peter's Pockets, Eve Rice, DRA 20
Uncle Elephant, Arnold Lobel

More Information to Help You Choose the Library That is Best for Your Readers

Library A

Library A is appropriate if your children enter kindergarten in October as very emergent readers with limited experiences hearing books read aloud. Use the following chart to help determine if Library A is about right for your class.

Approximate Distribution of Reading Levels of a Class Matched to Library A		
Benchmark Book	*Reading Level*	*Percentage of the Class Reading at about This Level*
The Cat on the Mat, by Wildsmith	TC Level 1	45%
Fox on the Box, by Gregorich	TC Level 2	30%
Mrs. Wishy-Washy, by Cowley	TC Level 3	25%

Library B

Library B is appropriate for a class of children if, in October, they are reading books like *I Went Walking*. Use the following chart to help determine if Library B is about right for your class. (Note to New York City teachers: Many of your students would score a 3 on the ECLAS correlated with titles such as, *Things I Like to Do* and *My Shadow*.)

Approximate Distribution of Reading Levels of a Class Matched to Library B		
Benchmark Book	*Reading Level*	*Percentage of the Class Reading at about This Level*
The Cat on the Mat, by Wildsmith	TC Level 1	10%
Fox on the Box, by Gregorich	TC Level 2	10%
Mrs. Wishy-Washy, by Cowley	TC Level 3	30%
The Carrot Seed, by Krauss	TC Level 4	25%
Goodnight Moon, by Brown	TC Level 5	15%
Henry and Mudge, by Rylant	TC Level 6	5%
Nate the Great, by Sharmat	TC Level 7	5%

Library C

Library C is appropriate for a class of children if, in October, many of your students are approaching reading books like *Mrs. Wishy-Washy* and *Bears in the Night*. (Note to New York City teachers: Many of your students would be approaching a 4 on the ECLAS that would be correlated with *Baby Bear's Present* and *No Where and Nothing*.)

Approximate Distribution of Reading Levels of a Class Matched to Library C		
Benchmark Book	*Reading Level*	*Percentage of the Class Reading at about This Level*
Fox on the Box, by Gregorich	TC Level 2	8%
Mrs. Wishy-Washy, by Cowley	TC Level 3	8%
The Carrot Seed, by Krauss	TC Level 4	20%
Goodnight Moon, by Brown	TC Level 5	20%
Henry and Mudge, by Carle	TC Level 6	20%
Nate the Great, by Sharmat	TC Level 7	15%
Pinky and Rex, by Howe	TC Level 8	5%
Ramona Quimby, by Cleary	TC Level 9	2%
James and the Giant Peach, by Dahl	TC Level 10	2%

Library D

Use the following chart to help determine if Library D is right for your class.

Approximate Distribution of Reading Levels of a Class Matched to Library D		
Benchmark Book	*Reading Level*	*Percentage of the Class Reading at about This Level*
Good Night Moon, by Brown	Level 5	8%
Henry and Mudge, by Rylant	Level 6	20%
Nate the Great, by Sharmat	Level 7	25%
Pinky and Rex, by Howe	Level 8	30%
Ramona Quimby, by Cleary	Level 9	10%
James and the Giant Peach, by Dahl	Level 10	2%

Library E

Library E is appropriate for a class of children if, in October, a readers list tends to look approximately like the following chart.

Approximate Distribution of Reading Levels of a Class Matched to Library E		
Benchmark Book	*Reading Level*	*Percentage of the Class Reading at about This Level*
Nate the Great, by Sharmat	Level 7	10%
Pinky and Rex, by Howe	Level 8	25%
Ramona Quimby, by Cleary	Level 9	30%
James and the Giant Peach, by Dahl	Level 10	22%
Shiloh, by Naylor	Level 11	5%
Baby, by MacLachlan	Level 12	5%
Missing May, by Rylant	Level 13	2%
Scorpions, by Myers	Level 14	1%

Library F

Library F is appropriate for a class of children if, in October, a readers list tends to look approximately like the following chart.

Approximate Distribution of Reading Levels of a Class Matched to Library F		
Benchmark Book	*Reading Level*	*Percentage of the Class Reading at about This Level*
Pinky and Rex, by Howe	Level 8	2%
Ramona Quimby, by Cleary	Level 9	20%
James and the Giant Peach, by Dahl	Level 10	25%
Shiloh, by Naylor	Level 11	30%
Baby, by MacLachlan	Level 12	20%
Missing May, by Rylant	Level 13	2%
Scorpions, by Myers	Level 14	1%

Library G

Library G is appropriate for a class of children if, in October, a readers list tends to look approximately like the following chart.

Approximate Distribution of Reading Levels of a Class Matched to Library G		
Benchmark Book	*Reading Level*	*Percentage of the Class Reading at about This Level*
James and the Giant Peach, by Dahl	Level 10	10%
Shiloh, by Naylor	Level 11	10%
Baby, by MacLachlan	Level 12	30%
Missing May, by Rylant	Level 13	30%
Scorpions, by Myer	Level 14	20%

About the Guides

Soon we'd begun not only accumulating titles and honing arrangements for dream libraries, but also writing teaching advice to go with the chosen books. Our advice to the contributors was, "Write a letter from you to others who'll use this book with children. Tell folks what you notice in the book, and advise them on teaching opportunities you see. Think about advice you would give a teacher just coming to know the book." The insights, experience, and folk wisdom poured in and onto the pages of the guides.

A written guide accompanies many of the books in the libraries. These guides are not meant to be prescriptions for how a teacher or child should use a book. Instead they are intended to be resources, and we hope thoughtful teachers will tap into particular sections of a guide when it seems fit to do so. For example, a teaching guide might suggest six possible minilessons a teacher could do with a book. Of course, a teacher would never try to do all six of these! Instead we expect one of these minilessons will seem helpful to the teacher, and another minilesson to another teacher. The teaching guides illustrate the following few principles that are important to us.

Teaching One Text Intensely in Order to Learn About Many Texts

When you take a walk in the woods, it can happen that all the trees look the same, that they are just a monotony of foliage and trunks. It is only when you stop to learn about a particular tree, about its special leaf structure and the odd thickness of its bark, about the creatures that inhabit it and the seeds it lets fall, that you begin to see that particular kind of tree among the thickets. It is when you enter a forest knowing something about kinds of trees that you begin to truly see the multiplicity of trees in a forest and the particular attributes and mysteries of each one. Learning about the particulars of one tree leads you to thinking about all of the trees, each in its individuality, each with its unique deep structure, each with its own offerings.

The same is true of texts. The study of one can reveal not just the hidden intricacies of that story, but also the ways in which truths and puzzles can be structured in other writings as well. When one book holds a message in the way a chapter ends, it gives the reader the idea that any book may hold a message in the structure of its chapter's conclusions. When one book is revealed to make a sense that is unintended by the author, we look for unintended sense in other books we read. Within these guides, then, we hope that readers like you will find truths about the particular books they are written about, but more, we hope that you find pathways into all the books you read. By showing some lengthy thinking and meditations on one book, we hope to offer you paths toward thinking about each and every book that crosses your desk and crosses your mind.

Suggesting Classroom Library Arrangements

Many the attributes of a book, detailed in a guide, can become a category in a classroom library. If a group of students in a class seems particularly energized by the Harry Potter books, for example, the guide can be used to help determine which books could be in a bin in the library marked, "If You Like *Harry Potter*—Try These." The similarity between the *Harry Potter* books and the other books in this group may be not only in difficulty gradient, but also in content, story structure, popularity, or genre. That is, a class of children that like *Harry Potter* might benefit from a bin of books on fantasy, or from a collection of best-selling children's books, or from a bin of "Long-Books-You-Can't-Put-Down," or from stories set in imagined places. As you browse through the guides that accompany the books you have chosen, the connections will pop out at you.

Sometimes, the guides will help you determine a new or more interesting placement for a book. Perhaps you have regarded a book as historical fiction, but now you realize it could alternatively be shelved in a collection of books that offer children examples of "Great Leads to Imitate in Your Own Writing." Or, perhaps the guides will suggest entirely new categories that will appeal to your class in ways you and your students haven't yet imagined. Perhaps the guides will help you imagine a "Books That Make You Want to Change the World" category. Or maybe you'll decide to create a shelf in your library titled, "Books with Odd Techniques That Make You Wonder What the Author Is Trying To Do."

Aiding in Conferring

Teachers' knowledge of what to ask and what to teach a reader who says, "this book is boring" comes not only from their knowledge of particular students but also from their knowledge of the text they are talking about. Does "boring" mean that the book is too easy for the reader? Perhaps it means instead that the beginning few chapters of the book are hard to read—confusing because of a series of flashbacks. A guide might explain that the book under discussion has mostly internal, emotional action, and, if the reader is accustomed to avalanche-and-rattlesnake action in books, she may need some time to warm up to this unfamiliar kind of "quiet" action. The guide can point out the kinds of reactions, or troubles, other readers have had with particular books. With the guides at our fingertips, we can more easily determine which questions to ask students, or which pages to turn to, in order to get to the heart of the conference.

Providing a Resource for Curriculum Planning

One Friday, say, we leave the classroom knowing that our students' writing shows that they are thirsting for deeper, more complicated characters to study and imitate. As we plan lessons, we can page through the guides that correspond with some of the books in our library, finding, or remembering, books that students can study that depict fascinating characters.

On the other hand, perhaps we need a book to read aloud to the class, or perhaps we need to recommend a book to a particular struggling reader.

Maybe a reader has finished a book he loves and has turned to you to help him plan his reading for the next weeks. When designing an author study or an inquiry into punctuation and its effects on meaning, it also helps to have the guides with you to point out books that may be helpful in those areas. In each of these cases, and many more, the guides can be a planning aid for you.

Reminding Us, or Teaching Us, About Particular Book Basics

No teacher can read, let alone recall in detail, every book that every child will pick up in the classroom. Of course, we read many of them and learn about many more from our colleagues, but there are far too many books in the world for us to be knowledgeable about them all. Sometimes, the guides will be a reminder of what you have read many years ago. Sometimes, they will provide a framework for you to question or direct your students more effectively than you could if you knew nothing at all about the book. "Probably, you will have to take some time to understand the setting before you can really get a handle on this book, why don't you turn to the picture atlas?" you might say after consulting the guide, or "Sharlene is reading another book that is similar to this one in so many ways! Why don't you go pair up with her to talk." You might learn to ask, "What do you think of Freddy?" in order to learn if the student is catching on to the tone of the narrator, or you might learn you could hint, "Did you get to chapter three yet? Because I bet you won't be bored any more when you get there. . . ." The guides provide a bit of what time constraints deny us: thoughtful insights about the content or unusual features of a given book.

Showcasing Literary Intricacies in Order to Suggest a Reader's Thinking

Sometimes, when we read a book, our idea of the author's message is in our minds before we even finish the story. Because we are experienced readers, much of our inferring and interpreting, our understanding of symbols and contexts, can come to us effortlessly. In the guides, we have tried to slow down some of that thinking so that we can all see it more easily. We have tried to lay out some of the steps young readers may have to go through in order to come to a cohesive idea of what the story is about, or a clear understanding of why a character behaved the way she did. As experienced readers, we may not even realize that our readers are confused by the unorthodox use of italics to show us who is speaking, for example. We may not remember the days when we were confused by changing narrators, the days when it took us a few chapters to figure out a character wasn't to be believed. In these guides, we have tried to go back to those days when we were more naïve readers, and have tried to fill in those thoughts and processes we are now able to skip over so easily.

By bringing forth the noteworthy features of the text, features experienced readers may not even notice, we are reminded of the thinking that our students need to go through in order to make sense of their reading. It gives us an idea of where to offer pointers, of where readers may have gone off in an unhelpful direction, or of where their thinking may need to go instead of where it has gone. By highlighting literary intricacies, we may remember that every bit about the construction of texts is a navigation point for students, and every bit is something we may be able to help students in learning.

Providing a Community of Readers and Teachers

The guides are also intended to help teachers learn from the community of other teachers and readers who have used particular texts already. They make available some of the stories and experiences other teachers have had, in order that we might stand on their shoulders and take our teaching even higher than they could reach. These guides are intended to give you some thinking to go with the books in your classroom library, thinking you can mix with your own ideas.

In the end, we don't all have a community of other teachers with whom we can talk about children's literature. The guides are meant not to stand in for that community, but instead to provide a taste, an appetizer, of the world of supportive professional communities. We hope that by reading these guides and feeling the companionship, guidance and insight they offer, teachers will be nudged to recreate that experience for the other books that have no guides, and that they will ask their colleagues, librarians, and the parents of their students to talk with them about children's literature and young readers. Then, when teachers are creating these guides for themselves, on paper or in their minds' eyes, we will know this project has done the work for which it was created.

Bibliography

Atwell, Nancie. 1987. *In the Middle: Writing, Reading, and Learning with Adolescents*. Portsmouth, NH: Boynton/Cook.

Calkins, Lucy. 2001. *The Art of Teaching Reading*. New York: Addison-Wesley Educational Publishers, Inc.

Cambourne, Brian. 1993. *The Whole Story: Natural Learning and the Acquisition of Literacy in the Classroom*. Auckland, NZ: Ashton Scholastic.

Krashen, Stephen. 1993. *The Power of Reading: Insights from the Research*. Englewood, CO: Libraries Unlimited.

Meek, Margaret. 1988. *How Texts Teach What Readers Learn*. Thimble Press.

Smith, Frank. 1985. *Reading Without Nonsense*. 2nd ed. New York: TC Press.

...And Now Miguel

Joseph Krumgold

Book Summary

This story, narrated by the character Miguel, is based on a documentary the author made of the Chavez family. Twelve-year old Miguel, neither the oldest nor the youngest son, longs to be a part of the clan of men in his family who herd the sheep into the heights of the Sangre de Cristo Mountains for summer grazing. This is the story of how he achieves that dream, as well as the mistakes he makes along the way. Filled with details about the life of a sheepherder in the 1950s, the story unfolds in Miguel's voice. We see events occurring through his eyes and judge them in light of his naiveté. There is a strong sense of the spiritual in this tale, a sense that reflects the beliefs held dear by Catholics. The reader is given glimpses into ways Latino families like the Chavezes celebrate their religion and honor their beliefs. Stronger yet are the many examples that demonstrate the unquestioning respect that younger family members have for their seniors. The father's word is law; no one opposes it, least of all Miguel. This coming-of-age story is one young students can both relate to and learn from.

Basic Book Information

...And Now Miguel is one of two Newbery books that Krumgold wrote. Fourteen chapters, over 245 pages, are needed to tell Miguel's story. Some sentences are quite long-forty words or more. Others have only three or four words. Charlot's small line drawings head each chapter. Some illustrations also appear within the chapters and help the reader visualize what the narrator describes. Each chapter, although untitled, has a focal point-an episode that moves the story forward to its conclusion. The opening line of a chapter frequently gives an overview of that episode, while chapters often end with a line that rouses the reader's curiosity about what comes next. Chapter 11 begins with the words: "And now what there is to explain is how the worst thing happened, and then how the best thing happened, and then how everything got mixed up, what was good and what was bad." It ends with the line: "There is only one thing left that I must do." In the next chapter that "thing" is revealed.

Noteworthy Features

The first-person narration gives a strong sense of voice to this story. The reader may feel they are hearing, rather than reading Miguel's words. Krumgold is careful to note the passage of time with words and phrases like "for a day or two after that," or "I studied about it for a couple of days," or "on the morning of the third day it happened." There are pages of descriptions with only a line here or there of dialogue that may well

Illustrator
Jean Charlot

Publisher
Thomas Y. Crowell Company, 1953

ISBN
006440143X

TC Level
12

challenge some readers. There are also lengthy passages of reflection that are, at times, difficult to follow.

Spanish phrases appear occasionally but it is not difficult to discern the meaning. Because the narrator is Latino, the language used to tell the story has a formality that suggests that English is a second language. In referring to his disappointment that his wish to go to the mountains had not been fulfilled, for example, Miguel tells us: "People come to the fiesta not only from Los Cordovas but from all around, more than come to the church"; or: "For myself, I wasn't hungry"; or, "I found out from which direction was the wind." This style does not make the text more difficult to understand-only different from the usual syntax found in books for readers in this age group. There are also moments of humor, as when Miguel, feeling proud because he has been given an important job, falls into the bag of shorn wool and cannot get out. Or when Miguel mistakenly thinks Gabriel is talking about a cow when he refers to Carlotta, a girl he is fond of.

Teaching Ideas

A coming of age theme is one which could be easily documented in this book. In Chapter One, Miguel tells us, "But to be in-between, not so little anymore and not yet nineteen years, to be me, Miguel, and to have a great wish-that is hard." In a conference with a child who has just begun reading this book, a teacher might cite this passage and ask a reader to think about why it is not easy to be Miguel. Miguel's wish is to go to the mountains, and again, a teacher might engage a reader in conversation about why this wish was so important to Miguel. In the end, the reader may realize that growing up is really a series of ups and downs, never a smooth journey. This conversation could set a reader up to notice the ups and downs in Miguel's story. Miguel is struggling toward being grown-up, and like so many others his age, he sometimes acts in mature ways and sometimes acts in ways that seem young. A reader could keep a jagged timeline reflecting the passages in the book which represent Miguel's highs and lows, or alternatively, could mark and discuss either those highs and lows, or the times he seems more or less mature.

The setting is an important element in this story. The story takes place in New Mexico. Since geography plays such an important role in the story, a teacher might take time in a conference with a reader to point out New Mexico on the map and to particularly point to the Sangre de Cristo Mountains, a branch of the Rockies. The setting of a story involves not only its geographic location but also its location in the timeline of history. The book was written in 1953, long before the changes brought about by the decade of the sixties occurred. Readers may study how the setting of the story helps them understand the events and the attitude of the characters.

Students may study how culture and religion have influenced Miguel's character, placing post-it notes where there is evidence in the text.

Book Connections

Baseball in April, by Gary Soto, contains a collection of short stories set in Fresno, California. Some of these stories are coming-of-age in nature, and students may be able to see thematic and cultural connections.

A Field Guide to the Classroom Library, Lucy Calkins and the Teachers College Reading and Writing Project, Heinemann, ©2002 Teachers College, Columbia University; http://www.heinemann.com/fieldguides

Genre
Nonfiction; Chapter Book

Teaching Uses
Independent Reading; Partnerships

A Field Guide to the Classroom Library, Lucy Calkins and the Teachers College Reading and Writing Project, Heinemann, ©2002 Teachers
College, Columbia University; http://www.heinemann.com/fieldguides

A Blossom Promise

Betsy Byars

Book Summary

The book's central characters include the Blossom children (Junior, Vern, and Maggie), their mother (Vicki), and their grandfather (Pap). Each chapter focuses on an episode of an individual character's actions across the span of a day, but by the 17th chapter ("By Snake Creek's Rushing Waters"), the author weaves in an event that causes the whole family to cross paths. Vern, the youngest, is tired of being the on-looker to his elder siblings' antics, and yearns to do something to impress the family. Junior, the middle, tries to establish his independence and confronts his own concomitance with maturity. Maggie, the eldest, teeters on the threshold of the adult world by becoming the newest member of the rodeo circuit and by sorting out her feelings of resentment toward her mother's new relationship and her own feelings of love. Both Vicki and Pap reflect on their own lives and yearn to be young and carefree again. It is when Pap suffers a heart attack that each Blossom member realizes that it is the bringing together of all of their unique qualities that makes their family strong.

Basic Book Information

A Blossom Promise has 145 pages and is divided into 28 self-titled chapters. There are about five pages per chapter. The chapters are cumulative, describing moments of each Blossom family member over the course of a day. The plot unfolds across the sequence of this time frame. Because chapters are not numbered, the chapter titles provide some insight as to the events and happenings. There are illustrations throughout the book that support the text.

Noteworthy Features

The passage of time spans the course of one day and is demonstrated by cumulative chapters, so students who are attempting to build reading stamina or focus closer attention to text may choose to take this book in as a "project." This book is the last of the *Blossom* series, and if it is read out of its series order the reader will need to rely on inferential skills when certain family situations and relationships are discussed. Each chapter in the book does act as a cadence to following chapters, enabling readers to develop predicting and questioning skills. Furthermore, the dialogue is free-standing in structure and helps the reader maintain meaning.

The narrator describes the actions and the thoughts of the entire Blossom family and even tells the actions and emotions of the family's pet dogs,

Series
Blossom

Illustrator
Jacqueline Rogers

Publisher
Bantam Doubleday Dell, 1987

ISBN
0440401372

TC Level
11

A Field Guide to the Classroom Library, Lucy Calkins and the Teachers College Reading and Writing Project, Heinemann, ©2002 Teachers College, Columbia University; http://www.heinemann.com/fieldguides

Dump and Mud. The individualistic characters and the setting-off of chapters devoted solely to each reflect the sense of each person feeling like a "vestige" of a family. There are real-life situations: death, new relationships, and a family member afflicted with a heart attack, all of which seem to drive the family's disconnectedness. This "outside-looking-in" viewpoint holds the reader to the story, pulling him or her along to find out how all of them will come together as one whole family.

The story is set in present day Arizona during the spring. The reader is exposed to river haunts and rodeos-settings that may not be familiar to some. However, the author writes each character with dimension and humor and the reader will find some antics of this eccentric family funny. This may encourage readers to read the other three books in the *Blossom* series.

Teaching Ideas

If this story is read as part of the series sequence, readers may want to talk about how the Blossom family characters have changed over the course of the books. Readers could also trace the family's progress toward coming together as a unit in this particular book (which happens during "The Rope Trick of the Year"). Independent readers or book clubs might be interested in collecting evidence for the role of each of the characters within the family unit. The title of the book will remain a mystery until the last chapter. A book club may wish to discuss what the title means in relation to the experience the family has gone through.

Another line of thinking that students could pursue is how each character sees him/herself as opposed to how he/she is perceived by family members. There is plenty of evidence to mark that shows both how the characters see themselves, and how they are seen by their families. Students can discuss how the Blossom children want to break out of the image their family has painted for them (and, ironically, that they have painted for each other).

Interesting work can be done with the story elements in this book. The way in which the story moves through time may be particularly interesting to some readers. While many chapter books take place over the course of weeks or more, readers may notice how Betsy Byars has slowed time for this particular book. How does this movement of time affect the plot? What does the author (and reader) gain by slowing the story down?

Book Connections

There are three other books in the series beginning with *The Not-Just-Anybody Family*, *The Blossoms Meet the Vulture Lady*, and *The Blossoms and the Green Phantom*. This book is the last of the series.

Genre

Chapter Book

A Field Guide to the Classroom Library, Lucy Calkins and the Teachers College Reading and Writing Project, Heinemann, ©2002 Teachers College, Columbia University; http://www.heinemann.com/fieldguides

Teaching Uses

Independent Reading; Book Clubs; Character Study

A Field Guide to the Classroom Library, Lucy Calkins and the Teachers College Reading and Writing Project, Heinemann, ©2002 Teachers College, Columbia University; http://www.heinemann.com/fieldguides

A Drop of Water

Walter Wick

Book Summary

Each of the short sections in this book describes a characteristic of water. It begins with the look of a drop as it falls, and moves through an explanation of surface tension and waters' attraction to itself. Readers learn about capillary action, bubbles and thin films, ice, vapor, and crystallization, condensation, precipitation, snow, ice, and clouds, and much more. Each explanation is accompanied by a stark photograph illustrating the property and an experiment that explains it further. Terms relevant to the explanation are defined within the text of the book.

Basic Book Information

This is a forty-page picture book of science. It has no table of contents and no index, although the text is divided into units of approximately one page each. Each page has about a paragraph of text and a large, clear-as-a-bell photograph of whichever property of water is being described.

The text itself serves as a caption to the photograph. The last two pages of the book describe experiments readers can embark on to further understand the properties and principals of water explained in the book. These experiments are printed in small font, and the pages aren't illustrated. The very last section of the book is a note from the author describing how he got the idea for the book and how he managed to take such unusual and beautiful photographs.

Noteworthy Features

The photographs in this book are spectacular without being flashy. They reveal the invisible marvels in everyday water. Because they are full color without including colorful objects, they are simple and scientifically descriptive.

The text, though full of abstract and concrete scientific concepts, is broken into small sections that are easier to grasp than large groups of text. While the properties of water are clearly interrelated, the book explains enough about each property so that any one topic can be read individually. This makes the book a good one for browsing. Readers can let the pictures catch their interest and then read the paragraph about them. The book could be used for a reference to find answers to particular questions if the reader is willing to page through the book looking for the heading that would address her particular topic.

The experiments in the book are a unique feature that will undoubtedly help children feel involved with the concepts in the book. Each of the experiments uses no more than a few easily obtainable objects, many of which can be found around the house or classroom. The book also has

Publisher
Scholastic, 1997

ISBN
0590023195

TC Level
9; 10; 11

recommendations for children who are interested in preparing and designing their own experiments. The introduction to this section even includes safety precautions.

In addition to helping children understand the concepts in the book, the existence of the experiments in the text reinforces the idea in readers that the text is about the real world, not only about abstract ideas, but about physical things readers can touch and see and experiment for themselves.

Teaching Ideas

As mentioned previously, the experiments in the text could be a marvelous way to help children understand their reading.

The last line of the book gives photo credit to Bentley. Readers who are familiar with the recent Caldecott winner about *Snowflake Bentley* may be excited to see this reference, or to read the two books side by side.

Genre
Nonfiction; Picture Book

Teaching Uses
Reading and Writing Nonfiction; Partnerships; Content Area Study; Read Aloud

An Angel for Solomon Singer

Cynthia Rylant

Book Summary

In this gentle, resonant picture book the author recounts the story of Solomon Singer, who resides in a hotel for men in New York City. Lonely and friendless, depressed by his drab room, Solomon wanders the city at night, dreaming of his boyhood home in Indiana. One evening he chances upon the Westway Café and a friendly waiter named Angel. The cozy café becomes a regular destination, and the warm welcome Solomon finds there satisfies his painful yearnings and alters his view of the city.

Basic Book Information

This 28-page picture book is an ALA Notable Book, an NCSS-CBC Notable Children's Trade Book in Social Studies, and a Child Study Association Book of the Year. Cynthia Rylant is the 1993 Newbery medalist for *Missing May* and the author of many highly regarded picture books (*When I was Young in the Mountains* among others) and books for older readers. The rhythmic prose and poetic language of this story make it a fine choice for a read-aloud session.

Catalanotto's rich-hued watercolor illustrations provide a dream-like complement to the author's memorable text. In the opening spread, for example, Solomon Singer's elongated body and face are seen in an image reflected in a steaming teakettle. Later his reflection appears, upside down, in a puddle. Other illustrations mingle Solomon's wishes and memories with the real-life details of his present surroundings, blending, for example, a view of a city street by night with an image of Solomon's boyhood home in Indiana. Sharp-eyed readers will point out that the tiger cat following Solomon on the street in the beginning of the story looks like the cat Solomon is holding on the final page of the book, after the story's conclusion.

Noteworthy Features

Children will enjoy focusing on the vivid details the author uses to make Solomon believable. Solomon dreams of a balcony, a fireplace, a porch swing, and a picture window for watching the birds. He wishes the walls of his room were yellow or purple. In the café he orders two biscuits, some bacon, and a large glass of grapefruit juice. Also noteworthy is Rylant's command of prose style. For example, she uses many long, rhythmic sentences with repeated grammatical elements, sometimes followed by a very short sentence (*The menus told him how much hamburgers and bowls of soup and pieces of pie and other things cost. But it didn't put a price on dreams.*)

Illustrator
Peter Catalanotto

Publisher
Orchard Books, 1992

ISBN
0531070824

TC Level
9

Teaching Ideas

Teachers in the Teachers College Reading and Writing Project community often regard this as one of Cynthia Rylant's best pieces of fiction, and it is often used as a touchstone text in Writing Workshops. For example, children who are trying to write short fiction have studied the craft in this book to learn strategies they too can use in their own stories. It helps that *An Angel for Solomon Singer* is a short story and that it is written in third person like the stories students write. Children (and teachers) especially notice that Rylant's book moves through time beautifully. Like many other favorite books, it has just a bit of magic in the text.

The setting of this text is New York City and this is valuable to us because there aren't many stories written about the city that students can enjoy. A teacher may want to help readers understand the implications of living in this kind of residential hotel for men. This can become a grand lesson on how a writer takes from the real (characters based on real people) and creates fiction.

Each of the story elements in this book is clear and easy to follow and find. A teacher could help students to think about the following things in this book:

How do stories begin (this one begins by describing the character)

How a story must, at some point, move from "everyday" to the "one day." In this book, it's "One evening..."

How to use parenthesis to create an aside

The name of the character is really a part of the story (Angel, the waiter's name is significant.)

How to include a list inside a story

How to move from writing that stretches time out making it move slowly (each night he visits the restaurant), to writing that shrinks time ("For many, many nights Solomon Singer made his way west, carrying...")

How to show the change that the character is undergoing

Although this book is perfect for craft studies within the writing workshop, a teacher could also spend an equal amount of time focusing on the story and its message.

An Angel for Solomon Singer also lends itself to work with the story elements, and would provide for an interesting study of character. While students often get to know characters through dialogue with others, we get to know Solomon through his dreams. These dreams provide rich opportunities for making inferences about Solomon's character. The story tells readers that Solomon was a wanderer by nature. How might Solomon's wandering have influenced the course of his life-the jobs he took, the places he lived, and the relationships he formed or didn't form? For what reasons might Solomon have landed in New York City-far, in many ways, from his boyhood home in Indiana? Some students may have connections to people who live alone, and seem to have no friends or relatives, like Solomon. Knowledge of such people may contribute to their understanding of Solomon.

Children may be coached to notice that Rylant's spare portrait of Solomon omits a great deal. Rylant gives no explanation for how he came to reside in the hotel in New York City or how he supports himself. The story tells readers only that Solomon was a wanderer by nature. Teachers could use this as an opportunity to encourage thinking outside of the text to seek answers to unresolved questions. What are *some* of the reasons that may lead a person to live in a hotel? What are *some* of the ways Solomon may be supporting himself? Students can use their knowledge of the world to infer possible explanations.

In reviewing the book, a teacher might think that there are several aspects that might cause challenges for students, and when she talks with children who read the book, she may want to dig a bit to see if these parts were in fact confusing. One thing that can confuse readers is the references to Indiana. Students may not know what Indiana is like (or know the term *Midwest*). The teacher might start off by talking about Solomon's boyhood home in Indiana, far different in many ways from New York City. This can help students understand why Solomon Singer is lonely in New York City. Students might also get confused with the parenthesis that appear sporadically. It might be helpful if the teacher talked with a reader about the text that sometimes appears in parenthesis. Finally students may find trouble with Rylant's use of the word *dreams*. Solomon Singer carries "a dream in his head, each night ordering it up with his supper." Teachers may want to talk about the fact that not everything is meant to be taken literally.

Readers may also be interested in discussing the role that Angel plays in the story. While he is not the central character, Solomon is changed by his interactions with Angel. Authors include minor characters for a reason. Why did Rylant choose to make a waiter Solomon's Angel? What can Angel's impact on Solomon tell us about the role minor players can play in our own lives?

One teacher decided to have a small group of students read this book on their own. She decided to introduce the book to help them have a fluent and meaningful first read of it. She said to the small group, "Today you're going to have the chance to read a book by Cynthia Rylant, *An Angel for Solomon Singer*. It is a book about an older man named Solomon Singer. Solomon Singer lives in a hotel here in New York City but he doesn't like where he lives and he is lonely. He is sad and misses where he grew up. If you look on page 4, we learn he is from Indiana-which is a state where there are lots of fields and trees. It's a good place to walk around-to wander. One day when Solomon Singer is in New York City, he comes to a café. It reminds him of being in Indiana. This makes him feel good so he eats and dreams. Do some of you have dreams? Do you ever dream of a place you want to go or what you want to be when you grow up? That's what Solomon Singer does in this book while he is eating. The café makes him happy and reminds him of home. Today you can read this wonderful book all the way through by yourself. If you finish the book, read it again and mark bits that you notice. Then we'll talk a lot about it."

Book Connections

Students who liked this book might want to read other books that Cynthia Rylant and Peter Catalanotto worked together on, *All I See* and *Soda Jerk*.

For a different take on a person who spent much of her life wandering and who has wound up living alone, try *Miss Rumphius* by Barbara Cooney.

A Field Guide to the Classroom Library, Lucy Calkins and the Teachers College Reading and Writing Project, Heinemann, ©2002 Teachers College, Columbia University; http://www.heinemann.com/fieldguides

Genre
Picture Book

Teaching Uses
Author Study; Teaching Writing; Interpretation

A Field Guide to the Classroom Library, Lucy Calkins and the Teachers College Reading and Writing Project, Heinemann, ©2002 Teachers College, Columbia University; http://www.heinemann.com/fieldguides

Anastasia Again!

Lois Lowry

FIELD GUIDE

Book Summary

In this second installment of the *Anastasia* series, twelve-year-old Anastasia discovers that her artist mother and English professor father are planning to move the family from sophisticated Cambridge to the suburbs. Anastasia is convinced that, in the suburbs, every living room is dominated by a huge television set, all walls are hung with paint-by-number art, and all housewives wear pink hair curlers to the supermarket. To vent her feelings, Anastasia begins to write a mystery story-the title and content of which change in amusing ways over the course of the book. Anastasia's regret over leaving their much-loved apartment and her friends is tempered by her pleasure over the big house her family buys, complete with a tower room for Anastasia.

Anastasia and her little brother Sam meet the next-door neighbor Gertrude Stein, a lonely and grouchy old woman, and Anastasia becomes friends with Steve Harvey, who will be in her seventh grade class. Meanwhile, Anastasia keeps in touch with two classmates from Cambridge, Jenny and Robert. She invites them to visit. Trying to help her lonely neighbor, Anastasia also invites members of the local Senior Citizen Center to come to her house for Kool-Aid, intending to introduce them to Gertrude. Only later does she realize that she invited her old friends and the seniors to come on the same day. The get-together turns out to be a huge success.

Afterward, touring the house, Robert, Jenny, and Anastasia discover a declaration of love for Gertrude Stein written on the wall of Anastasia's tower room many years ago. Gertrude enjoys the note, which recalls the neighbor boy she always loved, even after he married another woman. And so the Krupniks are happy with their new house, Gertrude has broken out of her shell, and Anastasia has made new friends while keeping the old. The book ends with Anastasia winding up her mystery novel, the final title of which is "The Mystery of Saying Good-bye."

Basic Book Information

This book contains 145 pages and twelve chapters. Many chapters are divided into shorter segments, the breaks marked by white space and an asterisk. The book is very humorous.

The book received excellent reviews and was named an American Library Association Notable Book for Children. The book is part of an *Anastasia* series, which has been in print almost twenty years. Lowry has written many books for young readers. She received the Newbery Medal for *Number The Stars* and *The Giver*.

Series
Anastasia

Publisher
Houghton Mifflin, 1981

ISBN
0440400090

TC Level
12

Noteworthy Features

The story is told in third person with Anastasia as the character whose viewpoint we see through. The sequence of events unfolds chronologically during the summer before Anastasia starts seventh grade. Lowry's gift for making ordinary situations funny enhances the lively, engaging plot, and the dialogue between characters is witty. Anastasia lives in a warm, loving household. Her cosmopolitan parents bicker amiably from time to time, sometimes losing patience with Anastasia's exaggerated behavior.

Teaching Ideas

Independent readers or book clubs may choose to embark on a character study of Anastasia. They may end up documenting Anastasia's proclivity to make snap judgements, and seeking evidence to determine whether or not this aspect of her changes throughout the story. Anastasia's father informs her that she is making "premature assumptions" about the suburbs when she tells them she is unwilling to move. The phrase "premature assumptions" recurs throughout the book as Anastasia observes her own attitudes and the behavior of other people and realizes the errors that can result from hasty conclusions. Another line of thinking students may pursue is to seek evidence that supports or discredits Anastasia's stereotypes about the suburbs.

Lowry's inclusion of Gertrude Stein stands out in this story, as most of the *Anastasia* books stick closer to characters Anastasia's age. Students may want to consider why Lowry chose Stein as a character, and what her presence in the book reveals to us about Anastasia. What did the author want Anastasia, and us, to learn from Gertrude? In addition to looking at Gertrude, readers may wish to look at other characters in this text.

Readers may also use post-it notes to mark important places in Anastasia's writing, to discuss the effect of Anastasia's experiences on the mystery book she is writing for catharsis. The title and content of the book change (quite humorously) as Anastasia experiences various emotions in connection with her experiences.

Book Connections

Lois Lowry is a prolific writer for children. Her *Anastasia* series includes *Anastasia Krupnik, Anastasia Ask Your Analyst, Anastasia on Her Own, Anastasia at Your Service, Anastasia Has the Answers, Anastasia's Chosen Career*, and *Anastasia at This Address*. Although Anastasia's age changes as the series progresses, children who like this engaging heroine may take pleasure in exploring both earlier and, later (more challenging) stories about her life.

Genre
Chapter Book

A Field Guide to the Classroom Library, Lucy Calkins and the Teachers College Reading and Writing Project, Heinemann, ©2002 Teachers College, Columbia University; http://www.heinemann.com/fieldguides

Teaching Uses
Independent Reading; Character Study

Appalachia: The Voices of Sleeping Birds

Cynthia Rylant

Book Summary

Appalachia is a nonfiction book told as a story of a people and follows a circle structure in its plot. It begins by introducing the good dogs of Appalachia who are then present throughout the story. At the end, the good dogs run through the mountains.

It is a clear story that evokes images of how the people of Appalachia live. Regardless of circumstance, the mountains and nature surround all, and this seems to unite and give common values to the people in the story.

Basic Book Information

This book is 23 pages long. Each 2-page spread contains one page of illustrations and the other of text. The vocabulary is very simple and there is no use of technical or erudite terms. There are no main characters in this story. It is possible to see the mountains as the main character, for they are there on every page.

The information of this book is given subtly and it becomes an overall picture, rather than a series of discrete pictures or assembled facts. There is evidence of research behind the scenes that comes out as the two characters talk to one another.

Noteworthy Features

This is a gentle nonfiction book, which helps the reader to appreciate and love the people and mountains of Appalachia. This is a book written for people curious about Appalachia and results in appreciation and a whetting of the appetite for more information. From this book, resulting studies could develop, including perhaps studies of coal mining, agriculture, religion, quilting, canning, hunting, or weather. All these topics are given a light touch.

Barry Moser was raised in Appalachia and his illustrations are of actual people and scenes in this area. For every page of text, there is an accompanying illustration on the other page. These illustrations are directly and indirectly tied to the text. For example, there is an illustration of a dog lying on the ground in front of a house porch. The porch is made of wood and sits up off the ground on unseen legs. There is no foundation evident. The accompanying text simply states, "some are wood and some are brick" of the houses. The illustration serves to elaborate more by showing a tiny corner of a house. Both author and illustrator work together to give more to the reader.

Illustrator
Barry Moser

Publisher
Harcourt Brace, 1991

ISBN
0152016058

TC Level
9; 10; 11

A Field Guide to the Classroom Library, Lucy Calkins and the Teachers College Reading and Writing Project, Heinemann, ©2002 Teachers College, Columbia University; http://www.heinemann.com/fieldguides

Cynthia Rylant is a gifted writer and Appalachia is a well-crafted book. Rylant brings the tools of writing poetry, memoir, and fiction to this nonfiction text. Her literary and artistic style is present in every sentence of this book, and readers will create a richer story if they take the time to envision the scenes Rylant portrays. For example, "Night in these houses is thick, the mountains wear heavy shawls of fog and giant moths flap at the porch lights while cars cut thought the dark hollows like burrowing moles." This is a fairly complex sentence, with layers of visuals piled on top of each other. It may be too rich for readers unused to the form of prose.

Teaching Ideas

Appalachia would serve well as a touchstone text to teach students to write literary nonfiction, and specifically to write narrative nonfiction. There are hundreds of passages that can take one's breath away. "What has Rylant done to make me gasp over this line?" readers ask. "Where else did she use a similar technique?" "What purpose does she accomplish when she does this?" Soon readers may take out their own drafts and reread them, thinking, "Where could I borrow on one of Rylant's techniques, using it within my own text?"

Some of the most important craft lessons in *Appalachia* are not the ones that readers will cite if they begin with the questions, "Where is her writing especially notable? What has she done?" Teachers may then want to draw readers (and apprentice nonfiction writers) to notice the way Rylant weaves information about the everyday life in Appalachia into this story of one day. Rylant guides the reader thru Appalachia; she writes "The houses..." "Inside their homes," "In their bedrooms," "The kitchens," "Mommy's," "If it is Sunday. ..." Rylant is the friendly guide bringing the reader inside homes to new rooms and personal belongings, going inside churches and onto front porches to observe what the people are doing.

It can be especially important for readers to notice the way Rylant, as a writer, paints the world of Appalachia with her words. She shows rather than tells. She also writes for people who read-with-their-ears, and readers can note and discuss what Rylant does to create rhythm and songs with words.

As a source for a study of Appalachia in social studies, this would be a great introductory book to start an inquiry. Using it as a read aloud in the content area can get students understanding more about this area and its people as well as creating researchable issues and questions.

This book could also be used as a way to teach note taking and processing (and interacting) with information. Finally, it would fit well into an author study on Cynthia Rylant.

Book Connections

Cynthia Rylant and Barry Moser have both written or illustrated numerous other books for children.

Genre
Nonfiction

A Field Guide to the Classroom Library, Lucy Calkins and the Teachers College Reading and Writing Project, Heinemann, ©2002 Teachers College, Columbia University; http://www.heinemann.com/fieldguides

Teaching Uses
Content Area Study; Reading and Writing Nonfiction; Author Study; Read Aloud; Teaching Writing

Arthur for the Very First Time

Patricia MacLachlan

Book Summary

Arthur's parents need time to themselves to prepare for the imminent birth of his new baby sister. They leave him with his Aunt and Uncle for the summer, and the story begins. Through his relationships with Aunt Elda, Uncle Wrisby, and Moira, Arthur learns to watch less and do more, participating in life instead of sitting still as events unfold around him. This book is about taking the risks necessary to true growth, as well as the power of relationships to affect change. These themes are embodied, respectively, by Arthur's initial fear of climbing out his window onto a bordering tree branch, of literally "going out on a limb," and by Aunt Elda's story of the prism. She says, "All of us touch each other. Just like the colors of the prism. Don't you forget that."

Arthur's writing grows increasingly reflective as he begins to see the world through new eyes. His emerging ability to glimpse life from new perspectives is the gift intended by Uncle Wrisby when he hands Arthur a pair of binoculars. He says, "Look in the little end if you want to see things up close. ...The other end makes everything far away." Arthur wonders why anyone would want to see things from far away. Uncle Wrisby replies, "Sometimes you see just as well. ...Sometimes better."

This book is about the discoveries Arthur makes when he looks up from his notebook and steps into life, eventually coming to terms with the coming birth of his baby sister. Toward the end of the story Arthur is beginning to take action, and is initially despondent when things don't always work out the way he had planned. Bernadette, Uncle Wrisby's pig, does not seem to like the pen Arthur builds. He attempts to treat Pauline, the sick, french-speaking chicken, with Uncle Wrisby's tonic, but makes her drunk instead.

The book climaxes when Bernadette gives birth in the midst of a thunderous downpour. She is standing in the pen Arthur built, and Arthur and Moira discover one of her piglets laying still in the mud. Arthur remembers what to do from a book Moira loaned him, and is able to rescue the pig from near death. Moira exclaims, "Arthur did it! Arthur really did it all!" She has never before uttered his name, aptly referring to him instead as Mouse, and it is here that the story ends and Arthur's life as himself begins. "He looked up to grin at Moira, who called him Arthur for the very first time."

Basic Book Information

This book is 117 pages, divided into fifteen chapters. The chapters' titles frequently signal important themes or ideas to be glimpsed within them.

Publisher
Harper & Row, 1963

ISBN
0060240458

TC Level
12

There exist both illustrated and non-illustrated editions of this text. A table of contents precedes the title page, indicating chapter numbers, titles and page numbers in italics. MacLachlan also uses italics to set poems and songs apart from the body of the story, and to provide readers with a glimpse into Arthur's thinking. The story is told in third-person narrative. Arthur's journal entries and letters are printed in bold font.

Noteworthy Features

Randall Jarrell's *The Mockingbird*, read by Aunt Elda, is about distinguishing the truth from its reflection as perceived within our limited perspective. This poem is reflective of the questions Arthur poses as he begins to glimpse the world from a changing, more inclusive point of view. Although he does not understand it immediately, and will never fully discern its full meaning, Arthur returns to its words at important moments in the text. This facilitates students' understanding of the poem, and encourages them to make connections between it and the changes taking place within the character.

Arthur inwardly recites, "*Which one's the mockingbird? Which one's the world?*" after Moira asks, "O real...what's real?" After unfocusing his eyes and seeing Uncle Wrisby's garden from a new perspective, "He could still see the roses, looking like watercolor flowers in the background. But now he saw the tall, dark-green onions. ...It was almost like looking through the far away end of the binoculars. Far away, but near somehow. ...Look one way, look the other, he said to himself, remembering the poem Aunt Elda had read to him. ...*I wish*, he thought, *I wish I could unfocus my eyes just enough to make that tree look smaller. Then maybe I could climb it.*" Arthur is learning that his fear is only as big as he imagines it to be; he is seeing for the first time that it is possible to change his perspective and overcome it. He writes in his journal, quoting *The Mockingbird*, "Look one way, look the other," then wonders: *How do my parents see me?*

Early on in the text, MacLachlan provides an outstanding opportunity to empower students with the language of metaphor, enabling them to put words to ideas and feelings for which there are not words. She writes, "And suddenly, something seemed to move, to shift, to open a bit like a door opening in a dark room and letting in a sliver of hall light." Taking time to discuss the meanings intended by the opening door and emergent light will deepen their ability to recognize these common themes in other books and empower them with the language to talk about it.

Randall Jarrell's *The Mockingbird* is replete with myriad layers of meaning, and was written for an adult audience. Arthur himself does not understand it right away, and never fully discerns its implications. He records in his journal, "I don't understand the poem either." He continually returns to the line most relevant to his life, eventually understanding that things are not always what they seem to be as glimpsed through the narrow, limited perspective of his vision. This is all that is necessary to students' understanding of the text. They should not be expected to understand it before Arthur does, nor should undue time be devoted to other possible interpretations. Also, Uncle Wrisby speaks to his chicken only in French, occasionally singing to her. No melody is provided. When reading these passages aloud to students, the teacher may need to think ahead toward how these passages will be read and sang.

Teaching Ideas

This book might best be taught as a daily read aloud, as it is rich with literary themes and requires heavy teacher support to do justice to its significance. MacLachlan provides strong evidence in support of Arthur's journey toward a new perspective, a vision in which he is not only observing life, but taking risks and becoming part of the action as it unfolds.

Arthur shows his journal to Uncle Wrisby. He explains, "I write about people, things I see, everything I think about." Uncle Wrisby takes a pair of binoculars out of a leather case and replies, "Don't believe in anything written, only what I see...I've got these instead of a journal." Aunt Elda climbs onto the tree branch outside Arthur's window. She encourages him to do the same. "Arthur's mouth felt dry. Dry with fear. He's never climbed this high before. Never for himself. Never for a silly bird."

Readers will soon see Arthur's perspective is beginning to change. MacLachlan writes, "And for a moment, his binocular eyes turned inward on himself: A small boy, sitting on a hay mound with a russett chicken." After making homemade braces with Moira, Arthur studies his reflection in the mirror. "His hair was uncombed, and with his smiling face, he didn't look much like Arthur anymore."

Throughout the book Arthur is continually surprised by his own thoughts, "It came as a great surprise to Arthur, and it wasn't until Uncle Wrisby reached out to take Arthur's hand that he realized he said 'I love you' right out loud." When Arthur and Moira plan the pen they will build for Bernadette, Arthur realizes, "He had never planned anything in his life. For Arthur everything happened one way or another, either way it should be or the way it shouldn't without any help on his part." At the end of the story, after Arthur saves the life of a baby pig, Moira exclaims, "Arthur did it! Arthur really did it all!"

It is easy to see why this book makes for a perfect character study.

Book Connections

In Patricia MacLachlan's *Journey*, the title character learns to see things as they really are through his relationship with his grandfather, who teaches him to look through the lens of the camera to the truth. *The Monument*, by Gary Paulsen, is the story of Rocky's journey toward a new perspective, and the important relationship that made this possible.

Genre
Chapter Book

A Field Guide to the Classroom Library, Lucy Calkins and the Teachers College Reading and Writing Project, Heinemann, ©2002 Teachers College, Columbia University; http://www.heinemann.com/fieldguides

Teaching Uses
Independent Reading; Read Aloud; Character Study

At Her Majesty's Request: An African Princess In Victorian England

Walter Dean Myers

Book Summary

Sarah Forbes Bonetta was an African Princess who as a child was rescued from a ritual in which she was to be put to death, by an officer in the British Navy. She is taken back to England and given the name Sarah Forbes Bonetta. Queen Victoria takes an interest in the young princess and supports her throughout her life in England and Africa. Her story is one that deals with royalty, class, race, and equality.

Basic Book Information

This 146 page book is organized in chapters with titles that represent the main focus of the chapter. The story unfolds chronologically from when the Princess is captured at about age 5 until her death at about age 37.

Noteworthy Features

The subtitles of the chapters and the letters and excerpts from Queen Victoria's diary support a reader's understanding of the story. The pictures also support the understanding process. However, because this story is pieced together from historical information there are some holes in the story that can make it hard for readers to understand.

Teaching Ideas

This biography tells the story of Sarah Forbes Bonetta. The introduction explains how the author gathered information from letters he found in an antique shop and from historians in England. Her actual date of birth and her actual name were never learned. The book includes letters written to and by Sarah to the various people she lived with and to and from Queen Victoria. Excerpts from Queen Victoria's diary are also included in the telling of the story.

This book can be used to show the breath of nonfiction which includes biography and stories that are "real." It can be read aloud in grades 3 or above, and a read-aloud of the book could lead to an in-depth conversation regarding life in Victorian England, class, royalty, cultures, and so on.

This book demonstrates how research and information gathered from primary sources, can be incorporated into the story, not just told. It can also support the Social Studies curriculum.

Publisher
Scholastic Press, 1999

ISBN
0590486691

TC Level
13; 14; 15

A Field Guide to the Classroom Library, Lucy Calkins and the Teachers College Reading and Writing Project, Heinemann, ©2002 Teachers College, Columbia University; http://www.heinemann.com/fieldguides

Book Connections

Walter Dean Myers has written many books for young readers.

Genre

Nonfiction; Chapter Book

Teaching Uses

Reading and Writing Nonfiction; Content Area Study; Read Aloud; Independent Reading

A Field Guide to the Classroom Library, Lucy Calkins and the Teachers College Reading and Writing Project, Heinemann, ©2002 Teachers College, Columbia University; http://www.heinemann.com/fieldguides

Autumn Street

Lois Lowry

FIELD GUIDE

F G

Book Summary

While her father is off fighting in World War II, six-year-old Elizabeth lives with her grandparents on Autumn Street in a small town in Pennsylvania. Now an adult looking back on that time, Elizabeth conjures up in luminous detail the people who filled her life: her mother and older sister, her grandparents, the three spinster great-aunts, and-especially-her beloved Tatie, the black cook, and Tatie's young grandson Charles, Elizabeth's best friend. With the world she knew disrupted by war, the imaginative Elizabeth suspects danger everywhere. She worries that her father will never return and that her pregnant mother will die in childbirth. She is terrified by tales she hears of flesh-eating turtles, and a man ground flat by a train.

As the months pass, significant events, both good and bad occur. Elizabeth's mother safely delivers a baby boy. Her grandfather buys Elizabeth an autograph book, but she is dismayed to discover that Tatie doesn't know how to write her name in it. She and Charles ignore the cries of a neighbor boy who is ill because they despise him for his cruelty to animals; when the boy dies, they believe they are to blame. Charles and Elizabeth visit her three great-aunts, who make such a fuss over Charles that Elizabeth, in a fit of jealousy, calls him a nigger. Elizabeth's elegant grandfather suffers an incapacitating stroke, and Elizabeth struggles to make contact with him.

When fall arrives, both Elizabeth and Charles start first grade, but in separate, segregated schools. Elizabeth makes friends with a girl named Louise and encounters the town crazy man, Ferdie Gossett, of whom she has heard many stories. During Thanksgiving dinner at the home of the great-aunts, Elizabeth learns a family secret concerning an engagement between her grandfather and one of the great-aunts. And finally, with chilling inevitability, comes the painful event alluded to in the opening of the book.

Despite a sore throat, Elizabeth goes sledding with Charles, taking him to the local park. Older boys mistreat him and order him off the hill because he is black. Enraged and humiliated, Charles runs off into the woods. Elizabeth, feverish and fearful of some nameless threat, turns back. While Elizabeth lies ill, the police discover Charles in the woods with his throat slit, a victim of Ferdie Gossett. Elizabeth struggles with her illness and with the awful news of the tragedy. On her seventh birthday, her father arrives, using a cane because he has lost part of one leg. "Bad things won't happen any more," he assures Elizabeth and the adult narrator.

Publisher
Dell Yearling, 1986

ISBN
0440403448

TC Level
14

Basic Book Information

Seventeen chapters and 188 pages long, this novel looks back at a year in a child's life as seen from adulthood. The main character is only six, but the richly nuanced story and sophisticated writing make the novel more appropriate for readers from age nine and up. Although the narrator and central character is a girl, there is also a male character of the same age who figures prominently in the plot. Boys who enjoy challenging themes and high-quality writing will like this complex story. The book received starred reviews from *Booklist* and *School Library Journal*. Lowry has written many books for young readers from lower middle grades up to young adult. She received the Newbery Medal for *Number The Stars* and *The Giver* and won acclaim for *A Summer to Die*.

Noteworthy Features

The first-person story is told in the voice of the adult narrator. The opening and closing sections frame the tale and set the tone for the often painful memories that will be recounted. Characters are strongly developed.

Stylistically, Lowry accomplishes a difficult feat, unifying the adult voice of the narrator with the perceptions and emotions of the child she was at six.

Teaching Ideas

The story is set in a small town in Pennsylvania during World War II, a setting unfamiliar to many young readers. Teachers may find it helpful to readers to provide some orientation to the setting to prepare students for the story.

This book is full of symbolism and deeper meanings for an astute reader who is willing to dig below the surface. It is, therefore, a great book for readers who are learning to do interpretive work. In a conference, a teacher could ask, "Why did the author do this? What do you think she is trying to say?" One challenge, when a reader interprets, is to go from saying something about one part of a text to saying something about the entire text. "Why are the woods portrayed in such a foreboding way, do you think?" a teacher might ask and then respond to *whatever* the child says by asking, "so go from that to saying something about the book as a whole. How do your ideas of the woods, for example, fit with the title?" There are no right and wrong answers but readers need to learn to justify their interpretations with evidence from the text and to try to compose interpretations that account for as many parts of the text as possible.

When helping youngsters to think about the deeper meanings in a book, it is helpful to remind them that nothing in the book is accidental. The way the book opens and closes, the names of the characters, the metaphors Lowry uses etc. are all chosen for deliberate reasons. Lowry could have done all of these things differently. Why might she have made these choices?

The opening section makes it clear that the story will culminate in tragedy, and the description of the murky color the narrator would paint the woods ("the hueless shade that I know from my dreams to be the color of pain") hints that the tragedy will happen there. However, Lowry withholds the exact nature of the painful event and builds suspense by including other elements and incidents that suggest horrifying possibilities, but which don't prove central to the ultimate tragedy. Students can analyze the way she accomplishes this by listing those elements and incidents: the giant flesh-eating turtles Elizabeth believes inhabit the woods; the statement that baby boys are often born during the war to replace fathers killed in conflict; Willard B. Stanton's gruesome death under the wheels of a train; the knife found by Charles; Noah Hoffman's cruelty to animals and to his brother. In the opening section the narrator describes the painting she would make of Autumn Street in a way that suggests a Chagall painting. A reader might briefly research works by Chagall to help imagine the way that painting would look.

Teachers have used selective excerpts from this book as examples of good writing. Children could spend days discussing the passages in which Tatie shows Elizabeth the taste of cinnamon (and she in turn shows her grandfather) or Elizabeth's description of the awful taste of school milk.

Book Connections

Lois Lowry is a prolific writer for children. Her *Anastasia* series includes *Anastasia Krupnik, Anastasia Again!, Ask Your Analyst, Anastasia on Her Own, Anastasia at Your Service, Anastasia Has the Answers, Anastasia's Chosen Career*, and *Anastasia at This Address*. She has also written *Number The Stars* and *The Giver*. A book that takes a similar, but light-hearted, look at two kids staying with their grandmother during the 1924-42 era, is Richard Peck's *A Long Way from Chicago*.

Genre
Chapter Book

Teaching Uses
Independent Reading; Interpretation; Teaching Writing

A Field Guide to the Classroom Library, Lucy Calkins and the Teachers College Reading and Writing Project, Heinemann, ©2002 Teachers College, Columbia University; http://www.heinemann.com/fieldguides

Baby

Patricia MacLachlan

Book Summary

The story begins at summer's end. The tourists have left the island, and Larkin's family returns home to find a baby on their doorstep. A note reads, "This is Sophie. She is almost a year old and she is good. I cannot take care of her now, but I know she will be safe with you." Although it has not yet been revealed to the reader, the family has recently suffered, yet not acknowledged, the loss of their own baby. They are as yet incapable of even mentioning his brief presence in their lives, as the grief is too big for words. Larkin's father warns her against loving Sophie. It will be too painful, he thinks, when her mother returns and removes her from them. What he doesn't yet realize is that by allowing himself to love her, then leave her, he will be able to name and experience his grief. He will be capable of mourning the loss of his son.

The book begins its journey toward resolution when Larkin's teacher, Ms. Minifred tells the story of her own brother William, who has died. She says, "He wanted to be a writer, and he once said to me that words were comforting. Words had power, he told me. There was no way I could accept his death. . . . And then I found a poem among my brother's books. . . . When I read it I felt a strange and powerful comfort-not because it made me feel better, but because it said what I felt." She then recites "Dirge Without Music," by Edna St. Vincent Millay. Although Ms. Minifred will never accept William's death, she can now find the words to name it. The poem provided her with a mirror, through which she can see and ultimately accept the unnamable magnitude of her grief. Through this experience, Larkin is now able to do the same. She names the family baby William. At the conclusion of the story, her family marks his grave with a headstone bearing his name. In naming the baby, they are acknowledging his brief existence in their lives and are ultimately able to mourn his loss.

Basic Book Information

This book has 132 pages, divided into seventeen chapters. The chapters are not titled, and signal new phases in Larkin's family's journey toward naming and accepting their grief. The story is told in four parts: Summer's End, Winter, Spring, and Summer-Ten Years Later. It ends where it begins, yet the characters are not the same, thus reflecting the circular, transformative nature of time. The seasons are also reflective of the characters' experiences of their loss.

An excerpt from "Dirge Without Music," a poem by Edna St. Vincent Millay, precedes the title page, and is cited in its entirety on page eighty-five. MacLachlan uses italics to set poetry, songs, and glimpses into Larkin's thinking apart from the rest of the text. The first chapter, and every second chapter after that, begins with a brief, italicized passage clearly describing a

Publisher
Bantam Doubleday Dell, 1993

ISBN
0440411459

TC Level
12

memory. These are Sophie's memories of the family that was for a brief time her family, as told from a future, undisclosed place and time.

Noteworthy Features

The text begins with a stanza from Edna St. Vincent Millay's "Dirge Without Music." MacLachlan clues her readers into the central theme of this story, namely, Larkin's family's inability to face and accept the death of their infant son. Through Larkin's character, it is this poem that provides them with the language to express a feeling for which there are no words.

Students may not understand the poem at the opening of the book. MacLachlan probably intends for her readers to uncover and discover its meanings along with Larkin, who also does not understand the poem when it is first read to her. Teachers can encourage students to use the context of the poem to build their own theories about what it means to be resigned to something. When the poem finds its place in the story, it is probably not necessary to discuss it in its entirety. Instead, readers can look at it through Larkin's eyes, focusing primarily on the two lines she repeats to herself. These are essential to her story.

Along with providing her readers with a deeper understanding of the journey Larkin's family needs to take, MacLachlan creates an outstanding opportunity to discuss the real purpose literature serves in their lives. The characters feel that among other things, books and poems make them feel less alone helping them to hold mirrors up to experiences and feelings, empowering them with the language to talk. As Byrd says to Larkin, "You will have to find your way. Your dream is like a poem, you know. It puts in words what you think about but can't say. Maybe that's what poems do."

The italicized passages that precede every two chapters are also a potential source of difficulty. These are Sophie's memories of Larkin's family, as remembered from a future time and place. They are written from Sophie's point of view. MacLachlan begins, "The memory is this: a blue blanket in a basket that pricks her bare legs, and the world turning over as she tumbles out." While to a more experienced reader it is clear that these are Sophie's future memories of the story that is presently unfolding, MacLachlan's playfulness with both time and point of view will most likely confuse young readers. Teachers can provide students with a moment to develop hypotheses concerning the function of these passages, then explain them. This will probably greatly facilitate their understanding of the text, and free them to focus on the questions that are closer to the heart of the story.

Finally, MacLachlan does not initially reveal the secret that hangs heavy in the air surrounding Larkin's family. Although it will be tempting, teachers should be wary of telling students the story of William's death before the author does. She intends to keep her readers guessing, all the while providing clues toward the development of their own theories. By the time the plot is fully explained, most students will have accurately guessed the specifics of its content.

Teaching Ideas

This book is absolutely perfect for reading aloud and studying closely

A Field Guide to the Classroom Library, Lucy Calkins and the Teachers College Reading and Writing Project, Heinemann, ©2002 Teachers College, Columbia University; http://www.heinemann.com/fieldguides

through daily, whole class book talks. Its subject matter is extremely emotional, and it is filled with metaphors, layers of meanings and themes that less experienced readers may not discern independently. Some teachers have found it helpful to gently guide conversations toward the fact that Larkin's family will not articulate a secret that needs to be articulated, then support readers as they gather evidence toward the resolution of this central tension.

Some teachers have found that after spending time reading aloud and discussing this book, it is worthwhile to encourage children to harvest all their insights into literary essays. Each reader will need to review his or her jottings and notes and scan the pages of the book asking, "What is an insight or an idea about this book that snags my attention, that seems to matter?" Hopefully a class of readers will have a whole array of beginning ideas. One may notice that this is a book about the events that break the circles and patterns and rhythms of life. Another may notice that this is a book about Baby-an unnamed infant-who has the power that all babies have, the power to turn life around. Another may notice that the book is knit from Sophie's memories, and that what she remembers and doesn't remember is significant. Some will see this as the story of a family learning to accept a loss. Yet others will see this as a book about the silences in our lives, about the words that can bridge awful silences, and about families needing to communicate.

Larkin already knows the deafening sounds of silence. When Ms. Minifred moons over the power of words, Larkin thinks, "What about when there are no words?" "Silence can change you too, Ms. Minifred." Over time, Larkin begins to learn that words are powerful as well. A reader could gather evidence of this growing appreciation. After Ms. Minifred shares the experience of her brother's death and use of poetry as catharsis, Larkin runs home to read Millay's poem. She finally becomes equipped with the words to confront her mother. "I never saw the baby!" she said softly. "And you never named him! And you never talked to me about him!" Larkin learns to speak into the silence choking her family.

Book Connections

MacLachlan's *Journey* also addresses the title character's journey toward facing and accepting the truth. As Larkin's family is initially incapable of finding the language to cope with their loss, the boy Journey initially refuses to acknowledge the fact that his mother is never coming back. In both books, the transformative power of relationships and the arts eventually allow characters come to terms with their grief. For Journey, it is photography as introduced by his grandfather. For Larkin it is Sophie, and the poetry that empowers her with words for a previously unnamable loss. *The Monument*, by Gary Paulsen, is also a story of acceptance and change as made possible through Rocky's relationship with Mick and her emerging artistic sensibility.

Genre
Chapter Book

A Field Guide to the Classroom Library, Lucy Calkins and the Teachers College Reading and Writing Project, Heinemann, ©2002 Teachers College, Columbia University; http://www.heinemann.com/fieldguides

Teaching Uses
Read Aloud; Teaching Writing; Book Clubs

Baseball in April and Other Stories

Gary Soto

Book Summary

This collection of short stories focuses on the everyday lives of Hispanic children and teens growing up in Fresno, California. Many of the stories revolve around the main character's yearning for something (a guitar, a Barbie doll, a new dress for a dance, a chance to play Little League) and tell how the character goes about trying to achieve that goal.

In "Barbie," Veronica "had wanted a Barbie for as long as she could remember." Her Uncle Rudy does eventually buy her the doll she wants, while at the same time announcing his upcoming wedding, but at the end, Veronica's Barbie's head falls off and is lost.

In "The No-Guitar Blues," Fausto wants a guitar so badly he tells a small lie to gain the money to buy one. Consumed with guilt about his wrongdoing, he puts the money into the church collection. This story ends on a happy note, though, when his mother remembers that his grandfather has an old "guitarron" stored in his garage.

In "Mother and Daughter," Yollie and her mother share a special closeness. Mrs. Moreno is so poor she often can't afford to buy her daughter the clothes she needs, especially a new dress for the upcoming outdoor dance. They dye Yollie's white summer dress black, and for a while the dress is a big hit, until it begins to rain. The dye runs out, leaving Yollie's dress and her mood, gray.

Basic Book Information

This collection of short stories, 134 pages long, was named an ALA Best Book for Young Adults, A Booklist Editors' Choice, and A Horn Book Fanfare Selection. It also won the Beatty Award. Each chapter is a separate story from nine to fifteen pages long. The chapter titles hint at the focus of each story and draw readers in with names like "Broken Chain," "The Karate Kid," and "The No-Guitar Blues." While some figures later reappear as minor characters in other chapters, each story stands on its own. Except for the cover, there are no illustrations. However, Soto, who is also a poet, describes characters with such telling details that he provides readers with strong images. In the first story, young Alfonso keeps trying to push his crooked teeth back into place with his fingers. In a later story, Lupe works so hard to strengthen her thumb (in order to become a marbles champion) that her mother thinks her thumb is broken. There is an appealing simplicity and innocence to the children Soto describes. The stories are funny and ring true to life. Children will enjoy reading them and will probably identify with the characters.

Publisher
Harcourt Brace & Company, 1990

ISBN
015205720X

TC Level
12

A Field Guide to the Classroom Library, Lucy Calkins and the Teachers College Reading and Writing Project, Heinemann, ©2002 Teachers College, Columbia University; http://www.heinemann.com/fieldguides

Noteworthy Features

"Baseball in April," set in Fresno, California, is rich in details drawn from Hispanic life.

While each chapter stands on its own as an independent story, it is also possible to trace the common themes of growing up, love and friendship, success and failure throughout the anthology. Although the vocabulary and sentence structure are not complex, there is a maturity level to the stories that stems from the fact that some characters are as old as fifteen and also from the adult nature of some of the themes, such as being poor and falling in love for the first time. At times the author uses Spanish words and expressions; however, the characters who use them usually follows up immediately with the English words. There is also a glossary of Spanish words and phrases at the back of the book.

These stories reflect Gary Soto's own experiences growing up in California's Central Valley. Although the incidents in these stories have broad appeal and could have happened to practically any child at any time, there is a rich strain of Latino culture threaded through the narrative. Food plays an important role. One mother is cooking papas and chorizo con huevos. In another story, "a pile of tortillas lay warm under a dishtowel." Although poverty is common among the families in the stories, what stands out is their strong sense of family bonds; their pride, loyalty, and respect; and the way family and friends support each other. An offshoot of this is that these children are polite and respectful. Extended family is highly visible throughout the stories. In "La Bamba," the whole family comes to see Manuel pantomime Ritchie Valens's "La Bamba" in the school talent show. When Lupe shoots her way to victory in the marbles tournament in "The Marble Champ," her brother and father come along to cheer her on. "Growing Up" tells the story of Maria, a tenth grader who considers herself too old to go on the family vacation this year. After a heated argument with her father, she is allowed to stay behind with an aunt, but she winds up missing her family and worrying that something terrible has happened to them.

Teaching Ideas

Gary Soto creates rich characters, placing them in true-to-life situations. These stories could support work with students "putting themselves in their character's shoes," and emotionally empathizing with them. In doing this, they can help to create the world of the story in their minds. Some students may have connections to their own lives that help them in this endeavor. Several of the stories appear to have "unsatisfying" endings, such as "Baseball in April," "Two Dreamers," "Barbie," and "The Karate Kid." It might be useful for readers to consider why he or she thinks Gary Soto ended some stories this way (and not others).

In addition, Soto uses strong, vivid details in his stories, such as Lupe's swollen thumb and Alfonso's crooked teeth, which look like "a pile of wrecked cars." Yollie's mother is portrayed as "a large woman who wore a muumuu and butterfly-shaped glasses." Students who are trying to create the world of the story in their minds may find it useful to visualize these

A Field Guide to the Classroom Library, Lucy Calkins and the Teachers College Reading and Writing Project, Heinemann, ©2002 Teachers College, Columbia University; http://www.heinemann.com/fieldguides

details, making pictures of the world they wish to visit.

The short stories in "Baseball in April" also provide an opportunity for students to look at author choices in crafting a text. Teachers can encourage students to dig for the deeper message in the story, and to think about what Soto is *really* trying to say. Book clubs or partnerships who are experienced with these types of discussions may hold themselves accountable for the author's meaning. While this can be done with each story on its own, students may weave together meanings they discuss for each story and integrate them into a larger statement about the book as a whole.

A teacher may also choose to use these short stories to support story element work, and to encourage broader discussions of how the story elements influence each other. How does the setting, in a Latino neighborhood in Fresno, California, influence the plot? Can we always expect significant change with the passage of time? A related line of thinking some students may wish to pursue is seeking to document subtle, rather than overt, changes in character. For example, in "Barbie," Veronica gets the doll she always wanted, but the doll's head falls off. This may or may not have a profound influence on Veronica's character, but may have more subtle implications.

Book Connections

Students may want to read other books by Gary Soto. In *Taking Sides*, athlete Lincoln Mendoza must deal with conflicting loyalties when the basketball team at his new, suburban school plays the team from his old neighborhood school. In *Pacific Crossing*, a sequel to *Taking Sides*, Lincoln studies karate and travels to Japan.

Genre
Short Story Anthology; Memoir

Teaching Uses
Whole Group Instruction; Small Group Strategy Instruction; Partnerships; Book Clubs

A Field Guide to the Classroom Library, Lucy Calkins and the Teachers College Reading and Writing Project, Heinemann, ©2002 Teachers College, Columbia University; http://www.heinemann.com/fieldguides

Basket Moon

Mary Lyn Ray

Book Summary

A young boy lives with his mother and father deep in the woods. Every full moon, or basket moon, his father goes into Hudson to trade the baskets he has made for the goods the family needs. Every month, the boy asks to go along and the father says no. Then, when the boy is nine and beginning to learn the trade for himself, the two finally go to Hudson together. At first the trip is exciting and wonderful, but then, as they are leaving, a man in the square makes fun of the boy and his father for living in the hills and making baskets. The boy becomes ashamed of who he is and even messes up the baskets in the shed. Eventually, he comes to hear that the wind is also calling him to the trade and he once again feels proud to be a basketmaker.

Basic Book Information

This title has 32 pages filled with beautiful illustrations. Barbara Cooney's precise and tone-setting illustrations make this book inviting to many readers; it usually needs no help in gaining an audience.

Noteworthy Features

Some readers puzzle a bit over the setting. They ask each other if the family was very poor, or if the story just takes place a long time ago. Usually, this question is resolved when readers get to the part of the story that describes what is available in the stores in Hudson.

The book could almost be considered a book of nonfiction. A main focus of the story is the techniques and lifestyles of the basket makers of the Hudson. Children may find value in using this book as a model for the ways that nonfiction can be written, or the ways that research of real life can enrich a fictional story. This may serve as a guide for them when they carry out their own nonfiction or historical fiction writing projects.

Teaching Ideas

This is a coming of age story. Many discerning readers will struggle to understand the source of the boy's life-lesson. What caused his change of heart? This is a reasonable question, and some will be skeptical over how the boy could so easily go from feeling so upset to quickly accepting that he will be a basket maker. Readers may instead want to discuss the boy's response to the man who ridiculed him. Why is the man making fun of the father and son not the object of the boy's scorn? Why did the man's ridicule make the boy scorn his own family?

Some small groups of readers have discussed why the father waited so long to take the boy to Hudson. Maybe, they argued, if the father had taken

Illustrator
Barbara Cooney

Publisher
Little, Brown, and Company, 1999

ISBN
0316735213

the boy earlier, he could've gotten used to people making fun of him and it wouldn't have hit him so hard. Since he waited until he was nine, the boy had a lot of anticipation built up, and the bad experience really tore him down. Other readers say that the father didn't wait long enough because the boy wasn't ready to handle the teasing. Still others say he did handle it, didn't he? Teachers can use these ideas to complicate discussions of the issues in the books.

The Author's Note at the story's end is to be read by all readers of the story, not just adult readers. The level of difficulty of this portion of the text is not substantially different from that within the story, and the typeface and placement of the Note make it likely that children will read it, if they have enjoyed the story. Since the Author's Note is where the readers find out that the story is basically true, most readers will benefit from reading it, and a teacher may want to nudge children to notice this section. Children have even been known to start discussions based on the information in the Author's Note. These discussions have revolved around questions such as "Why did the people keep themselves so secluded?" or "Why did the author call the baskets 'art'?" and "Why were the basket makers in the story men when the one in the Note was a woman?"

Book Connections

This book has similarities to ...*And Now Miguel*, by Joseph Krumgold. ...*And Now Miguel* is also a coming of age story, about a boy who can't wait for the day to herd sheep with the men in his clan.

Genre
Picture Book; Historical Fiction; Nonfiction

Teaching Uses
Independent Reading; Content Area Study

Black Hoops: The History of African Americans In Basketball

Fredrick McKissack Jr.

Book Summary

This chapter book tells the history of African Americans in basketball from its roots to present day, including the WNBA. This straightforward text is easy to follow and packed with information, without being overwhelming.

Basic Book Information

Black Hoops is 154 pages long. The table of contents sets the flow of the book and informs the reader of what information will be presented. The chapters have titles that represent the main idea contained in them. While the flow of the chapters move across time chronologically, they can also be read independently of one another.

Noteworthy Features

Photographs and captions add flavor to the text. However, they may confuse some readers by not always relating directly to the main point being presented in the chapter. Some photos are generally described but not specifically named.

The chapter titles support comprehension because they let the reader know what information will be presented in the section. The sentence structure and flow of paragraphs are easy to follow and their meaning is apparent. The writing style can be described as reader friendly. Vocabulary specific to a topic or idea is explained or defined in the context of the text. The author provides the background knowledge for comprehension of the text.

Teaching Ideas

This book can be used to show how readers read nonfiction texts differently according to individual purpose and the text itself. Given their purpose, readers can make decisions about whether to read the book from beginning to end, or to identify specific chapters or sections that he or she will read. In addition, readers can be taught to use a table of contents or index to find the information they seek, and skimming and scanning skills will also prove valuable.

Readers may be interested in documenting the events that pushed African Americans in basketball to new heights. Independent readers or books clubs may want to create a chronology of events, or take notes from this book to use as a basis for discussion. Students interested in pursuing sports-related

Publisher
Scholastic Press, 1999

ISBN
0590487124

TC Level
12; 13; 14

topics (perhaps as part of a "reading project") will find this book helpful for gathering information. For these purposes, conferences which address topics such as note-taking, deciding what is important in text, working through difficult text, and organizing information would all be helpful.

Book Connections

Some other books that could be read as a follow up to this one are: *Black Diamond: The Story of the Negro Leagues*, Fredrick McKissack, Jr. and Patricia McKissack, *The Story of Baseball*, Lawrence S. Ritter, or *The Wright Brothers: How They Invented the Airplane*, Russell Freedman.

Genre
Nonfiction; Chapter Book

Teaching Uses
Independent Reading; Reading and Writing Nonfiction; Content Area Study

A Field Guide to the Classroom Library, Lucy Calkins and the Teachers College Reading and Writing Project, Heinemann, ©2002 Teachers College, Columbia University; http://www.heinemann.com/fieldguides

Bridge to Terabithia

Katherine Patterson

Book Summary

In the very opening of *Bridge to Terabithia* by Paterson, Jesse awakens early on a summer morning to rush outside and practice running. He is determined to be the "fastest kid in third, fourth and fifth grades" by the start of the school year. And he is only a fourth grader. In pursuit of this secret goal Jesse must leave the house early, practice and still milk Miss Bessie before breakfast. We quickly learn that sneaking past his four sisters is as difficult as getting past the screeching floorboards of the old house. Jesse feels isolated in his own universe. "Sometimes he felt so lonely among all these females-even the one rooster has died, and they hadn't yet gotten another." Jesse struggles to build space for himself and find connection with his father. His running he hopes will make his father "so proud he forgets how tired he is."

Jesse explores the world and attempts to create a degree of control and ownership, or at least as much as his teacher, the dreaded Monster Mrs. Meyers and the bullying classmate, the gorilla-like Janice Avery, will allow. As friendship develops between Jesse and his new neighbor, Leslie Burke they decide to create a special world for themselves; "a secret country and you and I [are] the rulers of it." And so comes to life the kingdom of Terabithia. It is a magic country, like Narnia and they enter it by swinging on the enchanted rope across the creek. Here the "dogwood and redbud play hide and seek with the oaks and the evergreens and the sun steams through and splashes on their feet." They are king and queen of a kingdom that is entirely of their own magical creation. In this land they call upon their imagination and the spirits to conjure up plots against Janice and to pray for the Spring rains to stop. As they swing themselves in to Terabithia they become "taller, stronger and wiser." Here nothing can defeat them.

During the endless rains of their Spring break Ms. Edmunds, Jesse's music teacher, phones and invites him on a short trip. It is his first time to Washington. It is also an escape from Terabithia, which frightens Jesse. The glory of his outing is paled by tragedy. Jesse returns home to discover that Leslie has drowned. The enchanted rope broke while swinging across the creek. But in his disbelief he dreams that "Leslie could not die any more than he himself could die." At the end of the story, in order to come to terms with Leslie's death, Jesse builds the bridge to Terabithia, making it safe to return. He brings his sister, May Belle, puts flowers in her hair and sets upon a path that will bring discovery of beauty, within her. Jesse decides that the world around Terabithia is, "like a castle where you come to be knighted. After you have stayed a while and grew strong you had to move on." Jesse realizes that he now has the strength to confront his fears.

Basic Book Information

Bridge to Terabithia is a 128 page chapter book. Each chapter ranges in length from eight to twelve pages. Paterson won the Newbery Award for this book in 1978. She is the well-known author of many young adult books including, *The Great Gilly Hopkins*, *Jacob Have I Loved* and *Flip-Flop Girl*. Katherine says of her work, "Eventually a character or characters will walk into my imagination and begin to take over my life. I'll spend the next couple of years getting to know them and telling their story. Then the joy of writing far outweighs the struggle, and I know beyond any doubt that I am the most fortunate person in the world to have been given such work to do."

Noteworthy Features

Jesse goes to Terabithia in search of meaning. Terabithia had turned him into a king. And it was here that Leslie had pushed "back the walls of his mind and made him see beyond the shining world-huge and terrible and beautiful and very fragile." She had brought the magic. Jesse decides that it is time for him to go forth. He must "pay back to the world in beauty and caring what Leslie had loaned him in vision and strength." He will make bridges.

For Jesse, the "whole mob of foolish little fears running riot in his gut" are quelled through his friendship with Leslie. And in turn Jesse offered Leslie the chance to be herself as she grapples in a new and unfamiliar environment. Each in their own way, struggle to come to terms with the world, which for all its injustices, still offers hope. Jesse and Leslie learn through the magic of discovery of both themselves and their environment, how to make a place for themselves in the world.

Teaching Ideas

This book is so layered, significant, sad, and beautifully written that it cries out to be closely studied. Therefore, most teachers regard it either as a whole-class read aloud or as a book for a small group book club.

Either way, children will probably find and follow themes in the book. One obvious theme that children often follow is that of the relationship between Jesse and Leslie. Children who explore this will want to think about ways in which Jesse and Leslie and their respective families are alike and different from each other. What role does each character play in the other's life? Jesse, for example, draws upon his friendship with Leslie to make sense of the world and his feelings. Leslie was more than just his friend. "She was his other, more exciting self-his way to Terabithia and all the worlds beyond." She had, Jesse explains, "tried to push back the walls of his mind and made him see beyond the shining world." Some readers will wisely see this as a coming of age book in which Jesse grows up.

Some children also become interested in Terabithia as a book about the human need to make a home in the world. Jesse looks for a home, onein which he can conquer his fears. Jesse explains to Leslie that he had once feared that the space they call Terabithia was haunted. "Oh, but it is," she says. "But you don't have to be afraid. It's not haunted with evil things."

A Field Guide to the Classroom Library, Lucy Calkins and the Teachers College Reading and Writing Project, Heinemann, ©2002 Teachers College, Columbia University; http://www.heinemann.com/fieldguides

Nevertheless, the deep and dark spaces continue to move the fears within Jesse. Terabithia is the magic home, the castle, where fears and monsters become personified. The creek is akin to a cellar in a house, wherein lies the unconscious, dark and damp in its subterranean forces. Fear of crossing rises with the height of the creek. The grove of pines likens itself to the attic. It is the source of cerebral fears, more easily rationalized but none the less monstrous for all that. What bothers Jesse more than telling Leslie he is afraid, is the very fact that he *is* afraid. "It was though he had been made with a great piece missing...Lord, it would be better to be born without an arm than go through life with no guts."

When away from Terabithia, Leslie's home provides yet another metaphor for the security that Jesse yearns to live with. The Burke's have time to fix up their old farmhouse and paint the living room sun-gold. Leslie's parents are fortunate to have the time to explore books and music. They are "smart in a way that he had never known real live people to be." By contrast, Jesse wonders what it would be like to have a mother whose stories were inside her head instead of marching across the television screen. In Jesse's house his older sisters, Brenda and Ellie, argue and beg for an extra dollar so they can buy something new for the start of school. His younger sisters, May Belle and Joyce Ann hope and cry for new toys. His father drives to Washington to make extra money and when he is laid off he still leaves early in the morning looking for any work that might come his way. In the evenings, his parents, exhausted by the toll of their lives, retreat to the television. Leslie's parents don't even own a television.

Book Connections

These are many other books which lend themselves to similar work: *The Great Gilly Hopkins* also by Paterson, *The True Confessions of Charlotte Doyle* by Avi, *War Comes to Willy Freeman* by Collier, *Toning the Sweep* by Johnson, *On My Honor* by Bauer, *The Taste of Blackberries* by Smith, *Mick Harte Was Here* by Park, *When Zachary Beaver Came to Town* by Holt, *Fig Pudding* by Fletcher, and *My Louisiana Sky* also by Holt.

Genre
Chapter Book

Teaching Uses
Small Group Strategy Instruction; Read Aloud; Book Clubs; Partnerships

Bunnicula

Deborah Howe; James Howe

Book Summary

A reader who cannot follow E.M. Forster's advice and "set aside disbelief" will not appreciate the humor of this delightful story. Harold the dog and Chester the cat, contented pets of the Monroe family, find their lives disrupted when a new member, a tiny rabbit, joins the household. Chester is convinced that Bunnicula whom the family found in a movie theater where the movie Dracula was playing, is, like Dracula, a vampire. Mysteriously, vegetables, drained of color, appear strewn on the Monroe's kitchen floor. The evidence is all circumstantial: the coloring of Bunnicula's fur-black and white-makes him appear to be wearing a black cape. The fur between his ears is also black and is in the shape of a V, all features reminiscent of Dracula. And, when Chester discovers that Bunnicula has two sharp fangs, he is convinced that the tiny rabbit is evil. The story of Chester's failed attempts to trap and destroy the rabbit, as told by Harold the dog, is one that has tickled the imagination of young children since it was published in 1979. The story ends on a positive note, one that has led to four sequels.

Basic Book Information

The book is a relatively short chapter book with only 98 pages. The authors tell the story in nine chapters that range in length from four to fifteen pages. Each chapter title announces the focus of the chapter. The story is told in sequential order, with the exception of the first few pages of Chapter 3, where we learn a bit of background about Chester and his ability to read.

Chapters end with a puzzling question or event that leads the reader to the next episode. There are black and white illustrations in various places in the text that help young readers visualize the action. While the authors use common words and simple sentence structure for the most part, there are occasional phrases like "character analysis," "tropical zygodactyl bird," and "obscure dialect" which make the text more interesting and a bit more challenging for the less able reader. The story is told with tongue-in-cheek humor. From the start, the reader knows this could not have happened, yet the reader reads on from one absurd incident to the next, all the while chuckling. *Bunnicula* has received numerous awards and was the subject of a TV special.

Bunnicula is the first in a series of books detailing the adventures of Chester and Harold. *Howliday Inn, The Celery Stalks at Midnight, Nighty-Nightmare, Return to Howliday Inn,* and the newest book, *Bunnicula Strikes Again.*

Noteworthy Features

While each chapter is complete in itself and leads logically into the next

Series
Bunnicula books

Illustrator
Alan Daniel

Publisher
Simon & Schuster, 1979

ISBN
0689806590

TC Level
10

A Field Guide to the Classroom Library, Lucy Calkins and the Teachers College Reading and Writing Project, Heinemann, ©2002 Teachers College, Columbia University; http://www.heinemann.com/fieldguides

chapter, the book is an unusual one because it is Harold the dog who tells this story. An editor's note at the beginning, which includes an explanatory letter from Harold, lets the reader know that this is a fantasy-with cats who read and dogs who write. Harold writes in first person so we witness the action from his point of view. The authors indicate the passage of time at the beginning of each chapter with phrases like "the next few days" or "that night." The entire case against Bunnicula is based on circumstantial evidence, challenging the reader to make inferences throughout the story. Youngsters with little or no prior knowledge of vampires might miss the humor of the story. Readers need to catch the absurdity to enjoy the humor-Chester spreading garlic all over the house, appearing in the kitchen with a towel draped like a cape around his shoulders, or misinterpreting "stake" and so trying to pound a beefsteak into the little rabbit, the total obliviousness of all the human family members to what is going on, tomatoes, lettuce, zucchini, mysteriously turned white, all add up to a delightful story never meant to be taken seriously. The dialogue between Chester and Harold add to the humor reflecting as they do the myths that surround dogs and cats-cats being far more intelligent, dogs just happy creatures, content to live and let live.

Teaching Ideas

One teacher did a promotional talk to her class on this book, which included a picture of the rabbit, and asked the class if the title *Bunnicula* reminded them of anything. Immediately, students thought of Dracula and filled their teacher in with all the details they had learned about vampires, thanks to movies and TV. She then read the editor's note to them and asked them to anticipate the kind of story this might turn out to be. This whetted the children's appetite for the book and also served as a whole-class book introduction supporting eventual readers with the two biggest challenges in the book. Now children who chose the book during independent reading would realize that Harold the dog tells the story and they'll bring their knowledge of vampires and of Dracula to bear on the story. Children were also ready for this to be a story that couldn't have "happened."

The authors introduce clues that link Bunnicula to vampires. Students may notice this pattern and mark such clues with post-it notes, explaining on the note why they think this is a clue. In Chapter 1, for example, Harold explains how the family, in the back row of a movie theater, found the rabbit with a note-written in "an obscure dialect of the Carpathian mountain region." Later we learn the movie was Dracula. Some students may identify that as a clue but may not know why until later, in Chapter 4, when they read that Transylvania-the home of Dracula-is the region name. Students can discuss these and other clues with their partners.

Chester is obsessed with the notion that Bunnicula is really a vampire. In a conference with a reader of this book, a teacher might want to describe the difference between "hard" and "circumstantial" evidence. The reader can then read, thinking about whether Chester's evidence is "hard" or "circumstantial" and deciding whether Chester is justified in his conclusions. It is possible to argue either way, and an argument for or against should be supported with details from the story. If a teacher wanted to help a child defend his or her ideas with references to the text, this book

A Field Guide to the Classroom Library, Lucy Calkins and the Teachers College Reading and Writing Project, Heinemann, ©2002 Teachers College, Columbia University; http://www.heinemann.com/fieldguides

would provide a neat context for such work. Students could argue for or against Chester's actions.

The rich dialogue between the characters could work well in reader's theater presentations. After students finish reading the book, partners might select sections such as the conversation the dog and cat have in Chapter 4 or the dialogue in Chapter 5 between the Monroes. Using minimal props, they could prepare a script and do an oral reading of the dialogue before the class as a whole.

Book Connections

Bunnicula is the first in a series of books about Chester, Harold, and their vampire bunny friend. Students might enjoy reading the sequels.

Genre
Chapter Book; Fantasy

Teaching Uses
Independent Reading; Book Clubs

Children of the Dust Bowl: The True Story of the School at Weedpatch Camp

Jerry Stanley

Book Summary

The text's introduction is about John Steinbeck and his role in drawing attention to the plight of the Oklahoma immigrants to California.

This book tells the story of the migration of families of "Okies" to California. It begins in Oklahoma and describes the conditions there that led people to leave in desperation. It then moves to the story of the trip West and the hardships and hopes of the travelers. The next chapters tell of life and death in the migrant labor camps, and of the attitudes of many Californians to the "Okies." Then, the book moves to the specific event of the conception and building of Weedpatch Camp School by a far-seeing, wise humanitarian Leo Hart. The next chapters describe the hands-on, self-esteem building curriculum of the school that led it to be one of the best around and one of the best ways to help get the "Okies" out of their vicious cycle of poverty.

The credits tell of what happened to some of the attendees of the school, and of the lives of some of its outstanding teachers.

Basic Book Information

This illustrated nonfiction book is eighty-five pages long. It is divided into nine chapters of about five to ten pages each. These chapters are each titled with a heading that is more of an attention grabber than a provider of information about what the chapter will contain. There is a photograph, usually two, on nearly every one of the double-page spreads. These photographs have captions and are reproduced from various sources and photographers. The text itself is densely spaced and plentiful. The chapters are followed by an afterward, a set of credits, a set of acknowledgments, an index, and a note about the author.

Noteworthy Features

This book brings humanity to a period of history for readers. It tells of everyday details of life that help readers understand how it was to be alive in the times and conditions described in the book. The pictures are well-chosen to help make the details feel real and easy to imagine. Many of the photographs and photographers are quite famous and the pictures will be ones that readers will see again and again if they continue exploring the Depression and the times in the West that surrounded it. While no book or

Publisher
Trumpet Club, 1992

ISBN
0440830435

TC Level
12

reading experience can totally capture the feelings of the times, this book is probably as close as a nonfiction book can come.

Teaching Ideas

Some teachers select this text to help readers begin to think about issues of prejudice in a way that is not immediately threatening to the here and now. The treatment of the "Okies" can easily lead into discussions of the treatment of various other minority groups in our society, and what should and shouldn't be done in reference to it.

Some readers will feel compelled to act in some way to remedy injustices in the world as the teachers in this book did. These readers may simply write letters or speak out, not establish schools, but their actions show that they read with a consciousness and what they read matters to how they live their lives. Teachers who are looking for books to help inspire that consciousness in readers will appreciate this book.

Teachers can help readers navigate the many primary sources integrated into the text, from quotations from diaries to excerpts from interviews. This "changing narrator" can be tricky for some readers to understand. Who is talking now? And now? For others it lends more truth and immediacy to the history. In either case, it is certainly a feature of good nonfiction with which readers will need to eventually become familiar.

Although the book is designed to be read cover to cover, it need not be read that way. Readers could easily read the beginning sections about life in the Dust Bowl and the challenges and troubles of immigrants' journeys and lives without reading the last few chapters about the specifics of Weedpatch School. Likewise, if the focus of the curriculum is on what makes for good learning, the parts at the book's beginning about the life of the "Okies" could be skipped. Most of the time, chapters are best left intact themselves, whatever order in which they are read.

When children read historical nonfiction, this provides teachers an opportunity to coach them toward reading-as-a-historian. Following are some of the skills and strategies we may want to teach:

The reader's challenge includes devising a course of study for oneself. In real life, no one says, "Read these four texts in this order." Instead, the reader needs to devise a plan making wise decisions. For example, one might first read an easy overview of a topic and then dig deeper.

The reader looks between sources asking, "Are there some questions of fact?" That is, the reader realizes that what one person might take as a fact may not be taken as fact by another person.

The reader tries to understand the point of view of the author and asks, "How does the point of view influence this text?" Often the point of view isn't stated. Sometimes a reader can infer this point of view by learning about the author's job. As part of this line of thinking, the reader also asks, "What bias might this author show?"

The reader might notice the historian's treatment of quotes. Usually a historian won't have characters saying what they think because the historian would need to fictionalize to do this. A historian may take what a character has written in diaries or letters and act as if it is speech.

Readers of history are wise to bring knowledge of geography to whatever they read. It's helpful to look between a text and a map.

A Field Guide to the Classroom Library, Lucy Calkins and the Teachers College Reading and Writing Project, Heinemann, ©2002 Teachers College, Columbia University; http://www.heinemann.com/fieldguides

Book Connections

This book would work well alongside Hesse's *Out of the Dust* and Turner's *Dust for Dinner.*

Genre

Nonfiction; Chapter Book

Teaching Uses

Reading and Writing Nonfiction; Content Area Study; Book Clubs

A Field Guide to the Classroom Library, Lucy Calkins and the Teachers College Reading and Writing Project, Heinemann, ©2002 Teachers College, Columbia University; http://www.heinemann.com/fieldguides

Children of the Fire

Harriette Gillem Robinet

Book Summary

During the Fall of 1871 in Chicago, Illinois, many fires were breaking out all over the city. An eleven-year-old orphan girl named Hallelujah (whose family was born into slavery) escapes one night from her guardians Mr. Joseph and Miss Tilly in search of an adventure. Hallelujah becomes witness to the Great Chicago Fire. In this event she plays a part in history, learns about life and death and forms an interesting friendship. She befriends Elizabeth, a wealthy, newly homeless white girl who lives with Hallelujah until her parents track her down.

The story takes place during the Great Chicago Fire of 1871. Legend has it that Patrick O'Leary's cow kicked over a lantern which began a fire that raged for three days (October 8, 9, 10) burning a section of Chicago, Illinois, that was four and a half miles long and about one mile wide. Rain on the early morning on October 11 stopped the fire.

Reconstruction is the American historical time period after the Civil War (1865-1877) when the southern Confederate states were controlled by the Federal Government before being readmitted to the Union. This was a time of rebuilding in the Southeastern states. Many African Americans living in Illinois during this time had either escaped slavery on the Underground Railroad or had been born free to former slaves.

Basic Book Information

This book is 134 pages long, and divided into seventeen chapters. The chapters are not titled. A map entitled "Burned District I in the Great Chicago Fire, 1871" adapted from a map in the collections of The Chicago Historical Society proceeds the opening of the story. There are no illustrations. The story is told in the first-person narrative, from Hallelujah's point of view.

Noteworthy Features

The author uses descriptive language in the form of similes, metaphors, and personification throughout the entire novel.

Robinet has her "lower class, uneducated" characters speak with one form of English, while her more "privileged" characters speak another form of English. Some readers may have to do some extra reading work in switching between the two dialects.

Publisher
MacMillan, 1991

ISBN
0689316550

TC Level
12

A Field Guide to the Classroom Library, Lucy Calkins and the Teachers College Reading and Writing Project, Heinemann, ©2002 Teachers College, Columbia University; http://www.heinemann.com/fieldguides

Due to the historical time period of this book, the reader will be exposed to the racial prejudices and social conflicts that existed in America after the Civil War and during Reconstruction.

Teaching Ideas

This book allows the reader to experience what life was like for an orphaned African American child living in Chicago among people of wealth, Polish and Irish immigrants, and other African Americans after the Civil War. In chapter one Hallelujah does not understand why she is instructed by her guardian Miss Tilly to leave a pot of food on the porch for the starving white immigrant family next door, instead of actually handing it over to them. Or why must she deposit it rather than an adult? Sometimes readers react by saying the book itself is racist. This may be an ideal time to talk about racism in texts. When is the book perpetuating it, and when is it depicting it to a positive end? How can readers tell the difference? This may also be a good book in which to help readers understand that when characters, even good characters, speak, what they say isn't always the truth.

As the readers experience the racial prejudices and class conflicts of this time (revealed through the characters' dialogue and actions), it is easier to unravel the author's message. This message happens to be the lesson learned by both Hallelujah and Elizabeth, two eleven-year old girls from very different ethnic and socio-economic backgrounds.

This story is told in the first person narrative from Hallelujah's point of view. Interpretative work can focus on what the reader knows and believes about a character (i.e., Hallelujah, Elizabeth) and how that knowledge can help us understand what motivates the character and explains their actions.

The author Harriette Gillem Robinet creates strong images with her writing. This book could be used in a writing cycle with a focus on craft and beautiful language.

Book Connections

Harriette Gillem Robinet has written three other books that also deal with the experiences of black people during important historical time periods in American History. These are: *Washington City Burning*, During slavery/ The War of 1812; *Forty Acres and Maybe a Mule*, During Reconstruction; and *Walking to the Bus-Rider Blues*, Montgomery, Alabama in 1956.

Jim Murphy's nonfiction book *The Great Fire* could be used along side *Children of the Fire* to give readers a better understanding of the 1871 Chicago Fire.

The Sunday, August 17, 1997 National Report section of the New York Times revisits the causes of the Great Chicago Fire.

Genre
Historical Fiction; Chapter Book

A Field Guide to the Classroom Library, Lucy Calkins and the Teachers College Reading and Writing Project, Heinemann, ©2002 Teachers College, Columbia University; http://www.heinemann.com/fieldguides

Teaching Uses
Independent Reading; Content Area Study; Book Clubs

Childtimes, A Three-Generation Memoir

Eloise Greenfield; Lessie Jones Little

Book Summary

This three-generation memoir, beginning in the 1880s and ending around 1950, revolves around the childhood memories of three Black women: Pattie Frances Ridley Jones, Lessie Blanche Jones Little and Eloise Glynn Little Greenfield. A preface for the book entitled "Landscape" tells how people are a part of their time, shaped by big and small things that happen in their worlds, such as a war, an invention like radio or television, a birthday party or a kiss. Subsequent chapters also begin with a "landscape" section, which gives an overview of the world each woman was living in at the time. Readers then follow the family through three generations, with each woman recounting the memories that most strongly affected her.

Pattie's section, for example, notes that the 1880s were a time of westward movement for the United States. But they were also a time of disappointment for many Black people in the post-slavery South. Wages for Black workers were low; jobs were hard to come by; Black schools and homes were burned; and people were dragged from their homes and murdered by the Ku Klux Klan. Pattie's family plants sweet potatoes and butter beans. They sweep their dirt yard every day, and Pattie and her sister, Mary, do all the cooking and ironing. Memories include picking mulberries, candy-pulling parties, reading and memorizing poems, and playing Sunday School with her little sisters. Pattie's story tells of a hard life of strenuous work, but one filled with good times, too.

Pattie's daughter, Lessie, lives in happier times. Her "landscape" section describes the bright beginning of the twentieth century, which brought the advent of the airplane, telephones and the automobile. Black people, looking for ways to end racism, had begun to demand rights, such as education for their children. Lessie describes herself as always singing at the top of her voice, jumping rope or running so fast she thinks her feet wouldn't touch the ground. Her days are filled with playing dolls and paper dolls, school, hide-and-go-seek and jacks. However, her father has trouble finding work, and even when he does, the pay is scarcely enough to buy what the family needs. Often Lessie is so hungry it is hard to play because of the pulling feeling inside her stomach. She has strong, fond memories of her parents. Her mama, a waitress at the local café, teaches the children how to draw and make rag dolls. She sits the children in chairs around her to tell them stories, read to them or recite poems. Papa is a quiet man who likes to read and study his Bible. He calls his children his "little duckies" and is the first one up on frigid winter mornings to build a roaring fire in the two stoves. One of Lessie's fondest memories is of school. They are proud of their school with its radiators and wide desks, and when Lessie graduates from high school, she receives a pin for having the best grades.

Publisher
HarperCollins Publishers
(Harper Trophy), 1979

ISBN
0064461343

TC Level
12

The third section of the book involves Lessie's daughter, the famous writer Eloise. She, too, was born in Parmele, North Carolina, right before the Great Depression, but her family soon moved to Washington, D.C., so her father could find work. But they often returned to Parmele, where their granny would make apple jelly and green tomato pickles, and their grandfather would entertain them with ghost stories. Eloise's fondest memories of her childhood are from Langston Terrace, the low-rent housing project where her family lives. With the playground in front of her house and a library within walking distance, Eloise is happy. She and her friends play hide-and-seek, paddle tennis, shuffleboard, dodge ball and jacks. They jump rope, have parties and take bus trips to the beach. For Eloise, Langston Terrace is a good growing-up place. Her happy memories include vendors coming through selling apples, fish and fruit-flavored snowballs. The organ grinder comes, too, his monkey on his shoulder, and the photographer, taking pictures of children sitting on his pony. And yet, behind the good times, linger traces of segregation. Eloise and her Black friends can't sit down at the drugstore soda fountains. The schools are segregated. The ads for the best jobs say, "White Only." But people still work together for Black freedom. "There was always, in my Washington, a sense of people trying to make things better."

Basic Book Information

Each part of this 176-page story is broken into vignettes with self-explanatory titles, such as, "Chores," "School," "Getting Baptized," "Spanish Flu," "Candy" and "Horses and Cows." The vocabulary and sentence structure are fairly simple as the stories are told in a conversational manner. A black-and-white photograph of each of the three women is included at the beginning of her section. There are also six pages of black-and-white photographs of other family members. At the beginning of each section is a sketch of where the person lived. Also, at the beginning of the book is a family tree. Although the book pretty much proceeds in chronological fashion, within each section the author may jump around a little in her memories.

Eloise Greenfield has received a citation from the Council on Interracial Books for Children in recognition of her "outstanding and exemplary contribution to children's literature." Lessie Jones Little's first book, *I Can Do It By Myself*, also a collaboration with Eloise Greenfield, was named a Notable Children's Trade Book in Social Studies by the National Council for the Social Studies/Children's Book Council Joint Committee.

Noteworthy Features

Each section of this lyrical memoir is told in the first person. Indeed, each voice is so strong that the readers feel as if they are sitting around a fire, while the author spins out her tale. In spite of hard times, these women are humorous. They use the dialect of Black people of their time, and place, which adds to the flavor of the stories and is never hard to understand.

A Field Guide to the Classroom Library, Lucy Calkins and the Teachers College Reading and Writing Project, Heinemann, ©2002 Teachers College, Columbia University; http://www.heinemann.com/fieldguides

Teaching Ideas

This book is a staple in classrooms in which children are invited to draft, revise and publish the stories of their lives. To do this well, children need models, and the short vignettes in *Childtimes* make this one of a small handful of texts that is regarded by many teachers as absolutely essential in a writing workshop. Teachers have found countless ways to use particular excerpts of *Childtimes*. "The Play," for example, has been used by many teachers as part of a lesson on the elements of story. "All stories have plot, character, setting, movement through time, and a change that is central to the plot and the characters," teachers have told children, and then they've asked children to listen to a reading of "The Play" and to later retell it, weaving together all the story elements. In "The Play," the passage of time needs to be inferred, and teachers remind children to draw on all they know about school plays in order to speculate how much time passed between the first rehearsal and the performance. Later, teachers have told children that when they read stories, it can help to keep an eye out for these elements of story. "You should be able to retell the stories you read, weaving together a mention of these elements."

The excerpt, "Mama Sewing" is another favorite. Children have spent many days noticing the features of this text and inferring the features of a memoir from it.

Every teacher who owns this book will go to it often, as one might go to an attic treasure chest, confident that each time it's opened, new treasures will be found.

Book Connections

Students may enjoy reading more books by Eloise Greenfield, such as *Africa Dream*, *Me and Neesie*, *Talk About a Family*, *Under the Sunday Tree*, or *I Can Do It By Myself* by Eloise Greenfield and Lessie Jones Little.

This book is a memoir, and its structure resembles a favorite memoir-like novel, Sandra Cisneros' *The House on Mango Street*, which is another favorite teacher resource for writing workshops.

Genre
Memoir; Chapter Book

Teaching Uses
Author Study; Teaching Writing; Read Aloud; Partnerships

A Field Guide to the Classroom Library, Lucy Calkins and the Teachers College Reading and Writing Project, Heinemann, ©2002 Teachers College, Columbia University; http://www.heinemann.com/fieldguides

Crocodilians

Joan Short; Bettina Bird

Book Summary

Crocodilians discusses crocodiles, alligators, and gharials. For each kind of creature, the book offers information about physical features, habitat, life processes, and the conservation measures being taken to preserve it. There is much less information provided about the gharial than about the crocodile and alligator.

Basic Book Information

This nonfiction picture book has about fifty pages. For many readers, it will be one of the harder books in the Mondo animal series. The pages are about half text and half photographs. The text itself is small and closely spaced, and therefore may appeal to more experienced readers. Perhaps the hardest part of the text is the many different headings and subheadings that divide it. If read continuously, the text's categories can seem to repeat and overlap and be disconnected from each other.

The photographs in the book are vivid and help to clarify the concepts and information in the text. At the book's end, there is a twenty-five word glossary of terms-many of which are also defined in the text. Following this, there is a fairly comprehensive, small-font, one-page index of information and photographic references.

Noteworthy Features

Since the focus of the book is on crocodilians and not simply one of the three kinds of creatures in this group, the book presents its information in an unusually broadened context. While the category isn't so broad as to diminish the importance of the particular creatures, it is broad enough to allow readers to learn about relationships among types of animals. This perspective also allows reader to easily compare and contrast and think of one creature in relation to another. Not many nonfiction books make this kind of thinking while reading so easy.

Teaching Ideas

Teachers may want to help readers build on the kind of thinking the book encourages by teaching students about ways to collect information that aids in creating comparisons and contrasts-creating tables, charts, and graphs can be especially helpful in doing this.

Many books about animals end with messages about conservation of the animals and environments described within the book. Sometimes readers may want to act on these messages by taking on conservation projects of their own.

Illustrator
Deborah Savin

Publisher
Mondo, 1988

ISBN
1572552174

TC Level
10; 11; 12

A Field Guide to the Classroom Library, Lucy Calkins and the Teachers College Reading and Writing Project, Heinemann, ©2002 Teachers College, Columbia University; http://www.heinemann.com/fieldguides

Genre
Nonfiction

Teaching Uses
Content Area Study; Partnerships; Reading and Writing Nonfiction

A Field Guide to the Classroom Library, Lucy Calkins and the Teachers College Reading and Writing Project, Heinemann, ©2002 Teachers College, Columbia University; http://www.heinemann.com/fieldguides

Daddy Is a Monster . . . Sometimes

John Steptoe

Book Summary

Two children, Abweela and Javaka, are talking to each other about their daddy. They discuss times when he is a monster- those times when he gets angry with them. They remember a time when their daddy bought them each an ice cream cone. Because it looked so good while they were eating it, he decided to get one for himself. A lady couldn't believe a man was buying ice cream for himself and not for Abweela and Javaka, so she bought some for the two children. Daddy turned into a monster when they accepted. When the kids start bickering at bedtime, Daddy turns into a monster, as he does when they are playing with their food at restaurants or if they are messy, noisy, or careless. Daddy says he only turns into a monster when his kids turn into monsters.

Basic Book Information

Steptoe has written numerous other picture books including, *Mufaro's Beautiful Daughters*, *Story of Jumping Mouse*, *Stevie*, and *Baby Says*.

Noteworthy Features

The pictures in this book are complicated and detailed. They draw some children into the story and they turn some children away because of their complexity. The divided panels on some pages make the pictures tell a sequential story, almost like a comic book. In most comic books, however, the general rule is that pictures "underneath" are read first, whereas pictures inset on top are read last. In this book, although it is fairly obvious, the pictures are read from left to right, just like the text.

Teaching Ideas

The pictures sometimes illustrate the text, and sometimes illustrate a supplemental story or information to the text. For example, in some pictures the children, not just the daddy, turn into monsters. Furthermore, the pictures often detail the transformation of the father or the children from human into monster, and the in-between panels can be quite odd-looking. The style of the drawing, with outlines and many straight-edged shadows, makes the pictures a bit surreal and not altogether realistic. The pictures probably don't help children understand the story because, unlike in most books, they illustrate the metaphor, not the meaning of the book. In other words, the pictures don't show the father being angry; they show him turning into a werewolf-like beast. For these

Illustrator

John Steptoe

Publisher

HarperTrophy, HarperCollins, 1980

ISBN

0064430421

A Field Guide to the Classroom Library, Lucy Calkins and the Teachers College Reading and Writing Project, Heinemann, ©2002 Teachers College, Columbia University; http://www.heinemann.com/fieldguides

and other reasons as well, teachers often overhear kids saying, "These pictures make no sense at all! What is going on here?" in the midst of their discussion about the book. Children who never bring up the topic of what the illustrations mean or what they add to the story can be encouraged to do so, as they would in a discussion of any other picture book.

Another aspect of the book that will make it easier for some children to read and harder for others is that it is told in Black English. Teachers often will overhear, "They talk different" or "They talk Black" or "They talk cool." While the meaning of the sentences is perfectly obvious even for children totally unfamiliar with Black English, the grammar may seem odd to them and may catch their attention frequently, continually breaking the thread of the story until they can get the hang of it. Reading the book aloud or having the children read it aloud to each other might sometimes help them with the flow of the language more easily than reading silently. Children sometimes want to discuss why the author chose to write with this particular form of grammar.

The topic of the book itself might be a tough one for many readers. It is not immediately obvious what exactly is going on with this werewolf-father and his children. Is he really turning into a hairy beast? Are the children lying? Why is he turning into a beast? The idea that the children see their father almost like a beast when he is angry often takes several readings to register.

In the pictures, the children turn into beasts. It takes several readings to figure out that in each picture in which they turn beastly, they are doing something they shouldn't be doing. This is especially true because the father's words near the end of the book are probably the biggest textual clue to what is going on. ("I'm probably a monster daddy when I got monster kids.") Re-reading the story after reading those words will probably shed light on the text and pictures for children. Some children never, on their own, would think of the transformation as a metaphor, and they are apt to instead decide that the father really turns into a beast, when he is angry. Teachers will have to decide whether or not children will benefit from hearing an adult interpretation.

There are some tricky parts in the structure of the story as well. Through most of the story, the two children are talking to each other and remembering. However, in one part, Abweela is talking directly to her daddy. This change comes without transition and without explanation. There is a page break, but no other indicator that things will be changing. As the two children remember, they also recall what their daddy has said, so sometimes all three are having a conversation together. In these cases, the dialogue is not always marked, and sometimes readers won't know who is speaking without careful reading. At the end of the story, it seems that the two children have come to their daddy to talk over what they have discovered about him being a monster. This is the final time change in the story.

Genre

Picture Book

A Field Guide to the Classroom Library, Lucy Calkins and the Teachers College Reading and Writing Project, Heinemann, ©2002 Teachers College, Columbia University; http://www.heinemann.com/fieldguides

Teaching Uses
Independent Reading; Partnerships

Dinner at Aunt Connie's House

Faith Ringgold

Book Summary

When Melody and Lonnie hear voices coming from the attic of their aunt the artist, they go up to explore. Inside, they see twelve paintings of famous African American women, each of whom briefly introduces herself to the children. The children feel proud to be African Americans.

Basic Book Information

Faith Ringgold was born in 1930, in Harlem. She went to City College in New York to study art and earned her degree from the School of Education. She followed the family tradition of teaching, but never stopped creating her own art or telling stories. Some of her books include, *Tar Beach*, *If a Bus Could Talk*, *Cassie's Colorful Day*, and *Aunt Harriet's Underground Railroad in the Sky*. Ringgold won the Caldecott Honor Book Award and Coretta Scott King Illustrator Award for *Tar Beach* in 1992.

Noteworthy Features

This story, originating from one of Ringgold's well-known "story quilts," has colorful, strong illustrations that make the book look appealing to children from the cover to the last page.

The structure of the text is patterned so that once children see the pattern they will have some hints about the kinds of text that will be found from one page to the next. The first four pages introduce the characters and set the stage for the magical event-their Aunt Connie's portraits talking about themselves. The next twelve pages are the paintings talking about the people they represent, one painting to a page. There is a summary of the paintings and then the story ends in the last seven pages with the children voicing their own aspirations and pride in their black predecessors. Once readers feel the pattern of the middle twelve pages, they will have caught on to the main content of the story.

At the end of the book, the author has written a short note that explains the differences between her original "story quilt" and *Dinner at Aunt Connie's House*. This note is followed by some extensive notes about the author herself. Both of these write-ups are slightly more difficult to read than the body of the text because they are in a smaller font with less predictable structure and content, and a more advanced vocabulary. Neither of these two supplementary pieces of writing is necessary to the understanding of the main story itself, but they do contribute to the depth at which the reader can understand it.

Illustrator
Faith Ringgold

Publisher
Scholastic Inc.

ISBN
0590137131

TC Level
9

Teaching Ideas

This book can contribute well to a study of interpretation. Ringgold has a clear and conscious agenda and message in writing the book, so children may find this message easier to uncover. Eventually, children will probably decide that the message of the book is, more or less, that people can feel better about themselves and what they are capable of when they learn about people like them who have been brave and good. It might be worthwhile to help readers discover that even the author's note (about her aunt) and the publisher's note (about Ringgold herself) may be seen to support that interpretation of the book, in that they are teaching children about two more strong people that could serve as their mentors and inspirations.

Of course, this is also an excellent reference book for the lives of these women heroes, and can serve like a nonfiction text as well.

Some students may want to use the fictional frame this story has to write their own nonfiction pieces.

Book Connections

Ringgold has written other books for young readers, such as *Tar Beach*.

Genre
Picture Book; Nonfiction; Biography

Teaching Uses
Independent Reading; Interpretation; Content Area Study; Reading and Writing Nonfiction

Duncan's Way

Ian Wallace

Book Summary

Duncan's family has fished off the coast of Newfoundland for seven generations. This year however, the cod have begun to disappear, and Duncan's father is out of work and depressed. It seems that all the family can do is move to a new place, but Duncan hatches a plan. Duncan's father changes professions, from fisherman to baker. The family refits his fishing boat to become a floating bakery, out of which Duncan's father sells bread and buns. Duncan's scheme is successful and hope returns to his father's life.

Basic Book Information

Duncan's Way is a picture book told in the third person and in the past tense. It is about Duncan, a boy who appears to be between nine and twelve years of age. *Duncan's Way* would be an excellent choice for a read aloud.

Noteworthy Features

The story begins with a string of colorful but somewhat abstract language, and it might be worth a teacher's time to pause after the first page and review the background the author gives. The pictures are attractive and realistic and are likely to make the book an easy sell once the background has been established.

    Duncan's Way fits neatly into a group of books about children who take charge of their lives. Readers will appreciate Duncan's perseverance, as well as his ability to take full advantage of his cleverness when his family needs him most. Whether or not children directly discuss the messages in the story, the characters of Duncan and his family offer any classroom solid role models in several respects. Duncan models positive pro-social behavior: talking out a problem, thinking of solutions with a friend. Also, those of us with feminist sympathies will be pleased as punch to see a man in the kitchen.

    The reason why Duncan and his family serve as such good role models is precisely because of their flaws, their humanness: the brothers bicker, the father gets depressed, the mother snaps-just like in everyone's family. For these reasons, this story lends itself to a character study, especially for those students who have never done one before.

    One part of the text that may leave some kids a little confused when they read it comes toward the middle of the story. Duncan tells Mr. Marshall, a retired fisherman and friend of his, about the troubles Duncan's family is having. The text reads, "Everything Duncan had been thinking about. . . spilled out of him like a dam bursting." Some readers may pass over this part and fail to grasp the meaning of this simile. With younger readers

Illustrator
Ian Wallace

Publisher
DK Publishing, 2000

ISBN
078942679X

especially, it might be worth a teacher's time to ask her students what exactly the author meant by that choice in language.

Teaching Ideas

Duncan's Way is satisfying in that it can be read on more than one level. The events of the story almost always have some kind of hidden supporting meaning. Mr. Marshall throws Duncan a little wooden boat, in the same way he tosses an idea his way. Duncan catches the boat on the fly, perhaps symbolizing his grasp of the idea. When Duncan starts home with a new hope in his heart, the waters in the sea around him calm. As his plan becomes clearer to him, and he begins to believe it will succeed, he steers around a huge iceberg, just as if he were steering around his family's troubles. Students could be given the freedom to make similar interpretations of deeper meaning, just so long as they are supported by the text.

As with many great stories, the end of *Duncan's Way* is a beginning of sorts. At the conclusion of the story, readers may be left wondering to what extent the floating bakery actually succeeds. This is one of a number of topics worthy of discussion. As always, discussions that emanate from students' concerns and questions are those that are likely to be most dynamic and most successful.

Genre
Picture Book

Teaching Uses
Independent Reading; Interpretation; Critique; Book Clubs; Partnerships

Dust For Dinner

Ann Turner

Book Summary

Dust For Dinner is a historical fiction story of a family's struggle during the Dust Bowl. Jake, the first person narrator, his sister Maggy, his Mama and his Papa live happily, growing wheat and dancing to their radio in their little house in the Mid-West. But when the rain stops and the wheat stops growing, the family starts to worry. Finally a storm comes, but it is not a rainstorm, it is a dust storm. The next year it still does not rain. Papa tells the family that "no crops means no money" and they have to sell the farm in an auction and go to California. Everything is sold at the auction except the family radio, Sam the dog, and their truck. Jake and Maggy worry on the trip west that Papa will not find a job in California. When they arrive in California, Papa gets a job as a watchman at a big store. In their new house Mama sets up the radio and the family sings a song about "hard times . . . and traveling . . . and still being together."

Basic Book Information

Dust ForDinner is 64 pages long. The text is divided into five chapters with short titles to clue the reader in to what the chapter will be about. There are realistic, color illustrations on every page that add tremendous support to the plot. Although this book appears to contain simple sentences, it does have some difficulties to watch out for.

Noteworthy Features

The reader is supported in this book because the story is a series of events in a sequence following a single plotline. The large color pictures scaffold the reader; for example, if the reader is unsure what an auction is, the pictures provide clues. The sentences are short and for the most part the vocabulary is simple. This historical time period is portrayed in a way that young readers and older struggling readers will gain an accurate look at this time period. The author's note at the end of the book, although written with more complex vocabulary (suffocated, withered, debts), provides a nice summary of this period of drought, dust, and depression.

Although the text is simply written some words may be difficult, such as: auction, hayloft, orchard, funeral, stern-and a reference to the song "She'll be coming 'round the mountain." Many of the simple sentences contain carefully chosen figurative language, which will be challenging to readers who are used to more concrete literal language. Turner also uses similes, "You are growing like a weed," and "I'm as tall as corn." Students who read more literally might also have difficulty with "the dust stung my face." The author's note might be better understood if read aloud since it is written at a higher level than the rest of the text.

Publisher
Harper Trophy, 1995

ISBN
006444225X

TC Level
8

Teaching Ideas

Dust For Dinner makes an excellent addition to the study of this time period. Other historical fiction *I Can Read* Level 3 books could be included in the study of this time period. *Dust For Dinner* would be an excellent choice for guided or independent reading to go alongside a read aloud of *Out of the Dust*, an exquisite and complex award-winning novel by Karen Hesse.

A possible minilesson could be on the use of figurative versus literal language. Readers could make a T-chart in their notebook with figurative language on one side and their interpretation of its literal meaning on the other. Also, the strong sense of place and the ideas about "home" could lead to in-depth conversations and connections to other books especially, *Sarah Plain and Tall* and *What You Know First* by Patricia MacLachlan.

Also, another possibility is for the readers to use post-it notes in places in the text where the family's feelings change. Students could mark each change from being happy to worried to sad and so on throughout the text until finally the happy ending.

Book Connections

As mentioned earlier, this book addresses the same historical time period as Hesse's *Out of the Dust*, but it is considerably easier. This book is similar in difficulty to the *Commander Toad* series as well as other *I Can Read* Level 3 books such as *The Josephina Story Quilt* by Eleanor Coerr and *Wagon Wheels* by Barbara Brenner. We recommend that the reader first experience success with books such as the *Nate the Great* series or the *M&M* series before tackling a book such as this one.

Genre
Historical Fiction; Chapter Book

Teaching Uses
Independent Reading; Content Area Study

A Field Guide to the Classroom Library, Lucy Calkins and the Teachers College Reading and Writing Project, Heinemann, ©2002 Teachers College, Columbia University; http://www.heinemann.com/fieldguides

Einstein Anderson, Science Sleuth

Seymour Simon

Book Summary

Einstein Anderson, Science Sleuth is written by Seymour Simon, who is know for his nonfiction books like *Mars, Jupiter*. *Einstein Anderson* is like *Encyclopedia Brown* by Donald Sobol, except that all of the mysteries can be solved by understanding science and science principles, rather than deduction. All of the chapters are self-contained and could be read separately. The first chapter gives readers the background of the main character Einstein (Adam) Anderson. All of the scientific principles are explained, as is Einstein, for the reader to understand. The stories (chapters) are all structured similarly: first the dilemma or the case is set up and the question posed: can you solve the question of the chapter? The page always ends there and the reader has to turn the page to get to the answer. The final page of the story continues on that last page.

The author uses the character of Stanley (one of Einstein's friends) to explain many of the scientific principles. It's a good device for conveying this information and showing Einstein in a sympathetic light because he doesn't get preachy. At the front of the book, right behind the table of contents is a page that lists all the areas of science covered in this book. Simon has made this list go with the chapter arrangement. For example, the first chapter is about motion and friction and the second is about astronomy. This helps give a name to the ideas and make it possible to continue research on them fairly easily. Like Encyclopedia Brown, Einstein Anderson solves every case, so this is a predictable format.

Basic Book Information

The book is 73 pages long. There are ten chapters, ranging from six to ten pages in length. Each chapter is a case. There is a table of contents. Each chapter (case) has approximately two illustrations (by Fred Winkowski). The illustrations support the text by depicting what the text says. The print is small with medium spacing between words and lines.

Noteworthy Features

Each chapter has the same story structure with the problem/challenge, question and answer. All of the science is written so that a layperson can understand, and in a common sense way so the reader doesn't feel inadequate. The main character, Einstein, is twelve years old, making this a great book for kids in fifth, sixth, and seventh grade who like science yet need short episodic chapters. The character encounters issues germane to the middle school years: bullies, younger siblings, and friendship. The illustrations in this book give it a light-hearted feel. All vocabulary introduced is explained immediately in context so readers won't be

Illustrator
Frank Winkowski

Publisher
Trumpet, 1992

ISBN
0440848490

TC Level
11

guessing.

One of Einstein Anderson's favorite pastimes is corny jokes and puns. At the end of each chapter, he says something "punny." Not all students will get, or appreciate, this humor. It is an attempt by the author to show Einstein as a regular guy.

Teaching Ideas

This book is good for independent reading, conferring on stamina and chapter length, and holding onto acquired information from the previous chapters. This is a high interest, moderate readability book and would be a good episodic chapter book for older or struggling readers.

This would also be a good choice for short read alouds in science. A study of motion could be started by reading, "The Frictionless Roller Skates," or it could rev up the interest in the subject later in the study. Used this way, it would introduce scientific principles by way of fictional characters that are fairly dynamic and entertaining.

Book Connections

There is a newer edition: Einstein Anderson #1: the Howling Dog and other Cases, Published by Aron Camelot in 1998. The chapter titles are different; "The Frictionless Roller Skates" is now, "The Case of the Rotating Roller blades." There is no page after the table of contents that lists the areas of science. The new edition is a pepped-up version, with stars surrounding all page numbers at the bottom of the pages. Every first letter of the new chapter is in bubble letters as well. The structure, format, and context are the same, barring changes like roller skates to roller blades.

Genre
Chapter Book; Mystery; Nonfiction

Teaching Uses
Independent Reading; Read Aloud; Content Area Study

Everywhere

Bruce Brooks

Book Summary

This is a realistic fiction book by Bruce Brooks, who is known for his *Wolfbay Wings* series, *The Moves Make the Man*, as well as many nonfiction articles. The story is about two boys, Dooley and Peanuts. (This is consistent with Brooks' other writing that is either about boys or that have boys as the principal characters.) The story is set in Richmond, Virginia. The central story happens in one day. It begins in the morning of a specific day, and then time accelerates, morning from this one day to weeks later, at the end of summer, when one of the boys goes out to the garage to make a pencil box with his grandfather, who has recuperated from his heart attack.

Basic Book Information

This book is 70 pages long. It is deceptively simple, both in appearance and in content, and the reading is not complicated. Chapters range from twelve to twenty-five pages in length; there are four chapters without titles. Awards and recognition for *Everywhere* include: Notable Children's Books of 1991 (ALA), Best Books of 1990 (SLJ), 1990 Books for Youth Editors' Choices (BL), 1990 Golden Kite Award Honor Book for Fiction (SCBW), and was listed on the 100 Books for Reading and Sharing 1990 (NY Public Library).

Noteworthy Features

The story is structured in a straightforward, chronological way and it tells about the events of two days in one boy's summer. Dooley is an appealing character and Peanuts is intrigued with him, the reader may be too. There is no reference to the year and so readers are left to figure this out.

Teaching Ideas

If a teacher wants to study a book in preparation to support the readers' experience of it, it can sometimes help to think about the elements of all of the stories as they are played out within this particular text. The teacher can ask, "What difficulties might this element cause for readers of *this* book?" Such a study of this book would help teachers realize that the setting of *Everywhere* will pose some challenges to readers and provide some teaching opportunities for teachers. Often children barely take note of a book's setting in time and place, and it's helpful for us to coach them to see that when we pause to really take in and think about a book's setting, that knowledge can help to situate and explain a great deal that happens in the

A Field Guide to the Classroom Library, Lucy Calkins and the Teachers College Reading and Writing Project, Heinemann, ©2002 Teachers College, Columbia University; http://www.heinemann.com/fieldguides

Publisher
Scholastic, 1992

ISBN
0590451634

TC Level
10

story. In this book, the setting will in many ways feel like the present, and readers will need to be alert to big clues that show that it is set in the 1950s and 1960s. Of course, some children won't make much of the fact that the book is set during these decades in the southern United States.

This book provides us with teaching opportunities because a reader's job is first to search for clues which signal the setting of a book, and then to assess whatever they know about that setting and to bring it to bear on their reading. With help, children will probably be able to recall something about the segregation and racism of the South in the 1950s. A teacher may want to add to a child's knowledge by explaining the Jim Crowe laws since they become theme in the book. The historical context of pre-Civil Rights South matters a great deal in this story, but the words on the page don't emphasize this. The central characters are a white boy and a black boy and this issue is brushed over very quickly. Because there are many references to cities in Virginia such as Richmond, Charlottesville, and Newport News, a map close by would greatly help the reader.

All stories move through time, and some do so in ways that pose challenges to young readers. This book takes place during two days of one boy's summer, and a great deal happens very quickly. The quickness of the events in this book may confuse the reader. For instance, the boy (Peanuts) and Dooley meet and immediately launch into a soul switch for his sick grandfather. Readers may need to re-read Chapter 1 to fully comprehend the text, because readers need to do a lot of work in this chapter.

Brooks makes use of colloquial language, especially in Dooley's case. "You strung pretty tight," or "Why the flip nut?" may sound familiar to city kids though not to suburban kids. However, through context, readers should be able to figure out the language. This language usage presents an interesting study in slang, its origins, and how it fades away and comes back in future generations. Studying slang will give students an appreciation of the evolution and creativity of language, as well as an ability to make substitutions for many words in daily speech.

In general, there is a lot to discuss and mull over in this book, and some readers will be tempted to read the book quickly and be done. If this happens, readers will miss the big ideas that this book can engender. To overcome this, it might be wise to use this book in a more social way than through independent reading-perhaps in a book club, a read aloud or at least by having serious partner conversations.

It is important to point out that one character in the book voices an attitude about obesity, which should be noted. Dooley says of his Aunt Lucy, "she knows better than to take up with a fat man. She says they don't feed you." This brings up a different kind of prejudice than the racial prejudices which are foregrounded in the book, and this passage could open the door to conversations about societal prejudices in general.

Genre
Chapter Book

A Field Guide to the Classroom Library, Lucy Calkins and the Teachers College Reading and Writing Project, Heinemann, ©2002 Teachers College, Columbia University; http://www.heinemann.com/fieldguides

Teaching Uses
Independent Reading; Book Clubs; Partnerships; Read Aloud; Critique

Five True Dog Stories

Margaret Davidson

Book Summary

The book *Five True Dog Stories* tells the stories of five unrelated dogs. Their stories are told in five separate chapters in this nonfiction book. Dox, the first dog, is called the greatest dog detective in the world. The author writes about his training by Giovanni Maimone in the city of Turin in Italy. The exact years that Dox worked as a detective are not revealed but we do learn that Dox could track criminals using his wonderful sense of smell even on highways filled with car fumes. The next chapter is about Grip, the dog who was a thief. He lived in London, England, more than 300 years ago. His master, Tom Gerrard, taught Grip how to rob men of their leather money pouches. When Tom Gerrard was finally captured, Grip wandered the streets. He finally became the dog of a minister. Wolf is the dog described in the third chapter. He was a dog who appeared not to care for humans or other dogs. However, throughout his life, Wolf saved many dogs from being killed by automobiles. Wolf's life ended when he was saving another dog from being killed by a train. Barry, the St. Bernard who saved people, is described in the next chapter. He lived in the Swiss Alps before roads and tunnels were built. He saved many men after avalanches buried them in snow. Barry also saved a child who rode on his back to safety. The last dog remembered is Balto, whose life-sized statue is in Central Park in New York City. He is the dog that led a team of dogs to the city of Nome, Alaska, during a terrible snowstorm. The citizens of Nome needed the medication that Balto carried because of a diphtheria epidemic in their city. Balto saved many people from certain death.

Basic Book Information

Margaret Davidson has written this nonfiction book for children who are just beginning to read chapter books. This book is really a collection of short stories. The only illustrations are the black and white sketches found in each "chapter." Margaret Davidson has written many other easy nonfiction chapter books including biographies of Jackie Robinson, Benjamin Franklin, Helen Keller, Martin Luther King, and Thomas Alva Edison. She also wrote a book called *Five True Horse Stories*. Ms. Davidson was born in 1936.

Noteworthy Features

At the end of the story about Wolf, there is an explanation about the dog's owner. He is Alfred Payson Terhune, the author who wrote many stories about Wolf and other collies who lived at Sunnybank Farm. The explanation continues by telling the children that these books can be found in the library.

Illustrator
Susanne Suba

Publisher
Scholastic, 1977

ISBN
0590424017

TC Level
8

A Field Guide to the Classroom Library, Lucy Calkins and the Teachers College Reading and Writing Project, Heinemann, ©2002 Teachers College, Columbia University; http://www.heinemann.com/fieldguides

Teaching Ideas

A teacher who pulls alongside a child who is reading this book may want to check to be sure the child notices that this is an anthology of short stories. The teacher might point out that the book is not about the five dogs on the cover but that it has five stories about each one of five different kinds of dogs.

These short texts can be perfect to use as a vehicle for small group strategy instruction. Also, read aloud, these stories can be used in a minilesson to teach children about the special demands of nonfiction reading.

Genre
Nonfiction; Short Chapter Book; Anthology of Short Stories

Teaching Uses
Whole Group Instruction; Content Area Study; Reading and Writing Nonfiction

A Field Guide to the Classroom Library, Lucy Calkins and the Teachers College Reading and Writing Project, Heinemann, ©2002 Teachers College, Columbia University; http://www.heinemann.com/fieldguides

Flight: The Journey of Charles Lindberg

Robert Burleigh

Book Summary

This Nonfiction book is the story of Charles Lindberg's first flight across the Atlantic. It tells the story from the moment just before he gets into the plane until he finally falls asleep after his arrival. The amazing thing about this beautiful picture book is the author's style and voice. The book is beautifully written. It begins, "It is 1927." The book incorporates Lindberg's actual words from the diary he kept as he crossed the Atlantic.

Basic Book Information

The book deserves to be categorized as a sophisticated biographical picture book. It has full-page paintings that capture the mood and make us feel as if we are standing in the world of the story.

The print is set rather like a poem without stanzas and it may be that the author intends for this to be read not only as a biography but also a romantic poem.

Noteworthy Features

This book is an extraordinary read-aloud text. The words, written with lyrical lilt and intimacy, create a mood and draw readers into a drama. The language is heart-shaping. The pictures are breathtaking. Meanwhile, every bit of the text is informational: "Lindberg is nearly as tall as the plane itself."

Burleigh gives us the precise time, down to the minute, throughout the text (e.g., 7:52, 12:08), so that we can sense how slowly time passes during this 33-hour flight. We are there with him looking at his watch.

Teaching Ideas

This book could be one of several texts that weave its way across the entire school year, serving as a mentor text to teach children countless lessons about the craft of good writing. For the text to work as a mentor text, however, children must first fall in love with it. This is sure to happen if a teacher rises to the occasion of reading it aloud. Practice reading it. Read it slowly. Read it with your mind fully attuned to what the book is saying, pausing with the line breaks, "Across the Atlantic / Alone."

The line break requires that we pause-pause and think about making a flight clear across that wide, wide sea. Then we add the word "alone," a word that says it all.

This is probably not a book that provides stopping points for mid-way

Illustrator
Mike Wimmer

Publisher
Putnam Publishing, 1991

ISBN
0399222723

TC Level
12

A Field Guide to the Classroom Library, Lucy Calkins and the Teachers College Reading and Writing Project, Heinemann, ©2002 Teachers College, Columbia University; http://www.heinemann.com/fieldguides

conversations. Read it in one long luxurious read. And then be silent. On another day, re-read it and invite kids to re-read their favorite pages to feel this text in their mouths. Invite them to find the lines they love most and to write them in their writer's notebook.

Later, return to sections to study the craft. Your writers will notice the repetition, which at times is almost like an echo. "Later, they will call him" (1). There is other more subtle repetition such as the repetition of the time and date. The end then circles back to the beginning. Because this is a true Nonfiction biography, this is surprising.

Burleigh uses the craft that one might expect in a pretty fictional picture book, but there aren't many true Nonfiction books that are written with these craft elements. Burleigh chooses simple but powerful words, often selecting particularly precise verbs. He savors detail. Burleigh balances short and long sentences. He makes readers read quickly, then slowly, then pause. His punctuation is worth noting, and young readers could profit from discussion about why he chose a dash instead of a comma, or why he chose a fragment instead of a whole sentence.

This text could teach fluent readers a great deal about how to read with phrasing and intonation. "Find a page you love and practice reading it aloud so, so well." We could also ask children to do the same with a page of their own writing. This may make them want to revise their own text.

Book Connections

This book could initiate independent studies of the complex character of Charles Lindberg. Readers may want to read James Cross Giblin's marvelous book, *Charles A. Lindberg: A Human Hero*.

Burleigh is the author of other books, and all deserve to be studied and admired. He's written *Black Whiteness* about Admiral Perry in the Antarctic and *Home Run* about Babe Ruth, where again, he chooses individuals who are independent.

Genre
Nonfiction; Biography; Picture Book; Poetry

Teaching Uses
Read Aloud; Independent Reading; Teaching Writing; Language Conventions

A Field Guide to the Classroom Library, Lucy Calkins and the Teachers College Reading and Writing Project, Heinemann, ©2002 Teachers College, Columbia University; http://www.heinemann.com/fieldguides

Freedom Crossing

Margaret Goff Clark

Book Summary

The story begins as Laura hears a sound in the middle of the night. She has just returned from her aunt and uncle's house in Virginia, where she was sent when her mother passed away. Now that her father has remarried, she is back home, but everything is strange and unfamiliar. She quickly discovers that their house is a station in the Underground Railroad and that her childhood best friend, Joel, along with her father and brother are helping slaves escape to the North. This goes against what her aunt and uncle have taught her: that slaves are property and are better off with their masters. She must decide if she is going to help their fugitive or turn him in.

Basic Book Information

Freedom Crossing is a 148-page historical fiction chapter book. All seventeen chapter titles hint at the chapter's meaning. The book is chronological and takes place over two days.

Noteworthy Features

Freedom Crossing is an interesting glimpse at how the Underground Railroad movement affected families-especially children-and how families were divided between Northern and the Southern mentalities. This division creates the urgency in the story as Laura's family must hide their fugitives, before their uncle visits.

Because this book deals with slavery, students may need some background on the Fugitive Slave Law (a law which made it harder for people to help slaves escape) and the Underground Railroad. Some students may not understand that the "Underground Railroad" was not a railroad at all but rather a nickname for houses that hid slaves trying to escape to the North.

Teaching Ideas

Freedom Crossing is well-suited for a character study of Laura, as she changes dramatically in the course of the book. What are Laura's initial attitudes toward the other characters and how do they change? How does reaching out to Martin change her own sense of identity? How does her sense of home and alienation change? How does she begin to see her childhood friend, Joel? If students create their own T-charts to compare Laura before and after, they will come up with their own set of interesting contrasts. For example, some students may notice that when she went to see Joel for the first time, she was concerned with her appearance, but in the end, Laura is referred to as Joel's sweetheart (which he embraces literally as

Publisher
Scholastic, Inc., 1980

ISBN
0590445693

TC Level
9

A Field Guide to the Classroom Library, Lucy Calkins and the Teachers College Reading and Writing Project, Heinemann, ©2002 Teachers College, Columbia University; http://www.heinemann.com/fieldguides

he puts his arm around her in the buggy).

As students read, if they write journal entries from Laura's perspective, they will be more aware of how she changes. For example, if students interrupt their reading to do a quick journal entry about Laura's brother (from Laura's perspective), they may be more likely to notice how her attitude changes. After sharing their entries with partners or as a class, the students can fill in the "before" column of their T-chart, and then read on to see what changes and what remains the same. Does Laura ever take her brother seriously? When she left for Virginia, he was still a child. Does she ever realize that he is growing up?

Another activity that may be an enjoyable and useful is for students to write character sketches (assuming they are first modeled by the teacher). Sometimes, even a paragraph is enough to describe the characters' hopes, fears, and identity. To draw connections to their own lives, students can also be guided to do character sketches of their own families and friends. They may, for example, discover that their own little brothers are growing up in similar ways. They may also discover that they, like Laura, are a part of something larger than themselves.

Students could also do research on this specific time period or about the history of slavery in general. A good place to start would be a study of *Uncle Tom's Cabin* (the gift Laura received from Joel). Students could study this text, finding passages that may have helped Laura to understand the truth about slavery.

Within *Freedom Crossing*, many prominent figures of the time period are discussed. Martin tells Laura and Bert about Moses, or Harriet Tubman, a slave who risked her own life to lead her people to freedom again and again, and about Frederick Douglas, editor of *The North Star*, an abolitionist paper that supported rights for all people. After doing research about Harriet Tubman and Frederick Douglas, students can share what the story's characters left out.

Students could also discuss the role of the slave hunters, and the laws created to punish those who were suspected of helping slaves escape. How does the threat of jail affect Laura's family and friends? (When the slave hunters find an escaped slave hidden in Joel's house, Joel is kept under watch and his father is put in jail. Laura's own brother is sent to jail.) What is Martin risking to escape the prison of slavery? All of these questions can be answered from the character's point of view, as well.

As teachers, how can we help students connect it's history with today? One question, which would require some research on the students' behalf, could be, "How has the role of prisons changed in modern society?" Another could be, "Is there anything like the Underground Railroad that has existed in the recent past?" These kinds of questions will help your lessons become more interdisciplinary.

Another exploration of the text could include hidden meanings. If the teacher takes care to help the class notice that the note that Laura and Bert receive from Joel is in code, then a discussion of hidden meaning in all forms of expression could be explored. In the story, they must uncover the secret that will help them lead Martin to safety. The book also talks about the hidden meaning of the slaves singing "Go Down, Moses" when they were planning to escape. Students may enjoy a three-minute free-write on the topic of "hidden meanings," where they may write about anything from

A Field Guide to the Classroom Library, Lucy Calkins and the Teachers College Reading and Writing Project, Heinemann, ©2002 Teachers College, Columbia University; http://www.heinemann.com/fieldguides

subliminal messages in advertisements to the latest lingo at school.

Book Connections

There are many texts that deal with the issue of slavery during this time period. Autobiographies about Harriet Tubman, Frederick Douglas, Sojourner Truth, or Nat Turner may serve as useful comparison texts.

Genre
Historical Fiction; Chapter Book

Teaching Uses
Independent Reading; Content Area Study; Character Study

A Field Guide to the Classroom Library, Lucy Calkins and the Teachers College Reading and Writing Project, Heinemann, ©2002 Teachers College, Columbia University; http://www.heinemann.com/fieldguides

Fudge-A-Mania

Judy Blume

Book Summary

First, Peter Hatcher, soon to be a seventh grader, learns that his little brother, Fudge, has concocted a plan to marry Sheila Tubman, Peter's sworn enemy. Next, Peter learns that his family and the Tubmans will be sharing a house in Maine for three weeks in the summer. But once in Maine, Peter finds that the situation is not as he imagined: he discovers that a famous retired baseball player lives in the house next door, he helps Fudge out of a few scrapes, he meets Isobel who has eyes like "the best chocolate," his friend Jimmy comes up for a visit and Fudge gives up the idea of marrying Sheila Tubman.

Basic Book Information

Fudge-A-Mania is final installment in a three-book series: *Tales of a Fourth Grade Nothing*, *Superfudge* and *Fudge-A-Mania*. *Fudge-A-Mania* has 147 pages broken into 14 chapters. The chapters range in length from 3 to 15 pages. A table of contents lists chapter titles and page numbers.

Noteworthy Features

Fudge-A-Mania takes place over a three-week period. While there is no central plot line, the chapters do build on and refer back to one another to some extent. Though some children will mistakenly regard each chapter as quite separate, they are, in fact, parts of a whole.

Fudge is a central character in this book, but *Fudge-A-Mania* is really Peter's story. Peter narrates, and some readers miss out on this essential characteristic of the story. Because of the title, readers sometimes expect Fudge to be the narrator. Readers may want to discuss why the book is named for Fudge and not for Peter.

The dialogue in the book is realistic and amuses most readers. Among the realistic spoken parts of the book are that Fudge asks a lot of questions and causes some verbal mix-ups, that Peter teases Fudge and that Peter argues with both Fudge and Sheila. Also realistic is the fact that Sheila and Peter do not become friends at the end of the book. In fact, they promise always to hate each other. Readers may enjoy that the ending is not pat.

Explanations of idiomatic expressions and definitions of terms are woven into the text, as are reminders of safety rules. For example, when the group goes sailing, hypothermia is defined, and everyone is instructed to wear life jackets. Chapter titles are catchy and intriguing, such as "Dizzy from Izzy" and "Green Gurgling Gas." The title of one chapter, "The I.S.A.F. Club," may confuse readers until they learn that I.S.A.F stands for "I Swallowed a Fly."

Teachers should be aware that some of Peter's private thoughts appear in italics. However, italics are also used for emphasis in dialogue between other

Series
Fudge books

Publisher
Yearling/Bantam
Doubleday Dell, 1990

ISBN
0440404908

TC Level
10

characters. The multiple uses of italics may be confusing to some readers and may need to be explained. Readers may also have a hard time keeping track of the minor characters who appear in the book.

Teaching Ideas

If students have read these books as a series, they may want to talk with partners or in small groups about how Peter has changed since his introduction in *Tales of a Fourth Grade Nothing.* They could talk about the most memorable messes Fudge has created for Peter, and discuss what is happening to the boys' personalities as they mature.

Students can also discuss how the antics in *Fudge-A-Mania* are different from the antics in *Superfudge.*

During teacher-student conferences, it is important to ask, "Who is telling this story?" Students can be asked to cite evidence in the first two chapters that indicates that it is Peter who is telling the story. They should understand that Peter's thinking and point of view color everything we learn as readers. Then they might be asked to think about how the story might be different if it were Fudge or Sheila Tubman telling it. In fact, in Chapter 9, Fudge begins writing his own book called *Tell Me a Fudge.*

There are several occasions in the book when Peter acts like a typical big brother. Sometimes that means losing patience with Fudge, and other times it means helping him out of a mess. Readers can connect Peter's role in his family to their roles in their own families. In what ways does Peter feel both protective of and frustrated by Fudge, and do readers feel this way about their siblings, too? How can this personal connection with the character inform their reading and inform their lives?

Time passes in this story and readers can note how the author makes that happen. Phrases such as "the next morning" in the beginning of Chapter 8 can be pointed to as signals that indicate the passage of time.

Since *Fudge-A-Mania* contains so much dialogue, students who read it in a book club might assume roles of particular characters and read their parts aloud. Chapter 5 would lend itself nicely to being read aloud. First, students could scan the chapter and then list all the characters that appear. Then they can discuss what is happening in the chapter, what the characters are feeling, and how a reader could express those feelings. Next, students could be selected for the various parts. Before the readers begin, they can quickly review the use of quotation marks, reminding each other that they are only reading aloud what is in quotation marks. For example, when the text says, "'I can't stand that smell,' Sheila said," the reader playing the part of Sheila needs to be reminded only to read aloud, "I can't stand that smell." "Sheila said" falls to whomever is reading the part of Peter; that person is responsible both for Peter's spoken dialogue and for the narration. Besides bringing the story alive for those who participate and those who view the drama, this activity might reinforce an understanding of direct quotations, help students to differentiate clearly between characters, and encourage reading with expression.

Book Connections

Students will be able to understand the characters' development better if

A Field Guide to the Classroom Library, Lucy Calkins and the Teachers College Reading and Writing Project, Heinemann, ©2002 Teachers College, Columbia University; http://www.heinemann.com/fieldguides

they have already read the first two books in this series, *Tales of a Fourth Grade Nothing* and *Superfudge*. *Forever Amber Brown*, another later book in a series, is written at a comparable level to *Fudge-A-Mania*, as is *Ramona Quimby, Age 8*.

Genre
Chapter Book

Teaching Uses
Partnerships; Read Aloud; Independent Reading

Gooseberry Park

Cynthia Rylant

Book Summary

Kona, a Labrador retriever, who lives with Professor Albert, and shares his home with Gwendolyn, a wise hermit crab, visits Gooseberry Park often to see his friend Stumpy, the squirrel. Stumpy is preparing to have her children in her nest in the sugar maple at the park. Shortly after the babies are born, an ice storm destroys her home. Her friend Kona, Gwendolyn, and neighbor Murray the bat, all come together with plans to save her children (to bring them to Kona's house) and to find Stumpy, who has wandered away, seeking help. They arrange a sign for Stumpy to find Kona's house. When she is finally reunited with her children, her loyal friends find a new home for the squirrels in a sugar maple in Gooseberry Park, a "split level" with room for Murray, too.

Basic Book Information

Gooseberry Park is written by well-known author, Cynthia Rylant. Other books by Rylant include: *Missing May, When I was young in the mountains, Every Living Thing, The Henry and Mudge Series,* and many more.

Gooseberry Park has 133 pages, and has 19 titled chapters. The story is told through an omniscient narrator, from the point of view of the animals. Each character has a distinct personality; Kona is the caring friend, who ventures out on the ice to look for Stumpy; Gwendolyn is the gossip lover, who is thoughtful and inventive; Murray is a lover of pop-culture, who protects the babies, although he would rather be eating Mars bars and drinking Pepsi; Stumpy is a collector of objects, she wants to have her cozy nest just right for the day when she will become a mother.

Noteworthy Features

There is some challenging vocabulary that may cause difficulty including: "funereal glow," "senile," "desolation," "exasperation," chapter titles such as: "Rescue and Remorse," and "Yet Another Muckraker." Humorous expressions such as "danced like a Bolshevik," and several others that are uttered by Murray ("He cooks Italian?" " Can't you just call a cab or something?" "Domestic animals-who can figure 'em?") may need explanation. The illustrations by Arthur Howard blend fantasy and reality throughout the story. The beginning chapters slowly introduce the various characters. Chapter 7 "Ice" brings the reader into the ferocious ice storm, with writing that is fast paced.

Teaching Ideas

Teachers may want to introduce this book by telling students about Cynthia

Illustrator
Arthur Howard

Publisher
Scholastic Inc, 1995

ISBN
059094715X

TC Level
10

Rylant and some of her other books, with which many will be familiar. The introduction might include a description of the characters, that this is a fantasy fiction story, and the understanding that dangerous events test the strength of friendship

There can be discussion of the omniscient narrator's role in describing the characters through their dialogue and actions, as well as what she/he feels; "Together the two gazed out the window in silence...Each was full of thoughts: thoughts...about mothers and their children, about the profound comfort of shelter and sustenance and the familiarity of home."

Kona and his friends can be compared to characters in *Charlotte's Web* by E.B. White. Students can discuss the ways humor, courage, and persistence enable the friends in both novels to overcome tremendous obstacles. They may notice how the personalities of the characters were clearly developed; Murray and his desire to consume Oreos, marshmallows, or whatever he could find in the professor's kitchen, compared with Templeton the rat who also persisted in his goal of feasting during his nightly forays on the farm.

Readers can discuss the impact some of the other characters have on the plot such as Professor Albert, "...a retired biology professor who loved to grow daylilies and listen to the saxophone"; the wise owl who said to Kona, "She is wandering, my boy, and no one can find a wanderer. The wanderer must first find you"; or the weasel who told Kona, "Yeah, I heard about that squirrel. So What?" Discussions can include Kona and his friends' understanding of the personalities of the other characters and how they use that knowledge to achieve their goal of finding the stolen watch that glows, or to provide a sign for Stumpy to find them.

At the end of the story, spring has turned to summer and Cynthia Rylant leaves the reader with a sense of fulfillment. Students might have a conversation about the changes that have taken place. Readers could explore the significance of the watch that glows in the dark; how it becomes the sign that helps Stumpy find her way back to the children and return to Gooseberry Park, to live near her friend Murray, near the house on Miller Street where Kona and Gwendolyn spend their evenings retelling their adventures.

This book can make a perfect read aloud for very young students. The animals and their antics tend to fascinate and stimulate youngsters.

Genre
Chapter Book

Teaching Uses
Independent Reading; Author Study; Read Aloud

A Field Guide to the Classroom Library, Lucy Calkins and the Teachers College Reading and Writing Project, Heinemann, ©2002 Teachers College, Columbia University; http://www.heinemann.com/fieldguides

Habibi

Naomi Shihab Nye

Book Summary

This is a realistic fiction chapter book, best for experienced readers in late elementary and middle school grades. The story involves a bit of dating and a lot of beautiful reflective passages. Liyana is "half and half," half Arab and half American. She has not experienced her Arab half until her family moves from St. Louis, Missouri, to Jerusalem. They have moved back to her father's Arab family and village. Liyana makes her transition as new émigré, learning about her heritage, her family, and herself. There are times when she does not feel one bit at home in this new and foreign culture, but that changes over the course of the book. As Liyana's sense of home expands, so, too, does her sense of herself and of her family. As Liyana struggles to find friendship in this new world, she learns that she and everyone else must learn to write a new story for themselves and for the war-torn Middle East.

Basic Book Information

Naomi Shihab Nye has written numerous poetry anthologies including, *Come with Me, Salting the Ocean, Fuel, Red Suitcase,* and *Hugging the Jukebox*. She was born in St. Louis, Missouri, in 1952, to a Palestinian father and an American mother. She has twice traveled to the Middle East and Asia for the United States Information Agency promoting international goodwill through the arts. Nye has received awards from the Texas Institute of Letters, the Carity Randall prize, and the International Poetry Forum.

Noteworthy Features

Habibi is a strong and significant book. One of its strengths lies in the way Nye has developed her characters. Through Liyana's eyes, the reader can experience life in Jerusalem, life as an Arab, and life as an outsider. Liyana herself is brought to life so skillfully that an identification with and concern for her will carry the reader forward into this rather subtle and sometimes slow-moving book, sustaining the reader's interest.

Teaching Ideas

This book contains many terms from Arab culture. It holds the thoughts and fears of a newly immigrated teenager. Issue of tolerance, war, and peace are omnipresent.

   This book is unusual because the plot revolves around character development. The main story line of this book follows Liyana and her family's progress as they grow into their identities. This makes *Habibi* especially suited to supporting work with characters. Liyana is a complex character, exemplifying the contradictions of teenagers. The book chronicles

Publisher
Aladdin (Simon & Schuster), 1999

ISBN
0689825234

TC Level
14

A Field Guide to the Classroom Library, Lucy Calkins and the Teachers College Reading and Writing Project, Heinemann, ©2002 Teachers College, Columbia University; http://www.heinemann.com/fieldguides

her growth, from asking closed questions and answers to a more open and inquiring way of being. Throughout the book, Liyana models a sensitive and literate teen: she reads voraciously and writes in her notebook. She also rereads her notebook and reflects upon the entries and her life.

At the beginning of each chapter, there are italicized lines, which are from Liyana's point of view, although they are written in third person. These lines deserve attention. They can help readers focus on the events of the upcoming chapter and to grasp Liyana's changing attitudes. We recommend using these lines for support and letting them evoke lines of questions during teacher-student conferences.

The author has used drama and the beauty of the setting in Jerusalem to contrast (in a variety of ways) Liyana's past life in America. Jerusalem is ancient, full of mystique and story, which Liyana soaks up gradually. The setting can be seen as a metaphor for the contrast in lifestyle of Israel/Palestine and America. The central themes of the book are wrapped in with both the setting and the development of Liyana's character. *Habibi*, therefore, becomes a great example of the interdependence of all the elements of story. That is, an understanding of the setting is necessary for an understanding of the plot and theme and characters in this book. The setting, the plot, and all the other elements in this story (and in most stories) need to be seen as an intertwined braid, each influencing the others.

Although there are many rich avenues into a deep discussion of this book, *Habibi* is especially suited to a character study. One way to organize a character study would be for the teacher to read aloud a book or short story in which there is a nuanced, dynamic character and then to involve the class in lots of work around that character. Then the class could disperse to their small groups, and within each small group children would read and do character work with another text. *Habibi* might not be the most enthralling read aloud for a whole class, but it could be the book one of the groups of strong readers consider. Perhaps *Freak the Mighty* might work as the read aloud in a character study. In any case, some of the work with characters could include:

A journey of sorts in a book, and often the journey is an internal one. Are there stages in the journey? Turning points? Surprises? Who accompanies the character on the journey and how is that person's journey similar or different?

A discussion of the difference between static (stable) and dynamic (changing) characters. Which term fits the main character in your book and why? If he or she changes, what causes those changes? What resists those changes?

Objects or places that become an extension of a character's identity. Has your author done this?

An exploration of the characters' actions. We get to know characters not only by explicit descriptions of them but also by seeing how they act. Actions can reveal. Which actions in your book are windows to your characters' personalities?

Complexity of character. Although sometimes a book has evil characters and good ones, more skilled writers usually create characters that are more complex, and often in stories as in life, our strengths *are* our weaknesses. The loving father can also be overbearing. What are some of the complexities in your character; what are ways in which his or her strengths

A Field Guide to the Classroom Library, Lucy Calkins and the Teachers College Reading and Writing Project, Heinemann, ©2002 Teachers College, Columbia University; http://www.heinemann.com/fieldguides

are also weaknesses?

Book Connections

Other books that are similar in style to this one are: *Words Under the Words*, a book of poetry by Naomi Shihab Nye, and *My Louisiana Sky* by Kimberly Willis Holt.

Genre
Chapter Book

Teaching Uses
Independent Reading; Character Study; Book Clubs; Read Aloud

Half Magic
Edward Eager

Book Summary

In this story about a summer without prospects and a magic coin, four ordinary children find out what happens when their wishes come true-but strangely, only *halfway* true. With no father and a hard-working mother, the children are left to muddle (with the usual sibling clashes) through a series of funny, almost calamitous adventures, including a playhouse blaze, a joust with Sir Lancelot, and a glimpse of how life might be in a different family. Eventually, the four come together to outwit the rules of magic and restore family happiness.

Basic Book Information

Half Magic is a humorous story with elements of fantasy and adventure. It has episodic chapters, each of which covers one character's wishes and their consequences. *Half Magic* is one of six books by Edward Eager, all of which involve ordinary children and magical happenings. There is some overlap between characters, but the books stand alone.

Noteworthy Features

Half Magic is clear and accessible. Dialogue is dramatic and lively, and the four children are distinct characters. While the book is set in the 1920s and was written in the 1950s, the family situation has a fairly contemporary feel. Siblings bicker and complain. The mother works full-time, leaving the children with a bad-tempered housekeeper. The oldest daughter opposes her mother's remarriage out of loyalty to her absent (deceased) father.

The book plays interestingly with the notion of halfway-ness. When the children realize their wishes only come half-true, they double their wishes to compensate. Outcomes are unpredictable and humorous. What happens when one wishes a cat could talk? He talks, but is only half-understandable. And how do you wish him back to normal? When one child wishes he could only say "music," expecting him to say half of that, or "Mew," the cat says "Sick," and the children have to think again.

The characters don't change much, though it is through the shared adventures and shared difficulties that the children, mother, and future stepfather are unified. With each episode, the wisher has some sort of realization-that he should have considered more carefully first, that one shouldn't tamper with history, that she loves her family after all. These lessons are minor, and lightly handled. The characters' internal lives are less important here than the combination of magic and humor.

Publisher
Harcourt Brace, 1954

ISBN
0152020683

TC Level
11

Teaching Ideas

Half Magic is an entertaining choice for independent reading. It will appeal to fans of magic and fantasy, including those who like the *Harry Potter* books, *Mary Poppins*, and C.S. Lewis, but is slightly less challenging. Because of the episodic structure, snappy dialogue, and brisk plotting, it would be an appropriate choice for readers who like their reading in manageable bites.

Book Connections

Ambitious readers will want to go on to the writings of E. Nesbit, Eager's model. Written in the early 1900s, Nesbit's books also concern sisters and brothers left to their own devices, who stumble on a way to make their wishes come true, but whose wishes have unexpected outcomes. The book and chapters are considerably longer than Eager's, and the vocabulary is more difficult.

Genre
Fantasy; Chapter Book

Teaching Uses
Independent Reading

Henry Huggins

Beverly Cleary

Book Summary

Eight-year-old Henry Huggins leads an uneventful life on Klickitat Street until he befriends a scruffy dog in the drugstore. The humorously unruly dog, renamed Ribsy, comes home and accompanies Henry while he cultivates guppies, collects worms, and tries to get out of playing an embarrassing part in the school play. When Ribsy's previous owner comes to claim him, the whole neighborhood watches to see whether Ribsy will choose Henry and stay for good.

Basic Book Information

Henry Huggins, like other books by Beverly Cleary, is a gentle, humorous story about the lives of ordinary children. Chapters are long and loosely structured, and plots are quirky but realistic.

Henry Huggins and Ribsy are featured in five other books by Beverly Cleary. All involve the small world of Klickitat Street and familiar issues of childhood: school, friends, first jobs, and so on.

Noteworthy Features

Henry Huggins offers a comical view of the middle-elementary years of a boy and his dog. Although the setting and situation, Klickitat Street, is somewhat idyllic by today's literary standards, Henry's issues and interests are still relevant and will resonate with most readers. Most children can identify with Henry's love of animals and his wish to make money.

The book is set in a quiet, homogeneous neighborhood. All the households have two parents, there is no mention of television or societal influences, the children have considerable freedom to wander, and virtually all of the characters are good-natured and basically well-behaved. Henry's school puts on a Christmas play, and there is no mention of any religious or racial diversity. For children who aren't in similarly homogeneous environments, the scene may appear archaic.

Henry is a versatile and enterprising character. In the first chapter, he has to devise a way to get home on the bus, and though he fails repeatedly, he keeps trying. He is equally persistent in pursuit of guppies, money, and a prize at the dog show. Henry's no-nonsense attitudes make him a likeable figure. As is realistic for third- or fourth-graders, Henry doesn't ponder-he acts.

Themes of the book include the value of persistence and hard work and the benefits of taking good care of others-animals, in this case. Henry puts the work ethic in an appealing light. Cleary shows, through her detailed descriptions of Henry's thinking and activities, Henry's effort in taking care of Ribsy, his various enterprises, and the rewards he reaps. In each chapter,

Series
Henry Huggins

Publisher
William Morrow, 1950

ISBN
0380709120

TC Level
9

Henry sets himself a task and comes up with a way to reach that goal.

Teaching Ideas

Books about Henry are appropriate for read alouds, group reading, and independent reading.

Henry Huggins might appeal to readers who enjoy books like *How to Eat Fried Worms*. Henry's worm collecting venture involves a similar brand of humor, but *Henry Huggins* has longer chapters, more involved characterization, and a more complex (though still chronological and simple) plot.

After reading about Henry's enterprises, readers might write about a goal they have reached or would like to reach. Then they could describe what the process would be to get there. For example, when Henry raises guppies, he buys two who have babies, gets a book about guppy care, helps make a net, separates the fish into more jars, and so on. Observing this detailed writing can help students make their writing concrete and complete, reinforcing their ability to organize and order thoughts.

In discussing the benefit (and difficulty) of pursuing long-term goals, students might also choose a goal they can work on in school. For example, students might aim to read a certain number of books in one month, or work on a particular area of their choosing (math, or handwriting, or organization) for a set period each school day.

Readers can mark parts of the book with post-it notes that they find funny, and discuss similar mishaps or embarrassing moments they have had. What makes those events funny? Are they funny at the time or only afterward?

Book Connections

Students may want to read the rest of the books in the *Henry Huggins* series.

Genre
Chapter Book

Teaching Uses
Independent Reading; Read Aloud; Whole Group Instruction

A Field Guide to the Classroom Library, Lucy Calkins and the Teachers College Reading and Writing Project, Heinemann, ©2002 Teachers College, Columbia University; http://www.heinemann.com/fieldguides

Horrible Harry and the Christmas Surprise

Suzy Kline

Book Summary

Horrible Harry and the Christmas Surprise tells the story of Harry and his classmates in Room 2B. Harry's class has been preparing for a Christmas celebration. They will be performing a play for the younger grades. One day, their teacher, Miss Mackle, injures herself by falling off her "reading chair" and tearing a ligament. The class is dismayed to learn that she will have to spend the rest of the holidays in the hospital. Mr. Cardini, the principal, takes over the class, and Miss Mackle's role in the play! The class decides to sing Christmas carols to Miss Mackle in the hospital and Harry makes a present for her. It is a new "reading chair," decorated with bugs (Harry's favorite thing) and the names of the children in the class.

Basic Book Information

Horrible Harry and the Christmas Surprise is one of a series of books about Harry and his classmates in Room 2B. It is graded by the publisher as appropriate for readers in Grade 3, or ages seven to ten years old. The book has 55 pages with four chapters. The chapters have titles and are listed in a table of contents. The titles of the chapters support part of the plot in the chapter and give the reader something to hold onto as they begin reading. Each chapter is about eleven to sixteen pages long. There are several small black-and-white illustrations per chapter, but these illustrations do not support readers with difficult words or content. The story takes place over several days and is largely set in Harry's classroom, other areas of the school, such as the auditorium or the principal's office, and outside a hospital. There is dialogue throughout the text. Almost all of the dialogue is referenced, but the references are often embedded in the text as well as coming at the beginning or ends of sentences. There is a lot of text on each page and the font is smaller than the font in early chapter books. Some pages have sentences that begin on one page and continue to the next.

Noteworthy Features

The character of Harry, his teachers, and friends are well-written and believable. The voices of the second-grade characters are authentic, and readers who share a similar background to that of the characters will have no problem relating to and recognizing the children in Room 2B. The text is usually straightforward and direct and doesn't include too many unfamiliar or challenging words.

Each title of the *Horrible Harry* books is told by Harry's best friend,

Series
Horrible Harry

Illustrator
Frank Remkiewicz

Publisher
Scholastic, Inc., 1993

ISBN
0590466380

TC Level
8

Doug. In this particular book, it is not very clear that Doug is the one telling the story. The story begins: "...Harry leaned on his table and made a wide smile. I could see his pink gums where his two front teeth used to be. 'Don't you love that sound, Doug?' Krikkity krikk. Krikkity krekk. 'No,' I said, shaking my head."

Although the book is introduced this way, it still can be confusing for readers at this level, particularly because the whole story is being told by Doug. In some other places in the book as well, it can cause some confusion.

In some chapters, the passage of time is marked by a break, or space between paragraphs. This may be unfamiliar for readers at this level.

Horrible Harry is called "horrible" because he likes horrible things such as: slimy things, creepy things, "horrible" noises, and so on. Yet, he is *not* a bad, mean, or "horrible" kid. Although this is well-explained in the text, it still may cause some confusion, particularly because there are times in the story where Harry's feelings get the best of him and he *does* misbehave. The reader must infer that Harry's intentions though are always good.

The author frequently uses italics and all capital letters to indicate "horrible" sounds in the classroom such as: *krikkity krikk,* DEE *doo,* DEE *doo,* THUD, KABOOM, THUNK and BLUB!

Although the story is fairly straightforward and not particularly complex, teachers might find it somewhat hard to connect the plot line through the four chapters. Rather, the chapters seem to somewhat stand on their own as four separate events in Harry's life and the connecting plot line is somewhat poorly defined and supported. The series of events that lead from beginning to end is clear, but an overlying bigger plot is hard to define. For example, the first two chapters are about preparing for the play, Miss Mackle's accident, and Mr. Cardini taking over and insisting that the show must go on. The third chapter is devoted to Harry getting in trouble for chasing girls at recess and having to stay after school with Mr. Cardini. In this chapter, Harry talks with Mr. Cardini about his error and writes apology notes to the girls. There is no mention of the Christmas play or Miss Mackle. This chapter is thinly connected to the others but it may be a little difficult for readers at this level to hold onto the rest of the story as they read this chapter. It also may be difficult to continue from this chapter to the fourth chapter which is again devoted to the Christmas play and Miss Mackle's stay in the hospital.

Teaching Ideas

Horrible Harry and the Christmas Surprise can be used as a read aloud, a partner-reading book, or an independent reading book. Teachers can use this book to model good reading behaviors for any of these forms of reading. But, like many chapter books at this level, this is an especially good book for readers who have begun to read independently in a fluent, sustained way. There are many "jobs" that readers at his level need to practice and *Horrible Harry and the Christmas Surprise* affords them the opportunity to do so.

Readers at this level tend to race through their books and often miss information, meaning, humor, and more subtle themes. Teachers may use this book to teach the children to practice "knowing" themselves as readers. One of the ways to do this is to assess where a good stopping point is before they begin reading. This stopping point can be used to retell, to reflect, to reread interesting, funny, or confusing parts or to discuss their reading with a partner or group. This is a sophisticated skill and readers at this level need a lot of practice to do it well. Teachers may say to readers: "Before you begin reading today, look through the book and put a post-it or a bookmark on a good place to stop for a moment. If you are reading with a partner, discuss with him/her where would be a good place to stop and talk." At this stopping point, readers can practice one of the abovementioned strategies, as part of a strategy lesson or strategy study done in the class or as part of a small guided group or partnership.

Horrible Harry and the Christmas Surprise can be used by readers who are practicing how to infer characters' motivation, feelings, and actions. At many times in the story, Harry does or says things that are not clearly spelled out in the text. Readers must be able to infer-by practicing strategies that help them do this-to understand the character and the story fully. Some of these strategies include: studying the dialogue more closely, paying attention to one part of the story and trying to relate it to the larger text, looking for "evidence" in the text as to why a character is doing or saying what he is, even, if it is not clearly explained. Readers need to become good at asking themselves questions like: "Why is the character acting like that? How is the character feeling? Is the character acting or saying something that seems different from the way they usually act or the things they usually say? Has the character gone through some kind of change? Does that make sense to me?"

Readers can use *Horrible Harry and the Christmas Surprise* to do character studies. Readers can learn characters' names and their relationships to one another. They can study the various good and bad traits of the characters. (For example, Sidney is the class troublemaker. Song Lee is gentle and shy.) Readers can write and discuss a list of characteristics. They can compare the characters in the stories to themselves, other people they know, or characters in other books they've read. These are great opportunities for readers to reread, write, and have relevant discussions with reading partners or members of a reading group.

In *Horrible Harry and the Christmas Surprise* (as in other books about the same character), Harry struggles with some kind of moral dilemma based on his misbehaving, acting impulsively or trying to make up for some wrongdoing. Through his own reflection, talking with friends or teachers or just plain feeling sorry, he always ends up resolving his dilemma and doing the right thing and the story has a satisfying resolution. This is a great topic of discussion for the whole class, reading partners or reading groups. Teachers may also do a strategy lesson on how to use post-its and notebooks to chart when, how, and why the character has grown or changed. Teachers may want to discuss with readers how, why, and when the character solves his/her problem. Teachers may say: "I wonder if Harry will apologize to the girls he chased in the schoolyard? Do you think he meant to make Song Lee feel bad? Do you think she will understand?" The teacher can instruct or model how to find places in the text that support the reader's questions or predictions.

These are also great opportunities for the teacher to model how readers think as they read, their "internal dialogue" with the book. As the teacher is reading she can "think out loud" for the children to notice. For example, when Harry does something that seems out of character a teacher may say (as if talking to herself): "That is so strange. I wonder why Harry insists on making a Christmas present for Miss Mackle that is covered in bugs? I thought he really liked Miss Mackle." Or, more simply, a teacher may (exaggeratedly) laugh out loud or show a shocked face at a part that is important to the story.

All of the features mentioned in the "Noteworthy Features" section are excellent opportunities for teachers to do strategy lessons with the class, with a small guided reading group, with a partnership pair or in individual conferring during independent reading. Teachers can make xeroxed copies of parts of the text that may cause some difficulty for readers. Or the teacher can copy a section of text on overhead projector paper to use for looking at with a larger group.

Book Connections

Horrible Harry and the Christmas Surprise is part of a series. Other titles include: *Horrible Harry in Room 2B, Horrible Harry and the Dungeon of Doom,* and *Horrible Harry and the Ant Invasion.* Other chapter books that are similar to this one are the *Mary Marony* series by Suzy Kline and *The Kids of the Polk Street School* by Patricia Reilly Giff.

Genre
Chapter Book

Teaching Uses
Independent Reading; Read Aloud; Partnerships

A Field Guide to the Classroom Library, Lucy Calkins and the Teachers College Reading and Writing Project, Heinemann, ©2002 Teachers College, Columbia University; http://www.heinemann.com/fieldguides

How To Eat Fried Worms

Thomas Rockwell

Book Summary

After Billy bets he can eat 15 worms in fifteen days, he learns how to enjoy worms prepared in a variety of ways, and then how to outsmart the friends who put him up to the challenge. The brief chapters capture the interactions between the four friends (and competitors) during the course of the ordeal, highlighting the suspenseful eating of each worm. Suspense and turns in the plot keep this realistic story moving at a quick pace.

How To Eat Fried Worms is part of a loose series that includes *How To Get Fabulously Rich* and *How to Fight a Girl*. The books do not need to be read as a series.

Basic Book Information

This book is 116 pages. The 41 chapters are titled with Roman numerals and range in length from one to eight pages.

Noteworthy Features

How To Eat Fried Worms is a plot-driven, comical, fairly realistic children's story with a topic that will grab most children's attention-eating worms. The fact that the main characters are all boys may make the book particularly appealing to a male reader.

The extremely brief chapters will give some readers a sense of accomplishment. However, in several cases (e.g., Chapter XXV "Pearl Harbor"), individual chapters are incomprehensible unless read with the preceding and following chapters because they functions more as a scene than an actual chapter. While some chapters are continuous, others open at an unspecified time-15 minutes later, two hours later, or the next day. Some readers may need preparation for these leaps.

Teaching Ideas

Because much of the book consists of untagged dialogue, it will require special attention. In partnerships, students could read the book aloud so as to enjoy the colloquial language, and work out possible ambiguities related to the untagged dialogue. In both cases, teachers may want to give students advance preparation. The speakers can be unclear, even to sophisticated readers, and though the frequent interjections and incomplete sentences may make Billy and his friends sound real, they may create confusion. The interaction of the main characters, the four boys and Billy's family, are recognizably life-like. However, the sketchiness of the characterizations may add to the difficulty of knowing who the speaker is.

Another difficulty lies in the fact that Billy sometimes speaks in a kind of

Series
How To Get Fabulously Rich and How to Fight a Girl, How To Eat Fried Worms

Illustrator
Emily McCully

Publisher
Dell, 1973

ISBN
0440445450

TC Level
10

baby talk, as in the line "Id oo doughing home, iddle boys?"

How To Eat Fried Worms operates as a comic action story, and its themes are not a main focus, but can serve as topics of discussion. Several themes include how the rivalry between friends can affect friendships, and how perseverance pays off. Students may also enjoy a discussion of the boys' friendship and its opposing characteristics of loyalty and rivalry.

This text is appropriate for independent reading if readers are comfortable tackling the dialogue and continuity issues.

Book Connections

How To Eat Fried Worms is part of a loose series that includes *How To Get Fabulously Rich* and *How to Fight a Girl*.

Genre
Short Chapter Book

Teaching Uses
Independent Reading; Partnerships; Read Aloud

How Would You Survive as an Ancient Roman

Anita Ganeri

Book Summary

The topics addressed in this series are similar but vary slightly according to the needs of the topic. Every book addresses certain basic aspects of life such as food, family, clothing, sickness and health, housing, and religion. (The book on ancient Egypt includes discussions of mummification, superstitions and life under pharaohs.) The book about ancient Rome, on the other hand, includes pages devoted to the army, education, and law and order. Each book's section is apparently composed according to available information and topics of special interest to readers. Most of these topics will be predictable to teachers.

Basic Book Information

All of the books in this series have the same structure, format, and approximate difficulty level-although the different content of each will certainly make the reading more or less difficult for individual readers. The books open with a table of contents that lists clearly the topics of life that will be covered in the book. Each topic takes up two facing pages. All the books in the series open with a "Time Spiral" that is a general, illustrated time line that starts at 100,000 B.C. and ends with today. The time period of the book is marked clearly on this spiral. Next is a summary of basic facts about the time period, summarizing some of the topics that appear later in the book, and adding some about language and naming people. Next comes a general map of the area of the world described in the book, with timely landmarks pictured. Just before the topics begin to be covered in depth, one after another, there is a four page, panoramic spread of people engaged in their lives at the time. Interspersed throughout this panorama are questions and page numbers, such as "It's a tough life being a slave. How might you become one? Go to page 19." By starting with these pages and following curiosities, readers can launch themselves into the book. All the books end by explaining where the information about the time period comes from, offering a more detailed time line of the period in question, presenting a quiz-yourself section with answers provided, and then offering an extended glossary and index.

There are also standard features within the text of each of the books in the series. Every page has, in the lower left and right corners, an intriguing question (e.g., "There is a great feast in the villa in a few days' time. How do you make the fish sauce? Go to page 21."). Every set of pages also has, along its borders, sequential pictures with captions that detail certain processes or travels of the time period. Sometimes these strips of pictures aren't

Series
How Would You
Survive....

Illustrator
John James

Publisher
Franklin Watts, Grolier,
1995

ISBN
0531153053

TC Level
10; 11; 12

sequential and instead show varieties of footwear, or small portraits of famous emperors. In the center of the pages are some larger pictures with captions and usually some labeled drawings. Each page also has a paragraph or two of primary text about the topic.

Every book is written in a mixture of third person, about the people of the day, and second person, as if you the reader were there in the time period.

Noteworthy Features

The most unusual feature of the book is the direct placement of you, the reader, into the text of the book. In every case, the descriptions bring the reader in and try to help him/her to imagine life in the conditions and times of the book. This is a great help for most readers in making history real and finding personal understandings of past times and foreign cultures.

This book is absolutely perfect for browsing. The intriguing pictures, details, and labels, maps, explanations, and questions are precisely designed to hook the reader into the book in many different ways. The multi-level text provides reading for many different levels of readers as well, so there is something accessible on every page for nearly every reader.

The book is not intended to be read cover to cover, although that of course is possible and a perfectly fine way to read it, if the reader feels compelled to do it that way. Instead though, the reader is invited by the text to read what interests them, skipping to pages that answer an intriguing question, turning back to a map to figure out something from a later page, reading only the short, comic like strips the first time through or simply reading the captions of the most fascinating illustrations. The book is probably intended to be read more than once, each time adding new layers of information to the reader's growing understanding of the ancient civilization in the book. These multiple readings need not happen immediately following one another, but could occur over the course of a week or a year as long as the reader isn't in any particular hurry to attain a particular level of knowledge.

The book's design makes finding the answers to particular questions relatively easy. In other words, the table of contents and the index make finding the pages where the information lies fairly easy. Both structures are thorough, clearly organized, and well-labeled. Once the particular page is found, however, the reader will probably need to read the text on that entire page to find sought-after information, as the pages themselves are full of informational text in the forms of captions, sidebars, main text, labels and sequential, comic strip-like explanations.

Of course, children who have a hard time with visual fields that are varied, full, and colorful with lots of kinds and sizes of text will find all the books in this series distressing and difficult to read.

Teaching Ideas

This book would almost never be a good read aloud choice. Occasionally however, teachers xerox a page or two onto an overhead and then use those pages for whole-class mini-lessons about reading nonfiction when there are a lot of different kinds of text all happening at once. In this kind of lesson, teachers discuss following one of the sets of text on the page, for example the series of steps illustrating how buildings are made, and letting the other ones pass by unread. It sometimes works to move back and forth between sets of text, for example, reading some captions under pictures in the middle of reading the main text of the book.

This book is a great choice for book clubs and partnerships. Often, even when it is an individual's choice during independent reading time, students will end up grouped around the book discussing it and marveling over the information and illustrations. However, since the book is constructed around following an individual's personal questions about the subject ("Why are snails so important for fashion conscious ladies? Go to page 22."), it is sometimes easier for readers to each have a copy of the book in front of them, at least as they read it the first few times.

Genre
Nonfiction; Picture Book

Teaching Uses
Reading and Writing Nonfiction; Content Area Study; Whole Group Instruction; Book Clubs; Partnerships

If You Traveled on The Underground Railroad

Ellen Levine

Book Summary

This book answers about thirty common questions about the Underground Railroad. Of course, the questions are well-designed to make certain that the answers cover a wide range of information. The questions begin generally, "What was the Underground Railroad?" and as the reader learns more, questions become more specific, "Did you use special signals and codes on the Underground Railroad?"

Basic Book Information

This nonfiction picture book is a little more than sixty pages long. Each double-page spread has four or five paragraphs of text and at least one large illustration. (Some of the books in the series have an occasional two-page spread with no illustrations, just solid text.) There is a table of contents at the beginning, showing that the book is divided into sections of approximately two pages each, with each section answering a particular question about the topic. There is no index. The pictures add color and variety for the eye, but they don't necessarily make the comprehension of the text easier.

Noteworthy Features

The text presents the topic very thoroughly, with specific intriguing details and broad historic events blended together. Readers can choose to read only the answers to the questions that interest them, or they can read the book from cover to cover to get an overall understanding of the topic. The questions serve as headers and don't seem to make the reading choppy, as one might suppose.

Because the subdivisions of the book are dictated by questions, some readers can more easily imagine themselves asking questions, or can more easily find the answers to questions they already have. In this way, the book's design encourages the questioning mind.

The book also presents facts alongside some interpretation of those facts. The author describes how dangers could affect you if you were on the Underground Railroad route. She writes about what the events might feel like, and what you might be afraid of. There are comparisons and contrasts and a fair amount of exclamatory sentences to help the reader process the raw facts. The author explains enough to help the reader picture what is going on, not just memorize facts about it.

Illustrator
Larry Johnson

Publisher
Scholastic, 1988

ISBN
0590451561

TC Level
9; 10; 11

Teaching Ideas

While a book, even one devoted solely to the topic, could never convey the horror of slavery, this one does a fair job of pointing out the various categories of cruelty and injustice that made up slavery. The descriptions of the violence inflicted on the slaves are there, but are not described in vivid and gory detail. The book doesn't explain much about the mental damage slavery caused-the damage to a person's self-esteem and confidence and abilities due to the constant subjugation. Many teachers believe this aspect of slavery also merits discussion, even when the Underground Railroad is the main topic.

The table of contents makes this book quite suitable for use as a reference. As mentioned above, the book is also a smooth and interesting read, from cover to cover or in parts. The book could even be a suitable read aloud, although the writing contains no special attention to figurative language, suspense, or other elements of fiction that some teachers look for even in their nonfiction read alouds.

Many teachers make sure that this book, or any unit on or involving a discussion of slavery, is not the first time the class has discussed or studied African Americans and African American history. Many teachers believe that students should first and foremost hear of their ancestors, or the ancestors of their neighbors and classmates, in positions of dignity and strength. Some teachers feel the same about the history of white European Americans-that children should not hear first of the horrors of being oppressors.

All of the books in the series are of similar length and format, including the use of "you" and the structure based on readers' questions. The illustrations vary, but generally, they are not of the variety that draw readers to texts. Somehow, the series has the look of being a bit out-of-date. Actually, the writing is up-to-date and well-crafted, so teachers may have to make an extra effort to bring these particular books into readers' hands, with book introductions and recommendations.

Genre
Nonfiction; Picture Book; Short Chapter Book

Teaching Uses
Reading and Writing Nonfiction; Content Area Study; Read Aloud; Partnerships

A Field Guide to the Classroom Library, Lucy Calkins and the Teachers College Reading and Writing Project, Heinemann, ©2002 Teachers College, Columbia University; http://www.heinemann.com/fieldguides

Indian in the Cupboard

Lynne Reid Banks

Book Summary

Omri, the youngest of three brothers in an ordinary English household, receives a cupboard for his birthday that can magically turn miniature plastic figures into miniature live ones. When Omri becomes friends with the Native American named Little Bear and the cowboy Boone, he learns to respect different ways of life, and finds out how difficult and important it is to keep the secret of the cupboard.

The Indian in the Cupboard is the first of three books about Omri, Little Bear, Boone, and the magic cupboard.

Basic Book Information

This text is 181 pages in length. There are 16 titled chapters, which vary in length from seven to fifteen pages. There are also illustrations by Brock Cole.

Noteworthy Features

This classic narrative is an adventure/fantasy story that is well grounded enough to be almost believable. The details of Omri's life-his school experiences, hurried breakfasts, fights with his brothers-take the story beyond simple fantasy. As in other stories of the genre, such as Edith Nesbit's books or *Peter Pan*, the power of a child's imagination transforms ordinary materials into something marvelous-something beyond the reach or understanding of adults.

Omri and the magical figures of Little Bear and Boone have distinct personalities and undergo changes during the course of the book. Omri finds out that his "toys" are as feeling and real as he is, and learns, in a sense, how to be a parent to them. He finds a way to get Little Bear and Boone to become friends, and he helps heal their wounds, sympathize with their feelings, and worry about their future.

The characterizations of Little Bear and Boone dispel the cowboy and Indian stereotypes. Through these characters, Banks provides detailed information about the Iroquois, the French and Indian War, and the West in the late 1800s. Paragraphs are fairly long and descriptive, but the lively pace keeps the story moving. Teachers should be aware that at first Omri thinks of these characters only as the stereotypes he knows, and readers who give up the book before its end may have these ideas reinforced in their minds. Teachers should also be aware that the name "Indian" instead of "Native American" is generally considered offensive. Little Bear's speech patterns are also oddly stereotypical, in direct conflict with Banks' apparent goal of challenging stereotypes.

Vocabulary throughout is varied and quite challenging (e.g. "foreboding,"

Series
Indian in the Cupboard

Illustrator
Brock Cole

Publisher
Avon, 1980

ISBN
0380600129

TC Level
11

A Field Guide to the Classroom Library, Lucy Calkins and the Teachers College Reading and Writing Project, Heinemann, ©2002 Teachers College, Columbia University; http://www.heinemann.com/fieldguides

"gesticulating," and "tousled"). Some English vocabulary may be unfamiliar, such as the word "marrow" for "squash." Boone uses cowboy colloquialisms such as "varmint" and makes slangy statements like "Ah'm plumb full o' vittles." Some of the vocabulary is clear from context, but much is not, as in the line, "He gazed back imperiously at Patrick." The many delights of the book may make some struggling worthwhile for less accomplished readers.

Themes students may decide to explore include the power of the imagination, the pains and joys of responsibility, and the value of life, regardless of the form it takes.

Teaching Ideas

The Indian in the Cupboard is a good independent read for versatile readers. It also works as a read aloud for students who might have trouble making their way through the vocabulary. In either case, the rich detail, plot twists, and suspense will engage many readers' attention.

Students can take notes on the historical information. Omri begins by seeing Little Bear as his inferior not just in size, but in other ways. Students can discuss how Omri alters his views after he learns about Little Bear's culture.

The Indian in the Cupboard might be viewed as a book about overcoming cultural divides. Banks presents more than three very different cultures-Omri's, Little Bear's, Boone's and a handful of others-and shows how the differences in cultures can cause misunderstandings and conflict. Students might take notes on how those conflicts are resolved and apply them to their own lives. Does learning about other cultures or circumstances help people get along better?

Students can trace Omri's development as a character, comparing his behavior and his attitude toward the Indian in the first few chapters with his behavior and attitudes at the end of the book.

Book Connections

There are two other *Indian in the Cupboard* books that follow this one.

Genre
Fantasy; Chapter Book

Teaching Uses
Independent Reading; Read Aloud; Book Clubs

A Field Guide to the Classroom Library, Lucy Calkins and the Teachers College Reading and Writing Project, Heinemann, ©2002 Teachers College, Columbia University; http://www.heinemann.com/fieldguides

Insects

Bettina Bird; Joan Short

Book Summary

This book begins by describing the physical characteristics of insects. It then describes three common life cycles of insects, from those that undergo no change through those that undergo a complete change. The next section of the book details some typical kinds of insect behavior including catching prey and avoiding predators. The last section of the book discusses insects' ability to survive.

Basic Book Information

This nonfiction picture book is about forty-five pages long. It is probably one of the most difficult of the *Mondo Animal* series. The font is smaller and more closely packed than most of the other books. The table of contents is well organized and well laid-out. However, the text is also divided and subdivided into many more categories than the average book in the series. Each category or subcategory may also go on for several pages, with several different examples, so that by the time it has ended, it is hard to bring to mind the larger topic that it was organized under. Of course, the table of contents can help with this.

The language itself is also more technical than that of the other books in the series. There are more new terms and topics and concepts than in the other books. There are a lot of diagrams and illustrations with labeled parts. The end of the book has a chart to help clarify some of the organizations of the insects. After that, there is a twenty-word pronunciation guide to some of the words in the text. There is also a fairly comprehensive, one-page, small-print index.

Noteworthy Features

This text is more complicated than others in the series. This may be because the book is not just about one insect, but instead about a whole phyla of animal life. Explaining this to the reader involves explaining different classifications and characteristics instead of simply describing one family or species in particular.

As mentioned above, the table of contents is well organized and well laid-out. Holding that table of contents in mind while reading, however, is a bit more difficult because of the many different levels and categories of information. Most readers will want to refer back to that table of contents as they read to help keep a tidy organization of information in their minds.

The diagrams and labels in this book are particularly clear and helpful in understanding the text. Readers could be encouraged to consult the diagrams as they read in order to help them understand the text. Waiting until after all the text has been read to look over the diagrams may not be

Series
Mondo Animal

Illustrator
Deborah Savin

Publisher
Mondo, Animals, 1988

ISBN
1572552166

TC Level
13; 14; 15

the most helpful way to read this book.

Teaching Ideas

As with nearly any book that is dense, this one would be a good choice for a book group or a partnership to read. Discussing the information as it comes up will inevitably lend it more meaning and permanence for the reader.

Many readers will want to study and examine some living insects while reading or after reading this book. Readers may want to find some of the parts that are described and labeled in the text on the living creature. They may also want to try to place the living insect into the categories laid out in the text of the book.

This book is as helpful for teaching about classifying animals-or anything else, for that matter-as it is for teaching about insects.

Genre
Nonfiction; Picture Book

Teaching Uses
Reading and Writing Nonfiction; Content Area Study; Book Clubs; Partnerships

J.T.
Jane Wagner

Book Summary

J.T. is a ten-year-old boy who feels lonely around the Christmas holidays until he finds a badly injured alley cat and is distracted from his own sadness. J.T. identifies with the cat's external injuries as he battles with his own internal conflicts around being poor and abandoned by his father. To make matters worse, J.T.'s teacher does not understand what he is going through, and there are two neighborhood bullies after him. J.T.'s relationship with his mother is tenuous, and although he feels more comfortable because his grandmother from the South is staying for the holidays, he is still unable to express his deep feelings of longing. However, through his desire and attempt to care for the badly injured cat, J.T. begins to learn that he can share his feelings with those around him.

Basic Book Information

This book is written by Jane Wagner and illustrated with photography by the well-known photographer Gordon Parks, Jr. This book originated as a ballad, and then as an award-winning CBS Children's Television Special. The book tells the story of a young ten-year-old boy living in the inner city with uncertainty and loss. The photographic illustrations make real the plight of this vulnerable ten year old. J.T. is a sensitive but conflicted boy who, on the one hand, is able to show love and concern towards a wounded animal, yet on the other hand, leans toward crime and dishonesty when he steals a radio and buys on credit at the grocery store without his mother's permission.

J.T. is 125 pages in length and it is not divided into chapters or sections. The story has a serious tone as well as a mixture of mystery and conflict. *J.T.* is not exactly a happy story, but represents what could be considered realism.

Noteworthy Features

The book is written in narrative form and includes dialogue between the characters. Some very challenging words are used, withmeanings not easily identified through context such as *antimacassar*, *valiant*, and *meticulously*. Colloquial speech is also used.

The book lends itself to great book talks because it deals with some difficult life themes, e.g., loneliness, poverty, abandonment and death.

It may be difficult for a child to keep up with the events because the book is not divided into chapters or sections. Children may benefit most by stopping to define, discuss and interpret major events as they happen in the book. This may make it easier for the child to group or organize ideas about the book for greater understanding of the plot.

Illustrator
Gordon Parks Jr.

Publisher
Dell, 1969

ISBN
0440442753

TC Level
10

A Field Guide to the Classroom Library, Lucy Calkins and the Teachers College Reading and Writing Project, Heinemann, ©2002 Teachers College, Columbia University; http://www.heinemann.com/fieldguides

Teaching Ideas

J.T's character is complex and many-sided; readers will want to think about him for a while. Is he a good boy? After all, he feels sympathy for the injured cat. Or is he a bad boy? After all, he steals, lies and stays out of school. To what extent has his environment made J.T. the person he seems to be?

Readers may ponder over how other characters fit into J.T.'s story. A reader might choose just one of these supporting characters and reread to notice and analyze his or her relationship with J.T and the minor character's role in the book. What would this book be like without this character? This, of course, is a move readers can learn to make with any book they read.

Genre
Chapter Book

Teaching Uses
Independent Reading; Character Study; Partnerships

A Field Guide to the Classroom Library, Lucy Calkins and the Teachers College Reading and Writing Project, Heinemann, ©2002 Teachers College, Columbia University; http://www.heinemann.com/fieldguides

Journey

Patricia MacLachlan

Book Summary

Journey tells the story of the title character's inward journey, which begins with his memory of his mother's departure. She tells Journey she will be back, and he wants to believe her even though her actions are not consistent with her words. She sends envelopes containing only money, providing no return address, but Journey continues to hold on to his belief that she will come back. Journey's grandfather represents the truth, continually telling Journey that she will not come back. Journey moves between blaming his grandfather and blaming himself, until old photographs and the memories they evoke allow him to face and accept the truth.

Journey's grandfather introduces Journey to the art of photography, teaching him that "sometimes pictures show us what is really there. ...Maybe that is why people take pictures. To see what is really there." Journey's sister Cat also avoids facing the reality of their loss. Unlike Journey, she acknowledges that their mother is gone but avoids confronting her feelings, acting as if she doesn't care and distracting herself with constant activity. Cat acknowledges and accepts her grief at the conclusion of the book. This is the story of Journey's inward journey toward acceptance, in which he learns to see things as they really are rather than how he would like them to be. As Grandfather says, "Journey, a thing doesn't have to be perfect to be fine. That goes for a picture. That goes for life."

Basic Book Information

This book is 83 pages long, and divided into thirteen chapters. The chapters are not titled. Two italicized quotes precede the opening of the story, which begins with a passage also in italics. Italicized passages throughout the book indicate glimpses into Journey's memories and dreams. Three asterisks and spaces between paragraphs signal shifts in time and place. There are no illustrations. The story is told in the first-person narrative, from Journey's point of view.

Noteworthy Features

This book provides students' with an outstanding example of the power of metaphor. It is replete with images that mirror and highlight the understory of the text, empowering students with new language to address similar themes in other books and their lives. There exists strong evidence for both Journey's denial and his ultimate ability to face and accept the truth, allowing students to clearly follow and document this central theme. The different ways in which Journey and Cat cope with the difficult feelings evoked by their loss provide opportunities to discuss the reasons behind their behavior, and to compare them with our own reactions to life.

Publisher
Bantam Doubleday Dell, 1991

ISBN
0385304277

TC Level
11

A Field Guide to the Classroom Library, Lucy Calkins and the Teachers College Reading and Writing Project, Heinemann, ©2002 Teachers College, Columbia University; http://www.heinemann.com/fieldguides

Students may be encouraged to ask themselves: When I feel sad, do I hide like Journey, or do I stay busy like Cat? The quotes at the beginning of the book offer scaffolding for thought, and may be continually reread to deepen students' understanding of its central themes. Finally, the author chooses her words carefully, attending not only to their meanings but to their sounds as well. MacLachlan writes, "Cat began to cut carrots at the kitchen counter," and "Grandma stopped stirring the soup."

The beginning quotes tap into significant themes addressed throughout the book, and students should not be expected to discern their meaning right away. Instead, they can be encouraged to return to them again and again to uncover their significance, while allowing them to inform their thinking around the text. Teachers can explain that the author intends to plant a question mark within their minds; they can learn alongside Journey as the truths of his life unfold. However, students should not be discouraged from bringing these quotes into conversations, as they do provide a valid springboard for reasonable predictions and theories. Students may also need assistance understanding what function the italicized passages serve in this book. Rather than allowing this question to distract from the real story, explain that they set Journey's memories and dreams apart from the rest of the text. Finally, and perhaps most importantly, this is both a very short and a very rich book. In order to uncover the many layers of significance within each page, it must be read slowly and with attention to detail. Reread significant passages and encourage children to talk and write often. They will develop a language around this book that will facilitate future conversations around similar texts.

Teaching Ideas

This book provides concrete evidence for both Journey's denial and eventual acceptance of the truth, allowing students to easily document this line of thought. At the beginning of the book, Journey refuses to believe that his mother is gone. He then vacillates between denial and acceptance until ultimately facing his anger and the reality of his loss. Journey thinks, "I was silent, suddenly remembering that once in this barn Grandfather told me that Mama would not come back. That was not true. I knew it was not true." Later he asks Grandma, "Why did Mama do it? The pictures?...I'll have to ask her when I see her." And even further into the text he says, "I'll fix this, Cat. I'll tape these pictures back together again...I will put all these pictures back together and everything will be all right."

Slowly Journey is beginning to direct his anger away from his Grandfather and toward his mother, where it really belongs, when he says to her picture, "You...I *could* have a sore throat. I *could* have a temperature. ...Do you hear me?" When looking at the pictures his mother has torn he thinks, "*Murder*. That word washed over me. It did look like a killing. Inside that box were people." When Journey's mother calls and he explains, "A cat has come. ...And the cat is a very good mother. And she is staying here with me. Forever." He apologizes to Cat, "I'm sorry. I'm sorry I couldn't put the pictures together. I wanted to make things all right again." Throughout the book Journey returns to the memory of sitting on someone's knees. He can remember the buttons of the shirt, but is unable to glimpse the face. Then he realizes that it is his Grandfather who has been there all along. He says, "I sat on *your* knees...not on Papa's...and you sang 'Trot, trot to Boston.' It was your shirt, your button I remembered...It was *your* face."

This book also provides outstanding opportunities to enrich students' understanding of metaphor. When Journey's mother sends money he notices, "The paper clip over my name was bent, as if Mama may have tried to make it right and hadn't." Later, Journey hides under the covers after learning that his mother has torn up the pictures, tearing up their past together. Cat enters the room and whips the covers off. "She lets the window shade snap up, and sun clatters into the room." She is lifting the covers and letting in the light. She is forcing Journey to face the truth. MacLachlan again taps into the image of light as truth, writing "A standing lamp shines down, a yellow pool on the pictures...I work alone...sorting and shifting picture pieces like a giant puzzle. But I can only piece together a few." A teacher might encourage students to notice and inquire deeply into the author's use of light, photography, and other objects to invoke and highlight the central themes in this book.

Book Connections

In Katherine Paterson's *The Great Gilly Hopkins* and MacLachlan's *Baby*, the protagonists also learn to face, accept, and mourn losses in their families. *The Monument*, by Gary Paulsen, and *Arthur For the Very First Time*, by Patricia MacLachlan, both address the transformative, healing power of the arts. For Journey it is photography. For Rocky it is drawing, and for Arthur it is writing.

Genre
Chapter Book

Teaching Uses
Interpretation; Read Aloud; Language Conventions; Character Study; Teaching Writing; Book Clubs

A Field Guide to the Classroom Library, Lucy Calkins and the Teachers College Reading and Writing Project, Heinemann, ©2002 Teachers College, Columbia University; http://www.heinemann.com/fieldguides

Junebug

Alice Mead

Book Summary

Junebug is the story of an almost-ten-year-old kid nicknamed Junebug who lives with his mom and his little sister in a pretty scary housing project. He has a lot to deal with in his life-gangs, bullies, worries about his family-and he wishes he could do something to make his family's life easier.

Basic Book Information

This realistic fiction book is 102 pages in length with 11 chapters. Each chapter is about 10 pages. A former art teacher, Alice Mead has written more than seven books for young adults. Some of her other titles include *Adem's Cross*, *Junebug and the Reverend*, *Walking the Edge*, *Crossing the Starlight Bridge*, and *Soldier Mom*.

Noteworthy Features

This story is told chronologically and is very easy to follow. It doesn't have many characters to keep track of and is told in the first person from Junebug's perspective.

The text poses few difficulties, although there are many serious issues for Junebug and the reader to think about and wrestle with throughout the story.

Junebug is a good book to make available early in the year. It has a sequel, which is good for students to know since it helps them with book choice. It could be a good read aloud in fourth or fifth grade-it offers a lot to think about. Junebug has to deal with living in a rough neighborhood; harassment and peer pressure from older kids about gangs and drugs; his mother being hospitalized, etc. It offers a nice mix of both plot and character-action definitely happens here, but there is also a very thoughtful narrator.

Teaching Ideas

Junebug is a great book for readers who have begun to read independently, in a fluent and sustained way. A teacher may, in a conference, want to remind readers of the challenges of chapter book reading. Because readers of early chapter books are often focused on processing all that print, they sometimes can read along without doing the mind-work that reading involves. Sometimes when teachers ask such readers about the book, they say, "I read it, honest. I just can't remember it." Readers can be reminded that reading is comprehension; it's not an extra credit option to read with accuracy and intonation.

It is essential that all students are working with books that they can read and process independently if they are reading them on their own. Students

A Field Guide to the Classroom Library, Lucy Calkins and the Teachers College Reading and Writing Project, Heinemann, ©2002 Teachers College, Columbia University; http://www.heinemann.com/fieldguides

Publisher
Bantam Doubleday Dell, 1995

ISBN
0440412455

TC Level
9

with serious comprehension problems should be encouraged to "shelve" the book until later in the year, and then try again.

If a teacher wants to prepare a child to be actively thinking while reading, it sometimes helps to look over the book together in order to activate a child's expectations and involvement in the story.

Then, too, teachers may want to talk with readers about the fact that when reading a story, one should generally expect to learn the characters, setting and basic plot by the end of chapter one. If one comes to the end of the first chapter without knowing these things, it's often a good sign that some rereading is in order.

It could be, for example, that the teacher reads a book aloud and during the following book talk, shows children some of the ways good readers think about character. Afterwards, when children disperse for their independent reading, the teacher might remind them to do some of this work with characters as they read independently. Alternatively, the idea of reading with an eye towards understanding the characters could simply emerge out of a one-to-one conference between teacher and reader. Teachers could suggest that readers read like magnets, collecting bits of information about each character so that early on in reading, students pause and create a tiny character sketch of each character.

Book Connections

Several books that could be read alongside this one are: *Junebug and the Reverend* by Alice Mead (the sequel to this book), *Chevrolet Saturdays* by Candy Dawson Boyd, *Miracle's Boys* by Jacqueline Woodson, and *Scorpions* by Walter Dean Myers (a harder read than this book).

Genre
Chapter Book

Teaching Uses
Independent Reading

Justin and the Best Biscuits in the World

Mildred Pitts Walter

Book Summary

When ten-year-old Justin's messy habits get him into trouble with his mother and sisters, he is thrilled and relieved to be invited to visit his grandfather's ranch. There, he learns about his ancestors' struggle out of slavery, the traditions of Black cowboys, and the simple satisfactions of learning how to take care of his own things. With the help of his resourceful and attentive grandfather, Justin becomes someone who takes pride in his work and in himself.

Basic Book Information

Justin and the Best Biscuits in the World is a realistic story that incorporates American history and culture.

Noteworthy Features

Justin is an engaging character whose progress is believable and compelling. At the story's beginning, his frustration with the difficulty of daily tasks like washing dishes and making his bed will be familiar to many. The story shows how Justin's wish to please his patient grandfather, coupled with the grandfather's clear instructions and support, make it possible for Justin to learn how to do his work well.

The backdrop for Justin's progress is his family history. After slavery ended, Justin's great-great-grandfather and his family traveled to Missouri at great personal risk. Their bravery and hard work, described in a book Justin reads, reinforce the changes Justin makes. The historical grounding makes the book richer than the usual tale of self-improvement.

The character of the grandfather, who is both a rancher and a pro at domestic work, serves as a model. He is admirable without seeming air brushed. The care he takes with Justin supports the idea that Justin's troubles are understandable and solvable. The grandfather does not fault Justin for crying or for not knowing how to make a bed; he simply encourages Justin and shows him the skills he needs.

With the grandfather at the center, *Justin* is a story aimed at boys (though girls will enjoy it) that counters stereotypes about race and gender. Justin's family is part of a Black ranching tradition that Justin knew little about-and learns to appreciate. The grandfather is not only competent at fence-building, riding, and taking care of livestock, but cooks "the best biscuits in the world" and keeps his house neat and well-organized. The grandfather's emphasis on self-sufficiency, both on the ranch and in the

Illustrator
Catherine Stock

Publisher
Knopf, 1986

ISBN
0590465198

TC Level
9

house, argues against the notion of dividing tasks into "men's" or "women's" work. When Justin is embarrassed about crying, the grandfather shows sympathy and Justin feels better, demonstrating that boys too can benefit from expressing their feelings.

Teaching Ideas

Justin's development is a good subject for study. Readers can look at Justin's behavior early in the book and chart the changes. What are Justin's feelings at each stage? Justin's activities change as well. At the start of the book, he is sneaking out to play basketball instead of cleaning his room. At the end, he is surprising his family with a home-cooked meal. What else changes about Justin? Exploring the changes in a character's behavior and feelings is an excellent strategy to teach readers studying character.

Justin concerns the skills that allow us to be independent and contribute to the family. Readers can assess their own skills. What do they know how to do? What would they like instruction in? Students can practice sequential writing by compiling instructions on different tasks like cooking, bed-making or window-washing, and then test the usefulness of classmates' instructions by following them at home. Comments from classmates will direct revision.

Readers can also collect historical facts about Justin's family. How does Justin's family counter or reflect the readers' previous ideas about Black history? Interested readers can follow up with research on Black cowboys and rodeos. More generally, readers can think about how personal history affects us. Students might research their own personal histories and consider how what they learn shapes their lives.

Genre
Historical Fiction; Chapter Book

Teaching Uses
Independent Reading; Character Study

A Field Guide to the Classroom Library, Lucy Calkins and the Teachers College Reading and Writing Project, Heinemann, ©2002 Teachers College, Columbia University; http://www.heinemann.com/fieldguides

Knights of the Kitchen Table

Jon Scieszka

Book Summary

At the end of his birthday party, Joe discovers one unopened gift. Intrigued by the black and gold wrapping paper, and the fact that the gift came from his uncle who is a traveling magician, Joe excitedly opens the present. What he finds is a strange book entitled only *The Book*. As he opens *The Book* to a picture of a knight in black armor, a green mist begins to swirl around him and his two best friends, Fred and Sam. The next thing they know, Joe, Fred, and Sam find themselves in the middle ages facing a black-armored knight who is preparing to charge at them.

The boys soon figure out that *The Book* has magical powers and can transport them through time. What they don't know is how to get back to their own time. The Time Warp Trio, as they decide to call themselves, face the Black Knight, meet King Arthur, Guenevere, Lancelot, Percival and Gawain, defeat a dragon and a giant, try to teach the people of Camelot how to play baseball, and finally find their way back to their own time with the help of the magician, Merlin.

Basic Book Information

Knights of the Kitchen Table has 55 pages divided into ten short chapters. There is no contents page; the chapters are numbered but not titled. An amusing note about the author and illustrator is included at the end of the book.

Noteworthy Features

If students are planning to read all the books in *The Time Warp Trio* series, this might be a good place to start as it explains the origin of *The Book* that the boys will use to travel through time.

The format of these books will become familiar to the readers: the first chapter drops The Time Warp Trio somewhere in a time other than their own; the second chapter explains how they got there. In the third chapter, they resume their adventures and in the final chapter they get back home. Students who choose to read the entire series may come to enjoy the predictability of the format; they can use the format to make predictions about the action of the book. At first, though, readers may be a little disoriented by the first chapter. It may help to read the first two chapters as a class, or to at least review the action of those chapters if students are reading them independently to make sure that they have understood.

The action of the book is progressive-chapters do build on one another, though the action does not build to one single climax.

The language of the middle age characters may be unfamiliar to the readers. The following terms come up frequently: knave, vile, lance, infidel,

Series
The Time Warp Trio

Illustrator
Lane Smith

Publisher
Scholastic, Inc., 1993

ISBN
0590981293

TC Level
10

moat, and chain-mail.

The character Joe often translates for Sam and Fred who have some difficulty understanding the language, and this helps to clarify most of the dialogue, but a teacher may want to check with students to be sure they're keeping up.

The characters use clever ways to get out of their fixes. Students can be encouraged to apply creative problem solving to some of their own problems.

Teaching Ideas

This book can be read as a class or individually. Since there is so much dialogue, students may enjoy taking the parts of Fred, Sam, or Joe and reading them aloud.

Knights of the Kitchen Table can be read as an individual book or as part of *The Time Warp Trio* series. Students reading the entire series will learn bits of information about *The Book* that students reading just one book won't. Nevertheless, each book can stand on its own.

This book is great for partnerships or book clubs since kids seem to enjoy laughing over the puns and studying the historical details together. They also tend to ask each other lots of questions.

If students are reading the books as a series, they may want to keep a time line, placing each book in its appropriate place on the time line to keep track of what they have read and when it was situated.

Book Connections

The Time Warp Trio series includes: *Knights of the Kitchen Table; The Not So-Jolly Roger; The Good, the Bad, and the Goofy; 2095;* and *Tut, Tut.* Other connections outside of the series: *A Wrinkle in Time, The Time Machine, The Sword in the Stone, Excalibur, A Connecticut Yankee in King Arthur's Court.*

Genre
Short Chapter Book

Teaching Uses
Independent Reading; Read Aloud; Whole Group Instruction

Letting Swift River Go

Jane Yolen

Book Summary

Sally Jane describes the peace, fun, and beauty she and her family and neighbors found in their little town of Swift River. When she was only six she would walk to school alone, past the beloved landmarks and the places where she would catch fireflies and sleep under the trees. But then things changed. Boston, sixty miles away, needed water. The town of Swift River and its neighbors would all be drowned under the reservoir to be built. Sally Jane watched the graves being moved, the trees being chopped down, the buildings being wrecked. Then, the water came. Many years later, she and her father rowed out on the reservoir, feeling they could almost see the outlines of where the buildings and roads and trees had been. As the water covering her hometown flowed through her fingers, Sally Jane thought to herself that she had to let it all go. And she did.

Basic Book Information

This is a beautiful picture book with a lot of text.

Noteworthy Features

If children are planning to interpret *Letting Swift River Go*, they will probably find a way to do so, as interpretations are very near the surface in this book.

In the author's note at the story's beginning, that readers may well skip without harm to the story, Yolen herself offers an interpretation of the story, saying that trades are never easy, and never perfectly fair. If children come across these words, they may use them to gather evidence of this message in the book.

Teaching Ideas

Interpretations that rise to the surface may come from some of the very few quotations in the book, such as Sally Jane's mother saying, "You have to let them go." The fact that her mother's words come up twice, and are nearly the final words of the book should be a clue to the reader that they are important to its interpretation.

Children may at first be puzzled as to why Sally Jane is remembering her mother telling her to let the fireflies go for the second time when now there are no fireflies in sight. This kind of reading puzzle can help children move to a new understanding of literature if they stick with it. If they can feel convinced that the author has a good reason for this reference, and if they feel confident enough that they can find the reason, then they will be well on their way to being able to interpret books well. At least they will be well on

---

Illustrator
Barbara Cooney

Publisher
Little, Brown & Company, 1992

ISBN
0316968609

TC Level
10

their way to realizing that Sally Jane has called on her mother's words to help herself let go of the longing for Swift River, or to help herself let go of the other emotions and thoughts that aren't helpful to her world now. Once children have seen this interpretation or something close to it, it is an easier leap to see that the book's message could be that people all have problems and longings that they might do better if let go.

Some children feel furious at the town of Boston for flooding Sally Jane's small town. Sometimes, it is most helpful for children at this stage to help them realize that there are two sides to the story. Needing water is a serious problem, and the government offered nice things to those who lost their towns. Readers could even be led to notice that Yolen herself claims the reservoir is a beautiful place. Making sure the children see this story not just as good and evil helps them to understand the story, and life, more fully and compassionately. Of course, telling it to the children is not always the best way-sometimes partner or group discussions or critiques of the story (e.g., "Who benefits from the story being told this way, from this point of view?") are the most helpful.

Book Connections

It might be informative and provoking for children to compare this work to others by Jane Yolen as well. *Owl Moon* and some of her other books might bring out some of the childhood, nostalgic, nature-oriented themes she tends to favor. Children will notice many other factors that are similar or different in a collection of her books.

For thematic connections, Patricia MacLachlan's *What You Know First* might be an interesting match. The child in that story is sad at losing her family's farm and community. She too describes many things about the place that she loves, knows they will be moving to a "better" place, and finds a way to come to terms with the loss.

Although Barbara Cooney is an illustrator and a writer, the books she writes tend to have similar values and themes to the books she chooses to illustrate. These emphasize the beauty of the natural world, the cycle of life, and the hardships and good times that all people go through. It might be interesting for children to lay out some of the works of Barbara Cooney-either illustrated or written-and see for themselves what they have in common. Or, of course, see something else that only they could notice. These books could include *Island Boy*, *The Ox-Cart Man*, or *Miss Rumphius*.

Genre
Picture Book

Teaching Uses
Independent Reading; Partnerships; Interpretation; Critique

Lives of the Musicians. Good Times, Bad Times, (and What the Neighbors Thought)

Kathleen Krull

Book Summary

This text acts as a resource for learning about musicians' lives. A reader is introduced to a number of musicians including Vivaldi, Bach, Mozart, Beethoven, Chopin, Verdi, Schumann, Foster, Brahms, Tchaikovsky, Gilbert, Sullivan, Satie, Joplin, Ives, Stravinsky, Boulanger, Prokofiev, Gershwin, and Guthrie. The reader is given a positive view of each individual along with information about their lives and their music.

These mini-biographies present a glimpse into their personal lives, into their struggles to become accepted musicians, and into the work they created which has stood the test of time and has made them famous.

Basic Book Information

Lives of the Musicians is part of a series of research texts. The other texts are entitled, *Lives of the Artists*, *Lives of the Athletes*, and *Lives of the Writers*. This particular text is 96 pages in length with -three to five pages devoted to each musician. Within the section on each individual, the reader is given the birth and death dates, additional suggested reading, and listening, if the reader is interested in the particular individual. There is also a section entitled "Musical Notes" that gives relevant pieces of information about music, and an illustration of the writer. The text begins with an index of the musicians who are mentioned within the book. The text also has an index and a glossary of musical terms found at the end of the book. The vocabulary level is relatively high, since it is so specific to the topic.

Noteworthy Features

This text does an excellent job at placing a face with a name for the reader. The illustrations depict each musician, and this allows the reader to get a better understanding of each individual. Each vignette offers interesting facts and outlines the larger experiences that these particular people had. The "Musical Notes" section of the book helps the reader learn more about the subject of music so as to understand the biographies better.

Teaching Ideas

The text gives the reader an insight into the life of a particular musician and it brings those lives into reality. This text is also wonderful because it does

Series
Lives of . . .

Illustrator
Kathryn Hewitt

Publisher
Harcourt Brace

ISBN
0152480102

TC Level
11; 12; 13

not include only European composers or only classical music composers, as so many other books do. There are many cultures and races represented in the profiles, making it more comprehensive and realistic than many others.

Book Connections

This text is part of a series and, if a student enjoys *Lives of the Musicians*, he or she will be likely to enjoy *Lives of the Artists*, *Lives of the Writers*, and *Lives of the Athletes*.

Genre
Nonfiction

Teaching Uses
Reading and Writing Nonfiction; Content Area Study; Partnerships

Lon Po Po: A Red-Riding Hood Story From China

Ed Young

Book Summary

When Mother leaves the house to visit grandmother on her birthday, she tells her three daughters to lock the door tightly while she is gone. That night, a wolf disguises himself as the children's grandmother and tricks them into letting him inside. Shang, the eldest, notices his hairy face but pretends not to. They trick the wolf into falling from the tall ginko tree, and he falls and bumps his head and breaks his heart to pieces. When their mother returns, the children eat treats from their real grandmother and tell the tale of the wolf.

Basic Book Information

This is a lovely picture book with gentle-edged watercolor illustrations. There is a fair amount of text on each page.

Noteworthy Features

This book fits best into a collection of Little Red Riding Hood stories. When read in conjunction with others, this story has added dimensions and perspectives by playing off the many other versions of the fairy tale that exist. This tale also has as many similarities, if not more, to stories of the wolf who dressed in sheep's clothing, so those fables also could be added to the collection.

Teaching Ideas

Children's knowledge of how fables and folk tales tend to go will carry them through this story. Without this prior knowledge, without those layers of stories, the idea of children actually thinking that a wolf wearing a dress is their grandmother may seem ridiculous. The stories also help to make acceptable that the mother leaves her three children while she goes off to visit Grandmother-these things happen in fairy tales. With enough stories where these kinds of things happen, those not-so-relevant details slide to the background and don't take away from the flow and suspense of the story.

This book has some of the characteristics that often go with translations. The word choice, while fresh and full of flavor from the language from which it is translated, is at the same time unconventional to read and at times a bit awkward in its flow or doling out of information. For example, the first sentence of the story tells us of a woman who has three children, Shang, Tao, and Paotze. Perhaps, to those who are familiar with these

Illustrator
Ed Young

Publisher
Scholastic Inc., 1989

ISBN
0590440691

A Field Guide to the Classroom Library, Lucy Calkins and the Teachers College Reading and Writing Project, Heinemann, ©2002 Teachers College, Columbia University; http://www.heinemann.com/fieldguides

names, it is clear that the children are daughters. To the reader unfamiliar to the language, however, that question remains unanswered, hanging in the readers mind until near the end of the story when it is finally clear that all three are girls. It is not so important that the gender of the children be known for the reader to understand the plot of the tale, but for the reader to picture the children and feel attached to them, some basic knowledge of who they are is essential. For this to happen, then, readers either need an introduction to the story, or they need to read it more than once, so that they can develop and idea of the characters throughout the whole story in the light of the knowledge of them from the end of the story.

Perhaps because of subtleties lost in the translation, near the end of the story some readers find it is not entirely clear whether or not the girls are intentionally trying to hurt or kill the wolf. Perhaps the wolf's death is a happy accident. After all, when the wolf gets into the basket and the girls haul him up to the tree to get the ginko nuts, why don't they haul him up high and drop him the first time? Why wait for three times? And the final time, when the wolf finally is killed, the reason he falls is because Shang coughs, not because the girls let go on purpose. Is this passage written like this because that is the way the wolf sees it, or are the girls really trying to help him into the tree? Since they are lying about the magical qualities of the nuts, it seems odd that they would be sincerely trying to get the wolf in the tree. Children need to refer to the text to bolster their arguments on this issue.

Sometimes children find it odd that the children are able to go directly to sleep after their harrowing experience with the wolf, and they discuss why this could be. Some readers also find the end of the story abrupt; they are expecting some words of praise from the mother for the girls' brave behavior, or perhaps a burial of the wolf or a "happily ever after." This too could be for a number of reasons that children can discuss. Perhaps, again, translation is the reason for the seeming abruptness.

The words "Po Po" clearly mean "grandmother" in the story, yet the words "Lon Po Po" from the title never appear. Children sometimes try to figure out what the "Lon" might mean, and from there try to figure out why the author chose those words for his title. There is little to no textual evidence to support any one theory, however, so these discussions are not very helpful to children generally.

Genre
Fairy and Folk Tale; Picture Book

Teaching Uses
Independent Reading; Interpretation; Critique; Character Study

A Field Guide to the Classroom Library, Lucy Calkins and the Teachers College Reading and Writing Project, Heinemann, ©2002 Teachers College, Columbia University; http://www.heinemann.com/fieldguides

Lost! A Story in String

Paul Fleischman

Book Summary

The power goes out when a grandmother is visiting her granddaughter. When the little girl exclaims that she will die with no TV or VCR, the grandmother offers to tell her a story. The story is of a little girl who has nothing to play with but a string, and with the string, she makes all kinds of pictures to entertain herself. One morning, she sets out to find her lost dog. With the versatility that comes to her easily from making all those pictures with only the string, she finds her way through many hardships in the search for the animal. She braves a snowstorm, finds food, makes a shelter, navigates in the big woods, makes snowshoes, builds a sled to carry her wounded dog, and finally, makes her way home. In the end, the grandmother admits the girl was herself, and encourages her granddaughter to make her own stories out of the string she gives her that she had used to illustrate her story with. As grandmother naps, the girl begins on her own.

Basic Book Information

This book has two distinct elements: the story, and the activities for readers to engage in with the string.

Noteworthy Features

The elegant and serious black and white ink drawings make this story alluring and noble instead of allowing it to be overwhelmed by the do-it-yourself activity part of the book.

The story itself is two-layered. The first story begins in modern times, with the grandmother and the granddaughter together in a storm when the power goes out. Readers then move into the story that the grandmother tells to her granddaughter. It isn't necessary for readers to think that the little girl in the story is the grandmother when she was younger, that part comes out clearly at the end of the story. Readers must only be facile enough with reading to jump from the depiction of the grandmother to listening to her as a narrator of the other story.

Teaching Ideas

That opening page, which tells of the grandmother and the granddaughter in the storm with the power failure, is written entirely in dialogue. There is no indication of who is speaking, so readers need to be familiar with, or be instructed that, the convention that each line is a new speaker. The picture helps, in that there are only the two characters depicted in it, so readers won't have to wonder how many people are talking. Some teachers refer back to this page when young writers are learning to write and punctuate

Illustrator
C.B. Mordan

Publisher
Henry Holt and Company, 2000

ISBN
0805055835

dialogue of their own.

Within the dialogue, the grandmother uses a phrase that some readers will not understand: she calls the TV and VCR "Finicky beasts" when they don't run without electricity. This is not the sort of detail that readers need to know before they go on, or before they can comprehend the story, so encouragement to just read on probably will be the most helpful if they appear stuck on it.

The story itself is fairly straightforward for readers at this level, however, the string drawings at the bottom of each chunk of text can be greatly distracting, especially since the pictures they intend to depict aren't immediately apparent and so may require a length of thinking to figure out. Teachers may want to advise students to look carefully at the string drawings only after the first read through of the story to avoid breaking the flow and excitement of the tale.

Children sometimes wonder why the hunter had a bow, when the dog was wounded by a bullet at the end of the story. They can certainly guess why the author gave the hunter a bow in the story (the string picture to go with it is of a bow) and they can guess that the hunter wasn't the same person who shot the dog. Many explanations are possible. This topic is one that partners and reading groups sometimes pick up.

The activity aspect of the story should not necessarily be dismissed from reading time. The process by which children read and follow the directions for how to create the string pictures can be a very valuable one. Mistakes in the reading of these directions will make for the wrong string picture and will therefore lead to self-correction and careful reading. Some teachers liken following the directions to make the string pictures to reading math word problems, or to reading computer manuals or VCR programming directions. This type of reading is extremely important for children to learn as well as the kind of reading that comes from deciphering the story of the girl lost in the woods.

Book Connections

The last page of this book lists other books that give directions for how to make string pictures (most are written by Camilla Gryski; one is by Anne Akers Johnson).

Genre
Picture Book; Short Chapter Book

Teaching Uses
Partnerships; Book Clubs

Maniac Magee
Jerry Spinelli

FIELD GUIDE

Book Summary

Because Maniac Magee's parents were killed on a bridge when he was three years old, he goes to live with an unhappily married aunt and uncle, who will not divorce because they are Catholic. Frustrated, he runs away, and is from then on known only as Maniac. It is the birth of a legend in which Maniac runs to the town of Two Mills, where he continues to run, from one place to the next, in search of a home to call his own. Maniac does the unthinkable when he crosses the boundary between the East and West ends of town, which is strictly divided along racial lines. Ultimately, through a series of truly heroic feats, he brings the two sides together, opening the lines of communication between Blacks and Whites.

Basic Book Information

This 184-page book is divided into three parts and forty-six chapters. The chapters are not titled; they are episodic, and vary in length from two to seven pages. The parts also are not titled but are labeled with roman numerals and separated by a blank page.

Each part addresses a different phase of Maniac's journey. In part one he runs away. Part two tells the story of his relationship with Grayson. In part three, the tensions central to the plot are ultimately resolved. A short passage entitled "Before the Story" precedes part one, and contains a jump rope rhyme that is set apart from the rest of the text with line breaks.

In this third-person narrative, the author frequently uses italics to emphasize certain words and to provide the reader with a glimpse into Maniac's thinking. Jerry Spinelli's writing voice is deliberately crafted to sound as if he is speaking aloud, in a casual way, and his narrative is replete with the kind of incomplete sentences that speakers' really use. It creates the impression that, as readers, we are listening to the story of a local resident of Two Mills, as told on a street corner one lazy summer afternoon.

Noteworthy Features

This book taps into more than one literary theme, as students in a book club will undoubtedly discover. Maniac helps resolve tension between Blacks and Whites while continually searching for home. When he develops a relationship with Grayson, a retired baseball player responsible for the upkeep of the local fields, Maniac teaches Grayson how to read, and Grayson tells Maniac the story of how he almost-but-not-quite-made-it to the major leagues. Together they create a sense of family and Maniac finally feels that he has found his address, but then Grayson dies and he is again without a home. Maniac continually runs from his problems instead of facing them, remaining in constant motion to avoid facing the difficult

Publisher
Little, Brown, and Company, 1990

ISBN
0316807222

TC Level
12

truth of his aloneness.

It is solely his desire to reach out and help Russell and Piper McNab, two runaway kids, that prevents Maniac from following through with his death wish. He convinces them to remain in Two Mills and to continue going to school through a series of bribes, living in the McNab's roach-infested apartment in the West End. Maniac is perhaps the most selfless character to be found in a work of childrens' literature. He is a hero in the classical sense-an issue some children return to again and again in their conversations

This book provides its readers with plenty of incidents that involve the central themes. With support, students may easily follow and document the figurative bridge Maniac constructs between the East and West sides of town. If they do not invent this metaphor themselves, it may be useful to empower students with the image of the bridge. Teachers could point out that Maniac was born in Bridgeport, and that his parents were killed on a bridge. It is ultimately this very bridge that is responsible for the final reconciliation between Blacks and Whites.

The beginning of the book is deliberately crafted to spark readers' curiosity. It has been written "after the fact," and is meant to be returned to again and again, continually becoming more meaningful as the story unfolds. There are several other opportunities to point out Spinelli's craft: his use of the colon, his unique writing voice, and his exceptional ability to bring characters' voices to life.

Until the story has reached its conclusion, the "Before the Story" cannot be understood. The author makes shorthand reference to unknown events, circumstances and characters, but with encouragement, students will learn to continually return to the beginning as events unfold. If they re-read frequently, students will delight in uncovering the "clues" that enable them to make sense of this passage. The clues are interspersed throughout the book.

Teaching Ideas

Maniac Magee works well as a daily read aloud, as it is rich with literary themes and teacher support can help do justice to its significance. Whether reading the book in large/small groups or independently, students may be encouraged to document moments where Maniac is "building the bridge" between Blacks and Whites. It all begins on page ten, when Maniac first encounters Amanda Beale. She thinks, "Who was this stranger kid? What was he doing in the East End, where almost all the kids were black. ...Back in those days the town was pretty much divided. The East End was blacks, the West End was white."

There are many sections of the book that are worthy of a closer look. On page 70, Maniac takes on Amanda's challenge to untie the infamous knot at the Cobble's Corner grocery store, conveniently located on Hector Street. Hector Street marks the boundary between the East and West ends of Two Mills. This wasn't just any knot. "Here and there a loop stuck out . . .pitiful testimony to the challengers who had tried and failed." Maniac is famous for, among other things, his ability to untie the most stubborn of knots.

On page 72, Spinelli writes, "Not only white kids, but grown-ups, too, black and white, because Cobble's Corner was on Hector, and word was racing through the neighborhood on both the east and west sides of the street." Then, "a huge roar went up, a volcano of cheers. Cobble's Knot was dead. It was nothing but string." This is one of several metaphors for Maniac's singular ability to unravel the tension between Whites and Blacks. Students in partnerships or book clubs may be interested in documenting and discussing these metaphors.

On page 171, Maniac begins running alongside Mars Bar Thomson, who is the toughest and fastest kid on the East End. He also happens to be Black. "Morning after morning it happened this way-the two of them dovetailing at an intersection and without the slightest hitch in stride, cruising off together." The book climaxes and the "bridge" is finally complete on page 173, when Russell and Piper are trapped on the very bridge responsible for the death of Maniac's parents. Maniac is running with Mars Bar, and he keeps running. Mars Bar, the toughest kid on the East End, is left with no choice but to rescue the McNab brothers, who hail from the toughest family on the West End. Children will enjoy recognizing how the book has come full circle, and the tensions are resolved exactly where they began.

Students may be encouraged to follow and document not only the resolving tension between Blacks and Whites, but also the ways in which Maniac runs from his problems, and the absolute heroism of his acts. There exists ample evidence to support each strand of thought.

Another difficulty is presented by the content of the story. A teacher can explain to students that the prejudiced attitudes of its characters are due to their ignorance, that if they only knew each other, this irrational, unfounded hatred would most likely not exist. Also, the Grayson's death is nothing short of heartbreaking, as is Maniac's subsequent desire to end his own life. If the book is being read aloud, the teacher will need to take time to discuss these sensitive issues.

Book Connections

The Great Gilly Hopkins, by Katherine Paterson, is also a story of the search for home, family, and acceptance. In Patricia MacLachlan's *Journey*, the title character, like Maniac, refuses to face the truth. Karen Hesse's *The Music of Dolphins* centers around Mila's resolution of the tension between the human and dolphin sides of herself, while Maniac's resolution of the tension between Blacks and Whites is what empowers him to become whole. Much can be learned from reading these books alongside each other.

Genre
Chapter Book

Teaching Uses
Book Clubs; Read Aloud; Interpretation; Critique; Language Conventions

A Field Guide to the Classroom Library, Lucy Calkins and the Teachers College Reading and Writing Project, Heinemann, ©2002 Teachers College, Columbia University; http://www.heinemann.com/fieldguides

Marianthe's Story: Painted Words, Spoken Memories

Aliki

Book Summary

Marianthe's Story is made up of two books. The first, *Painted Words,* tells the story of Marianthe adjusting to an American school and to the English language for the first time. The second book, *Spoken Memories*, depicts Marianthe telling her classmates and kind teacher about the life she left behind in her village in Greece.

Basic Book Information

Marianthe's Story is a 64- page book illustrated by the author.

Noteworthy Features

Aliki is a well-known and well-respected children's book author and illustrator. This two-book volume is constructed so that a reader can read one story and then turn the book to the back and flip it over in order to read the other. The second story is upside-down and backwards in relation to the first. An end paper separates the two stories. Because of this construction, it is easy to pick up the book and read the second story first. While this is not at all devastating to the understanding of the books, it is slightly easier for children to understand them if they are read in order.

Teaching Ideas

In Uri Schulevitz' book about picture books, he points out that the form of a picture book should support its content. And so, for example, the picture book *Knots on a Counting Rope*-a story of Native Americans galloping their horses-has an oversized cover with an illustration that bleeds off the edges and is in black, dark blue, and gray colors. On the other hand, Tasha Tudor's stories about the rabbit family of Flopsie, Mopsie, and Peter Cottontail are printed on tiny books, and the cover includes a little oval with miniature paintings of the rabbits, all painted in pastel blues, pinks, and yellows. The form of *Marianthe's Story* is its most dramatic feature, and children could be encouraged to ask why Aliki intertwined the two stories in this way. What was she trying to say?

Aliki would be a worthwhile subject for an author study because she writes in a huge range of genres. Readers might want to read several of her texts representing very different genres, noticing how the same skills and tendencies as a writer play out differently when writing a nonfiction book on corn or a picture book telling the story of a newcomer to America.

Illustrator
Aliki

Publisher
Greenwillow Books, 1998

ISBN
0688156614

TC Level
9

A Field Guide to the Classroom Library, Lucy Calkins and the Teachers College Reading and Writing Project, Heinemann, ©2002 Teachers College, Columbia University; http://www.heinemann.com/fieldguides

The text of this book requires some inferences. A teacher might want to duplicate a page or two of the text, display it on the overhead, and show children how she reads it, saying, "huh?" and then make mental leaps, almost as if she was getting across a stream by jumping from shore to shore. The author explicitly says one thing and then another, and leaves us, as readers, to bridge the gap.

On the first page of the first story, for example, the reader isn't told right away that Marianthe is about to go to a new school for the first time. We also aren't directly told that she cannot speak or understand English, and readers may miss that. Without readers inferring these bits of knowledge, the rest of the story can be challenging to understand.

Later in the book, as Marianthe learns English, the text says that the words she has been hearing and the bumps and lines that she has been seeing in books "change." Children will again need to infer that in fact these words and lines have stayed the same and Marianthe's way of understanding them has changed.

Here again, Aliki does some fancy work with the form of her text. This second story is a story within a story. The story begins in italics in Marianthe's class as Marianthe is about to tell the story of her life in her village in Greece. Then the text switches so that Marianthe is talking, in the first person, of how her life was a long time ago. These switches, from third person to first person narrators, from America to Greece, from now to the time when Marianthe was a baby require a lot of work. This same switch happens at the end of the story, when we are taken back to the present day, back to the American classroom, and back to the third person narrator. The gentle illustrations help children to move through these switches, as do the italics themselves, if children know how to use them as cues to shifts in the text.

The way Marianthe is treated by the other children in her class-well, by some and poorly, by others-will undoubtedly set off discussions. The idea that alphabets are completely different in some languages may be new to some children, and may also generate conversation.

The second story is set in a place where people live differently than many of the book's readers. This can make the story harder to visualize. A teacher, coaching a child who is reading the book, might caution the child that the second story is harder to really understand and might nudge the child to stop often to generate a picture in his or her mind's eye. "Famine touched everyone," Marianthe says, and later adds, "We hauled water from the spring." To really understand what is behind these words, most readers may have to pause to imagine the world Mari is describing.

This book could become part of a study on point of view. Such a study might also include *Ereth's Birthday* (Avi), or any of the *Poppy* books.

Alternatively, the book could be used as part of whole class work on the various ways authors use italics and parentheses. It might be interesting for a teacher to make overheads showing the use of italics and parentheses in any or all of these books, and for the class to notice the different choices authors make; this could help children become more intrigued by conventions in general. Other books that could be used are *Fourth Grade Rats* by Spinelli, *Fox on Wheels* by Marshall, *Fudge-A-Mania* by Blume, and *Adaline Falling Star* by Osborne.

A Field Guide to the Classroom Library, Lucy Calkins and the Teachers College Reading and Writing Project, Heinemann, ©2002 Teachers College, Columbia University; http://www.heinemann.com/fieldguides

Book Connections

Ereth's Birthday (Avi), or any of the *Poppy* books.

Genre

Chapter Book; Picture Book; Memoir

Teaching Uses

Independent Reading; Book Clubs; Partnerships; Author Study; Read Aloud

Mick Harte Was Here

Barbara Park

Book Summary

Mick Harte Was Here is about the death of a young boy, Mick Harte. Phoebe Harte's tender story about the loss of her brother makes the reader feel her pain.

The book opens with the circumstances surrounding Mick's accidental death. He fell off his bike while riding to a friend's house after school. Phoebe is playing soccer when she hears the sirens signaling an ambulance. An eerie feeling begins to overcome her. She is hoping that the sirens will get softer, but they never do. In fact, the sirens stop right in front of the school; feelings of dread overcome her as the coach begins to approach her with life altering words. The coach comes over to her, and tells her, "Phoebe, honey. It's Mick." She answers simply, "I know."

From that point on the reader learns about how a family, and in particular an adolescent girl, deals with the loss of a loved one. Phoebe's mother deals with the loss of Mick by sleeping through the days and nights...effects of the antidepressants her doctor prescribed, while her father seems to have immersed himself into his work. Phoebe is left alone to deal with this tremendous loss, as well as the guilt because she blames herself for Mick's death. Phoebe turns to her best friend Zoe and the suggestions made by the grief counselor at her school.

Basic Book Information

This book has 90 pages, and is divided into nine titled chapters. It is told from first-person point of view. This book is a work of fiction and is not illustrated. The author's note at the end of the chapter informs the reader of the real dangers of riding a bicycle without using a helmet.

Noteworthy Features

This book is a powerful story of a young girl's rite of passage into adulthood. Unfortunately, there is nothing in the world that can prepare her for the sudden loss of innocence, and the only person who is really able to help her through the transition is her best friend Zoe who is also a child.

Phoebe is unable to turn to her parents for support throughout this difficult transition. Her mother sleeps almost the whole day and night, and they barely speak to one another. Her father, who usually takes great pride in himself, goes through days on end without shaving, or ironing the usually present creases in his pants. When Phoebe finally returns to school, most of her "real" friends remain distant. The only person that she can count on is Zoe

Of course, the death of Mick makes the whole family see life in a different way. Mrs. Harte learns that every single aspect of life cannot be pre-planned,

Publisher
Random House, 1996

ISBN
0679882030

TC Level
14

and Mr. Harte learns that in the big scheme of things, it does not matter if your pants have perfect creases in them. Phoebe notices these things, and her observations provide insight into her development into an adult.

Phoebe's passage into adulthood is further exemplified in a scene where she teaches her mother that it is all right to remember Mick as he was. She helps her mother see that Mick would not want them to just remember his good traits-it would not be true to who he was as a person.

One of the most striking parts of the whole book is when Phoebe decides that she will speak at a bicycle safety assembly. She proceeds to show the audience a hat and a glow-in-the-dark bow tie, both of which Mick did not use because they made him look like a "dork" or "doofus." The audience laughed. Finally, she pulls out another birthday present that he was given and did not use-a brand new bicycle helmet.

Teaching Ideas

It can be important for a reader to have opportunities to talk about the book. The reader may notice that the book outlines three stages of grief: denial, anger, and eventually acceptance.

At the beginning of the book, Phoebe is very angry at the way in which her school is teaching the students how to deal with Mick's death. She is angered that they were told to talk about Mick...remember him...keep him alive by talking about the memories we have of him.

At first, she prefers to deal with Mick's death the same way her parents are through avoidance and denial. However, this soon has an adverse effect on her. She is confused, angry, but above all she deeply misses Mick. She finds a need to surround herself with his memory. She begins to think of the funny things Mick did, and how he himself dealt with the death of his dog, Wiggles. Phoebe tries to share these memories with her mother but it is clear that this offends her. The mother says one night after catching Phoebe in Mick's room, "Why are you doing this?" Phoebe then becomes extremely angry and is out to spite her mother. On another occasion, Phoebe's mom awakes to the sound of laughter coming from Mick's room. As Phoebe sits on Mick's bed remembering a time he took pictures of Wiggles with a cowboy hat on the dog's head, she is overcome by a case of the giggles. Her mother is now showing resentment towards Phoebe. With nowhere else to turn, Phoebe finds solace in her best friend Zoe. Zoe provides Phoebe with the opportunity to talk about Mick and the zany things he did. This begins the healing process for Phoebe. Yet, she notices that people at school now treat her differently. When her principal expresses sympathy by saying, "I'm sorry about Mick's death," Phoebe responds, "Why, you didn't kill him." All this information would undoubtedly come out as part of a character study of Phoebe.

Alternatively, a reader may notice the different ways in which Phoebe and her parents cope with the difficult feelings evoked by their loss.

Book Connections

This book connects very well with Katherine Paterson's *Bridge to Terabithia* where one of the main characters, Jess Aarons, learns to deal with the loss of his best friend. These two books could provide the opportunity for a possible compare/contrast literary essay.

In Patricia MacLachlan's *Baby*, Larkin and her family learn to face, accept, and mourn losses in their family. As with the parents in *Mick Harte Was Here*, Larkin's parents also try to avoid the death of their son by not talking about it.

Genre
Short Chapter Book

Teaching Uses
Book Clubs; Read Aloud; Independent Reading

A Field Guide to the Classroom Library, Lucy Calkins and the Teachers College Reading and Writing Project, Heinemann, ©2002 Teachers College, Columbia University; http://www.heinemann.com/fieldguides

Mirette on the High Wire

Emily Arnold McCully

Book Summary

Mirette and her mother keep an inn in France. One day, a man comes to stay with them who walks on clotheslines in the courtyard! Mirette is full of admiration and is determined to learn this amazing skill. With great determination and lots of practice, she learns to walk on the line. When she shows the man, Bellini, he is impressed and decides he will teach her. They work together and Mirette learns many tricks. One day she hears from the other roomers about the amazing feats Bellini has performed in the past. She runs to him and begs him to let her come with him. He refuses her, saying he cannot do his acts anymore for he is afraid. Mirette is heartbroken, and Bellini feels terrible for letting her down. He resolves to overcome his fear and the next night attempts a tightrope walk in front of the townsfolk. Suddenly, he freezes. Mirette runs to the other end of the line and coaxes him across by stepping on the rope by herself. Now happy, they go on tour together.

Basic Book Information

This Caldecott Medal-winning picture book has gentle, colorful pictures that bring to life this child's fantasy-adventure of running away to the circus and becoming a famous performer. Any child who has dreamed of such a thing will undoubtedly be interested in this book, especially since the title and cover picture show enough so that the reader can guess it is about circus performers.

Noteworthy Features

One might guess that the story's setting in France would add an element of foreignness to the story, at least in passing words and traditions or even in the pictures. Truly, though the setting is there if the reader wants to focus on it, it otherwise offers no strangeness to the story. The name of the inn, Gateau's, and of the girl herself are nearly the only French elements of the story.

Teaching Ideas

One of the first things readers tend to notice about the story is that Mirette's mother doesn't seem to be very involved in her life. Her mother seems to have no problem with her practicing walking on the tightrope in the backyard, or working with Bellini on her tightrope-walking skills. When Mirette runs up the many flights of the building and steps onto the high, high tightrope to meet Bellini, where is her mother? Doesn't she care that she could fall to her death? How could her mother allow her, and even

Illustrator
Emily Arnold McCully

Publisher
Scholastic, 1992

ISBN
0590476939

TC Level
9

A Field Guide to the Classroom Library, Lucy Calkins and the Teachers College Reading and Writing Project, Heinemann, ©2002 Teachers College, Columbia University; http://www.heinemann.com/fieldguides

encourage her to do such a thing, even once? And how could her mother let her go on tour?! Some readers decide that the story is really a child's wish, so of course the mother doesn't interfere in what is happening. What kind of a fantasy would it be if the mother were always there telling her she was forbidden to do it because it was too dangerous? Other readers decide that perhaps the parenting is different in France, after all, Mirette seems to have a lot of work to do running the inn! Some readers even think that maybe Mirette is old enough to make her own decisions, so her mother doesn't bother her. After all, it seems that maybe she has finished school, since she doesn't attend in the story.

Readers who wonder about Mirette's mother also tend to wonder about Mirette's lack of fear. Why was it so easy for her to walk out on the wire so many stories above the ground without even thinking twice about it, with her only thought about it being how nice it was! Mirette wasn't normal, they suppose. They also remember that Bellini says that once you are afraid it is very hard to do, so maybe that is Mirette's talent, she doesn't realize that she should be afraid. Sometimes readers even think that maybe Mirette is not too bright.

There are places in the story where readers are sometimes a bit confused. The first instance might be when Bellini tells Mirette that he is afraid. Some readers think: Afraid of what? Afraid of taking Mirette with him? Afraid she will get hurt? They don't assume he is afraid of the high wire because after all, he has been walking on it in the back yard, hasn't he? When they reread the book, however, they will see that the wire in the back courtyard isn't so high after all, and that Bellini has been sad from the beginning of the story. He is even pleased that his room is on the ground floor. That, in combination with what he says after he tells Mirette he is afraid, makes Bellini's fear clear. It can take some working out for some readers, however.

The second part of the story where readers sometimes incorrectly guess what is happening is when Bellini freezes on the high wire. Mirette says she knows just what is wrong in a way that seems to suggest there is a specific problem, and not just the general one of fear. "Is the wire slipping? What is wrong?" some readers wonder. But of course, it is only his fear. Mirette reminds herself of his advice and gets him to think only of the end of the wire, not of the ground. If readers still have that key bit of advice in their minds, the last lines of the book will make sense, and Bellini's sudden fear will seem understandable. Bellini has forgotten to concentrate only on the end of the wire.

Genre
Fantasy; Picture Book

Teaching Uses
Independent Reading; Read Aloud; Partnerships

A Field Guide to the Classroom Library, Lucy Calkins and the Teachers College Reading and Writing Project, Heinemann, ©2002 Teachers College, Columbia University; http://www.heinemann.com/fieldguides

Missing May

Cynthia Rylant

Book Summary

Aunt May has died and Summer and her Uncle Ob try to make sense of the world without May. Both Ob and Summer are depressed in their own ways, but with the help of their friend Cletus Underwood, they go in search of some sign that May is still with them. This is a realistic, yet hopeful portrayal of grief and how two people go through it together.

Basic Book Information

Missing May won the 1993 Newbery Award. This 89-page chapter book is made up of twelve untitled chapters that are divided into two parts, which are named, "Still as Night," and "Set Free." The story in narrated in the first person by Summer. There is a dream sequence that occurs in part two, which moves time back and forth from past to the present. The rest of the story moves chronologically through Summer's grief, interspersed with memories of her Aunt May.

Noteworthy Features

Summer's memories of her Aunt May are interspersed throughout the book and can create difficulty in understanding the time and the setting in this book. These memories take on the feel of the present, as they are extended and just as vividly rendered as the present in the book.

Ob experiences what he calls encounters with the spiritual world and is convinced that May is trying to get in touch with them from the other side. Some readers have difficulty relating to this.

The characters may seem outlandish to readers not from the South, as Rylant paints her characters in the colors of Appalachia and they seem similar to the characters of *When the Relatives Came* and *When I Was Young in the Mountains*.

This book is about grief and grieving. The theme is strong and some readers, especially if they are young, may need support in comprehending the emotional weight of this subject. Older readers and readers familiar with the hard terrain of life will probably not need support in this area.

Teaching Ideas

Since the echoes of her other writings are so strong, *Missing May* could easily be a part of an author study of Cynthia Rylant.

The themes in this book are weighty, and it is recommended that this book be read aloud to readers younger than fifth grade. *Missing May* would make an appropriate independent read with older students, and discussions of it tend to flourish because of the serious content.

Publisher
Dell, 1992

ISBN
0440408652

TC Level
12

 A Field Guide to the Classroom Library, Lucy Calkins and the Teachers College Reading and Writing Project, Heinemann, ©2002 Teachers College, Columbia University; http://www.heinemann.com/fieldguides

Many teachers enjoy reading *Missing May* aloud since it tends to make rapt listeners out of even the rowdiest bunch. The writing is also careful, beautiful, and spare.

Book Connections

Other books by Cynthia Rylant have similar flavor, like *When I Was Young in the Mountains* which is set in the Appalachians, as is *Appalachia. The Islander*, also by Cynthia Rylant, carries many of the same themes (grief, imagination, the power of love), and would be a good book to read subsequent to *Missing May*. Other books carrying similar themes to *Missing May* are *A Taste of Blackberries* by D.B. Smith and *Bridge to Terebithia* by Katherine Paterson. *The Library Card* by Jerry Spinelli has some characters that could be from Rylant's world, and so this too would be a good book to read after *Missing May*.

Genre
Chapter Book

Teaching Uses
Read Aloud; Independent Reading; Partnerships; Teaching Writing

A Field Guide to the Classroom Library, Lucy Calkins and the Teachers College Reading and Writing Project, Heinemann, ©2002 Teachers College, Columbia University; http://www.heinemann.com/fieldguides

Mr. Popper's Penguins

Richard Atwater; Florence Atwater

Book Summary

Mr. Popper's Penguins is the comic story of a semi-employed house painter whose passion for Admiral Byrd's polar adventures leads him (and his surprised family) to become caretaker of, at first one, and thentwelve, mischievous penguins.

With the help of practical Mrs. Popper and their children, Janie and Bill, Mr. Popper ingeniously creates a proper polar home in the basement of their house. It isn't long before the financial strain of a large, fresh-fish-eating family leads the Poppers to a brief career on the stage, and to a solution that pleases everyone.

Basic Book Information

This Newbery Honor book has 132 pages and 20 numbered, titled chapters of between four and nine pages each.

Noteworthy Features

Mr. Popper's Penguins is a rare combination of humor, science, history and fantasy. Although the slapstick antics of the Poppers and their penguins are in the foreground of the story, a reader also gets a taste of the 1930s atmosphere, learns something about the explorer Admiral Byrd, and gets information on penguin diet and behavior.

Set in a small town during the 1930s when Admiral Richard Drake was exploring Antarctica, *Mr. Popper's Penguins* contains what might be unfamiliar vocabulary and settings (e.g., "Pullman" train and "vaudeville" stage shows), but its delightful wackiness should keep readers involved. Engagingly comic illustrations, chronological narration, and short chapters will be assets to less patient readers. In general, there are fewer reading challenges (in terms of vocabulary, structure and dialogue) than in other books in this grouping.

Teaching Ideas

Mr. Popper's Penguins makes a good read aloud, but is also appropriate for independent reading.

Mr. Popper's Penguins can accompany other nonfiction research on the 1930s, penguins and the Antarctic. This research may help with comprehension of the book. For example, if readers collect information on penguins, they can then discuss how Mr. Popper accommodated the penguins' needs.

Kids can work on interpreting the message of the story. Commonly, students decide one message is that with enough enthusiasm, one can

Publisher
Little Brown, 1938

ISBN
0590477331

TC Level
12

A Field Guide to the Classroom Library, Lucy Calkins and the Teachers College Reading and Writing Project, Heinemann, ©2002 Teachers College, Columbia University; http://www.heinemann.com/fieldguides

accomplish nearly anything. Mr. Popper's eccentricity and passion, while bringing strange looks from the plumber, are assets to himself, his family and the penguins. Other readers decide on different messages, for instance, that odd people learn more. As long as kids are supporting their interpretations with textual evidence all of the messages they point to are fair game, and should generate lively discussion.

The characters of Mr. and Mrs. Popper are well drawn. Mr. Popper remains an irrepressible dreamer while Mrs. Popper is an utterly down-to-earth woman who ends up sharing Mr. Popper's love of the penguins. Students may want to study these characters and come to these conclusions about Mr. and Mrs. Popper's natures. Some students even do little character studies about the individual penguins!

Genre
Chapter Book; Fantasy; Historical Fiction

Teaching Uses
Read Aloud; Independent Reading; Character Study; Content Area Study

A Field Guide to the Classroom Library, Lucy Calkins and the Teachers College Reading and Writing Project, Heinemann, ©2002 Teachers College, Columbia University; http://www.heinemann.com/fieldguides

New Shoes for Silvia

Johanna Hurwitz

Book Summary

One day, a package from another America comes to young Silvia from Tia Rosita. It contains a new pair of red shoes. Everyone agrees that the shoes are beautiful, but they are too big for Silvia. She plays with them, tries them on all the time, and finally, one day they are not too big any more. Now she can wear them! As she walks, she thinks about someday getting another package from Tia Rosita, this time with blue shoes.

Basic Book Information

This is a large, beautifully illustrated picture book with plenty of details on weach page to keep the reader enticed and engaged.

Noteworthy Features

This story has a very straightforward opening, and the story unfolds chronologically with no twists, flashbacks, or secondary narrators. The words and sentence structure in the story are common and generally familiar to most readers. The few Spanish words are followed by their English equivalents, for easy understanding. When characters speak, it is always clear who they are. In every case, the pictures carefully reflect the story's words. Overall, the text is set up for children at this level to have a highly successful read.

Teaching Ideas

Though the text itself may be considered relatively simple, there is plenty to discuss in the story. The topic for discussion that kids often come up with first is to name the setting of the book. There is plenty of evidence on each page and several textual clues to place the story in South or Central America and children sometimes spend productive time trying to figure out in which country in particular Sylvia lives. Sometimes they use the dedication as a clue, but more often they use what they know about the artifacts in the pictures, the terrain, plants, animals, and clothing.

Another question readers sometimes use to launch their discussion is "Why does Sylvia care so much about a pair of shoes that doesn't even fit her?" This often turns into an examination of the shoes of the other characters in the story and a discussion of the readers' own experiences buying new shoes. It is sometimes helpful for teachers to guide children into finding reasons why they think they have had different reactions to new shoes than Sylvia has. Finding not just the differences but also why differences exist between ourselves and characters in books often helps readers analyze characters and their lives more fully and deeply.

Illustrator
Jerry Pinkney

Publisher
Scholastic Inc., 1993

ISBN
0590487493

TC Level
8

A Field Guide to the Classroom Library, Lucy Calkins and the Teachers College Reading and Writing Project, Heinemann, ©2002 Teachers College, Columbia University; http://www.heinemann.com/fieldguides

Sometimes children focus on Sylvia's hope at the end of the book that her aunt will send her some new blue shoes as well. They tend to ask many questions like: Is that greedy of her to want new shoes again right away? Is it just the way kids are? Is she only wishing once again that she could have the anticipation of having a new pair of shoes? Does that mean she enjoys the anticipation more than the actual gift? For productive discussions, readers will have to use evidence from the pages of the story to reinforce the validity of their ideas.

Genre
Picture Book

Teaching Uses
Independent Reading

A Field Guide to the Classroom Library, Lucy Calkins and the Teachers College Reading and Writing Project, Heinemann, ©2002 Teachers College, Columbia University; http://www.heinemann.com/fieldguides

No Mirrors in My Nana's House

Isaye M. Barnwell

Book Summary

As a little girl looks into the eyes of her Nana, she sees beauty in everything because that is what her Nana sees. The Nana doesn't see any negatives in the child or the world, but instead welcomes the beauty that is there for everyone to see if they want.

Basic Book Information

No Mirrors in My Nana's House is a colorful picture book that can be used for all grade levels. Isaye Barnwell is well known for singing in Sweet Honey in the Rock, an a capella singing group of African American women. Synthia Saint James has illustrated this book but is also well known for her illustrations and for her own books, including *The Gifts of Kwanzaa*.

In the final pages of this book, Barnwell uses some African American dialect particular to the South, "Chil'" for child.

Noteworthy Features

This picture book is also a poem, using rhythm and rhyme to add meaning to the story of the young girl who looks for beauty in the world at large.

The setting for this book will be very familiar to city dwellers. "I was intrigued by the cracks in the wall..." shows the unvarnished world of the housing project building. While city kids will find this familiar, suburban children who have not experienced this may find it more than odd; not understanding how someone could find cracked walls appealing. This new setting can help suburban readers expand their horizons a bit, seeing beyond the microcosm of their world.

Teaching Ideas

Children all feel the effects of peer pressure, no matter what age. Students in the upper grades (grades 4, 5, and 6) feel this pressure especially in regard to their appearance, and *No Mirrors in My Nana's House* can be used for its content to address children's fears and apprehensions. Fortunately, there is an audio CD recording of Isaye Barnwell singing the words to *No Mirrors in My Nana's House* that students can listen to. The music is appealing and it could become a class anthem, further ingraining the message.

Using *No Mirrors in My Nana's House* in the upper grades can help to take away some of the stigma that picture books have for older readers. This can help struggling readers pick up easier books. This book clearly deals with the issues that adolescents deal with daily; this book *is* for them. Barnwell uses everyday speech to tell the story from the point of view of a young girl, so it doesn't have the same feel as many picture books.

Illustrator
Synthia Saint James

Publisher
Harcourt Brace, 1998

ISBN
0152018255

TC Level
5

A Field Guide to the Classroom Library, Lucy Calkins and the Teachers College Reading and Writing Project, Heinemann, ©2002 Teachers College, Columbia University; http://www.heinemann.com/fieldguides

One class of sixth graders listened to this book in a read aloud and decided that they wanted to look at picture books, seeing why they sounded so different from the chapter books they were reading in their independent reading lives. Picture books became a class inquiry–together they searched for picture books that appealed to older elementary students.

Genre
Picture Book; Poetry

Teaching Uses
Independent Reading; Read Aloud; Partnerships

A Field Guide to the Classroom Library, Lucy Calkins and the Teachers College Reading and Writing Project, Heinemann, ©2002 Teachers College, Columbia University; http://www.heinemann.com/fieldguides

Number the Stars

Lois Lowry

Book Summary

This story is set during World War II and centers around ten-year-old best friends Annemarie Johansen and Ellen Rosen who live in war-torn Copenhagen. The book begins as they come home from school one afternoon during the early stages of the German invasion and are stopped by armed soldiers. After they are questioned as to why they are running, the soldiers eventually let them go, but all of the sudden, the war doesn't seem a million miles away. It is right in front of them, and this particularly worries Ellen because she is Jewish.

A few days later the girls discover that a local Jewish shopkeeper they know has "disappeared" overnight and there are rumors that other Jews will also be taken away to concentration camps. Ellen and Annemarie's mothers are also good friends and together they devise a plan to hide Ellen with the Johansen family while the Rosens plan their escape. Even though Annemarie is not Jewish, she sees the terror her friend Ellen is experiencing and adopts it as her own. Eventually Annemarie and her family take Ellen out to the countryside where Ellen is reunited with her family. In the climactic scene, Annemarie saves the lives of her friend and her friend's family. Both young girls prove to be courageous during this horrific time in history.

Basic Book Information

The story is told in the third person and follows a traditional, linear form. This Newbery honor book is broken into seventeen chapters. All of the chapters are titled with quotes (e.g.,: "Why are you running?" is the title for chapter one and is what the Nazi officer says to the two girls the first time they are truly fearful). There are no pictures or sketches in the story.

Noteworthy Features

Although this story is not true, it is based on historical findings. The secondary story in the book is the mysterious death of Annemarie's older sister, Lise. Annemarie's parents never speak of their deceased daughter or her death in a car crash a few years previous. Lise's fiance, Peter, still visits the Johansen family. He is involved in an anti-Hitler organization that helps Jews escape from Copenhagen and other cities throughout Europe. Peter is the mastermind behind Ellen's family's escape. At the end of the story, Annemarie learns that her sister's death was affiliated with this anti-Hitler group. It turns out Lise was involved with this group and was killed by Nazi supporters. Peter's character is based on a real person who aided thousands of Jews in escaping Copenhagen and other nearby cities. He was eventually caught and killed at point-blank range by the Nazis. Peter was in his early twenties when he died. It must be noted that this story does not go into the

A Field Guide to the Classroom Library, Lucy Calkins and the Teachers College Reading and Writing Project, Heinemann, ©2002 Teachers College, Columbia University; http://www.heinemann.com/fieldguides

history of the Nazis and the genocide.

Teaching Ideas

This book can be very moving for some readers. It is likely that nearly every reader will need to talk about its contents in order to process the story and how it relates to real life.

Number the Stars contains a number of discussion threads which students may pick up. For example, one book club looked at the way in which Annemarie's family placed themselves in danger in order to help Jews. Students in the club used post-it notes in places where members of Annemarie's family were placing themselves at risk, and met together to talk about them. Another club followed the way in which people lied to or tricked the Nazis in order to escape or help others escape. When Nazis saw dark-haired Ellen living with Annemarie's family, they became suspicious. Papa, thinking on his feet, found a baby picture of Lise, in which she had dark hair. The Nazis were convinced that Ellen belonged to Annemarie's family.

This book frequently inspires young readers to learn more about the Holocaust. Those who read this book alongside nonfiction Holocaust books (or have previous background knowledge) may be interested in tracking what is historical fact, and what likely came from the author's imagination.

Book Connections

Yolen's *Devil's Arithmetic* could also be read along side *Number the Stars*. *The Diary of a Young Girl* by Anne Frank and Esther Hautzig's *The Endless Steppe* are also books about young girls' experiences with World War II. Frank and Hautzig's books are more difficult than Lowry and Yolen's.

Genre
Historical Fiction; Chapter Book

Teaching Uses
Independent Reading; Book Clubs; Whole Group Instruction; Read Aloud

A Field Guide to the Classroom Library, Lucy Calkins and the Teachers College Reading and Writing Project, Heinemann, ©2002 Teachers College, Columbia University; http://www.heinemann.com/fieldguides

Pennies for the Piper

Susan McLean

Book Summary

Ten-year-old Bicks must deal with her mother's sickness and eventual death, and then her new home with her Aunt in Iowa.

Basic Book Information

This book is 150 pages long and has 19 chapters that range from eight to ten pages in length. There is no table of contents; untitled chapters are numbered only. There are no illustrations except for the cover by Diana McKee that shows a girl wearing a simple sundress over rolled up blue jeans. Print size is small, with small spacing between words and lines.

Noteworthy Features

This is a realistic fiction book that feels similar to Betsy Byars' *Cracker Jackson* and Conly's *Crazy Lady* because it holds the issues of poverty, death, and child abuse within it without being sensational. The characters are portrayed as part of their setting and not in contrast to them. This would be an interesting study of character in relation to setting from author to author, as long as students explored the author's probable intent behind these portrayals and their relationship to the setting.

The title "Pennies for the Piper" is an old saying that young people may not be familiar with, but its meaning is closely tied to the motivation behind the main character Bicks (short for Victoria). According to the story, "It's just the notion that you pay for all your good times." This premise is Bicks' motivation, and is embedded in her life of poverty. This rationale is important to point out early (as the author did) because it is Bicks' thinking that needs to be examined. Questions like, "Is that really true?" or "Do I agree with that?" should be asked by the reader throughout the book.

The structure of this book is chronological, with some turns back to the past. There are fleeting memories that occur often (one or two per chapter). Bicks lives in the present looking over her shoulder at the past and readers need to be alerted to this. The story is told in third person point of view by an omniscient narrator.

This is a dense and psychological text packed with action that young readers will probably enjoy and relate to. Bicks' memories are woven expertly throughout the book and it would be easy for a reader to overlook them or become confused by all of the shifting. Creating a time line may be helpful, as well as pointing out words identifying this shift-the verbs are written in past tense in the memories. The part when Bicks' mother dies moves from past to present a number of times and this can get confusing. Students may need to re-read this part several times to really understand it (pages 68 and 69).

Publisher
Sunburst, FSG, 1993

ISBN
0374457549

TC Level
12

Bicks' grief combined with her ignorance and poverty can be difficult to understand for many readers. Readers need to understand and expect that they are going on a journey of Bicks the character, not necessarily their own. Perhaps identifying Bicks (rather than Bicks being just like them) as a character can help readers understand more. Why doesn't Bicks call her aunt when her mother dies? Why doesn't Bicks ask anyone for help? Discussions about this book are generally heated.

Teaching Ideas

This is a good book to use to examine author's intent and developing a critical lens on fiction. *Pennies for the Piper* is a rationale for living that people will agree and disagree with. Some people think this system of thinking is helpful, others will think it dysfunctional. The author poses this question to the reader and the reader must answer. To support critical thinking, the reader will need to cite evidence in the book, for which (on either side and position) is plenty. If *Pennies for the Piper* were used in read aloud, it could be the source of a debate (and discussion) about outlook on life, point of view, and perspective. It can also be used for book clubs. Because of its realistic portrayal of poverty, it can spark conversation about politics, community, and social activism, as well as possibly creating a more balanced understanding of people in the world.

Genre
Short Chapter Book

Teaching Uses
Independent Reading; Author Study; Read Aloud; Book Clubs; Critique

A Field Guide to the Classroom Library, Lucy Calkins and the Teachers College Reading and Writing Project, Heinemann, ©2002 Teachers College, Columbia University; http://www.heinemann.com/fieldguides

Picnic with Piggins

Jane Yolen

Book Summary

In this book in the *Piggins* mystery series, the Reynard family of foxes takes Piggins and other friends on a picnic. After each eats, everyone takes a little nap. They wake up with a start to find that little Rexy is missing! They all try to figure out what has happened to him, but of course in the end the clever sleuth Piggins figures it out, clue by clue. What seemed at first to be a tragic disappearance eventually turns out to be a happy birthday surprise for Piggins-a delicious, fancy cake. The Reynards had planned the trick to give Piggins his favorite, a mystery.

Basic Book Information

This book is part of the Piggins series of mysteries. Like the others, it has colorful, detailed, cute illustrations that offer readers more information from which to build their theories.

Noteworthy Features

This book, like the other two Piggins books, can easily be enjoyed on its own or out of sequence. On the other hand, because this one is a bit of a twist on mysteries in that the mystery turns out to be just a trick, a fake, it's twist is more effectively felt if the reader reads it after the other mysteries. Finding the correct sequence of the *Piggins* books, however, can be part of the clue-finding work that children do with these stories. The author has left little clues about time in the text, relating to the fox children's "fox pox" and other things. In the end, as long as children do the reading and rereading intended in these books, the sequence of the reading doesn't matter at all.

This book has the same special features as the others: the picture clues, the ritual beginning and ending of the story, the cross-section of the house with descriptions of what every character is doing, the intertextual jokes about the characters, the multilingual names, the unusual Queen's English vocabulary, and of course, the mystery itself.

Teaching Ideas

This book is perhaps the most difficult of the three because the mystery is two-layered-the apparent mystery and then the fact that the mystery is a hoax. The clues are first misinterpreted by Pierre Lapin and then correctly interpreted by Piggins, so the mood and plot and context of the story change dramatically from one section to the next. If readers are just barely holding on to the plot, these drastic changes might be subtle. However, the events are all carefully explained by the end of the story, so a second or third reading should make everything clear to the reader who is still trying to

A Field Guide to the Classroom Library, Lucy Calkins and the Teachers College Reading and Writing Project, Heinemann, ©2002 Teachers College, Columbia University; http://www.heinemann.com/fieldguides

Series
Piggins books

Illustrator
Jane Dyer

Publisher
Harcourt, Brace & Company, 1987

ISBN
0152615350

TC Level
9

understand.

The emotions of the animal characters are hard to read in the pictures, and the tone of all the illustrations is upbeat and colorful, even in dire circumstances, so the pictures don't give much clue as to the broader picture of what is happening, either tragedy or joke. (This is true for all three books, but is especially relevant in this one, as readers are most apt to be searching for other means to grasp what is happening.) Readers may well need to stop and talk with partners, or stop and make notes to themselves, about what the characters are probably thinking and feeling.

It's hard to imagine a reader who wouldn't be interested in attending closely to details of text and illustration with these Piggins books. The books are especially good for small groups because readers each notice their own details, and in reading mystery stories, one feels compelled to put important details together. This brings the readers in the group together, usually excitedly, without any contrived activity.

Genre
Picture Book; Mystery

Teaching Uses
Partnerships; Small Group Strategy Instruction

A Field Guide to the Classroom Library, Lucy Calkins and the Teachers College Reading and Writing Project, Heinemann, ©2002 Teachers College, Columbia University; http://www.heinemann.com/fieldguides

Piggins and the Royal Wedding

Jane Yolen

Book Summary

In this third book of the *Piggins* series, the Reynard fox family goes to a princess' wedding. Rexy is charged with carrying the royal ring on its elegant pillow, but just as it is time to hand over the ring, it is no longer there! Everyone blames young Rexy Reynard, even though he swears he didn't do it. Quickly, faithful Piggins the butler is sent for to save Rexy and save the royal wedding. With a little quick thinking and the discovery of a few clues, Piggins solves the crime, catches the thief, and saves the day. The Reynards feel lucky to have such a faithful and fast-acting sleuth for a butler.

Basic Book Information

This book is part of the Piggins series of mysteries. Like the others, it has colorful, detailed, cute illustrations that offer readers more information from which to build their theories.

Noteworthy Features

Nearly all the notes from the first book in the series, *Piggins*, are applicable here as well. However, this book needn't be saved for last. Although there are inside jokes and references to past books here and there, the jokes are such that they usually build on each other in any order. The first time you hear that Sara the scullery maid is a bit dirty herself, it may not be funny to the reader. By the third book in which Sara finds a new way to be a little dirty, however, it's silly and humorous. In any case, it doesn't truly matter which book is the first that the reader hears about Sara being a bit unclean, and other such references. This book could easily be the first in the series, although the best reading experience would be to read them in order.

It is a little tricky for readers to spot the culprit in the pictures, even after he has been named by Piggins at the end of the book. Once he is spotted, however, readers can find him back on the page in which Rexy saw the pickpocket dashing away. This kind of rereading and re-noticing the details of the text and pictures is as crucial to appreciating this story as it is to the others.

It is interesting for some children to know that the illustrator of this work did enormous amounts of research to draw the wedding costumes and the inside of the cathedral-information they can find on the back jacket flap of the hardcover edition.

Teaching Ideas

This book is perhaps the most difficult of the three in the series, because the mystery is two-layered-the apparent mystery and then the fact that the

Series
Piggins books

Illustrator
Jane Dyer

Publisher
Harcourt, Brace & Company, 1987

ISBN
015200078X

TC Level
9

A Field Guide to the Classroom Library, Lucy Calkins and the Teachers College Reading and Writing Project, Heinemann, ©2002 Teachers College, Columbia University; http://www.heinemann.com/fieldguides

mystery is a hoax. The clues are first misinterpreted by Pierre Lapin and then correctly interpreted by Piggins. So, the mood, plot, and context of the story change dramatically from one section to the next. If a reader is just barely grasping the plot, these changes might be too subtle. The events are all carefully explained by the end of the story, however, and a second or third reading should make everything clear to the reader who is trying to understand.

The emotions of the animal characters are hard to read in the illustrations, and the tone of all the illustrations is upbeat and colorful, even in dire circumstances. Therefore, the pictures don't offer many clues as to the broader picture of what is happening; either tragedy or joke. (This is true for all three books, but is especially relevant in this one, as readers are most apt to be searching for other means to grasp what is happening in this one.) Readers may need to stop and talk with partners, or stop and make notes to themselves, about what the characters are probably thinking and feeling.

It's hard to imagine a reader who wouldn't be interested in paying close attention to the details of the text and illustrations with these *Piggins* books. The books are particularly good for small groups because each reader notices their own details, and in reading mystery stories, it is helpful to put important details together. This can bring the readers in a group together, usually excitedly, without any contrived activity.

Genre
Picture Book; Mystery

Teaching Uses
Independent Reading; Small Group Strategy Instruction; Partnerships

Polar Express
Chris Van Allsburg

Book Summary

This extraordinary book begins one Christmas Eve a long time ago. A little boy lies in bed awaiting the sound of ringing bells from Santa's sleigh and "hissing steam and squeaking metal." Instead, he hears and sees a train outside his window called *The Polar Express*. The train whisks him and the reader far away to the North Pole, a magical *city of lights* where dreams are realized and Santa will give away the very first gift of Christmas. The boy is chosen to receive the gift and out of all the gifts in the world, he requests one of Santa's silver bells from his sleigh. Before the next page is turned, his wish comes true. The clock strikes midnight and the boy puts the precious silver bell into his pocket. But when the other children on the train ask to see the silver bell, it is gone-nowhere to be found until the miracle of Christmas morning when wondrous things can happen and often do for those who believe.

Basic Book Information

When asked how he comes up with ideas, Van Allsburg says he uses a "what if" and "what then" method (e.g., What if a young boy were to find himself aboard a train to the North Pole? What then?). From there, he works to weave his images together into a story line. He is well-known for his imaginative use of light and perspective to portray everyday objects in extraordinary, mysterious and mystical ways.

His text is filled with mystery and words of wonder just like his pictures. This brilliant author and illustrator feels that his books are surrealistic and he gains inspiration from Degas and Hooper. The words compliment the pictures, which in turn compliments the text and will intrigue readers of all ages. Chris Van Allsburg is the author of 15 books, most recently *Bad Day at Riverbend*. *The Polar Express* and *Jumanji* both won the Caldecott Medal.

This picture book is 30 pages long. The pages are not numbered. With the exception of the last page, text is written in a column, either on the left or right hand side of each spread. The remaining space on each spread is covered by Van Allsburg's classic pastel illustrations. The last page, simply illustrated with a small picture of the sleigh bell, serves as an epilogue explaining the bell's jingle, "Though I've grown old, the bell still rings for me as it does for all who truly believe." The book is often sold as part of a gift set, including an audiotape of the story and a sleigh bell.

Noteworthy Features

This book provides students with the outstanding quality of what good stories do-transport us to different worlds, make us question and wonder and want to reread the book over and over again. It is a simple story told in

Illustrator
Chris Van Allsburg

Publisher
Houghton Mifflin

ISBN
0395389496

A Field Guide to the Classroom Library, Lucy Calkins and the Teachers College Reading and Writing Project, Heinemann, ©2002 Teachers College, Columbia University; http://www.heinemann.com/fieldguides

first person but one filled with such rich language (most especially metaphors), and an air of mystery that it can be read over and over again as readers discover deeper meaning.

This is a text that raises many questions during and after reading and is a wonderful way for teachers to encourage students to question, wonder, and reflect. Why did the boy ask for the silver bell? Can we go back into the text and notice where we have clues that he will ask for the bell? There is a lot of evidence in the text that would need to be explored. (However, since the book does not have page numbers, teachers may want to attach very small post-it notes to the bottom of the pages so children can cite page numbers.) Also, the rich text enables teachers to explore with children making inferences, such as why the parents thought the bell was broken. [Ed: please check edits so that meaning is still intact. Original paragraph was: This is a text which that raises many questions during and after reading and is a wonderful way for teachers to encourage students to question, wonder, and reflect. Why did the boy ask for the silver bell? Can we go back into the text and notice where we have clues that he will ask for the bell? There is a lots of evidence from in the text work that would need to be doneexplored. (Hhowever , , since the book does not have page numbers, so teachers may want to post attach the very small very small post- it notes on to the bottom of the pages so children can cite page numbers..) Also, it the rich text enables teachers to explore with children making inferences, such as why the parents thought the bell was broken.]

This is a terrific read aloud with poetic language and metaphors that can help children understand how authors carefully craft their words by showing not telling the reader. An example is the line, "Lights look like a strange ocean liner sailing on a frozen sea." The illustrations are all works of art and readers will want to jump aboard The Polar Express. While many teachers may want to use this book as a read aloud during the holidays, it is really one that can be read all year round. Although certainly, teachers may not want to miss the opportunity that this book provides to discuss the deeper meaning of gifts and why this little boy preferred the bell to any toy or video game. Children may want to share their own personal stories about gifts they received that have great meaning to them not because of the gift but because it holds a special place in their hearts.

Teaching Ideas

The teacher might open a read aloud by showing the cover to the children sitting on the rug and asking them to look carefully, examining the picture as an entire spread (front and back contain the picture) for some noticings and wonderings. If children are familiar with some of the other books by the same author, they may predict that this book will have a sense of mystery like in *The Garden of Abdul Gazasi*, *The Wreck of the Zephyr*, and of course the beloved *Jumanji*. The book provides plenty of rich opportunities for inference work and questioning which aids comprehension. Young readers may come up with many questions like, "How would the other children feel who came all that way and did not get a gift and this kid who gets one loses it?" Children with older siblings may question, "Why didn't the boy take his little sister Sarah along?" "Why doesn't the young boy have a name?" "Why do we never see the conductor at all in any of the pictures?" (Readers can cite evidence from the pictures by researching picturesthe text mentions the conductor but there are never any pictures of him.) Some astute children, especially those who ride the subway may pose the question, "How can it be an express? It made lots of local stops to pick up all those children." Further questioning may explore, "What would I have asked for if Santa was going to give me the first gift of Christmas?" There are many opportunities for inference work especially at the end, "Why did the parents think the bell was broken?" "Where is the young boy now?" "How old is he?" "How come he can hear the bell but his sister and friends cannot?" "What do you have to believe in to hear the bell?" Some smart students may even raise the question to their teacher that even though she is a grown up, would she hear the bell?

The rich language and the way that the words are put together enables children to really listen in throughout the text to the beautiful imagery and create a movie in their minds such as the sounds of "hissing stream and squeaking metal" of the train. And "the train was wrapped in an apron of steam." (The teacher can pose, "Is the train really wrapped in an apron?) "Climbed mountains so high, it seemed as if we would scrape the moon." The teacher could pause for a turn and talk, "Turn and talk to your partner, what do you think that means, 'Looked like the lights of a strange ocean liner sailing on a frozen sea.'" When Van Allsburg uses language such as "broke my heart"-the boy's heart doesn't really break like a dish would break. The teacher can ask, "What does that feel like to the boy to have a broken heart?" Turn and talk opportunities abound throughout the read aloud as teachers can also ask, "What do you think figurative language is? Literal language?"

Students can also be encouraged to study the mood of the book. Van Allsburg's books are often described as "mysterious." Students can discuss how the use of light and shadow, color, figure placement, perspective, and so on work together to create a sense of mystery. Such conversation can lead to a discussion on reality versus fantasy in the text. Did the journey to the North Pole really take place? Or was it just a dream? How do you know? Students can discuss how and why the author blurs the line between reality and fantasy through changes in scene and perspective. Things look so normal-the boy's bedroom, the train, the forest, the mountain-until the train enters the North Pole. The distant lights viewed from the shadows of the bridge look somewhat dreamy as they are reflected in the icy water, yet the village itself looks like any other typical winter wonderland lined in outdoor lights and dusted with snow. Santa's reindeer look just as real as the wolves in the forest.

Teachers can also have children explore Van Allsburg not just as a writer but an artist and how he made his decisions on what to draw with what corresponding words. Do children think the pictures came first or the words? (Van Allsburg says he sees pictures in his mind so it could be that at times pictures come first then the text tags along.) Many children may notice the use of light and dark, "Where is the light in this picture? Why did Van Allsburg use only dark colors here? The sense of the magical stays with us long after we finish the book and gives plenty of rich opportunity to linger, reflect, talk, and go back to the text and rediscover.

There are so many more teaching ideas with this book such as following

A Field Guide to the Classroom Library, Lucy Calkins and the Teachers College Reading and Writing Project, Heinemann, ©2002 Teachers College, Columbia University; http://www.heinemann.com/fieldguides

the big idea and talking back to text. Ask children, "What is your theory about this story?" (Theory charts can be created.) Let children know that their theory may change as they get more and more information from the text.

Students could compare and contrast other books by Van Allsburg-some are all in black and white while some are all in color while some have a combination of both. Teachers can ask, "Why do you think he does that?" Van Allsburg repeatedly has the same character in many of his books. The character's name is Fritz from *The Garden of Abdul Gazasi* and he is hidden in most of Van Allsburg's books including *The Polar Express*. Children will love trying to find him in his other books. (In *The Polar Express,* Fritz is the puppet on page one on the bedpost.)

Readers could discuss story elements. Besides plot they could discuss character. What do we know about the character? Why do you think the author left out the boy's name but told us his sister's name? What kind of person is this boy? Where is he today? Movement through time could be examined. Until the last page the children will be able to understand movement through time but then there is a gigantic leap. A discussion of how the book jumps ahead so many years and where the evidence is can be very challenging, as children become movement-in-time researchers. A teacher might use the text to have children note the progression of time from the beginning to the next to last page and then the leap at the last page.

Setting plays an important role in this story. As students hear the story over and over again, they will have new wonderings and noticings. Teachers can suggest that children pay attention to setting since the story shifts to several settings, the bedroom, outside his bedroom, outside the train, inside the train, over mountains, wilderness, to the North Pole, and back inside the comfort and safety of his family living room. Where is the last page that is boxed taking place? Where can we imagine he is now? This can lead to a discussion of change. A teacher might ask, "How has the character changed from the beginning to the end of the story? Is he still a little boy?" Children can think about how old he may be now.

Book Connections

Introducing this book is a fabulous way to begin an author study on Van Allsburg and all his incredible books that have poetic text and pictures that could be in an art museum. Children can compare and contrast his work and find a basic theme that may underline his books and spark a reader's imagination. How does he do this? What are some of his crafts? There are fifteen books to choose from but children should not compare more than three. Children individually may become Van Allsburg fans and want to read all his books during independent reading time. Children with artistic interests may wish to explore his drawings and study the work of surrealistic artist, too.

Genre
Picture Book; Fantasy

A Field Guide to the Classroom Library, Lucy Calkins and the Teachers College Reading and Writing Project, Heinemann, ©2002 Teachers College, Columbia University; http://www.heinemann.com/fieldguides

Teaching Uses

Teaching Writing; Read Aloud; Author Study; Character Study; Independent Reading

Ragweed
Avi

Book Summary

Ragweed is the third book in Avi's *Tales from Dimwood Forest* series, which tells the story of a family of mice. In the first book, *Poppy*, Ragweed is killed by Mr. Ocax, the owl, for dancing in the moonlight with his fiancée, Poppy. Poppy takes on some of Ragweed's reckless bravery by fighting Mr. Ocax and getting her family to fight back. *Ragweed* is a flashback, to a time when Ragweed first went from his family nest to the big city. It is about how Ragweed acquired his own bravery and outspokenness. At the beginning of the book, the reader is introduced to Ragweed and his family. This flashback will seem logical to series readers because Ragweed's big city adventure was alluded to in *Poppy* and readers have been waiting for this story.

Basic Book Information

There are 178 pages and 27 chapters in this book. Chapters are short and can usually be read in one sitting. Chapter titles are supportive and preview the main idea or event in the chapter. There is a map in the front of the book. The illustrations are by Brian Floca and are consistent with the pictures and style of the other *Dimwood Forest* books. At least one picture appears in each chapter, and supports the text well. A chapter usually contains only one scene, and when the scenes change within a chapter, the new scene is set off with extra spacing.

Ragweed is the third book in the *Tales from Dimwood Forest* series, but it can be read as if it followed *Poppy*, the first book. The other books include *Poppy and Rye* and *Ereth's Birthday*.

Noteworthy Features

There are a lot of colloquialisms and slang terms used in this book. Readers can grasp the cadence once they get accustomed to the patterns of speaking. It may be helpful to read certain sections aloud to students.

There are also a lot of characters in this story. Members of Ragweed's family are present in this book and not in other books in the series. The point of view varies; different chapters are written from the point of view of different characters. Usually this shift occurs with a new chapter, but sometimes it happens within a chapter, most notably on page 127 in chapter 19. That chapter starts out being told through a third-person narrator who observes the cat. After double spacing and a new paragraph, the point of view changes from a narrator who observes the cat to the cat itself, voicing its thoughts.

The pictures are helpful in envisioning the story. They appear frequently and correspond to the text on that page. There's a lot of action in this story, which will keep the reader attentive and motivated to read on.

Series
Tales from Dimwood Forest

Illustrator
Brian Floca

Publisher
Harper Trophy, 1999

ISBN
0380801671

TC Level
13

Teaching Ideas

This book works very well in studies of either point of view or setting. They can do this independently, in read alouds or in book clubs or partnerships. Students can use sketches, Post-its, highlighters or various other reading workshop tools to help them focus on these elements. If, for example, students are investigating how the setting affects the mood of the story, the teacher might say, "As you read this book, each time you come to a place where you can really picture in your mind where the story is happening, mark it with a Post-it. Take a moment to jot down the moods and feelings it brings up. How are the characters feeling? How are you feeling? By looking at these markers, students realize that the mood of the book changes when the setting moves from the city to the country.

Book Connections

More advanced readers can be pointed to *Mrs. Frisby and the Rats of NIMH* as a follow-up to this series.

Genre
Chapter Book; Fantasy

Teaching Uses
Independent Reading; Book Clubs

Redwall

Brian Jacques

Book Summary

The bumbling mouse Matthias, an orphan who is a novice at the Abbey of Redwall discovers that a large army headed by the dreaded rat Cluny the Scourge is heading to conquer Redwall. As the forces of Cluny grow nearer, Matthias sets out on an epic quest to discover the famous sword of Martin the Warrior, the founder of Redwall. This search leads him to the very darkest basements of the Abbey to a terrifying climb to its roof, and even into the pit of a powerful Adder with hypnotizing eyes. The search is a race against time, because without the Sword the peaceful mice of Redwall Abby have little chance against Cluny's hordes. This book has the well-known fantasy theme of good versus evil, which will ring familiar chords with readers of the *Harry Potter* series. The book also follows the theme of the weak rising up and overcoming the strong.

Basic Book Information

Redwall is the lynch pin in a series of at least thirteen books. The entire series is named after this book. These books are popular among fourth through sixth grade audiences. Brian Jacques, a British writer, has just written his first book outside the *Redwall* series, *Castaways of the Flying Dutchman*.

The *Redwall* series is unusual because there is no single character that connects all the books. Instead, they are linked by a shared setting: an imaginary world inhabited by mice, rats, stoats, badgers, ferrets, and otters. This world centers around the medieval Redwall Abbey, a huge red-stone structure that houses the Brotherhood of Mice-a pacifistic order that was founded years ago by the legendary Martin the Warrior, who overthrew the vicious wild cats who ruled a castle that once stood in the same location as Redwall Abbey. The world also centers around Salamnadastron, a hollowed-out mountain stronghold-ruled by a dynasty of Badger Lords and filled with a garrison of Hares (rabbits). Between the Abbey and the mountain there are swamps, a mountain range, plains, and several rivers.

Brian Jacques is a master at creating characters that take on meaning to the reader. Many readers become emotionally attached the mother-like Badgers, and bumbling, yet trustworthy mice of Redwall, and readers come to hate Cluny as he uses attempts to use terror tactics against the indefatigable inhabitants of Redwall.

Redwall has 351 pages, with fifteen chapters, and thre "books." Instead of titles, the chapters have small black and white pictures that hint at either the character the chapter will follow, or the setting in which the chapter will take place. There are no other illustrations except for the map at the front of the book. The book jumps from character to character, sometimes following Cluny the Scourge, and sometimes leaping to Matthias, then to the Abbot.

Series
Redwall

Publisher
Philomel Books, 1986

ISBN
0399214240

TC Level
14

The subjects and settings change, as do the narrators. These can change between and within chapters.

Noteworthy Features

One problem that some readers have with the *Redwall* series is that animals speak dialects and these can be hard to read. The dialect of the Moles sounds like this; *"Yurr moles, get outten th' loight. Let'n um dog at bone thurr"* or the easier dialect of the Sparrows; *"What for ratworm want sentry?" War beak shrugged her wings. "Him catch Abbey, not know we come to catch back."* Any one of these sentences is not vital to the story, but obviously to read this series, readers need to begin to acclimate to the dialects in the text.

Teaching Ideas

If a teacher wants to introduce students to *Redwall*, she might begin with reading aloud even just a portion of the first chapter, as it introduces the reader to Matthias, and some important characters in his life. The teacher might nudge a child who is reading the book to make a chart of the characters, because throughout the books there are well over 50 separate encounters with new creatures, which may cause some readers to lose track. Reading aloud will also give students a taste of the dialects.

Students may choose to follow a single character's development throughout the book, using post-it notes to mark places in the text where events occur or which a character changes. The teacher may want to talk to readers and find out how the characters have changed. If a reader is following Matthias, the reader may notice that Matthias slowly grows to be more and more like his perception of Martin the Warrior. Once this student has finished the book, the teacher may encourage the student to go back over the text, and try to find places where Matthias takes on Martin the Warrior's attributes. Then the student could try and discover *why* Matthias grew to be like Martin.

It would also be worthwhile to compare *Redwall* to the *Harry Potter* books. Both are fantasy, but *Harry Potter* is more of a modern work then *Redwall*, and *Redwall* is closer to an epic fantasy then *Harry Potter*. The two series share battles between good and evil, which belong almost exclusively to fantasy, and both include characters that mature from a very childish start.

Book Connections

Redwall is, in part, another version of the famed *Harry Potter* books, with the same sense of adventure, and magic. But it is more similar to "adult" fantasy (such as the works of Robert Jordan and Terry Goodkind) than *Harry Potter*. Brain Jacques' other well known books in this series include *Mossflower*, *Martin the Warrior*, and *Marlfox*.

Genre
Fantasy; Chapter Book

A Field Guide to the Classroom Library, Lucy Calkins and the Teachers College Reading and Writing Project, Heinemann, ©2002 Teachers College, Columbia University; http://www.heinemann.com/fieldguides

Teaching Uses
Independent Reading; Book Clubs

Ribbons

Laurence Yep

Book Summary

Ribbons is the story of Robin, an eleven year old Chinese-Caucasian girl who is a talented ballet dancer. Her family can no longer afford her dance lessons because all of their money is going toward bringing Robin's Chinese grandmother to Oakland, California, from Hong Kong. Robin at first resents her grandmother's intrusion into her life, but she uncovers a secret that leads to a new understanding of the many ways in which she and her grandmother are alike. Robin's determination to pursue her dream makes this an uplifting story.

Basic Book Information

The book is 179 pages long, with titled chapters each nine to fourteen pages in length. The main character tells the story throughout and both the plot and the dialogue are easy to follow. The chapter titles hint at what is to come in the chapter.

Noteworthy Features

The original story of "The Little Mermaid" is referred to in this one as a story that parallels the story of Robin and her grandmother.

Teaching Ideas

If a teacher confers with a child who is just beginning this book, the teacher may decide to tell the reader a bit about the book in order to help the child get involved in the story. The Book Summary can be used as a book introduction, and if the child has read Robert Kimmel Smith's *The War with Grandpa* or another book in which a grandparent moves in with a family, creating some ambivalence, the teacher may want to remind the reader of that book. In *Ribbons*, the first three chapters show Robin before her grandmother arrives. Then in chapters four through eight, Robin and her grandmother are at odds with each other. Then beginning in chapter nine, Robin and her grandmother learn to understand each other. The teacher *could* conceivably overview these sections as part of a book introduction, but it would probably be more helpful to let the reader experience the book and then to say, "Sometimes I think back over a book and realize there were major sections in the book. If you were to divide this book into sections, how would you do it?" Of course, the divisions described above aren't the only possible way to map out the text.

Readers of this book will learn about Chinese culture. For example, they'll read about the custom of binding feet. Readers will also learn about ballet. Robin has an extreme concern with eating too much and getting fat.

Publisher
Putnam & Grosset, 1992

ISBN
0698116062

TC Level
12

She is tall and thin, but watches snacks carefully for her dancer's figure as do her friends. This may end up being a topic of conversation.

Book Connections

Like *Ribbons, The War with Grandpa* (Smith) and *Cry Uncle* (J. Ausch) also deal with elderly relatives moving in and disrupting the lives of a main character. *Alphabet City Ballet* (E. Tamar) and *Another Way to Dance* (M. Southgate) are, like *Ribbons*, books which deal with a character's struggles to achieve dreams of dancing despite the obstacles. *The Cook's Family* (L. Yep) continues the story of Robin and her family.

Genre
Chapter Book

Teaching Uses
Independent Reading; Book Clubs

A Field Guide to the Classroom Library, Lucy Calkins and the Teachers College Reading and Writing Project, Heinemann, ©2002 Teachers College, Columbia University; http://www.heinemann.com/fieldguides

Sammy Keyes and the Hotel Thief
Wendelin Van Draanen

FIELD GUIDE

Book Summary

Samantha, also known as "Sammy," Keyes is a seventh grader with problems. Her mother has deserted her, leaving her with her Gram who is hiding her in her government subsidized elderly living apartment. Sammy has also started seventh grade, and on her first day she is suspended for fighting with another girl. Sammy has also used her Gram's binoculars (which she isn't supposed to use) to look out the window and has seen a burglary in process across the street. To make matters worse, the burglar saw her too, as Sammy waved! Despite all these problems, Sammy never gives up, and instead she sets out to solve the mystery of the burglar, defend her reputation at school, and maintain her living situation with her grandmother. She does this in a spunky and unassuming way, with some great laughs.

Basic Book Information

This 163-page mystery novel has nineteen chapters, prefaced with a page-long Prologue, which does a nice job of introducing the reader to Sammy as the narrator. This is a fast-moving book, as Sammy seldom sits still to wallow in her problems. *Sammy Keyes and the Hotel Thief* won the esteemed Edgar Award for Best Children's Mystery in 1999. This is the first book of the *Sammy Keyes* series, of which there are now six books.

Noteworthy Features

This is a fast-moving book, and this can be a strength as well as a difficulty. The character of Sammy Keyes will pull many readers into the tangled web she weaves, and if readers are not quick enough, she will leave them behind in her dust. For example, in the first nine pages of the book, Sammy has described her illegal living situation with her grandmother, her mother's search for Hollywood fame and fortune, the Heavenly Hotel across the street from her grandmother's apartment, and how she saw a burglary in process. As Sammy describes her use of the binoculars, there is a flashback as she remembers the time she went into the Heavenly Hotel out of curiosity and was thrown out by the hotel manager. Mrs. Graybill, her grandmother's mean and nosy neighbor is introduced in these first pages also, as Sammy must use a different way into the apartment each time in order to avoid being seen too often. The remainder of the book is of a similar speed.

The scenes change constantly in this book, but the setting of a suburban town, remains the same for the whole book. Scenes change from Gram's Spartan apartment, the seedy Heavenly Hotel, the store on the corner, the Mall, Hudson's house, her best friend Marissa's house, and the junior high school. There are many scenes, and Sammy moves between them quickly. It

Series
Sammy Keyes

Publisher
Alfred A. Knopf, 1998

ISBN
0679892648

TC Level
12

would be helpful for readers to have familiarity with some of these scenes. The junior high school will be recognizable to many students in fifth and sixth grade, especially if they have experienced departmentalized teaching.

The language of this book is mostly vernacular, and there is not much in the way of vocabulary that proficient readers will struggle over. There is mention of pork beelines and futures and commodities trading, but this is as mystifying to Sammy as it is to any reader. Sammy's friend Hudson does a great job explaining it to her, and in turn to the reader.

Teaching Ideas

One upper-grade teacher decided to study the genre of mystery, using past read books as the basis of their investigation into *Sammy Keyes and the Hotel Thief*. To do this, she decided to reacquaint her class by re-reading one of the *Cam Jansen* series books and one of the *Encyclopedia Brown* books.

She began the study by saying, "This is a great book to study the genre of mystery with. *Sammy Keyes and the Hotel Thief* represents children's mystery on the cusp of moving into adult mystery: it contains deductive and inductive reasoning with only subtle evidence from the author that there is a different kind of thinking going on. Think of mystery of being on a line that goes from easiest to hardest. That's called a continuum. What do you think we should put at the beginning of the continuum?" The class responded with animated conversation, weighing the difficulty of *Cam Jansen* and the *Nate the Great* series (by M.W. Sharmat). They finally decided upon the *Cam Jansen* series by David Adler, because, as one student put it, "*Cam Jansen* shows the character of Cam thinking and remembering in a clear way, using the 'Click!' as a way to point the readers in to important information."

By studying *Cam Jansen* the class also found that these mysteries follow a predictable formula of setting up the mystery and its resolution. The class decided that this was important and that *Encyclopedia Brown* represented another mark on the mystery continuum. They decided that these books were more difficult because of the number of characters walking in and out of the stories, as well as the kinds of issues Encyclopedia encounters. But the formulaic outlay of facts and explanation of the mystery all create a predictable structure for the reader to work in. Always at the end of each chapter (mystery), Encyclopedia's thinking is explained, and readers can being to think in this way too, using Encyclopedia's deductive reasoning (using the clues presented to uncover the truth). The *Einstein Anderson* books (written by Seymour Simon) are harder than *Encyclopedia Brown* books because of their content and vocabulary, but they follow the same format and formula.

The class had created their continuum and it was time to examine Sammy Keyes. The teacher gave the following book introduction: "*Sammy Keyes and the Hotel Thief* is a fiction chapter book that is a mystery, containing clues throughout. And yet, Van Draanen introduces some inductive reasoning into the book, like what Encyclopedia Brown does. But there are many little stories going on and they can fool the reader. The things that are tricky in mysteries are called 'red herrings.' When Sammy remembers something, she doesn't say, 'Click' like Cam Jansen. Instead, this noticing is part of the story, it doesn't stand out at all. The clues are buried more than we've seen before, even with *Encyclopedia Brown*. This is the hard part of this kind of mystery, but what also makes it very interesting to read. Let's begin, being sure to jot down what you think could be a clue. We'll get a chance to talk to our partners about what we think."

Independent readers and readers in participation or groups may choose to carry out similar "mystery investigations," and could certainly do so on their own.

Genre
Mystery; Chapter Book

Teaching Uses
Independent Reading; Partnerships; Book Clubs

A Field Guide to the Classroom Library, Lucy Calkins and the Teachers College Reading and Writing Project, Heinemann, ©2002 Teachers College, Columbia University; http://www.heinemann.com/fieldguides

School Days

Adapted from the Little House books by Laura Ingalls Wilder

Book Summary

This book tells the story of Laura Ingalls and her family. It begins when they are living on the prairie. Laura and her sister Mary are going to school for the first time. Laura is apprehensive about leaving her "outdoorsy, untamed" life behind; but learns to love her days at school, where she learns to read, makes new friends, and plays fun new games at recess. About midway through the book, Laura is five years older and beginning school in a new place. Her family has moved from the prairie in Minnesota to a town in the Dakota territory. Here Laura makes new friends, has her first "schoolgirl crush," and encounters a big and dangerous blizzard. At the end of the story, Laura realizes that she has truly enjoyed her experiences-at school, with learning, and helping her sisters study-and decides that when she grows up, she will become a schoolteacher.

Basic Book Information

School Days is one book in a series that has been adapted from the *Little House* series by Laura Ingalls Wilder. Some educators refer to these books as "rip-offs" from the original series, and deliberately include only this one title in the library. The book is a simplified and condensed version of two books from that series: *Little House on the Prairie* and *Little House in the Town.* The book is nine chapters with 69 pages. The chapters are titled and these titles do a good job of foreshadowing the content. There is one black-and-white illustration per chapter. The book is graded by the publisher as being appropriate for grades 2 through5. The sentences range from short and simple to long and relatively hard. There is quite a bit of dialogue in the book, referenced by proper names and pronouns.

Noteworthy Features

Readers who are unfamiliar with historical fiction and/or this time in American history will need quite a bit of background information in order to fully understand the setting, the plot, and some of the vocabulary in this book. It takes place in the American Midwest in the 1880s, on a prairie settlement and in a prairie town. The text makes many references to things that may be unfamiliar to the reader. For example, Laura is eight and her sister Mary is ten and neither of them have ever been to school. Laura's "Pa" catches fish for dinner with a handmade fish trap "in the falls by the banks of Plum creek."

There is also a lot of unfamiliar vocabulary. In the first two chapters, the reader will come across word like: "blue-flowered calico," "slate pencil," "lumberyard," "prairie hen," and "sunbonnet." There are also several examples of characters speaking in colloquialisms such as: "For pity's sake,"

Series
Little House

Illustrator
Renee Graef

Publisher
Harper Collins Publishers, 1997

ISBN
0060271469

TC Level
9

"book-learning," and "hollering." Much of the text does a good job of explaining unfamiliar words and concepts in the context of the sentences. Many descriptions are contained in dependent clauses, following sentences or later in the chapter. Most of the unfamiliar words and concepts that are not explained through context, are less important to the reader's full understanding of the text.

Although the story line of the book is quite simple, there is an abrupt change in time in Chapter 6: "Another First Day." At this point in the story, Laura's family has moved from the prairie to the town *and* Laura is five years older. Although it is explained in the second and third paragraph of the chapter, it is not smoothly written. Otherwise, the passage of time is clearly stated in the first sentences of each chapter.

Finally, the last chapter "Studying at Home" contains quite a bit of difficult poetry and verse which may be hard for readers to decode and understand.

Teaching Ideas

School Days is a condensed adaptation of two books from the *Little House* series by Laura Ingalls Wilder. The Wilder books are much longer, highly detailed and more difficult. Although *School Days* does a good job in adapting the series to the needs of readers at this level, there are some concepts and vocabulary that will need explaining before reading the book. Teachers may want to use *School Days* as a follow-up to a read aloud of one of the books by Laura Ingalls Wilder. This will save a lot of time and also provide a good place to start, for children who want to compare the books in both series.

Teachers could also use *School Days* itself as a read aloud as part of a study of the American Midwest in the 1880s, American history in general, life on a prairie, or the genre of historical fiction.

If the class was doing a study of the historical fiction genre, readers could look for, chart, and discuss the features that historical fiction books have in common. Some of these features include: blending of fact and fiction, recognizable (or famous) characters, settings and events from history; sections where the author had to use their imagination to re-create the story, fictional characters, events and settings and so on. A study of the historical fiction genre is a great opportunity for reading partnerships, reading centers, and whole class read alouds. The historical fiction genre lends itself well to having lively discussions, comparing books about the same topic, finding more books about the topic and using the information they've learned for other things (future reading, reports, writing of their own, etc.).

Many chapter books at this level have chapters that are untitled. *School Days* has chapters with titles that "set the reader up" with a clue as to what the chapter is about. Teachers could model for readers how to read the chapter title and to briefly speculate or question what might happen next. For example, in the chapter entitled "The New School" a teacher could say; "It looks like Laura may be starting a new school. I wonder if her family has moved? Maybe, Laura is older in this chapter and she had to change schools like we do in older grades? I wonder if her new school is different from her old one?"

A Field Guide to the Classroom Library, Lucy Calkins and the Teachers College Reading and Writing Project, Heinemann, ©2002 Teachers College, Columbia University; http://www.heinemann.com/fieldguides

Because *School Days* has quite a bit of unfamiliar vocabulary, it would be a good book to use to instruct readers at this level in the various strategies for figuring out new vocabulary. Teachers can ask children to practice, and therefore develop, the skill of "noticing" an unfamiliar word, and making a note of it (on a post-it note or in a notebook). They may pause and make a note while reading or come back to it at the end of a paragraph or chapter. Children can practice: using the context to figure out unfamiliar words, making an educated guess, looking for the word in parts of the book they may have read already, asking a friend, or looking for it in the dictionary.

School Days is written for readers who are beginning to be comfortable reading independently in a fluent and sustained way. Yet, this is also a level where readers can tend to race through their books and often miss information, meaning, humor and/or more subtle themes. Because of this, teachers may use the book to work with children on "knowing" themselves as readers. This is a very sophisticated skill and readers at this level need a lot of practice to do it well. One of the ways to do this is to learn how to assess where a good stopping point is in their reading. This stopping point can be used to reflect, to re-read interesting, or confusing, parts or to discuss their reading with a partner or group. Teachers may say to readers, "Before you read today, look through the book and put a post-it note or a bookmark on a good place to stop for a moment. If you are reading with a partner, discuss with him/her where would be a good place to stop and talk."

Because *School Days* is longer than the early chapter books that readers at this level may be very familiar with, it is important to do some teaching about how to read on, without forgetting what has happened in the story so far. Teachers may have children practice doing a little re-reading, by either skimming from the beginning or completely re-reading a small section directly preceding the place where they left off.

Book Connections

There are many other books in this series. Some titles include: *The Adventures of Laura and Jack, Pioneer Sisters, Laura and Nellie,* and *Farmer Boy Days.* Other historical fiction series include: *The American Girls Collection* and *The Little House* [Ed: *The* okay here? Not included under Series info] series by Laura Ingalls Wilder. Both of these are quite a bit harder.

Genre
Chapter Book; Historical Fiction

Teaching Uses
Partnerships; Independent Reading; Read Aloud

Shiloh

Phyllis Reynolds Naylor

Book Summary

When eleven-year-old Marty Preston befriends a young beagle near his home in rural West Virginia, he suspects that the dog has been badly mistreated. Marty hides the dog in the woods and cares for him while he wrestles with a wrenching question: Should he be honest with his parents and return the dog, or will returning the dog to its owner, Judd Travers, mean the dog's death? Marty finds his way through his ethical dilemma, works out a bargain with the owner, and saves the dog's life.

Basic Book Information

Shiloh, winner of a Newbery Medal, is a 144-page book divided into 15 untitled chapters. There are no illustrations.

Naylor's work includes several series-the *Alice* books (*The Agony of Alice*, *Alice In Between* and *Reluctantly Alice*), the *Magruder* series (*Bernie Magruder and the Haunted Hotel*, *Bernie Magruder and the Disappearing Bodies*, and *Bernie Magruder and the Case of the Big Stink* among others) as well as the *Shiloh* trilogy, which includes *Shiloh Season* and *Saving Shiloh*, along with *Shiloh*. Some of her other titles include *Jade Green:A Ghost Story*, *Carlotta's Kittens* and *Walker's Crossing*.

Noteworthy Features

This suspenseful, well-written and thought-provoking story will hold the attention of many children, particularly animal lovers. Written in the first person, it has an intimacy that keeps readers close to the concerns of the narrator, Marty. The setting-rural West Virginia-is clearly evoked, and the unobtrusively colloquial speech contributes to the mood and setting.

Suspense drives the story forward. Will Marty get caught? Will his parents see through his lies? Will his lies about having the dog hidden backfire? The resolution of the story is uncertain until the last few pages, and should keep readers glued to the page. Because the suspense involves not just action, but Marty's internal dilemmas, there is always a sense of complexity that is convincingly "real-life."

The characterization of Marty is subtle, yet from it readers can sense the complexity of his feelings: his love for the dog; his guilt about lying to his parents; his interactions with family, friends and the dog's owner; and his relationship to the outdoors. Marty's growing maturity is unforced and his realizations are convincing. Judd Travers, the dog's owner, appears at first to

Series
Shiloh

Publisher
Bantam Doubleday Dell,
1991

ISBN
0440407524

TC Level
11

be purely evil, but through Marty's eyes, readers come to see his frailty, and his capacity for change.

The language is simple and evocative, with a few difficult words and phrases (such as *groveling*) but most of the language is clear enough from the context. Colloquial language, such as "You never eat more'n a couple of bites," may be difficult for many readers, and some teachers find that presenting a few examples of Marty's dialect to the group before they start reading can head off a lot of confusion.

Teaching Ideas

Shiloh is appropriate both as a read aloud and for individual reading. Children can consider and discuss the themes and ethical issues. Are there instances in which they are torn between conflicting feelings? Have they suffered negative consequences from lying? Have they ever felt lying was necessary?

The mistreatment of the dog and the attitude of Judd Travers may disturb readers, just as Marty is disturbed. However, this is a necessary part of understanding *Shiloh*. One theme involves how Marty learns to confront and understand evil, as personified by Travers, and not simply fear it. Marty must give up his fantasies of avoiding Travers, escaping with Shiloh or keeping Shiloh hidden.

A related theme involves honesty, as it relates to Travers, Marty and his parents. During the course of the book, Marty's lies cause trouble for Marty, his parents, Shiloh and Judd Travers, while honesty proves to be the key to rescuing Shiloh from danger. As a study of cause and effect, readers can collect instances of Marty's dishonesty and discuss the effects.

A third related theme worthy of discussion involves the conflict between personal conviction and the rules of family or society. Marty feels a sense of obligation toward the helpless dog, but his obligation runs counter to the wishes of his parents and the laws of society.

The changes in Marty's character might be another area of discussion. Some categories to look into include Marty's attitude toward Travers, his view of his father and his mother, his relationship with Shiloh, his attitude toward work and his attitude toward honesty.

Book Connections

Naylor's work includes several series-the *Alice* books (*The Agony of Alice*, *Alice In Between* and *Reluctantly Alice*), the *Magruder* series (*Bernie Magruder and the Haunted Hotel*, *Bernie Magruder and the Disappearing Bodies*, and *Bernie Magruder and the Case of the Big Stink* among others) as well as the *Shiloh* trilogy, which includes *Shiloh Season* and *Saving Shiloh*, along with *Shiloh*. Some of Naylor's other titles include *Jade Green: A Ghost Story*, *Carlotta's Kittens* and *Walker's Crossing*.

Genre
Chapter Book

A Field Guide to the Classroom Library, Lucy Calkins and the Teachers College Reading and Writing Project, Heinemann, ©2002 Teachers College, Columbia University; http://www.heinemann.com/fieldguides

Teaching Uses
Independent Reading; Read Aloud; Interpretation; Critique

Shoebag

Mary James

Book Summary

This story of a modern metamorphosis (change of form or body) draws its ideas from ancient Greek myths. It is also used in current mythology of shape shifters and superheroes and the popular "Animorphs." The shape shifting happens with an unlikely, and to most people repugnant, character of a cockroach who changes into a boy. The story is told in the third person, but from Shoebag's point of view. In this way the reader can see the world from the point of view of a cockroach, a small but smart creature.

There are several stories going on: the cockroach story and the parallel human being story. Both stories are of conflict and survival-cockroaches trying to find food and survive extermination and adolescents trying to survive in their own ways.

Basic Book Information

This book is 135 pages long. There are 22 chapters without titles. There is no table of contents. Chapter length runs from five to eleven pages. There are no illustrations aside from the cover by K. Sengler. The print size is medium with medium spacing between words and lines.

The "About the Author" page is the very last page of the book, and it has a tidbit about the author's own changes-Mary James is also know as M.E. Kerr who writes popular adolescent fiction, usually intended for students older than those reading *Shoebag*. The characters in *Shoebag* are younger than those in M.E. Kerr books, and they deal with issues that usually occur in the middle school years.

Noteworthy Features

This book is a lot of fun, flipping the worldview of the reader all the time. Because of this, the book moves along at a good pace and is never boring. It combines real life situations with pure fantasy. Mary James uses familiar settings-home and school-and this helps to steady things as the point of view shifts into that of an insect.

Teaching Ideas

Readers don't necessarily need to believe the book, but readers must suspend their disbelief to understand and enjoy it. The willing suspension of disbelief is intrinsic to reading any fantasy story. Many readers will have

Publisher
Scholastic, 1999

ISBN
0590430300

TC Level
11

suspended their disbelief before with picture books and early chapter books like *Stella Luna* and *Frog and Toad*. It may help readers to remind them of this.

There are two parallel stories in this book and that could pose difficulty to readers who are not aware of it. Shoebag acts as the bridge or connection between the two stories and worlds. Shoebag's inner conflict of which world to belong to is constant and can help raise readers' awareness of the two worlds. The parallel stories can serve up some interesting interpretations and this is the author's intent. Conversations about what the author is *really* saying with this book are usually complex and interesting for readers.

There aren't many fiction (or nonfiction) stories told from an insect's point of view. This point of view can help readers understand the world from another perspective. After all, if readers can fully jump into the world of a cockroach, won't they be able to jump into the world of some human who is only somewhat different from them?

While this is a great read aloud for about grades three and up, independent readers will also find much to think and talk about in this book. There is a lot of dialogue and this can be studied for fluency and phrasing as well as for character voice.

There are many characters and names in this book and this can be confusing. Independent readers or readers in groups may use character names to try to infer information about the characters. It is helpful to note that most of the characters have unique names, which gives some insight into their character (Pretty Soft is a child model and actress wannabe, very preoccupied in her looks). Even Gregor Samsa, another cockroach that can change shape (his real cockroach name is "in Bed"), gives a clue to his identity as shape shifter by alluding to another piece of literature, "The Metamorphosis" by Franz Kafka, whose main character changes from a man to an insect named "Gregor." Students won't know this piece of literature, but a quick chat about it can help them see the layering going on in this book.

A reader may be interested in searching for other literary allusions, learning to read with an awareness of them. Literary allusions are an author's intentional text-to-text reference. Once readers find these references, it is important for them to ask how the connection between the two texts changes the meaning of both. How does one story influence a reader's understanding the other?

Book Connections

Mary James is also known as M.E. Kerr who writes popular adolescent fiction, usually intended for students older than those reading *Shoebag*. The characters in *Shoebag* are younger than those of M.E. Kerr books, and they deal with issues that usually occur in the middle school years.

Genre
Chapter Book; Fantasy

Teaching Uses
Independent Reading; Read Aloud; Character Study

Sisters in Strength: American Women Who Made a Difference

Yona Zeldis McDonough

Book Summary

Herein lie the simple, well-told stories of the life and adventures and achievements of eleven women: Pocahontas, Harriet Tubman, Elizabeth Cady Stanton, and Susan B. Anthony, Clara Barton, Emily Dickinson, Mary Cassatt, Helen Keller, Eleanor Roosevelt, Amelia Earhart, and Margaret Mead. Together the inspiring stories of these woman show the many different ways that a person can be great, and the many different conditions and backgrounds from which a great person can grow. The stories are not only of the accomplishments of the women, but also give a taste for their personalities and motivations.

Basic Book Information

This colorfully painted, Nonfiction picture book has about fifty pages. In it are the life stories of eleven American heroines. The one-paragraph introduction (which is not at all critical to the book) pays tribute to all the women not chosen to be subjects in this text. Each story opens with a quotation from or about the woman described and is about three pages long, illustrated along the borders and with a full-page painting to open. The paintings are in the lavishly colored folk art style. The table of contents in the beginning of the book makes it easy to find the story of any one particular woman. The book ends with a time line recording important events in the lives of all of the women in the book.

Noteworthy Features

This book is of the finest quality. The two page sketches of the women are not told as biographies only, but also as stories to listen to for their suspense and interesting details. The writing is spare but precise. The stories start not with the year of each woman's birth as in many biographies, but with an intriguing hook, for example, the woman deeply involved in some unusual task or the woman as a baby being watched by her parents. Any unusual terms within the text are explained immediately. Details from the women's lives, and even odd quotations from them make the stories vivid and lively.

The bright and lively pictures are bound to attract and hold readers. The childlike style of the art may also inspire young illustrators as well.

Teaching Ideas

These short biographies, vignettes even, are perfect to read aloud. The

Illustrator
Malcah Zeldis

Publisher
Henry Holt and Company, 2000

ISBN
0805061209

TC Level
11; 12; 13

contents of each is inspiring and interesting. Once a teacher has read one or two portraits aloud, the book could be selected by several readers to read on their own. Teachers would need to emphasize the fact that great people, men and women can inspire other great people, both men and women. Books about great women are not only for other women.

The table of contents makes the book an easy one to use as a reference as well. It would be especially interesting to put this book alongside some of the biographies in the series of *A Picturebook of Helen Keller*, [or Eleanor Roosevelt, or Harriet Tubman] to let readers compare and contrast the information and the impressions they receive about the woman from the two different texts. It may be a surprise to readers to see the way the same facts can be put together to create different impressions.

This book also provides examples of ways that children can write about other people. Since each essay in the book is short, children can easily use these sketches as examples for their own writing of biography, or even autobiography.

Readers in partnerships or clubs may be interested in following the thread of what makes these women "great.". For some, it may be that they saw social injustices and tried to address them. For others, it may be that they overcame obstacles to achieve goals. It may be useful to readers to "look back" on this book following their reading of it, to draw conclusions about these women and their impact on society.

Genre
Nonfiction; Picture Book

Teaching Uses
Reading and Writing Nonfiction; Independent Reading; Teaching Writing

A Field Guide to the Classroom Library, Lucy Calkins and the Teachers College Reading and Writing Project, Heinemann, ©2002 Teachers College, Columbia University; http://www.heinemann.com/fieldguides

Skinnybones
Barbara Park

FIELD GUIDE

Book Summary

Alex Frankovich is a wisecracking fifth grader nicknamed "Skinnybones" by T.J. Stoner, the class athlete and Alex's rival for attention. T.J. brags constantly about his fantastic pitching, which drives Alex, the perennial winner of "Most Improved Player," to retaliate with humor. The story is full of Alex's jokes and quick comic comebacks to T.J.'s teasing and bullying. This is a fun story that shows a child reacting to bullying with humor, rather than with violence or avoidance. Even readers not interested in baseball will be delighted in Alex's antics on the field and off.

Basic Book Information

This is a 112-page book made up of twelve chapters. There are no chapter titles and no illustrations. *Skinnybones* was written by Barbara Park, beloved author of the *Junie B. Jones* series.

Noteworthy Features

This story is set at school and home, and there is frequent use of dialogue between Alex and his classmates and Alex and his parents. The dialogue works to move the story along, but it is at times quite lengthy and dense. The story is told in the first person, from Alex's point of view. Whenever the dialogue stops, Alex's thoughts pick up. Sometimes this can make a change of the scenes hard to recognize.

Humor is a prominent feature of this book; it is always present as Alex's personality is both funny and engaging. Some readers may not appreciate that Alex's brand of humor is a protective shield as well as an attention-getter. There is an episode where Alex misunderstands what "bunt" means, thinking that it means to vomit. This is slapstick similar to Abbot and Costello's "Who's on First?" which is hysterical, but only if the reader can follow the quick action and dialogue.

Teaching Ideas

There is a lot of internal thinking in this book, creating a strong persona for the reader to connect with. Despite this bond between reader and narrator, there are times when the reader must learn to distrust the narrator-his view of the world is not the most reliable. Because of this, *Skinnybones* could be used to introduce reader skepticism of narration.

T.J brags and Alex cracks jokes. A student may want to mark the behaviors and search for patterns in the two characters' actions. Does Alex crack jokes when he feels badly? When does T.J. brag? A student may develop a "theory" about these or any other aspects of the characters, and

Publisher
Knopf, 1982

ISBN
0394849884

TC Level
10

176

A Field Guide to the Classroom Library, Lucy Calkins and the Teachers College Reading and Writing Project, Heinemann, ©2002 Teachers College, Columbia University; http://www.heinemann.com/fieldguides

continue reading to see whether or not the evidence supports it.

Book Connections

Skinnybones is similar to *How to Eat Fried Worms* and *How to Fight a Girl* because of the similar antagonism between the characters. Barbara Park has also written the *Junie B. Jones* series.

Genre
Chapter Book

Teaching Uses
Independent Reading; Character Study

A Field Guide to the Classroom Library, Lucy Calkins and the Teachers College Reading and Writing Project, Heinemann, ©2002 Teachers College, Columbia University; http://www.heinemann.com/fieldguides

Slake's Limbo
Felice Hoffman

Book Summary

Aremis Slake "was born an orphan at the age of thirteen, small, dreaming, bruised, an outlander in the city of his birth (and in the world)." He sleeps on a cot in a kitchen overlooking the NYC subway tracks and he goes to school hungry. After a truck hits Slake's only friend, he has no one in the world; he has never known kindness from family, friends or peers.

One day, when a gang of bullies chases Slake, he escapes into a subway tunnel. There, he stays for 121 days, in limbo. Here, he never has to face his fears of the outside world. Slake makes his very first "home" in a hole blasted in one of the underground subway tunnels. He makes his living by selling found newspapers and gets meals from a job sweeping floors in a coffee shop in Grand Central Station. In his new life underground, Slake experiences his first sense of home, freedom from bullies, and the feeling of being satiated. He also learns about the kindness of strangers, like the coffee shop waitress who sneaks extra food into his bag lunches and the old woman he sells papers to who gives him clothing.

When Slake is finally faced with having to leave the subway when his tunnel is slated for construction, he becomes terribly ill. He is rescued from death when another stranger, a subway motorman, finds him. After Slake leaves the hospital, he thinks about where he is headed next, upwards perhaps-a rooftop?

Basic Book Information

Felice Hoffman is also the author of *The Escape of the Giant Hogstalk* and *I Hear Your Smiling*. Hoffman has written many poems for young readers including *The Future of Hopper Toote* and *The Cricket Winner*. *Slake's Limbo* is an ALA Notable Book, a YASD Best Book for Young Adults and the winner of the Lewis Carroll Shelf Award.

Noteworthy Features

The most notable feature of this book is that it is made up of two parallel stories. The book is split up into numbered chapters that follow Slake's experience living underground in the subway. And the book also contains chapters interspersed throughout the book entitled "On Another Track." These chapters are very brief (one to two pages in length) and give an ongoing personal history of the motorman that rescues Slake. The two stories are distinct from one another. This is illustrated by not only the different chapter headings ("On Another Track" versus numbering) but also a difference in font style. Not until the motorman finds Slake in the subway, at the end of the story, does the reader know that the two personal stories have any true connection.

Publisher
Scholastic Inc., 1974

ISBN
0590455885

TC Level
12

A Field Guide to the Classroom Library, Lucy Calkins and the Teachers College Reading and Writing Project, Heinemann, ©2002 Teachers College, Columbia University; http://www.heinemann.com/fieldguides

The book is a poetic one, filled with metaphors, imagery, and beautiful words. Hoffman's background as a poet is evident in lines such as "Slake knew his life was some persistent weed that grew in gravel, in broken sidewalks, in fetid alleys. ..."

The cover illustration warrants some discussion. There is a lot of description throughout the book that portrays Slake as a thin weakling and an outsider. There are also physical descriptions that suggest he is an African American. Yet, the cover illustration shows a light-skinned robust boy with pink cheeks. Some readers may find it difficult to align the two different images painted of Slake: one painted by the author's words and another by the illustrator's pencil. This often inspires hearty conversation.

Teaching Ideas

In a read aloud, the connections between the "On Another Track" chapters and the numbered chapters could generate wonderful book talks. If a solitary reader encounters this format on his or her own, it will probably cause some confusion and lead the reader to do good problem-solving work. What's going on? Why does the book seam to lurch about? If readers *don't* seem confused they may not be reading closely enough to realize the author has written the text in a complex way that makes us pause. There is no indication that the stories are at all connected in the beginning; the personal narrative of the motorman is truly "On Another Track" from Slake's. Readers, either in partnerships or individually, might at first think the stories have no connection but hopefully they'll begin to suspect that Hoffman probably has something in mind and they may note places in the text that support how the two tracks begin to merge and finally cross.

Teachers may want to use this book to teach readers about the way authors often foreshadow what is to come. There are elements in the "On Another Track" entries that foreshadow that the two stories are parallel and will eventually be connected (i.e., their two lives are both spent in the subway, they are both trying to escape from the drudgery of their lives). Foreshadowing can also be the focus of a writing workshop. Writers can learn to use devices like this to create a sense of suspense for their readers.

The "On Another Track" chapters are not the only places in the text that nudge readers to infer. Even skilled readers will find that they have to do a lot of inferring and rechecking of the text. Hoffman's use of metaphors, sophisticated sentence structure, and difficult vocabulary extends throughout the course of the book. The book does not supply very concrete descriptions or information. For instance, it is left to the reader's discretion whether or not Slake is a true orphan. Also, in introducing the protagonist, Hoffman writes "... for the purpose of this chronicle of events, it is simplest and most practical and even sufficient to believe that Slake was born an orphan at the age of thirteen. . . . In other ways he was not so different from the rest of the young raised with house keys around their necks, rearing themselves in the litter-strewn streets."

Hoffman skillfully captures the essence of her characters without supplying too many details. She leaves gaps in her text. She creates a sketch and lets her reader's mind fill in the details. Readers might want to consider ways in which this book is poetic, since a poet wrote it. Children may want to mark sections in which they encounter metaphors such as "On Another

Track" and then their interpretations of what they think the metaphors represent.

One of the prevailing metaphors in *Slake's Limbo* is that of the bird. This is not a real bird (children who are not accustomed to reading figurative language may be confused). At the beginning of the book, Slake has a dream of a bird that flies into his stomach and pecks away at him from the inside. The bird chokes Slake and screams when he is hungry or in danger. Finally, when Slake leaves the hospital, the bird flies away in freedom. Readers may notice how her deliberate use of metaphor provides a window into her characters. Why does she use this image of a bird to tell her readers more about Slake? Children can reference the places in the text when the bird image appears and note why on Post-It Notes.

The book also has many references to the New York City subway and locations that will be refreshing to urban readers who are often reading books situated in rural or suburban settings. It will also be helpful for suburban/rural readers who will benefit from the window this gives to another world.

Hoffman actually makes life in the subway seem like something with merit and beauty. Readers can explore why this underground world with a "green sky" may have been a better alternative for Slake than the real world. She creates a vision of a magical underground world. It will make readers wonder every time they step out onto a subway platform, what lurks in its "passages to everywhere."

Book Connections

Fly Away Home, by Eve Bunting, is a story about a father and son who live in an airport. Felice Hoffman is also the author of *The Escape of the Giant Hogstalk* and *I Hear Your Smiling*. Hoffman has written many poems for young readers including *The Future of Hopper Toote* and *The Cricket Winner*.

Genre
Chapter Book

Teaching Uses
Independent Reading; Language Conventions; Read Aloud

A Field Guide to the Classroom Library, Lucy Calkins and the Teachers College Reading and Writing Project, Heinemann, ©2002 Teachers College, Columbia University; http://www.heinemann.com/fieldguides

Stealing Home - The Story of Jackie Robinson

Barry Denenberg

Book Summary

Stealing Home - The Story of Jackie Robinson is the biography of Jackie Robinson, the first black man to play major league baseball. The story recounts Robinson's humble beginnings in California, where his athletic prowess was evident at an early age. At UCLA, he became the first athlete in university history to earn major letters in four different sports during one year.

When Branch Rickey, General Manager of the Brooklyn Dodgers, decided that the time had come to integrate major league baseball, his decision to pick Robinson was not solely based on his impressive athletic skill. Rickey knew that it would take a special man, "he was equally concerned about the player's personality, background, intelligence, and desire to succeed. ...Rickey also needed someone with enough drive and determination to manage to hold[ED: ok?] his head up high despite the abuse." Jackie Robinson was his man. The book recounts the abuse that Robinson had to contend with both on and off the field. His talent and drive made him a trailblazer, who successfully integrated America's favorite past time. At Jackie Robinson's funeral, Jessie Jackson said, "When Jackie Robinson took the field he reminded us of our birthright to be free."

Basic Book Information

Stealing Home - The Story of Jackie Robinson is a Nonfiction, biographical account of

Jackie Robinson's life. The book contains black and white photographs. Barry Denenberg is an award-winning author of other Nonfiction books for children including: *An American Hero: The True Story of Charles A. Lindberg*, *Voices from Vietnam* and *The True Story of J. Edgar Hoover and the FBI*.

Noteworthy Features

Every chapter contains pictures from Jackie Robinson's life. The photographs help readers picture what Robinson looked like during the period of his life the chapter is discussing. Oftentimes, the pictures depict significant events that the author is writing about on a nearby page. For example, there is a photograph of Branch Rickey and Jackie Robinson signing the contract, which broke the color barrier in major league baseball in the same chapter that discusses that landmark event.

The dialogue throughout the book is very sparse. For the most part, the

A Field Guide to the Classroom Library, Lucy Calkins and the Teachers College Reading and Writing Project, Heinemann, ©2002 Teachers College, Columbia University; http://www.heinemann.com/fieldguides

Publisher
Scholastic Inc., 1990

ISBN
0590425609

TC Level
11; 12; 13

narrator describes the events of Robinson's life. In his narration of events, the author provides a lot of detail. He often cites names, titles and dates. The abundance of information contained in this book may be overwhelming for some readers. They may find it difficult to retain the details of the story throughout their reading of the 116-page biography.

Children who are not sports' enthusiasts may still enjoy this biography. Jackie Robinson's story is significant to the civil rights movement and American history. There are however, some reference to sports that children may not understand if they are not well-versed on the topic.

Many readers will be shocked by the abusive language and behaviors that Robinson was forced to endure. When Jackie Robinson first begins to play with the Dodgers, he is insulted with names like "nigger," "coon," and "darkie." The Phillies "shouted from the dugout, asking him why he wasn't home cleaning out bathrooms or picking cotton." Children may need to process these upsetting image by talking with their peers or a teacher.

Teaching Ideas

Stealing Home - The Story of Jackie Robinson contains a lot of information about Jackie Robinson's life. Readers who feel that they have to digest all of the details of the story may find a biography such as this overwhelming. It is important for readers to realize that they do not have to remember every piece of information. The story happens in chronological order from birth to death. The dates are not meant to be memorized necessarily, but instead to give readers a general idea of the progression of Robinson's life. Readers who have a hard time doing mental math to figure out his age from the dates can rely on the pictures for support.

In *Stealing Home* the narrator sometimes lets you know what Jackie Robinson was thinking at a specific moment-"Although Jackie appeared calm, he was nervous inside." Readers may wonder how the author could have known such a thing. It is important to realize that biographies are not always strictly factual. Readers may realize that there are times throughout the book when the narrator states things that he could not have gathered from traditional research. A teacher might nudge readers-individually or in partnerships-readers may want to use post-it notes to mark places in the text that deviate from "just the facts." It may be interesting for readers to speculate how the author could gain such information, i.e. is it fictional? Did he interview Robinson? and so on.

Some readers may be surprised at the widespread discrimination and abuse that most black Americans faced less than fifty years ago. For children who do not know about this period of American history, it is important for them to know that the book is historically accurate and that they are not reading a fictional account of someone's life.

Jackie Robinson not only endured prejudice from the white community, but from the Negro American League, too. "It would ruin their (the Negro league's) business" if the major league was integrated. In addition, many whites were against the integration of major league ball for economic reasons. When white major league teams were out of town, the stadium owner rented the space to black teams. The Yankees alone brought in $100,000 in revenue from stadium rental to the Negro league. It is important for readers to realize that not all whites were negative (i.e.,

Branch Rickey was a major crusader for civil rights) and that not all blacks were positive. Also, readers may want to attach post-it notes to all of the forces at work against the integration of baseball to begin to understand the complexity of the situation. The post-it notes can help them go back to those bits of information to think about some more.

Many readers may be surprised to learn that Rickie chose Jackie Robinson for characteristics other than solely his athletic ability. During the course of a character study, a reader may be interested in marking and discussing passages in which Robinson displays these other characteristics.

Book Connections

It may be interesting to read other accounts of Jackie Robinson's life for comparative purposes. Readers may notice that authors tend to focus on different aspects of Jackie Robinson's life or certain biases. Also, they may begin to notice that there is sometimes a discrepancy in the way facts and events are recorded. Reading biographies from different authors may also begin to give readers a more complete picture of Robinson's life.

This book could become part of a child's personal reading project on sports (or even baseball) and race. Alfred Slote's books about the Negro Leagues belong in such a text-set as does *Baseball Saved Us* by Ken Mochizoki and the anthologies about sports players.

Genre
Nonfiction; Biography

Teaching Uses
Reading and Writing Nonfiction; Content Area Study; Independent Reading; Character Study

A Field Guide to the Classroom Library, Lucy Calkins and the Teachers College Reading and Writing Project, Heinemann, ©2002 Teachers College, Columbia University; http://www.heinemann.com/fieldguides

Stone Fox

John Reynolds Gardiner

Book Summary

Little Willy and his grandfather live together on a potato farm. When his grandfather falls ill from depression, little Willy has to save the farm.

The bond between little Willy and his dog, Searchlight, is a strong one. So strong that the dog helps to harvest the potato crop by becoming Willy's plow-dog. Thinking the harvest is the root of grandpa's depression, little Willy finds out he is wrong.

When the tax collector comes, little Willy understands that grandpa will not get better until the taxes are paid and the farm is saved. Little Willy finds a way to earn the money by entering a race with the help of Searchlight.

Stone Fox, the great Indian racer, with his five beautiful Samoyed dogs, becomes Willy's main competitor. Stone Fox is a legend in the state of Wyoming. He never speaks to the "white man" because of the treatment his people suffer, and he never loses a race.

The race is a hard one, but Searchlight gives his heart and soul to win. One hundred feet from the finish line, Searchlight's heart gives out and he dies. Stone Fox allows little Willy to carry his beloved Searchlight over the finish line to win the race.

Basic Book Information

The book contains 81 pages, divided into ten chapters. The illustrations look like charcoal drawings, adding to the rustic setting of the Wyoming landscape described in the text.

Noteworthy Features

The elements of story are well developed through the themes of person versus nature and person versus person. The changes in the story are the results of conflicts and resolutions. The plot or structure of the text supports the main message.

The illustrations, which look like charcoal sketches, enhance the image of the rustic setting. This encourages the students to inquire about how the illustrations highlight the central themes of this book.

When students read this book on their own, they sometimes miss the fact that beloved Searchlight dies at the very end of the book-it all happens so suddenly that sometimes readers are caught up in the excitement of the race and read right past the ending.

Teaching Ideas

Stone Fox is an excellent and powerful book to read aloud. The problems in each chapter are real-a grandfather too depressed to get out of bed and help

Illustrator
Marcia Sewall

Publisher
Harper Trophy, 1988

ISBN
0064401324

TC Level
11

A Field Guide to the Classroom Library, Lucy Calkins and the Teachers College Reading and Writing Project, Heinemann, ©2002 Teachers College, Columbia University; http://www.heinemann.com/fieldguides

pay the bills, mounting debt a young boy must deal with on his own, preparing for a physical challenge, and finally the loss of a true friend, Willy's dog. Many readers cry and nearly all feel touched forever at the end of the story. For this reason, reading this book aloud brings a community of students together as a class. This bonding can also happen when a book club chooses to read this book together.

Character studies on this book can be fruitful. The silent Stone Fox, Willy's grandfather, and Willy himself all have complexities to their character unusual for a book written as simply as this one. Readers will learn a lot in unearthing the depth in these characters.

Book Connections

Jack London's *Call of the Wild* and *White Fang* are on similar topics, person versus nature, and take place in similar settings, although both are at a much higher reading level. Stanford's *The Bravest Dog: The True Story of Balto* deals with a hero dog who risks his life to save his team from falling into icy water while carrying an antitoxin in the 1925 diphtheria epidemic in Nome, Alaska. Gary Paulsen's *Winterdance*, detailing the fine madness of the running of the Iditarod, *Woodsong*, and *Dogsong*, are three books with related themes.

Genre
Short Chapter Book

Teaching Uses
Independent Reading; Book Clubs; Partnerships; Read Aloud

A Field Guide to the Classroom Library, Lucy Calkins and the Teachers College Reading and Writing Project, Heinemann, ©2002 Teachers College, Columbia University; http://www.heinemann.com/fieldguides

The Best Christmas Pageant Ever

Barbara Robinson

Book Summary

This uproariously funny story is a splendid read aloud and an equally satisfying book for independent readers. When Mrs. George Armstrong breaks her leg, another mother (whose daughter narrates the story) reluctantly replaces her as the director of the children's Christmas pageant. The pageant has always been a predictable event-the same script, the same costumes, and the same two children playing Mary and Joseph. This time, however, the Herdmans get involved. The six Herdman children (Ralph, Imogene, Leroy, Claude, Ollie, and Gladys) have regularly terrorized kids in school. Now, having heard that desserts are served in Sunday school, they show up at church and decide they want to participate in the pageant.

Fearing Herdman wrath, the other children let the Herdmans take over all the major roles: Mary, Joseph, the three wise men, and the Angel of the Lord. Mrs. Armstrong is appalled, and her criticism angers the woman who has replaced her. She vows to make this the best Christmas pageant ever, complete with the Herdman children. As expected, the Herdmans turn rehearsals upside down, in part because they have no idea what the Christmas story is about. They ask amusing questions (what were the wadded-up clothes Mary wrapped the baby in?) and offer blunt comments (the wise men should tell the innkeeper where to get off and get the baby out of the barn).

At first, Alice Wendleken, the prissy girl who previously has played Mary, finds fault with everything the Herdmans do. But the Herdmans' insistence on using ordinary language to discuss the details of the Christmas story gradually leads other children to see the story in a fresh and meaningful way. After a disastrous (and funny) final rehearsal, the night of the pageant arrives. The Herdmans' unorthodox performance casts a new light on the Christmas holiday and leads to general agreement that this was, indeed, the best Christmas pageant ever.

Basic Book Information

The paperback version of the book is 80 pages long. The story is divided into 7 numbered chapters and includes 7 amusing, black-and-white illustrations. The narrative is structured in past tense and moves forward chronologically, but the narrator seems very close to events, almost as if they were unfolding as she relates them. Although the story involves Christmas, it has appeal for people who do not celebrate Christmas as well as for those who do.

Noteworthy Features

The first-person narrator is a classmate of Imogene Herdman and Alice

Illustrator
Judith Gwyn Brown

Publisher
Harper Trophy, 1998

ISBN
0064402754

Wendleken. The narrator appears to be a fifth grader, and the spoken language with which she tells the story is accessible to young readers. Although the narrator's name is never mentioned, her personality comes through strongly in the wry account she offers. For example, as pageant roles are being assigned, she says: "There was one Herdman left over, and one main role left over, and you didn't have to be very smart to figure out that Gladys was going to be the Angel of the Lord." When her mother tells Gladys that the Angel brought the good news to the shepherds, the narrator observes, "Right away all the shepherds began to wiggle around in their seats, figuring that any good news Gladys brought them would come with a smack in the teeth." The concluding episode, when the Herdmans take the Christmas pageant quite seriously, is managed with an effective shift in tone. The sweet ending of the story proves as memorable as the opening.

Teaching Ideas

This book makes a spectacular read aloud, one that can pull the classroom community together in shared laughter. For the book to work magic in a classroom, however, it is important to also honor books that focus on non-Christian holidays. Teachers should be sensitive to any guidelines in their school regarding the use of fiction built around a specific religion.

Expressed in an abstract way, one premise of the book is the fact that the language used to celebrate traditional cultural events is often so formal in tone that it is inaccessible to some, and may even blur historical reality. In Chapters 5 and 6, the Herdmans disrupt pageant rehearsals with questions and comments about the Gospel story. Students can follow the Herdmans' growing understanding of the holiday. How do those explanations change the way children perceive the Gospel story? Teachers can also ask children to share examples of texts read during their own holidays and festivals. Then they can discuss what "ordinary" truths underlie the formal language.

Characterization is central to this book, making it a text with which to do character studies. It is interesting to note that the author includes few details regarding the appearance of the Herdmans or Alice Wendleken. Instead, she brings these characters to life by describing their actions. Independent readers or book clubs may choose to focus on a particular Herdman, and learn about his or her character through what the text states, what the text leads readers to infer, and the response the character evokes from interactions with other characters. During a read aloud, students can turn and talk to partners about the same matters.

Readers might also wish to question the text and consider the author's decisions about point of view. Why did Barbara Robinson make this a first-person story? Who is the narrator? Why is she in a good position to tell the story? Perceptive readers will notice that narrator contributes little to the action-she simply tells what she observes-but the way she presents her observations frequently adds to the humor. For example, she notes that the Herdmans arrived ten minutes late for the first pageant rehearsal, "Sliding into the room like a bunch of outlaws about to shoot up a saloon." Children can look for other examples of colorful comments from the narrator.

A Field Guide to the Classroom Library, Lucy Calkins and the Teachers College Reading and Writing Project, Heinemann, ©2002 Teachers College, Columbia University; http://www.heinemann.com/fieldguides

Book Connections

Another book with a similarly touching and humorous pageant scene is *Ramona and Her Father*, by Beverly Cleary. Barbara Robinson brings the Herdman children-wildness and all-back for the sequel, *The Best School Year Ever*.

Genre
Short Chapter Book

Teaching Uses
Character Study; Independent Reading; Read Aloud

A Field Guide to the Classroom Library, Lucy Calkins and the Teachers College Reading and Writing Project, Heinemann, ©2002 Teachers College, Columbia University; http://www.heinemann.com/fieldguides

The BFG
Roald Dahl

Book Summary

Sophie, an 8-year-old orphan, is kidnapped by the BFG (Big Friendly Giant). The BFG takes Sophie to the land of giants where there are other giants that are mean and love to eat human beans (human beings) especially kids. Sophie and the BFG work together to end the nasty unkind deeds of the other giants. How do Sophie and the BFG solve the problem? You'll have to read this humorous fantasy to find out. And as an after thought, who really wrote this book?

Basic Book Information

The BFG is one of the many humorous fantasy books written by Welsh writer Roald Dahl. The 23 chapters are short and the story is fast moving. The length of the book is 208 pages. There is a short summary and author biography on the first page followed by a list of characters, humans and giants. Roald Dahl has written many other books such as *Charlie and The Chocolate Factory, James and The Giant Peach, George's Marvelous Medicine, The Witches*, and many more. Five of Dahl's books, *The Witches, James and the Giant Peach, Matilda, Charlie and The Chocolate Factory (Willy Wonka and The Chocolate Factory)*, and *Danny, The Champion of The World* have been made into films. Dahl has received a number of literary awards. In 1954, 1959, and 1980 he received the Edgar Allan Poe Award. In 1982 he won an award for *The BFG* and in 1983 he received the Whitbread award. He also won The World Fantasy Convention Lifetime Achievement award in 1983.

The illustrations by Quentin Blake are simple and cartoon like. Blake was the first Children's Laureate in Britain in 1999. Quentin Blake has illustrated some of Dahl's other books and has also authored many books.

Noteworthy Features

There are words mispronounced by the BFG, like "human beans" (human beings). This is because the BFG has tried his best to learn to speak on his own. He has no mother and there aren't any schools in giant land. "Words," he said, " is oh such a twitch-tickling problem to me all my life. So you must simply try to be patient and stop squibbling. As I am telling you before, I know exactly what words I am wanting to say, but somehow or other they is always getting *squiff-squiddled* around." There are also many nonsense words in the giant's vocabulary such as *cannybull, elefunt, cattlepiddlers*, and *scrumdiddlyumptious*. Students are challenged to sound out these nonsense words and use reading strategies to figure out what the word means. Then, too, some words have a British spelling (for example, *flavours* for *flavors*).

A Field Guide to the Classroom Library, Lucy Calkins and the Teachers College Reading and Writing Project, Heinemann, ©2002 Teachers College, Columbia University; http://www.heinemann.com/fieldguides

Illustrator
Quentin Blake

Publisher
Puffin Books, 1982

ISBN
0140315977

TC Level
11

Teaching Ideas

A teacher wanting to give a very brief introduction to this book might say, "*The BFG* is a fantasy story about an eight year old girl named Sophie that is kidnapped by a big friendly giant, hence the acronym BFG. He takes her to Giant Land where other giants reside who are mean and nasty. They love to eat people all over the world. This is the problem that the BFG and Sophie set out to end. In the story you will meet the Queen of England and her staff (footman, butler, guards, etc.). She lives in the palace by Hyde Park, a famous park in London. There is a list of characters at the start of the book. There are also many words that you will be unfamiliar with. Some are nonsense words and others are words with a British spelling (*flavours* for *flavors*). You will have to rely on reading strategies to figure out their meanings and pronunciations."

It would be helpful for students to be paired with another student reading the same book. Partners could retell parts of the story giving details to show they have a real sense of what the text holds.

The BFG is full of vivid descriptive language that "paints a picture in your mind." Readers may use post-it notes and talk about sections that "paint a picture in their minds." Roald Dahl also uses similes. One example is on page 88 when he writes that "they were snoring like foghorns" and on page 131, he writes, "he swiveled his huge right ear until it was like a great shell facing the heavens." Readers might want to pay special attention to Sophie and the BFG noting their character traits. How does their friendship compare to other literary friendships?

The nonsense books can give children opportunities to work with large, complex words without any pressure. There isn't the same sense of right and wrong if a child is trying to read a nonsense word.

Readers may also inquire into why the font changes into italics in particular places. How does this support the meaning of the text?

Readers may or may not notice the reference to "Jack and the Beanstalk" but this is worth noticing because it's a simple, early form of literary allusion.

Book Connections

Roald Dahl has written many books. Some of his chapter books are *The Witches, Charlie and The Chocolate Factory, James and The Giant Peach*, and many more. He has also written some picture books-*The Enormous Crocodile, Revolting Rhymes, Dirty Beasts,* and *The Giraffe and The Pelly and Me.* Dahl has written a memoir of his childhood in Wales titled, *Boy.* British illustrator Quentin Blake has illustrated many of Dahl's books and also books for other authors. He has written *Clown,* a book entirely of pictures. This is a good opportunity for students to create their own story. Blake also authored *Zagazoo* and *Mrs. Armitage and The Big Wave* among others. If a student likes *The BFG* and is a good reader he or she might enjoy reading the *Harry Potter* books by British author J.K. Rowling.

Genre
Fantasy; Short Chapter Book

Teaching Uses
Independent Reading; Language Conventions

The Chalk Box Kid

Clyde Robert Bulla

Book Summary

Gregory moves to a new neighborhood on his ninth birthday. The new house is in an older section of town and does not have a yard. He has to share his new room with his uncle and has problems being accepted at his new school. Gregory consoles himself by drawing on a wall blackened by fire in his neighborhood. In school the class is given seeds to plant a garden. Gregory cannot plant seeds in his yard so he draws a garden on the wall. At first people doubt his claim that he has a garden, but when they see the wall, everyone is impressed by his "garden" and he is accepted by his new classmates.

Basic Book Information

The text spans 58 pages and is divided into 9 chapters with supportive titles that clue the reader into what the chapter will be about, such as "The New School" or "The Burned Building." Black-and-white pictures appear every few pages and support the written text on the page. The sentences are simple and not too long. The dialogue is clearly referenced and on separate lines. Time flows chronologically.

Noteworthy Features

Readers may have difficulty understanding the beginning of the story because it is written in the past perfect tense: "He had wanted to go with Mother and Daddy. They were moving to another house, and he hadn't even seen it yet." The tense then changes to the simple past and remains in this tense throughout the rest of the book: "The house was small and it needed paint.... There was no yard at all." Although the story is told in a straightforward way and does not require much inference, the ending is inconclusive. Children sometimes say, "Is that the end?" as it occurs in the middle of an unresolved conversation with Gregory's new friend. Although the text is written simply, there is a serious theme: how the character copes with disappointment and rejection by creating art.

Teaching Ideas

Readers of this book tend to spend a lot of time making personal connections to Gregory's situation. Being new, being placed in a disappointing situation, and finding acceptance are themes that many children readily relate to. Many teachers encourage their readers to develop these connections beyond the "me too" statements many readers make at this level. Having students develop the reasoning behind the similarities and differences they see with Gregory can deepen and build their personal

Illustrator
Thomas B. Allen

Publisher
Scholastic, 1987

ISBN
0590485237

TC Level
9

A Field Guide to the Classroom Library, Lucy Calkins and the Teachers College Reading and Writing Project, Heinemann, ©2002 Teachers College, Columbia University; http://www.heinemann.com/fieldguides

response.

Because *The Chalk Box Kid* combines readability with a meaningful story, teachers may use this book for character study, theme work or read aloud with students of any age. The text is accessible enough for partner and or independent reading with newly fluent readers. This book is well written and offers the opportunity for young readers to experience the qualities of good writing and a universal theme.

Book Connections

Paint Brush Kid is the sequel to this book. Bulla also wrote the popular *Shoeshine Girl*, which also deals with the theme of a child finding a place in a new situation.

Genre
Short Chapter Book

Teaching Uses
Read Aloud; Independent Reading; Character Study

The Chocolate Touch

Patrick Skene Catling

Book Summary

The Chocolate Touch is a story about a well-behaved boy named John who has one major fault. He loves candy more than anything else in the world. His parents are constantly trying to get him to eat right and to think of how his actions may affect others. John doesn't listen.

Then, one day, John finds a strange-looking coin with his initials on it. He ends up in a candy store he's never seen before and buys a huge box of chocolates. To his dismay, there is only one little piece of chocolate in the box, but unlike any chocolate he's ever tasted before.

After John eats the chocolate, his whole life changes. Everything he put into his mouth turns into chocolate. At first, John is ecstatic, but he soon realizes that his life and the lives of the people around him will never be the same. John learns that there are more important things in life than candy. He realizes that his actions do affect other people and he becomes less selfish and more aware of other people's feelings.

Basic Book Information

This book is 87 pages long, and divided into twelve chapters. The chapters are not titled, but there are illustrations and numbers on the pages beginning each new chapter. The story is told in the third-person narrative.

Noteworthy Features

This book nudges reader to think because the author asks open-ended questions throughout the text. Also, the use of simple language and third-person narrative helps to lead the students to understand the changes occurring in John's personality. The text contains a lot of dialogue. The author writes in such a way that images of the text will float through student's minds as they read. For example, "the refreshing taste of cold, creamy milk," and " the bacon had been hot, crisp, and oily," can bring students to imagine tasting what they're reading.

Teaching Ideas

A teacher who confers with a child who is reading this book may want to ask the reader to talk about his theories about John. "Sometimes I pause when I'm reading to think whether the main character is changing," the teacher might say. "Is John changing?" The reader will probably respond yes. In the beginning, when everything that John puts into his mouth turns into chocolate, he is very happy. As the day goes on, John begins to realize that having chocolate all the time isn't as wonderful as he thought. His ordinary life is being affected and the "chocolate" is becoming a big problem.

Publisher
Bantam Doubleday Dell, 1996

ISBN
0440412897

TC Level
5

A Field Guide to the Classroom Library, Lucy Calkins and the Teachers College Reading and Writing Project, Heinemann, ©2002 Teachers College, Columbia University; http://www.heinemann.com/fieldguides

Finally, when he kisses his mother on the cheek and she turns into chocolate, the change is complete. John is distraught and finally blames himself for being selfish. He realizes that there are more important things than chocolate. Students could be encouraged to recognize the events that cause changes in his character. Talking about these events will lead to a deeper understanding of John's character, as well as his feelings during each of these events.

This book also provides opportunities through book talks for students to bring their feelings and prior knowledge to conversations. Some readers may talk about their own eating habits. Do they eat a lot of candy? Are there behaviors that they have that might be making someone else in their life unhappy? How would they react if suddenly everything they ate turned into chocolate? Some examples of questions students have generated:

Why did the coin John found have his initials on it?

Why did the candy store where he bought the big box of chocolate suddenly disappear?

Where did it go? Was it real?

Why did it hurt John's mother that he only ate candy?

Why was John miserable when he finally had the thing he loved the most (chocolate) all the time?

It was strange how the two times John went to the candy store and talked to the storekeeper, his father was missing. Was it magic or did his father have something to do with it?

All of these topics could lead to incredible conversations and a deeper understanding of the book.

Genre
Chapter Book

Teaching Uses
Book Clubs; Character Study; Independent Reading

A Field Guide to the Classroom Library, Lucy Calkins and the Teachers College Reading and Writing Project, Heinemann, ©2002 Teachers College, Columbia University; http://www.heinemann.com/fieldguides

The Door in the Wall
Marguerite de Angeli

Book Summary

In *The Door in the Wall,* Robin, the son of a nobleman, is about to leave home and learn the ways of knighthood when he is stricken by a crippling illness. The servants leave him, afraid of the plague, and Robin is alone until a monk named Brother Luke takes him in. At the hospice of St. Mark's, Robin gains strength and learns fine woodworking; his new abilities bring him a sense of pride that helps make up for the loss of the use of his legs. When the castle is attacked by the Welsh, it is up to Robin, despite his handicap, to find help and save them all.

Basic Book Information

The Door in the Wall, winner of the Newbery medal, is an historical novel about the Middle Ages.

Noteworthy Features

The Middle Ages are vividly and accurately depicted in this historic novel. The physical surroundings, food, clothing, education, professions, and health of the people of that time are chronicled in detail, thoroughly enough that background information is generally not needed. In one typically informative, economical passage, de Angeli writes that the characters stop "to pray at each wayside cross, just as if they had been on a pilgrimage." This shows readers for whom the word "pilgrimage" is new, that a pilgrimage is a journey that is focused on a Christian religion.

De Angeli has a wonderful feel for dialogue; without making the language overly difficult, she gives readers a taste of the vocabulary and diction of the Middle Ages. In the first chapter, for example, the monk says, "Good eve, my son . . . I have brought thee food, and, cause 'tis Friday, fish."

Robin's physical disability is an obstacle at first, but he learns to accept it and even benefit from it. One theme that this highlights is that disabilities require people to develop *other* abilities. When Robin loses the use of his legs, he can't become a knight, but he does learn woodworking skills he would otherwise have lacked; more importantly, he learns how to work, how to be patient, and how to persist. It is these skills that make it possible for him to slip past the castle's attackers and get help for his countrymen. In fact, Robin takes advantage of the enemy guard's misconception that Robin's handicap makes him harmless. More generally, Robin's achievements teach us that overcoming our obstacles makes us stronger, and that with persistence, we can succeed.

Publisher
Bantam Doubleday Dell, 1949

ISBN
0440402832

TC Level
13

Teaching Ideas

The Door in the Wall is a good choice for group study.

Readers might trace the evolution of the theme of "the door in the wall." They can begin with their initial impression of the title's meaning. In the first chapter, the metaphor is introduced-Brother Luke, the monk, tells Robin that "thou has only to follow the wall far enough and there will be a door in it,"-but the meaning is still unclear. At regular intervals, the metaphor resurfaces. Readers can keep track of each reference and write or talk about how they come to understand it's meaning, and how Robin come to understand it.

Another way of tracing Robin's development, other than through the theme of "a door in the wall," is to make a chart that traces both Robin's attitudes in each chapter and his acquisition of new skills.

A comparison study might be done with the development of the main character, Jimmy, of James Garfield's *Follow My Leader*. Both characters suffer a disability at the start of the book, learn new skills as a result, become independent, and use their skills to help others.

To take advantage of de Angeli's way of incorporating background information, teachers might have students define words or concepts, using the book alone as a reference. Students can collect information and then discuss, for example, a knight's training, the life of a monk, diet, the treatment of children in the Middle Ages, how books were written, or the plague. When reading in small groups, students can increase their comprehension of new information through discussion.

Genre
Historical Fiction; Chapter Book

Teaching Uses
Independent Reading; Content Area Study; Whole Group Instruction; Character Study

A Field Guide to the Classroom Library, Lucy Calkins and the Teachers College Reading and Writing Project, Heinemann, ©2002 Teachers College, Columbia University; http://www.heinemann.com/fieldguides

The Dream Keeper and Other Poems

Langston Hughes

FIELD GUIDE

Book Summary

The Dream Keeper and Other Poems is a collection of poems, written by the poet laureate of Harlem, Langston Hughes, that celebrates hopes, dreams, aspirations, life, and love. This is his only poetry collection specifically meant for younger readers. While it was originally published in 1932, it was re-issued in 1996 with seven additional poems as well as illustrations done by renowned artist, Brian Pinkney to complement the passionate yet sensitive words that Hughes used in his poems.

There is a general theme running throughout this collection, namely that of the importance of dreams and of keeping ones dreams (hopes) alive. The poems are about the universalities that all people struggle for and deal with no matter what their age or race. It is this universality that is so clearly evident in poems such as, "Dreams," "Reasons Why," and "Mother to Son" that makes this collection as worthwhile to share with the children of today as it did sixty years ago.

Basic Book Information

This book contains 68 poems, as well as an introduction by Lee Bennett Hopkins, a personal note by Augusta Baker, and Pinkney's aforementioned illustrations, all spread out over 83 pages. Most of the poems are short, none taking up more than one page in length. The poems are divided into seven sections (The Dream Keeper, Sea Charm, All Dressed Up, Feet, Jesus, Walkers with the Dawn, and the recent add-on, Additional Poems) with each section built around a different theme. One section, All Dressed Up, includes "Note on Blues" to help readers understand this genre of music, which is the base of all the poems in this section.

Noteworthy Features

This collection of poems has some truly outstanding examples of various poetic devices, such as metaphor and simile, personification, and repetition. It also has examples of poetry as song. Several of the poems in the book are well known and readily recognizable: "Dreams," "Poem," "Mother to Son," and "The Negro Speaks of Rivers." The variety of styles found within this text is remarkable; there are poems that are as soft as whispers, others that could be sung out loud as boisterously as any jazz scat or even those that are reverent prayers. All are infused with the voice of Hughes. This is a body of work strongly influenced by the many experiences of Hughes' life as well as the time and place in which it was published (the Harlem Renaissance period). As such, it is an excellent introduction to that period, in which Hughes played a major part; he is often thought of simultaneously when one speaks of this period in the 1920s. Among the many thoughts that this

Illustrator
Brian Pinkney

Publisher
Alfred A. Knopf, 1994

ISBN
0679944214

A Field Guide to the Classroom Library, Lucy Calkins and the Teachers College Reading and Writing Project, Heinemann, ©2002 Teachers College, Columbia University; http://www.heinemann.com/fieldguides

entire collection evokes, the weaving throughout of the theme of dreams come through very clearly. There are many poems that either explicitly contain a variation of the word or relate other aspects that radiate from this concept. It is a wonderful example, overall, of how to develop a body of work around a central premise.

Teaching Ideas

There are many ways to use this book to teach students about both the craft of poetry as well as the reading of it for meaning and expression. As all the poems are relatively short, any of the poems could be used as a short shared text within a minilesson. One string of minilessons might be designed to teach children that readers read poetry differently than we read most prose. We often read a poem over once to get the gist and then reread asking, "What's this about?" One graduate level poetry scholar encourages his students to read a poem asking the questions of who? where? when? and why? Then, too, readers of a poem look at the patterns in a poem. Are words repeated? The form matters too and the question can be, "How does the form support the content?"

Another string of minilessons could be designed to show children that as readers, we often gasp at the way an author has written a text and then return to notice the craft and to give words to what the author has done. As we continue reading we're apt to notice the author using the same technique again (and again). Later when we write, we, too, may try to use the technique.

This collection could also be part of a genre study on reading poetry. Everyone in the class could read some poems together and could then spend independent reading time reading poetry with an eye toward whatever the class noticed in the shared poems. For example, with a shared poem the class could do some work around how one reads a poem aloud (and in our heads). During the independent reading workshop, readers could choose a poem they love, think about its meaning and how they'd want to read it in a way that conveys the meaning, and then during partnership time children could read their poems aloud to each other. If this work continued across days through teacher modeling and partner response, students could gain insight in how changes in intonation, moderation, and pauses affect emphasis and meaning when reading aloud.

For the purpose of reading for comprehension, the use of poetry is an excellent approach as the texts are shorter than what most intermediate students encounter in the usual reading material. However, just because these are poems doesn't mean that there is any less complexity of meaning. For instance, "As I Grew Older" and "Mother to Son" provide richly layered texts to delve into with students (in a strategy or whole class mini-lesson) to discern both meanings and messages.

Readers could notice techniques Hughes uses across poems. For example, the author often uses the first person pronoun, *I*. There is subtle difference in how he uses this between his poems. In "As I Grew Older," Hughes is speaking from what seems to be the vantage point of his older adult self, while in "Mother to Son," *he* refers to the author writing in the voice of a mother giving sage advice to her offspring. In "The Negro Speaks of Rivers," Hughes writes from the point of view of generations of Negroes who have lived and toiled by the great rivers of antiquity and modern times.

Book Connections

In both Emily Dickinson's and Robert Frost's poetry, there are plenty of poems to explore in ways similar to what was discussed with Hughes' poetry. Both Dickinson and Frost have poems that are accessible for intermediate readers, especially the former as most of her work is shorter in length. For more advanced readers and/or to raise the level of students' thinking about poetry, try using some of Walt Whitman's poetry, such as "Oh Captain, My Captain" and "I Hear America Singing." The latter poem is particularly good to use with students to compare with Hughes', which he wrote as a response to Whitman's well-known poem. Watch as the fascinating conversations come about when these two poems are compared side-by-side.

Genre
Poetry

Teaching Uses
Teaching Writing; Read Aloud; Book Clubs; Interpretation

A Field Guide to the Classroom Library, Lucy Calkins and the Teachers College Reading and Writing Project, Heinemann, ©2002 Teachers College, Columbia University; http://www.heinemann.com/fieldguides

The Endless Steppe

Esther Hautzig

Book Summary

The Endless Steppe tells the story of an eight-year-old girl and her family who were arrested by the Russians because they were "capitalists" and were exiled to Siberia for five years. The story begins with Esther Rudomin recalling her final moments of freedom in Poland as an upper-middle class young girl. Her home was equipped with servants; she frequented the opera, ballet, and plays; and she had closets full of tailor-made clothes. All of this changed when Russian troops came in and forced her family out of their home and shipped them off in a cattle car to a desert in Siberia.

In Siberia, Esther and her family work for Russian comrades in the fields and sleep at night in a tiny, fly-ridden hut with thirty-some other Polish Jews. Slowly, the family works their way out of the labor hut, but only to find meager jobs that barely provide enough for them to survive. Here, they live with all different types of Siberians under the worst of conditions (brutal winters, scorching-hot summers, and with scraps of food at most).

Eventually, Esther attends a Russian school and makes friends, and though the conditions do not improve, she makes the best out of it. Five years later, when the war has ended, Esther and her family return to Poland, and another arduous journey begins-that of rebuilding their lives.

Basic Book Information

This is a standard chronological narrative without flashbacks. The narrator relates her life experiences in present tense. Esther rarely includes details about World War II, why it was being fought, who was involved, and so forth, so background research may be a good idea.

Noteworthy Features

The Endless Steppe incorporates many Russian and Jewish words (always in italics), but these words are either explained by Esther or can be understood in their context. Many character names are also Russian or Jewish.

As Esther narrates, she uses sarcasm to add levity to the horrific strain she and her family are under, and she also uses metaphors to begin chapters, but neither are difficult for the reader to understand.

Teaching Ideas

To support readers as they make their way through the text, one approach might be to do a book introduction. It may be valuable to first point out Siberia's location in Russia. Then, a teacher could begin her introduction by asking the students what they know about World War II.

As they read through the book, students will be more able to discuss how

Publisher
Harper Trophy (Harper Collins), 1968

ISBN
006440577X

TC Level
14

and why the Jews were so ruthlessly mistreated and systematically evicted from their homes, put into concentration camps, and so on. Students may also be guided to look at the relationship between prejudice and cruelty.

As they read, students can be asked what remains the same (e.g., Esther's determined personality) and what changes. Readers could mark sections with post-it notes in which Esther refuses to give up. By the end of the story the reader might realize that although what happened to Esther and her family was horrible, Esther remained courageous and strong.

Book Connections

The Diary of a Young Girl by Anne Frank is another great book written by a young girl during World War II, but it uses more difficult vocabulary and might be too challenging for some readers. Yolen's *Devil's Arithmetic* could also be read along side this book, as well as *Number the Stars,* which is much easier to read than *The Endless Steppe.*

Genre
Memoir; Nonfiction

Teaching Uses
Independent Reading; Content Area Study; Character Study; Critique

A Field Guide to the Classroom Library, Lucy Calkins and the Teachers College Reading and Writing Project, Heinemann, ©2002 Teachers College, Columbia University; http://www.heinemann.com/fieldguides

The Family Under the Bridge

Natalie Savage Carlson

Book Summary

Just before Christmas in Paris, a gruff hobo meets up with three homeless children and their mother and comes to care for them over the week described. His growing affection for the children leads him to exchange his carefree and solitary life for a more static one that keeps them all together.

Basic Book Information

This Newbury Honor book is 123 pages long. The nine chapters are untitled and range from twelve to twenty-three pages in length.

Noteworthy Features

The Family Under the Bridge is a classic tale with fairytale elements and a timeless quality. It begins, "Once there was an old hobo...." The setting takes readers to Paris-a kind of new world-and gives a good sense of its atmosphere. The beautiful and informative drawings place the story somewhere in the 1920s to 1940s. Descriptions are detailed enough to keep most readers grounded, though they may have difficulty with unfamiliar place-names.

This chronological narrative should not pose difficulty for most readers. Each chapter usually follows from where the previous chapter left off, or is well established at the outset (e.g., "The day before Christmas...").

The story is written in third person and is closest in point of view to Armand, the hobo. This may initially put-off readers who are used to stories that center on children, but it will provide a good stretch for many children.

The language is lyrical, interesting, and challenging (e.g., "fastidiously," "wheedled," "witless," "twittering," "crypt," and "pilgrimage"). It is not necessary to understand all of the vocabulary as the context often supports comprehension.

Several characters develop during the course of the story. Armand and the children's mother significantly alter their views and their lives, and the children become more resourceful. Armand gives up his rootless life, and the mother changes her attitude toward those she once despised: the homeless and the gypsies.

The story is rich in theme. The notion of family is addressed in various ways-through the depiction of the gypsy encampment and especially through the formation of the new family unit: the mother, the children, and Armand. Throughout the book, the idea that appearances can be deceiving is emphasized; well-dressed people behave badly, while people who appear dishonest prove to be loyal and kind.

A Field Guide to the Classroom Library, Lucy Calkins and the Teachers College Reading and Writing Project, Heinemann, ©2002 Teachers College, Columbia University; http://www.heinemann.com/fieldguides

Illustrator
Garth Williams

Publisher
HarperCollins, 1958

ISBN
0064402509

TC Level
10

Teaching Ideas

As a sort of fairy tale with difficulty vocabulary, *The Family Under the Bridge* makes a good read aloud. This would provide the opportunity for more information about the setting and would allow students to discuss themes and define new terms (e.g., "flying buttresses").

Some good topics of discussion might be homelessness, materialism, and first impressions. Students could investigate how the characters deal with being homeless, what makes something a home, and how their different encampments provide certain elements of home. In terms of discussing materialism, students could look into what the characters in the story (and people in general) feel they want and need, and what makes them happy. Students can consider how first impressions change like they do in the book as Armand alters his first impression of the children, and the mother's rethinks her views about the gypsies.

Students might also discuss how the story is like and unlike a fairy tale: how realistic is it? How realistic is the depiction of homelessness? How realistic is the resolution of the story? This comparison of a book to books that are typical of the genre often leads to fruitful discussions. Why has the author created the differences between this book and what is standard? Why has the author chosen this genre?

Another significant area of inquiry would be the changes in the main characters: Armand, the mother, and the children. Students might track these changes from chapter to chapter with post-it notes, and/or compare their own experiences of undergoing and learning from those difficulties.

Students reading independently may need advance notice of the complicated vocabulary, but can use context to begin the deciphering process. In partnership reading, students can work as a team to address unfamiliar vocabulary.

Genre
Chapter Book; Fairy and Folk Tale

Teaching Uses
Character Study; Independent Reading; Read Aloud; Partnerships

A Field Guide to the Classroom Library, Lucy Calkins and the Teachers College Reading and Writing Project, Heinemann, ©2002 Teachers College, Columbia University; http://www.heinemann.com/fieldguides

The Great Gilly Hopkins

Katherine Paterson

Book Summary

Gilly has been shuttled from one foster home to the next since she was born, and has developed an armor of sarcasm and intimidation to protect her from being hurt repeatedly. This book is about the relationship between Gilly and her most recent foster family and about the loving relationships that eventually alter the way Gilly perceives and reacts to the world. Gilly comes to learn that, even though this foster parent is not the mother of her dreams, she is her family. By the time she realizes this, however, it is too late. She has already written a letter of complaint to her "real" mother (her birth mother), and is forced to leave the family she has grown to love.

But Gilly's birth mother does not live up to Gilly's fantasies either. She abandons the girl again, as she did when Gilly was born, and at the end of the book Gilly is living with her grandmother and writing letters to her foster family.

Although the primary plot line revolves around Gilly's struggles to find a family (as evidenced by her relationships to Trotter, her foster mother, and Courtney, her birth mother), the book is also about Gilly's relationships with several other people. Gilly learns important life lessons through her relationships with these other characters, such as her foster brother, William Ernest. She comes to realize that William is not a "wimp," but is scared because he has been hurt in the past by the people closest to him, just as Gilly has been. This book is about the relationships that allow Gilly to learn, change and grow.

Basic Book Information

This book is 148 pages long, with 15 chapters. The chapters are titled and vary in length from 6 to 18 pages. The chapters are episodic, and their titles foreshadow the events taking place within them. For example, in the chapter entitled "Welcome to Thomson Park," Gilly moves to Thomson Park. Italics set poems and letters apart from the rest of the text. There are no illustrations. The story is told in a first-person narrative, from Gilly's point of view.

Noteworthy Features

The Great Gilly Hopkins lends itself to a study of character, motivation and change. Gilly's actions and words clearly reflect the lessons she is learning on the inside, and thus provide strong textual support for readers' ideas about these changes. Her sarcastic, intimidating manner is easily traced to past experiences, providing a solid springboard for conversations around the reasons behind characters' choices and behaviors. This is an excellent opportunity to discuss the fact that readers can understand and feel

A Field Guide to the Classroom Library, Lucy Calkins and the Teachers College Reading and Writing Project, Heinemann, ©2002 Teachers College, Columbia University; http://www.heinemann.com/fieldguides

Publisher
Harper Trophy, 1978

ISBN
0064402010

TC Level
12

compassion for characters, even when disagreeing with their choices. Because chapter titles foreshadow coming events, they lend themselves nicely to predictions and guesswork.

Gilly uses mildly offensive swear words, such as "dammit" and "hell," and refers to religious practices in less than flattering ways. The erroneous thinking caused by her past experience, or lack of experience, is responsible for the prejudiced attitudes and behaviors she demonstrates toward African American characters. When she first meets Mr. Randolph, Gilly thinks, "I never touched one of these people in all my life." Paterson writes, "It was bad enough having to come to this broken down old school but to be behind . . . to have to appear a fool in front of . . . almost half the class was black." Readers will protest Gilly's behavior and attitudes, rightly calling her racist, but as the story unfolds, Gilly becomes a more sympathetic character, leading readers to reach for explanations for her behavior. In time, Gilly shows signs of changing. "She's softening up," readers will probably say. "She's learning and letting her true feelings out." Readers will want to understand the various factors that contribute to Gilly's transformation, and to see how all elements of the story fit with this central plot line.

Some readers will want to puzzle over the rather complex (and significant) words of a poem recited by Mr. Randolph. Although the poem is clearly connected to Gilly's journey, it is not imperative for students to understand its every nuance. They need not be expected to, and it would take away from the real story to devote an inordinate amount of time to its interpretation. Gilly doesn't fully understand it herself.

Finally, readers will want to understand why Gilly holds so tightly to her fantasy of Courtney, her birth mother. It will be worthwhile for readers to spend some time on Courtney's letter to Gilly. She writes, "My Dearest Galadriel, the agency wrote to me that you had moved. I wish it were to here. All my love, Courtney." Students may come to understand that, although these are the words Gilly wants to hear, they are not supported by her mother's actions. Sometimes it's hard for readers (as it is for Gilly) to understand that when words are just words, unsupported by actions, they may not justify our putting too much trust in them.

Teaching Ideas

This book is so rich that it deserves to be the centerpiece of a daily, whole-class read aloud and book talk. Because the book is rich with literary themes, the book merits intense, teacher-supported conversations.

If the class develops the theory that Gilly is tough, students may be encouraged to stop and write at moments when Gilly's actions or words reflect inner change. For example, someone may claim that Gilly leaves people before they can leave her. Readers can find evidence for this. Paterson writes that the Nevinses "got rid of her. No. She'd got rid of them-the whole stinking place." And later she thinks, "But I can't stay. I might go soft and stupid, too. Like I did at Dixons'. I let her fool me with all that rocking and love talk. I called her Mama and crawled up on her lap when I had to cry . . . but when they moved to Florida, I was put out like the rest of the trash they left behind. I can't go soft-not as long as I'm nobody's real kid. . . ." Readers might also find and write about instances when it seems Gilly is starting to soften.

A Field Guide to the Classroom Library, Lucy Calkins and the Teachers College Reading and Writing Project, Heinemann, ©2002 Teachers College, Columbia University; http://www.heinemann.com/fieldguides

Book Connections

Gilly taps into more than one major literary theme and can be compared to several books along different lines. Texts addressing a search for home and family include *The Music of Dolphins* by Karen Hesse and Jerry Spinelli's *Maniac Magee*. The protagonists in Patricia MacLachlan's *Journey* and *Baby* are also forced to cope with loss and, in the process, ultimately learn to face and accept the truth.

Genre
Chapter Book

Teaching Uses
Book Clubs; Character Study; Independent Reading; Read Aloud

A Field Guide to the Classroom Library, Lucy Calkins and the Teachers College Reading and Writing Project, Heinemann, ©2002 Teachers College, Columbia University; http://www.heinemann.com/fieldguides

The Islander

Cynthia Rylant

Book Summary

While living with his grandfather on an island off British Columbia and dealing with loss and loneliness, ten-year-old Daniel Jennings sends a message in a bottle, and a mermaid appears. The mermaid gives him the gift of a magic key that helps him heal birds. He and his grandfather grow closer as they care for the birds together.

Basic Book Information

Rylant is the author of many favorites such as, *Nursing May*, *Dog Heaven*, and *Henry and Mudge*. This fantasy book is 97 pages long. There is no table of contents but there are 12 chapters that are separated into parts. These are: Part 1, The Mermaid (chapters 1-5), Part 2, The Key (chapters 6-8), Part 3, the Photograph (chapters 9 and 10), and Part 4, The Islander (chapters 11 and 12). The chapters are not titled. All pages have large margins and the text appears in the middle of the page looking rather isolated (like an island). There are illustrations on the pages that separates the parts which are all pictures of seashells, big and small: cockles for part 1, a clam for part 2, a turret for part 3, and 2 shells, a cone, and a periwinkle for part 4. It is important to note that there is a preface.

Noteworthy Features

Readers unfamiliar with the ocean, an island, or even the idea of being alone, may find this book bewildering. It may be difficult for a kid living in the city in an apartment building to know the quietness and beauty of an island and the ocean. Teachers should recognize this and take the time to introduce the setting of this story. One example may be to have students find a quiet place at home and experience it or take a field trip to the ocean.

The setting in this text is strong. Rylant portrays the island as a constant character, which will help the reader feel the pull of the fantasy. Most readers will not have lived on an island miles from the mainland and civilization. The theme of nature is very strong in this book. Daniel and the island are the principal characters and that makes it easy to hold onto. And even though this is a memory, the story is told in an active voice, as if it were happening right now.

Seldom is there dialogue, which helps the island theme, but when it is used, it is powerful. "You're a good boy, David," says Grandfather, which signals a change in their relationship.

The vocabulary used is fairly simple. Places where it could be unfamiliar, like "vibrated" is explained further down the page in context, "the key moved again." Poseidon is also explained in context to all readers.

Publisher
DK Ink, 1998

ISBN
0789424908

TC Level
10

A Field Guide to the Classroom Library, Lucy Calkins and the Teachers College Reading and Writing Project, Heinemann, ©2002 Teachers College, Columbia University; http://www.heinemann.com/fieldguides

Teaching Ideas

Cynthia Rylant designed the layout, illustrated the cover, and wrote this book. The cover is of a cormorant on a rock. The cormorant is a sea bird that hides in the water, coming out only to dry its wings in the sun. It likes to sun on outcroppings of rock in the ocean, preferably surrounded by the sea, like little rock islands. The setting of this book is very important and readers will want to ground themselves with a map. We suggest having an atlas with Canada and British Columbia ready for reference. Notice that Cynthia Rylant now calls the Pacific Northwest home (she grew up in North Carolina and so many of her earlier books are set in the Appalachian mountains like, *When I was Young in the Mountains*). It may be useful to go back and re-read *When I was Young* or *The Relatives Come* or *Missing May* after this, or even read them alongside this book to understand her intent with the setting.

A teacher might want the readers to notice the structure of the book (four parts) with its illustrations. A teacher can begin by talking about the cormorant and wondering about its significance to the book can lead toward investigating the other illustrations. There is much to take note of with this illustration (there are bivalves and univalves among the illustrations, what does that mean?). Why are these shells used and not another?

The story itself is set up by the preface, which explains that this is a record of a memory of a boy named Daniel Jennings looking back ten years or so. This is a fictionalized memoir and finding out or reviewing what a memoir is can be helpful, especially remembering that memoir is all about how one person remembers things, it is told from their singular point of view. Because of this, the book is written in first person point of view with Daniel as the narrator. The story begins ten years in the past and goes chronologically forward. As art 3 (chapter 9) begins, a large chunk of time passes and the boy is now 17.

This is a superb book for a read aloud because of Rylant's eloquence and the mysteriousness of the book and mermaids. Children (and adults too!) are fascinated by mermaids and their folklore. Listening to Rylant's words read aloud is captivating and apt to cause internalization of some of her beautiful language. Because it has a mermaid, it has a fantasy fairy tale-like quality that is enhanced by reading aloud, like a bedtime story.

Genre
Memoir; Fantasy; Chapter Book

Teaching Uses
Author Study; Teaching Writing; Read Aloud; Partnerships

A Field Guide to the Classroom Library, Lucy Calkins and the Teachers College Reading and Writing Project, Heinemann, ©2002 Teachers College, Columbia University; http://www.heinemann.com/fieldguides

The Just Desserts Club

Johanna Hurwitz

Book Summary

If sixth grader Cricket Kaufman is faced with having to eat boring zucchini one more night for dinner she thinks she might go crazy. So, she comes up with an ingenious plan...why not make desserts from them. After reading some cookbooks from the library, she finds that she can make zucchini cookies, brownies, and breads. Cricket's friends have so much fun guessing what the secret ingredient is that they decide to start the Just Desserts Club. The club raises money for the poor with a no-bake sale. Cricket woos a handsome eight-grader with "Be My Honey" cookies. And, the club throws an April Fools' party for their teacher, with such surprising desserts as cakes made with mayonnaise and tomato soup. *The Just Desserts Club* turns out to be a "recipe for a good time" for Cricket and her friends who share a love of cooking and fun.

Basic Book Information

The Just Desserts Club is written by Johanna Hurwitz. She is the author of many young adult books, including *Starting School, Llama in the Library, Faraway Summer,* and *Ever-Clever Elisa.* Johanna Hurwitz has received a number of child-chosen awards for her writing including, the Texas Blue Bonnet Award, the Kentucky Bluegrass Award, and the Garden State Children's Book Award.

Noteworthy Features

The Just Desserts Club is a combination of a traditional chapter book and cookbook. It is divided into a prologue (page xi) and four sections (One, Two, Three, and Four). Each section contains four chapters, which are outlined in a table of contents. It may be somewhat confusing for readers of traditional chapter books that only the first chapter in each of the sections contains the story. The other three chapters at the end of each section are the actual recipes that Cricket makes.

Since the story is interspersed with recipes, it may be difficult for emergent readers to retain a continuous story. In addition, there are big gaps in time between each section. For instance, "One" takes place during summer vacation, "Two" takes place at the beginning of the school year, "Three" takes place in the winter, and "Four" takes place in the spring. Most indications of time are clearly noted in the text, for example, "One December morning...". However, there are parts of the story where the time frame is not as clear. For example, when Cricket starts the school year Hurwitz writes, "Sixth grade was even better than Cricket imagined." Readers must pick up on clues such as this, to know time of the year it is.

The book contains many characters. Cricket, Lucas, Julio, Zoe, and Sara

Illustrator
Karen Dugan

Publisher
William Morrow, 1999

ISBN
0688162665

TC Level
10

Jane are all the Edison-Armstrong students who are part of the Just Desserts Club. There are however, a number of other characters including family members, teachers and other students who are secondary characters. Since the story is only four chapters long, this lengthy list of characters makes it somewhat difficult to keep everyone straight. Readers might have to go back and reread sections of the book where the characters are introduced for clarity.

The illustrations in the book by Karen Dugan provide limited textual support. There is only one illustration in each chapter that contains the story. Most of the illustrations are contained in the recipe chapters. They show the club members cooking and eating their recipes. This gives readers a good sense of what the finished recipes would look like. Also, the illustrations provide readers with a picture of the characters. This may act as a visual aide for helping readers keep track of the many players.

Teaching Ideas

Many children choose in their clubs or partnerships to create some of the dishes outlined in this book. The prologue, "Recipe for a Good Time" provides a good introduction to both the contents of the story and cooking the recipes. It reviews the basics of kid's cooking, that is, "1 parent to oversee use of stove, sharp utensils, and general activities." And, "Recipe for a Good Time" also lets readers know about the essential ingredients to having fun cooking which are "1 part sense of humor. 2 parts sharing."

Readers may have a tendency to skip over the recipes if they are not intending to use them. This may be somewhat problematic, since these are not "traditional" recipes. Hurwitz provides clear depictions of how Cricket and her friends make the recipes and gives you a good idea of how much fun could be had. Hurwitz has directions like "Fool your friends by telling them that this is apple pie!" and "...mix all the topping ingredients in a large bowl. This works best when done with your fingers. ..." It should also be noted that when a cookbook is within the context of a fictional book, it is important to read. The recipes tell a story, too. Readers can infer a lot about characters who uses their fingers to stir a recipe and makes an extra loaf of zucchini bread to "give one to a friend."

Teachers may want to have a discussion around the use of nonfiction reference books such as cookbooks. It could be discussed that sometimes recipes are just looked up in an index or table of contents when someone wants to cook something particular, like brownies. At other times, such as the case with this short cookbook, all the recipes can be read. Later when readers want to make a particular dish they may remember one of Cricket's recipes. Readers can then go back to the book and find all the important details about how to prepare the recipe.

The Just Desserts Club has a lengthy list of characters and much dialogue. It may be important for readers to go back when they are confused and reread character introductions in order to establish the speakers and their relationships. Oftentimes, the author does not say directly who is speaking. For readers who do not have much experience reading books heavy in dialogue, it may be somewhat difficult traversing through this text.

Book Connections

Readers who enjoy this mix of nonfiction cookbook entwined with a fictional story may also delight in *Salsa Stories* by Lulu Delacre. This story has a similar format and will surely delight any reader who takes pleasure in cooking and reading.

Genre
Chapter Book

Teaching Uses
Partnerships; Character Study; Independent Reading; Book Clubs

A Field Guide to the Classroom Library, Lucy Calkins and the Teachers College Reading and Writing Project, Heinemann, ©2002 Teachers College, Columbia University; http://www.heinemann.com/fieldguides

The Lion, the Witch and the Wardrobe

C.S. Lewis

FIELD GUIDE

E **F** **G**

Book Summary

This is Book Two of *The Chronicles of Narnia*, but it is generally regarded as the foundational book in the series because it is here that the reader is introduced to the four children: Lucy, Susan, Edmund, and Peter. Lucy discovers another world on the other side of a magic wardrobe in a friendly professor's house and she and her siblings begin their adventures in Narnia. Lucy's brother Edmund is enchanted by the White Witch, evil ruler of Narnia who has kept the land forever in a winter without Christmas. Together with Aslan, the magic lion, Lucy and her brothers and sister work to free the land and its inhabitants of their enslavement.

Basic Book Information

This book was originally published in 1950 and this edition is its 50th year anniversary. This is a full-color collector's edition, which, interestingly, is the first time that it has appeared with the complete interior illustrations and jacket that Pauline Baynes created for the book in 1950. Some of the illustrations (especially those of Mr. Tumnus) will look familiar to older readers because they have appeared in black and white in previous editions.

About This Series

Unlike many series, it is not necessary to read this series in order. For many years, it was thought that *The Lion, the Witch and the Wardrobe* was the first in the series, not the second. Although the children are introduced in *The Lion, the Witch and Wardrobe*, reading out of order will not have a detrimental effect. Rather, it makes for a more interesting, and sometimes more challenging read. *The Chronicles of Narnia* are considered classics. The United Kingdom thinks so, too, having bestowed the prestigious Carnegie Award in 1956 to the final book in the series, *The Last Battle*.

Noteworthy Features

There is a map of "Narnia and the Surrounding Counties" before the title page and it is worth examining and referring back to as the book is read. An island called "Terebinthia" appears within the Bight of Calormen and some readers may think of *The Bridge to Terebithia* by Katherine Paterson. Indeed, Paterson mentions Narnia as a reference point for both Leslie and Jess when they create their own magical land and it is no coincidence that the names are so similar.

There are seventeen chapters in this 189-page fantasy book, which is sometimes steeped not only in Briticisms, but sayings common to the 1950s.

Series
The Chronicles of Narnia

Illustrator
Pauline Baynes

Publisher
Harper Trophy Edition, 2000

ISBN
0064409422

TC Level
12

The children speak proper English, "Do stop grumbling, Ed," and "Indeed, indeed, you really mustn't," and may seem impenetrable to young readers. Even those who have read *Harry Potter* haven't been exposed to true British colloquialisms because J.K. Rowling created an American version for readers west of the Atlantic. A few students may need help deciphering "wireless," a radio, and "row," a fight, both which appear within the first pages of the book. Probably, though, they can speed over these words without needing to know exactly what they mean.

There is sophisticated vocabulary that readers need to be encouraged to "have a go" with by relying on context clues. Sometimes children will puzzle over words because they've grown up in a modern culture, and are unfamiliar with "marmalade" and "pavilions."

Readers come to meet mythical creatures who often populate fairy tales and fantasy books: centaurs, dryads, dwarves, elves, talking animals, and bewitching witches. Lewis also incorporates some references to the Old Testament as he names the children the Sons of Adam and the Daughters of Eve. C.S. Lewis is a Christian theologian and these books can be read as allegories, with Aslan representing Christ. Unless an adult tells children that deeper meaning, it's doubtful a child will find it on his or her own. The story does not require this interpretation and most readers find abundant meaning and significance in the fantasy story itself.

Teaching Ideas

The Lion, the Witch and the Wardrobe marks another step up into higher-level fantasy for readers. Readers who have read some fairy tales and legends and perhaps fantasy books such as *The Search for Delicious* by Natalie Babbitt will find this background helps them when they turn to *The Chronicles of Narnia*. A genre study of fantasy and how it weaves in elements of other genres could be fascinating to fantasy enthusiasts. Lewis incorporates important features such as the battle between good and evil, enchantment, talking animals, magical powers, delicious foods, and believable characters. His rich portrayal of Lucy, Susan, Peter, and Edmund also affords a character study that could cross over into the other books of the series. Readers could follow Lucy, or any of the other characters, and see how they develop in the future.

There are several rather obvious lines of thinking that a reader might follow when reading this book. Early in the book, Edmund is lured onto the Evil Queen's sleigh by the taste of Turkish Delight, and after that much of the plotline involves the other three children's efforts to rescue their brother from the Queen's power. Many readers read to find out if Edmund is freed, even though he has done some things that could make readers wonder whether he is worth all the risk and effort the other children go through to rescue him. The core plot of this story is not unlike the plot of *The Wizard of Oz*. In both books a cluster of characters journey through an enchanted land en route to their goal. All such journeys have their ups and downs, their internal journeys paralleling the external ones, artifacts that do and don't accompany the travelers, and so on.

One sixth grade book club took on *The Chronicles of Narnia* as a project, and each of the club members studied a particular character (Lucy, Edmund, Peter, or Susan). During one of their meetings, the club was discussing the changes in Edmund. One member of the club said, "In *The Lion, the Witch and the Wardrobe*, Edmund is a weak and greedy boy. He just wants the candy, the 'Turkish Delight,' and to be a prince. He doesn't care about his sisters or brother. That's why Aslan dies, because of Edmund and his dumbness. But, at the end of the book Edmund seems a little different than in the first book." Another club member chimed in, saying, "Yeah, I think so. I think he's sorry. See how he acts, look at this page. . . ." Following this exchange, the club decided to make a chart for Edmund and one for each of the other characters, to follow how, or if, they change through the series.

Indeed, the club discovered that in later books, Edmund develops into a hard-working and wise young man. He has learned through his experience with Aslan's death. Susan, however, is shown to be a virtuous and open-minded character in *The Lion, the Witch and the Wardrobe*, but in later books, her character deteriorates. She becomes selfish and unwilling to use her imagination so as to be a part of the adventures in Narnia.

With the inclusion of the map of Narnia, *The Lion, the Witch and the Wardrobe* becomes part of a growing collection of books that have maps in their frontispieces. All of the *Tales of Dimwood Forest* (by Avi) contain maps, as do Lloyd Alexander books, *The Search for Delicious* (by Natalie Babbitt), the *Oz* books, and the *Redwall* books. A study of these books, which are mostly all fantasy books, could be a rich one. In each of these books, a new world is created. What do these worlds have in common? How does the skilled reader come to envision and care about these worlds and the characters who live in them? A book club or an individual may take on these maps that are present in all the books as a project, patching them together to create the whole world of Narnia. (Students can also undertake this study with the *Redwall* series by Brian Jacques.) While these books are fiction, they utilize many geographical principles that readers and students need to be acquainted with (like physical features such as rivers, mountains, oceans).

Book Connections

See above for many book connections. Edward Eager's *Tales of Magic*, including *Half Magic, Knight's Castle, The Time Garden*, and *Magic by the Lake*, is about siblings who embark on a variety of magical adventures and could be another good companion series to this one.

Genre
Fantasy; Chapter Book

Teaching Uses
Read Aloud; Book Clubs; Independent Reading

The Monument

Gary Paulsen

Book Summary

The Monument is told in the first person by its main character, Rachael Ellen Turner, also knows as Rocky. Rocky is a thirteen-year-old girl who was abandoned as a baby and left in the back seat of a police car. She isn't really sure if Rachael is her real name or just a name the sisters at the orphanage gave her. She has "caramel colored skin, curly tight hair, and a bad leg," which is what she believes kept her from being adopted until she was nine. Then Fred and Emma Hemesvedts agree to adopt her and they bring her to her new home in Bolton, Kansas, the flattest place on earth. There, the lonely Rocky "adopts" a stray dog who becomes her faithful sidekick and protector.

After one of the townsfolk returns from a trip to Washington, D.C., where he was moved by the Vietnam Memorial, he convinces the other townspeople that Bolton should have their own monument honoring their war dead. The job of finding a professional artist to create this monument falls to Mrs. Langdon, the town's unofficial art expert. She hires Mick Strum, whose philosophy and art profoundly affect Rocky and the rest of the town.

Mick helps Rocky to see herself as something much more than an overlooked dark-skinned orphan with a bad leg. Moved by his deeply revealing work and passion for artistic truth, she too decides to become an artist. Under his tutelage and with the full support of her parents, Rocky experiences new emotions and learns to "see things in ways she never has before-including herself."

Basic Book Information

The Monument, an American Library Association Best Book for Young Adults selection, is 151 pages long and is divided into 17 untitled chapters, and 4 sections ("Rocky," chapters 1-3; "Python," chapters 4-5; "Mick," chapters 6-14; and "The Monument," chapters 15-17). This fictional story is told in the first person narrative, from Rocky's point of view. There are no illustrations in the book.

Gary Paulsen is a well-known author of many popular novels for young people, including the Newbury Honor books *Hatchet*, *Dogsong*, and *The Winter Room*.

Noteworthy Features

Paulsen's use of exaggeration and sarcastic humor capture the essence of how a13 year-old may react to the world. When Rocky talks about some of the larger families in town, she'll exaggerate the number of children they have as, for instance, "Emerson Garret has about 37 kids," or "The Walterses

Publisher
Bantam Doubleday Dell, 1991

ISBN
0440407826

TC Level
12

A Field Guide to the Classroom Library, Lucy Calkins and the Teachers College Reading and Writing Project, Heinemann, ©2002 Teachers College, Columbia University; http://www.heinemann.com/fieldguides

had about seven dozen kids. . . ." This may be a jealous reaction to those with large, stable families given her transient, orphanage background. There may also be an analogy between Python and Rocky. She describes the dog as "big, scruffy, ribs sticking out . . .curly tight hair . . .starving." When she frees the dog she states "either someone picks them up or they're shot." She could be describing herself and how she felt at the orphanage . . . awkward, older, bad leg sticking out, curly tight hair, and starving (emotionally). Her fear is that, if not adopted, the only way she'll escape the orphanage is by getting pregnant and kicked-out (abandoned). The author's use of simile and repeating images and phrases is evidenced throughout the book.

Teaching Ideas

When reading this or any book, students could be invited to develop ideas about the book, and to read expecting these ideas to gain weight and substance . . . or to be revised in the light of new information. Probably the ideas students develop about this book will have something to do with the general idea that people benefit from seeing and accepting the truth of themselves. A teacher may not want to predetermine the theme in a book and try to get children to parrot it. This can create passive, disenfranchised readers and little reason to talk, write, or think as one reads.

"Sometimes you don't see things and time will go by and by and then you'll look and see it." This realization by Rocky is repeated throughout this story. Her transformation from looking at things to really *seeing* them, and herself, is at the core of the story. When Mick says, "Well there's seeing and there's seeing," he's talking about getting to the truth of the subject, the essence of its being. Rocky learns to do this by studying Mick as he sketches the town, revealing the truth-both beautiful and ugly-of people and things she thought she knew so well. A reader who notices this theme may perhaps follow it to an exploration of prejudices. Alternatively, a reader may be most interested in the role of art in helping Rocky learn to see the world (and perhaps the parallels with writing), or in Python's importance in the story, or how Rocky is "apple-like"-hard on the outside, soft on the inside. There are examples throughout the story of "learning to see" that students can find and use.

There is irony in the line Rocky uses to describe the flat dullness of Bolton, Kansas, "There is nothing to stop your seeing," because her ability to see is obstructed until Mick opens her eyes to the richness and diversity of the town. Examples of simile can be found throughout the story, as for example, Mick being described as like a garden gnome, or the farmers' grain as their gold, and the light like as a blessing, like a kiss from the gods. There are many examples that can be used to show how they help the reader see what the author intended.

Book Connections

Two books by Patricia MacLachlan, *Journey* and *Arthur For the Very First Time*, use the arts to help the main characters deal with their issues. Where Rocky uses drawing, Journey uses photography, and Arthur uses writing.

A Field Guide to the Classroom Library, Lucy Calkins and the Teachers College Reading and Writing Project, Heinemann, ©2002 Teachers College, Columbia University; http://www.heinemann.com/fieldguides

Genre
Chapter Book

Teaching Uses
Independent Reading; Read Aloud; Book Clubs; Partnerships

A Field Guide to the Classroom Library, Lucy Calkins and the Teachers College Reading and Writing Project, Heinemann, ©2002 Teachers College, Columbia University; http://www.heinemann.com/fieldguides

The Pain and the Great One

Judy Blume

Book Summary

This funny, colorful picture book has two parts. Part one is written from the point of view of the older sister. She explains how annoying her younger brother is, and in the process reveals to everyone but herself that she enjoys playing with him at times, although she is jealous of the attention he gets. Part two is written from the point of view of the younger brother. He explains how annoying his big sister is, and in the process reveals to everyone but himself how much he admires her and also enjoys playing with her. He too is jealous of the attention she receives from their parents and even the cat. Both end their stories by saying that they think the parents love their sibling the most.

Basic Book Information

This is a short but two-chapter picture book.

Noteworthy Features

The well-known and well-loved Judy Blume offers this insightful picture book about sibling rivalry to young readers.

The structure of the book is unusual. The book opens with a title page with "The Pain and the Great One" written on it. Then comes a page with "The Pain" written on it, signifying the opening of part one. Many readers just turn past this second page without noticing it, because they assume that it is another title page. This doesn't usually end up being much of a problem initially because the point of view is fairly clear almost immediately-the first line says "My brother's a pain." and the picture clearly illustrates who she is and who her brother is.

The rub comes at the end of the first section when there is another divider page with "The Great One" on it signifying the beginning of part two. If readers have missed that there is a part one, it is often a bit tricky to go into this part with the correct expectation for the change to come. Many readers begin the section thinking that the girl, the older sister, is still talking and that she has an even older sister as well as a younger brother. This miscue can not continue for long and still make sense, especially if the reader is paying attention to the pictures, but it can throw readers off for a bit. A "heads-up" from the teacher may be welcome in some cases.

Illustrator
Irene Trivas

Publisher
Bantam Doubleday Dell, 1985

ISBN
0440409675

TC Level
8

Teaching Ideas

Another part of understanding the story that is difficult for many readers, is hanging on to the first story and giving it equal mental weight to the last story. Understandably, the second story tends to stay in readers' minds, since it is the most recent one read. Readers then conclude in accordance with the last idea that, yes indeed, the parents love the big sister better than they love the little brother. This can be the basis for minilessons or conferences about the ways and means to holding an entire story in one's head when thinking it over and making judgments about it.

Misreading this book may also be a product of readers taking everything the narrators say at face value. If the character says the parents love the sister best, then some readers assume this must be the absolute truth. One of the wonderful characteristics of this book is that a close study of it, or of the characters it contains, can bring about a change in readers who have always taken the narrators extremely literally. When these two narrators in the same story, even in the same events, tell different versions, the reader has to make some decisions about who or what to believe, and it can't be that both narrators are right. Gaining the understanding that a narrator can have a point of view that isn't necessarily the whole truth is an enormous step in comprehending literature.

To get to this point in their understanding of the book, readers will probably need to reread the story several times, and they may need help organizing their thoughts and notes so that related parts of each of the two stories can lay side by side. This may mean a teacher photocopying the page in each sibling's story that tells about the cat, or the page in each that tells about the blocks, or the telephone. Perhaps some children can collect these related bits of information and lay them side by side in their notebooks without teacher intervention.

In addition to showing contradictions in the versions of reality that prove that both narrators can't be right, laying the two characters' versions of events side by side can also offer insight into the behavior of each. As the reader reads about the little brother dancing around his sister and yelling while she's on the phone, most will conclude that he is just really annoying. When that incident is placed next to his thoughts about the telephone, however, some insight into why he might be behaving like that is possible. Any character study would have to involve some comparisons of incidents through both points of view.

Readers also tend to read through and miss the two siblings' like for playing with each other. This again may be because that information is in the text, but not in the narrator's attitudes. This aspect of the story is more likely to be seen by the reader once she understands that the narrators are not "right' about everything, and that they can make "mistakes" in their telling.

Genre
Picture Book

A Field Guide to the Classroom Library, Lucy Calkins and the Teachers College Reading and Writing Project, Heinemann, ©2002 Teachers College, Columbia University; http://www.heinemann.com/fieldguides

Teaching Uses
Partnerships; Independent Reading

A Field Guide to the Classroom Library, Lucy Calkins and the Teachers College Reading and Writing Project, Heinemann, ©2002 Teachers College, Columbia University; http://www.heinemann.com/fieldguides

The Rainbow and You

E.C. Krupp

Book Summary

This nonfiction picture book is a compilation of scientific explanations of what makes rainbows, everyday talk about rainbows, and even some of the folklore and mythology surrounding rainbows.

Basic Book Information

It is written in a continuous narrative form. There is a short paragraph of writing on each page, and a few captions under the illustrations and diagrams.

Noteworthy Features

Although this book is written as a continuous text, the informational bits presented often do not flow from one to another, and have no particular reason to be joined or follow from the preceding paragraph. This can make for a choppy read for children who are expecting a story or a smooth flow of facts and information. The narrative form of this nonfiction book can also make research a bit more difficult, since there is no table of contents or index to direct the reader to specific parts to get specific bits of information. On the other hand, the book is not exceedingly long or dense, so fairly experienced readers shouldn't be unduly burdened by having to read or skim the entire book if they are trying to get only a small bit of information.

Teaching Ideas

This book is exactly the kind of nonfiction book that is best read with a pencil in hand to write down questions as they come up. Sometimes the way the book is written seems to cue the reader to ask questions: "Most of the time people say the rainbow has seven colors..." seems to cue the reader to ask if there are other times when people say the rainbow has a different number of colors. This question isn't answered in the book, however, the answers to other questions that will undoubtedly arise are found in the book. Because the book seems to cue questions and only answer some of them, it may be a good first book to read on a topic, since it will probably get the ideas and curiosities of the children flowing in a way that won't be shut down by the end of the book. (Of course, if the book is a bit too hard for the reader, it wouldn't be a good one to start with as it will undoubtedly consume more energy than it gives.)

In reading this book, as in reading many other fiction and nonfiction books, stopping to make sure the reader has understood every word and concept before moving onto the next page is probably not a good idea. Within the scientific explanation parts, the book has a tendency to explain

Illustrator

Robin Rector Krupp

Publisher

Harper Collins, 2000

ISBN

0688156010

A Field Guide to the Classroom Library, Lucy Calkins and the Teachers College Reading and Writing Project, Heinemann, ©2002 Teachers College, Columbia University; http://www.heinemann.com/fieldguides

the whole thing and then explain it again in more detail later, maybe several pages later. For this reason, moving ahead and gathering more information is usually more helpful in dispelling confusion than reading and stopping to think too much about the information already read. If by the end of the book, the same questions linger or the same confusions still have root, then perhaps a slower more concentrated read of those parts is in order.

The captions in this book are sometimes seemingly irrelevant to the text and even to the subject of rainbows. The captions sometimes label places on the globe without explaining why they are depicted there. Children may be annoyed by this or they may find it a mystery to be solved. They might ask, "What is the relevance of that particular place in the world to the text?" It could be a topic for further research.

Near the end of the book, there is a list of research questions that readers can ask themselves if they see a rainbow. However, the text does not explain why gathering this information would be helpful. What does it matter whether or not the witness could see through the rainbow, for example? Again, students can therefore dismiss these questions as silly, or they can use them as the basis for further research-what would knowing those facts about the rainbow reveal to the witness? Where could they lead?

As in any book, recreating scenes, or experiments, can aid in text comprehension. There are many activities hinted at in the book. Although we can't create enormous rainbows in the sky for children to study and think about, a hose or thin film of the kind found on bubbles or in shallow pools of oil can also create rainbows. Children can also look at photographs of actual rainbows-some picture calendars feature a rainbow every month. Often, the reading of nonfiction should and will inspire some kind of real world observation or activity, and encouraging this is a good and powerful way to show kids the importance and relevance and meaning in texts, especially nonfiction ones.

At the end of the book, there is an attempt by the authors to help readers form social groups around their studies of rainbows. If children seem about to do this-on any topic-this idea from the authors of this book may help them move farther in that direction without any teacher intervention. In other words, this book can contribute to a general tendency to form clubs of kids that want to study a certain topic.

Genre
Picture Book; Nonfiction

Teaching Uses
Independent Reading; Reading and Writing Nonfiction; Content Area Study

The Secret Garden
Frances Hodgson Burnett

Book Summary

In *The Secret Garden*, Mary Lennox, a weak, disagreeable and recently-orphaned child is sent from India to live with her uncle in England. Lonely and struggling, she finds a secret garden by the old stone house. Her growing love of the garden proves the key to not only *her* happiness, but the happiness of her sickly cousin Colin and her grieving uncle.

Basic Book Information

The Secret Garden has 298 pages and twenty-seven titled chapters of between eight and nineteen pages.

Noteworthy Features

The Secret Garden is a beautifully-written classic. The story emphasizes character, motivation, and descriptive writing over plot and action. It will appeal to those readers who enjoy deeper explorations of character and an old-fashioned, lyrical style of writing.

The main character, Mary Lennox, will grab most reader's attention because she makes such an unlikely heroine-self-centered, bossy, and peevish. Her transformation from bratty child to altruist is gradual and accompanied by realistic setbacks. Mary's motivations are complicated and make that transformation meaningful. Growing up in India, she was both catered to and deprived of affection; in England, she learns to take care of herself and recognize the satisfactions of doing so. From there, she learns to care for the secret garden and enjoy the results. The reasons behind Colin's bad temper and self-pity, and the ensuing reasons for his recovery, are carefully developed.

In order to understand Mary's life before England, readers may benefit from some information about England's colonization of India. Some attitudes in the book are outdated, and readers should keep in mind the book's age as they read about India, Colin's illness and treatment, and the attitudes of masters and servants.

The language in *The Secret Garden* is sophisticated, and contains Indian terms, for example, "ayah" (p. 1), "obsequious" (p. 25), and "imperious" (p. 101). The Yorkshire accents and local vocabulary add another level of difficulty. For example, "Canna thy dress thysen!" (p. 26) means "Can't you dress yourself?" Readers need to have solid vocabularies and be fairly skilled at inferring meaning from context.

The earnest tone and resolutely happy ending-a "crippled" boy learns to walk-will be satisfying to some readers and too neat for others. An absence of irony, though, can be a welcome change from the highly ironic tone of much current material.

Publisher
Scholastic

ISBN
0590433466

TC Level
12

 A Field Guide to the Classroom Library, Lucy Calkins and the Teachers College Reading and Writing Project, Heinemann, ©2002 Teachers College, Columbia University; http://www.heinemann.com/fieldguides

A major theme of the story is that society is largely bad, while nature is basically good. Society spoils: Mary's sociable parents die of a contagious disease; Mary's behavior is spoiled by her upbringing by those sociable parents and by her luxurious lifestyle; Colin is spoiled by being kept indoors and by too much doctoring. On the other hand, nature heals: the uneducated housemaid and her "wild" brother are sources of wisdom; the garden and its animals help turn Mary and Colin into kind, resourceful people.

Teaching Ideas

The Secret Garden provides an excellent opportunity to study character development and motivation. In addition, Mary and Colin might be compared. How are they similar and different? Do they change for the same reasons, or not?

The book concerns upper-class characters, but it also provides glimpses of the working class. What does the book say about the classes? Is this book fair?

As part of an exploration of the theme concerning nature and society, readers might look at the descriptions of the inside of the house, including Mary's and Colin's bedrooms, and contrast them with the descriptions of the moor and the garden.

Genre
Chapter Book

Teaching Uses
Critique; Independent Reading; Book Clubs

A Field Guide to the Classroom Library, Lucy Calkins and the Teachers College Reading and Writing Project, Heinemann, ©2002 Teachers College, Columbia University; http://www.heinemann.com/fieldguides

The Secret Soldier: The Story of Deborah Sampson

Ann McGovern

Book Summary

The Secret Soldier is a biography that takes place during the Revolutionary War. After five-year-old Deborah Sampson's father dies, her mother becomes too ill to care for her or any of Deborah's four siblings. Deborah is sent to live with one of Mrs. Sampson's cousins and is treated well. When this woman dies, Deborah is taken in as a servant to the large family of a minister and his wife. She agrees to provide them with ten years of service in exchange for food and shelter. Over the years, as Deborah is working hard for her new family, dissatisfaction over the British rule of the colonies is growing, and war eventually breaks out. After ten years, Deborah earns her freedom. Desiring an adventure and in need of work, she disguises herself as a young man and joins the army. She is brave and loyal as a soldier, and she earns the respect of the other soldiers. It isn't until she becomes very sick after serving for a year that her secret is discovered. Deborah's fellow soldiers maintain their respect for her even after they discover she is a woman; Deborah recovers; the war ends. Later, Deborah marries, has children, and becomes the first woman to tour the states as a paid speaker; she talks about her experiences as a soldier, and denounces war, in general.

Basic Book Information

The Secret Soldier has 64 pages broken into 13 short chapters. There is no contents page; the chapters are titled but not numbered. The titles give a clear indication of the subjects of the chapters.

Noteworthy Features

The Secret Soldier starts out quickly and maintains a brisk pace throughout. The book begins with Deborah's mother having made the decision to give her children away. Some readers may feel immediately engaged in the action and the plight of Deborah. Curiosity and sympathy will be evoked right from the start.

Deborah is determined to learn to read and write at a time when girls weren't usually educated in those skills. Her strong desire to master those abilities should be pointed out to readers and discussed. Why was it so important to her to learn? Why would she want to go to school when she didn't have to? Her desire could lead to a discussion of the readers' own needs to learn and a renewal of their motivation.

The Secret Soldier puts Deborah in the midst of history. Students can be made aware that they, too, are in the midst of history, that history is

Illustrators
Harold Goodwin;
Katherine Thompson

Publisher
Scholastic, Inc., 1975

ISBN
0590430521

A Field Guide to the Classroom Library, Lucy Calkins and the Teachers College Reading and Writing Project, Heinemann, ©2002 Teachers College, Columbia University; http://www.heinemann.com/fieldguides

happening all the time. The author presents this history very matter-of-factly, and also makes it personal by including Deborah in it. Students who thought they were not interested in history may discover that when history becomes a story, they are, in fact, interested.

The Secret Soldier uses clear, simple language but does not condescend to the reader. Most readers should not have much difficulty with the language.

Time moves quickly throughout the book but the author makes a point of marking the years with particular events in Deborah's life and in America's history. It is not a whirlwind of years passing, yet it does not bog down with details that may bore young readers.

Deborah is separated from her siblings at the beginning of the story, and we don't hear anything about those siblings again. Students may want to know what happened to the other children. It can be surmised that they went to the homes of other relatives, but what happened to them after that, the readers can only guess. Deborah may not have known where her brothers and sisters went, but readers may still find it strange that she never mentions them or thinks about them again.

In some ways, Deborah's life parallels the lives of the colonists. While she is working for ten years providing service to a family that is not hers, the colonists are working to pay taxes to a ruler they didn't choose. When Deborah starts thinking about and planning for her freedom, so do the colonists. Students can be encouraged to draw a parallel between Deborah's life and the lives of the colonists.

This book can be a springboard for discussions on various topics: adoption, child labor, the Revolutionary War, life in the colonies, women's roles and rights.

Teaching Ideas

This book can be read individually, in pairings or groups, or as a class. However, since it moves so quickly, students will not want to be held back; they should be encouraged to read at the pace the book demands. Slowing down the reading will diminish the book's momentum and its impact.

A teacher could confer with a student, after the first chapter, asking them to use the chapter titles to speculate on what will occur in the coming chapter. The titles are clear and suggestive of the content, and making students aware of the title could help them to read more critically, and help them to discern what the important information is in that chapter. This is often a helpful exercise in reading nonfiction.

As the book begins with the mother having to place her children in other homes, students can be made aware that families often were broken up in times of sickness and poverty and that being raised by someone other than one's parents was not uncommon in the 18th and 19th centuries. In any case, this is an opportunity to point out to students that various family configurations-other than mother, father, children-have always existed and are as legitimate and (can be) as nurturing as what we think of as the traditional family. Unfortunately, Deborah is treated as a servant in her new "family," though she is treated with kindness, and so this might not be the best example of nurturing. However, if Deborah had remained at home, she would have had to assume many of the same chores she assumed with her new "family" as life on a farm was hard work. Later in her life, Deborah takes in a baby to her family. The parallel to her life as a child being taken in could be noted, and a discussion of why she would want to adopt a baby and how she would treat that baby could ensue.

Students might want to view a map of the United States in 1770 so that they could see how little of it was settled and where Deborah was living.

War builds up in *The Secret Soldier;* it doesn't just suddenly break out. This is an important concept for students, and sometimes book clubs choose to go through the story, noting how the tension mounts, and how that is conveyed in the story through the words of the author.

Students may wish to discuss why a woman was not allowed in the army at that time.

Book Connections

Johnny Tremain, Caddie Woodlawn, Sarah Plain and Tall .

Genre
Historical Fiction; Short Chapter Book

Teaching Uses
Content Area Study; Independent Reading; Partnerships; Book Clubs; Whole Group Instruction

A Field Guide to the Classroom Library, Lucy Calkins and the Teachers College Reading and Writing Project, Heinemann, ©2002 Teachers College, Columbia University; http://www.heinemann.com/fieldguides

The Top of the World: Climbing Mount Everest

Steve Jenkins

Book Summary

The text of the book takes the reader from the airplane heading toward Kathmandu in Nepal through the hike to base camp and up the mountain all the way to the summit. The book gives an account of the appearance of the mountain, conditions, dangers, and challenges along each part of the endeavor. It also providers sidebars about the geography, geology, Sherpa culture, world records, equipment, and climbers that have climbed Everest. The book is written as if the reader might someday climb the mountain, and ends with a warning about getting down from the summit quickly before altitude sickness or bad weather set in!

Basic Book Information

This picture book, illustrated with realistic, cut-paper pictures, is about 30 pages long. Most pages have a paragraph or two of text as well as a several paragraph-long captions that give more information about details of the text. Some of the pages offer diagrams, maps, or details about equipment in addition to the main picture. The text of each page is set off with a short heading. The captions too have short, defining headings. No text wraps across pages-every paragraph is fully contained on the page on which it begins. The text itself is fairly small, light, and without defining serifs on individual letters (most people believe serifs make text easier to read), and the caption text is the same font, but smaller. The background behind the text is sometimes mottled. However, the text is beautifully placed on each page, not at all cluttered or hectic, and its overall look is very appealing and inviting to most readers.

The beginning of the book provides some maps and background about Mount Everest, while the very last page of the book provides a diagram of each continent's highest peak, a table of records pertaining to the mountain, web sites for up-to-date information about the mountain, and a bibliography not intended as further reading for children, but for adults.

Noteworthy Features

The beautiful paper collages that the author has designed give the book a unique and beautiful appearance. The pictures seem to be modeled after photographs and offer a surprisingly realistic depiction of the scenery and landscapes of the mountain when compared with actual photographs. Most readers love the pictures, and are happy to read as much of the book as they can.

Illustrator
Steve Jenkins

Publisher
Houghton Mifflin, 1999

ISBN
0395942187

TC Level
10; 11; 12

Teachers should be aware that the book does not shy away from the deadly peril and ugly dangers that climbing Everest presents. The book honestly presents the fact that the bodies of climbers who have frozen to death can be found at base camp. It presents an image of frostbitten fingers and presents the number of climbers who have died on their way to the summit and back. Children prone to nightmares and overwhelming fears might be steered away from the book. On the other hand, for the less squeamish reader, these details are realistic depictions of the perils involved.

The full-color collage, double-spread illustrations are beautiful however, they can be distracting. It is difficult to see the main text on pages where black print is on blue/gray paper of the collage. It is also distracting when a lot of information is presented in the illustrations; the number of images can feel overwhelming and distract from written text on the page. Captioned pictures, the glossary, and charts often interrupt the flow of the information.

The subtitles clearly guide the reader through the text and name the information clearly. They set the reader up well to receive the information being given.

Teaching Ideas

This is a really good text to teach students how to negotiate the page. This layout is frequently seen in nonfiction texts and students can be taught how to negotiate the page. The teaching could begin with demonstrating to students how to orient oneself to a text as a whole, then how to orient to the page and plan how to read the text from that gathered information. Because it seems like something many students would be interested in, this book could be used with the whole class for the abovementioned purpose.

Some talk might be necessary (during the reading or in an introduction to the book) about how to read books that have substantial captions on nearly every page. Some readers can hold the main text of the story in their heads as they stop to read several lengthy captions. Other readers get disoriented when they do this. The headings on the text and captions tend to help make it easier for readers to remember what they are reading about or have just read about. Some readers might be better off reading only the text and not the captions the first time through the book, and then going back later to read through the captions. On the other hand, although the text is continuous in that it is a chronological progression up the mountain, the interruptions are not interrupting a story per se. There is no risk of forgetting characters or plot twists or details of events that may be important later. For this reason, the interruptions might be tolerable even for readers who couldn't normally incorporate them into a reading.

The captions themselves may not be immediately recognizable as separate from the text. The font is the same, only slightly smaller, and the background that separates it might at first seem to be a different part of the main picture. Once readers realize that nearly every page has its own sidebar with a different background from the main picture, this differentiation will most likely be easy.

This book starts a little slowly for some readers. The map, history, and geological data in the initial pages make some readers tune out early, or put the book away. If they push on until the narrator puts them on the plane flying to Nepal, they may be hooked. Teachers may want to tell readers ahead of time that the book will turn into a guidebook after the initial pages in order to hold their attention.

The book is well-designed for either browsing or reading. Since each paragraph on each page is labeled separately, readers can dip in and out of the story and still have a good understanding of what they are reading about. Since the captions are also similarly headed, they too make for short easy reading, and in their case, that reading is meant to be discreet from the rest of the text.

Many teachers appreciate the author's responsible depiction of both foreign and Sherpa climbers, of both native guides and visiting mountaineers. They also appreciate the book's realistic depiction of base camp as full of litter, despite efforts to remove the garbage left behind by climbers.

The text is written as if the reader may someday climb the mountain, bringing the reader right into the story. This approach can help readers to visualize the trek and imagine the experience.

Book Connections

National Geographic Society Destination: See *Jaguar In the Rain Forest*, by Joanne Rydle, or *Just For A Day* Books, published by Morrow Junior Books.

Genre
Nonfiction; Picture Book

Teaching Uses
Reading and Writing Nonfiction; Content Area Study; Partnerships

The Twits

Roald Dahl

Book Summary

The Twits is a terrible tale about two ugly old people. Their ugliness manifests itself into everything they do. First, the narrator introduces the characters and explains how they became so ugly: "If a person has ugly thoughts, it begins to show on the face. And when that person has ugly thoughts every day, every week, every year, the face gets uglier and uglier until it gets so ugly you can hardly bear to look at it." The Twits reign terror on each other, making their lives more and more miserable each day.

In between torturing each other, The Twits find time to spread their unhappiness to everyone and everything around them. Their pet monkeys, the Muggle-Wumps, are forced to stand on their heads all day long for no reason. The Twits terrorize innocent birds by spreading "Horrible Hugtight" onto the branches of trees, so when the birds land on the branch they stick and can't get away. Unfortunately, these birds end up in the weekly bird pie, the Wednesday night special. The plot starts to change when the Muggle-Wumps band together with Roly-Poly, a bilingual bird that swoops down and rescues his species. Together, the animals play a crafty trick on the Twits, leaving them to meet their timely demise.

Basic Book Information

Roald Dahl, a masterful storyteller, is the author of *The Twits*, a delightfully disgusting book about karma and revenge. Dahl has written several very popular books, such as *James and the Giant Peach*, *Matilda*, and *The Witches*.

The Twits has 76 pages with 29 chapters. The chapter titles are written in a way to give you small clues as to what will come next, without totally giving the book away. Then again, each chapter is as unpredictable as the next. Almost every page has an illustration by Quentin Blake that captures the expressions of each character.

Noteworthy Features

The text is rich with ongoing alliteration, such as "squiggly spaghetti," "filthy feathery frumps," and "fearful frumptious freaks," to name a few. Students will find this a delightful read, even if they do tend to stumble over some of the expressions.

This book contains some material that is borderline offensive. The pet monkeys speak a "weird African language," according to the author. This could unfortunately give students a negative connotation to African languages. Different does not mean weird. In addition, Roly-Poly, the bilingual bird makes this comment: "It's no good going to a country and not knowing the language." Again, this type of subversive comment might make

Illustrator
Quentin Blake

Publisher
The Penguin Group, 1980

ISBN
0141301074

TC Level
10

A Field Guide to the Classroom Library, Lucy Calkins and the Teachers College Reading and Writing Project, Heinemann, ©2002 Teachers College, Columbia University; http://www.heinemann.com/fieldguides

the reader question the values of the author.

Teaching Ideas

The short chapters make this an easy read for children. Students will want to explore the text on their own, probably imitating the voices of the characters, including the talking animals. It would also make a great book for partners to read together.

Dahl provides foreshadowing when Mr. Twit is scaring Mrs. Twit by telling her about the shrinks and "in the end there's nothing left except a pair of shoes and a bundle of clothes." Ironically, this is how the book ends. There are a few good book talks that could revolve around the use of foreshadowing.

The book has a great lead-"What a lot of hairy-faced men there are around these days." It could be used for just that-a mini-lesson on leads.

It would be interesting to explore the relationship the Twits have with one another. Do they love each other or hate each other? Is it a love/hate relationship? Can two people be happily miserable together? What about Mr. Twit-would he really have let Mrs. Twit float away from earth? What would his life be like without her, or her life without him?

Although this is a book and not a poem, readers could explore the use of alliteration and onomatopoeia. How do these techniques help make language come alive?

Another interesting discussion could revolve around the everyday habits of the Twits. Why do they have less than humanistic characteristics? Why do they like to catch birds and eat them? Readers can discuss the idea of not being accepted in society, and the impact it has on you as an individual.

Lastly, there is the topic of revenge. Did the Twits get what they deserve? Is there such a thing as karma? Were the Twits predestined to die a miserable death, because of the misery they bestowed on others? All these questions and more tend to come up in book club discussions children have.

Genre
Fantasy; Short Chapter Book

Teaching Uses
Book Clubs; Independent Reading; Character Study

A Field Guide to the Classroom Library, Lucy Calkins and the Teachers College Reading and Writing Project, Heinemann, ©2002 Teachers College, Columbia University; http://www.heinemann.com/fieldguides

The Voyage of the FROG
Gary Paulsen

Book Summary

David Alspeth's Uncle Owen is suddenly struck with a fatal cancer. When 14-year-old David sees his uncle for the last time he so struck with grief that he throws up. He feels it is so unfair that the cancer claims the life of his uncle who lived down the block from him, shared meals with his family, and taught him to sail. Owen's final wish is that David have his boat, The FROG, and scatter his ashes in the sea. Dedicated to his uncle's final wish, David sets sail for a two-day solo voyage that will be Owen's "last trip."

David, an inexperienced sailor, doesn't anticipate the weather and soon a ferocious storm blows him violently off course. When David recovers from the storm, he realizes that The FROG is lost at sea with only ten cans of food and no radio. The days that David spends at sea are a lesson in self-reliance and will. He and The FROG course through rough waters, ride alongside killer whales, battle shark attacks, and get hit by an oil tanker. The voyage helps David to understand his uncle and his attachment to the sea. When David is finally rescued after nine treacherous days at sea, he cannot abandon The FROG. He decides to sail his boat all the way home, for he has become its "captain." David cannot give up the boat that he has faced so many challenges with. The FROG, David, and Owen are one.

Basic Book Information

The Voyage of the FROG is written by Gary Paulsen and won the American Association Best Book for Young Adults. The book also was acclaimed the Best Book of the Year by the School Library Journal. Gary Paulsen is a three-time winner of the Newbery Honor Award. He has written many books for children including: *Dogsong*, *Hatchet*, *Brian's Winter*, and *The River*.

Noteworthy Features

The Voyage of the FROG is divided into three main sections in the table of contents. The first section is entitled "The FROG" and is a labeled diagram of the sailboat. The second part is "The Voyage of the FROG" and is the story of David's voyage. Then, the final section of the book is called "The Voyage" and is a map of the waters off the California coastline. The map charts David's voyage at sea with markings of where all the significant events of the trip took place. "The FROG" and "The Voyage" are handy reference sections that help guide readers through the text.

The language in *The Voyage of the FROG* is very technical. Paulsen uses many nautical terms and makes many references to the various parts of the boat. It is notable that while many of these terms are contained in the ship diagram (in "The FROG" section) there are many words that are not.

Publisher
Bantam Doubleday Dell, 1989

ISBN
0440403642

TC Level
12

There is one significant jump in time at the beginning of the book. The story begins with David looking at The FROG for the first time after his uncle's death. The sight of it sparks the memory of his uncle's final days. These days are a flashback in time. Then, the story proceeds in the present as David sets sail. While David is lost at sea, jumps in time are not always clear.

Since David is lost at sea *alone* for the duration of the book there are not many characters for readers to keep track of. Readers only come to know Owen through David's memories. The narrator lets you in on David's thoughts and tells about his hardships and adventures at sea.

Teaching Ideas

The Voyage of the FROG is a story that may be difficult for readers who are unfamiliar with sailing. Readers may find it helpful if teachers point out the diagram of The FROG at the beginning of the book. It may be necessary for readers to make reference to the sailing boat parts as they encounter foreign terms in the text. A reader who is unfamiliar with sailing may have difficulty with figuring out the terminology from the context and will find the diagram useful.

The map at the back of the book may also be helpful for readers. It may give them a clearer picture as to where the events of the story are taking place. The map is a solid tool that shows just how far David manages to get off course. By using the legend at the bottom of the map, readers can see that David is driven hundreds of miles from California's coastline by the first storm.

Readers may notice the way jumps in time are noted while The FROG is at sea. Before the storm, Paulsen cues readers into time leaps with precise calculation, such as "at *nine* in the morning." However, after the violence of the storm knocks David unconscious and breaks his watch, Paulsen writes, "Time seemed to telescope. It was dark when his eyes opened again, or partially opened, but it didn't seem to have been that long." From this point on, the story records time by day and night blocks, like "Another night and another full day and yet another evening passed...." What is interesting to point out to readers is that by the end of the voyage, time is measured precisely, "He sailed west slowly for two hours." Readers either independently or in partnerships may want to note how these notations of time correspond to David's experience sailing. As time measurements become more precise, so does David's sailing expertise. Readers can see how a small detail such as this gives them a window into the character and helps them chart David's path to becoming "captain" of the FROG.

Paulsen also, uses unique sentence structures. He often sets apart phrases in the text. For example, the word "Hunger" sits alone on it's own line. The use of italics is another way that Paulsen distinguishes phrases from the rest of the text-"*Sun broiling down*," "*Time,*" and so on. It may be helpful for teachers to point out that Paulsen uses these devices to create emphasis. Readers can note the significance of the terms he chooses to do this with. This sentence structure and italic use can also be subjects of study in a writing workshop.

Whether as a read aloud, or read independently or in partnerships, *The Voyage of the FROG* can be a wonderful text to explore how people can breathe life into inanimate objects. This boat becomes so much a part of

David that he risks his own safety to sail it home. Readers can note the events that bring him more in tune with the boat. They can explore how the death of a loved one makes holding onto an object that belongs to them more significant. It is all David has left of his uncle and it generates memories.

Readers of *The Voyage of the FROG* may also want to explore how David's experience at sea brings him closer to his uncle. Paulsen writes, "...this was Owen's trip. His last trip." The significance of these lines cannot be overstated. Uncle *and* nephew shared this voyage.

There are places in the story where David's experiences aid in his understanding of his uncle. Such as, when David sees the sea at night for the first time: "And it came to him then, came to his mind like the leaping dolphin, why Owen-who found such beauty in life-wished to end his days amidst the leaping dolphins and the blue fire and the lines of sun-gold across the water." Uncle and nephew are united in many shared experiences throughout the voyage. Owen hoists the same sail his uncle did, looks upon the same ocean, and finally survives because he comes to know The FROG as well as his uncle did before him.

The Voyage of the FROG is a timeless novel for young readers with vivid imagery and deep sentiment. Paulsen takes his readers on a voyage they surely won't forget.

Book Connections

Paulsen has written many other books for young readers. Jean Craighead George is another author who writes stories about people surviving in the wilderness.

Genre
Chapter Book

Teaching Uses
Independent Reading; Partnerships; Read Aloud

A Field Guide to the Classroom Library, Lucy Calkins and the Teachers College Reading and Writing Project, Heinemann, ©2002 Teachers College, Columbia University; http://www.heinemann.com/fieldguides

The Wall
Eve Bunting

Book Summary

A boy and his father visit the Vietnam War Memorial in Washington D.C. The boy describes the black wall with the names engraved in it, and he describes some of the people visiting the monument alongside him. The two make a rubbing of the boy's grandfather's name. They leave a picture of the boy under some pebbles to keep it from blowing away. The father tells the son that yes, the place is sad, but it is a place of honor too. The boy would rather have his grandfather alive.

Basic Book Information

This is a picture book with illustrations on every page that depict the scenes from the text.

Noteworthy Features

The power of this book comes in part from the reader's knowledge of the gravity of war. Perhaps it is not necessary for the reader to know the particulars of the Vietnam War, but it is certainly necessary for them to know of the concept of people dying in war and of other people missing them and building monuments in their honor. Without this prior knowledge, the book has substantially less meaning. The power of the book is further amplified if readers have been to the Vietnam War Memorial or are planning a trip there. Without this experience, the book also has less resonance. If the children have not been there, it would perhaps help them to read the Author's Note at the end of the book first. This Note will give readers a bit more orientation to the place.

Teaching Ideas

This book could be the perfect example for children who are trying to make a piece of writing from collected observations. It seems likely that Eve Bunting created this book with the help of notes she took while at the Vietnam Memorial itself, and children too might be able to see that with a careful rereading of the text.

The format of the book is a good example for children who want to write nonfiction. Putting a child into a situation and describing it, or an event, through his or her eyes is a format the young writers can try as well. This can be a readable way to impart information, and an easy concept to grasp, especially with this example.

Some teachers use Bunting's books to teach students qualities of good writing. One teacher for example, pulled the class together for a minilesson. She began with the connection part of a minilesson saying, "Yesterday, I stayed after school to read the first drafts of your pieces for our author study publication and I noticed one thing I want to talk to you about." Then the teacher proceeded to the next component of her minilesson in which she did some teaching. She said, "Sometimes, when I'm writing a piece that really excites me, I tend to cram a lot of information into it because I don't want to miss telling my readers about one thing. For instance, last night I wrote about our class trip to the aquarium. First I wrote about how we went to see the beluga whales and how excited everyone was to see the new calf swimming with his mom. Then, I remembered how John forgot his lunch and was really upset. And, I added how nice Katie was to share her lunch. Then, I also added the part about how we couldn't find the bus at first. When I reread my piece, I noticed that I had three really different ideas in one piece. And I remembered what the class noticed about Eve Bunting's writing-that she takes a single precious moment in time and writes 'long' about it. John had noticed that in her book, *Flower Garden* Eve Bunting took an idea as small as a window box garden and nurtured it into a whole book. So I went back to my piece and decided that I really wanted to explore the moment when I saw the baby Beluga whale swimming with his mother because it was a special moment. And I realized I could save the other ideas for possible future pieces."

By now it was time for children to work in partners for a few minutes, practicing this strategy. The teacher said, "Writers, I want you to go back to your entries of writing and put a star next to one tiny nugget within the entry that you think you could develop into a whole piece of writing."

Finally it was time to send the writers all to their work. The teacher said, "By a show of hands, how many students think that they sometimes do like I do and try to cram too many ideas into one piece? For those of you raising your hands, I want you to get right to work zooming in on the details of your marked section and developing it into a piece. Let's share how the strategy worked at the end of the workshop."

Later, after that day's writer's workshop, the teacher pulled her class together on the rug for a follow-up discussion. She began, "For those of you who tried out the strategy of writing long about a single nugget of an idea, can you share with the class how it worked?"

In the next minilesson, this teacher wanted to make sure that student writers were developing their precious moment in time using rich detail. Eve Bunting provides a wonderful illustration of how a writer can use "show not tell" to make their writing powerful. The teacher drew students' attention to the part of *The Wall* where Eve Bunting writes about the Dad putting paper over the wall and rubbing in the grandfather's name: "We've brought paper. Dad puts it over the letters and rubs it with a pencil so the paper goes dark and the letters show up white. 'You've got parts of other guys names on there too.' I tell him. Dad looks at the paper. 'You're grandpa won't mind.'" The teacher first tried to create a reverence in her voice during a read aloud of this passage and in the minilesson tried to encourage students to find places in their writing to do this kind of "show not tell" work.

Children may find it helpful and interesting to examine the reactions different people that the boy observes have to the monument. How are the people reacting? What does it seem they must be feeling? Why are the people responding differently to it? Questions like this tend to arise on their

A Field Guide to the Classroom Library, Lucy Calkins and the Teachers College Reading and Writing Project, Heinemann, ©2002 Teachers College, Columbia University; http://www.heinemann.com/fieldguides

own when the boy presents to us the scenarios of the different visitors. The process of thinking through these questions may resemble character studies, or it may more closely resemble personal response.

Older children can examine the perspective on the war presented in the book. What is this book's presentation of the war? Who benefits from the war being presented this way? How else could it be presented? If these questions seem too difficult for children, they might instead ask themselves what the father or son's attitude toward the war is. There is little fuel for this discussion beyond the few words of the father and the few thoughts of the son near the end of the book, but it may still be a question worthy of discussion. This discussion might be supplemented by a discussion of what other people's attitudes of the war might be.

Book Connections

Faithful Elephants, by Yukio Tsuchiya, is a story that unfolds as zoo visitors notice a tombstone for animals. This tombstone commemorates the death of zoo animals in Tokyo during World War II. The power of war resonates throughout the text.

Genre
Picture Book; Nonfiction

Teaching Uses
Author Study; Partnerships; Content Area Study; Reading and Writing Nonfiction

The War with Grandpa

Robert Kimmel Smith

Book Summary

Fifth grader Peter Stokes loves his grandfather and is happy that he is coming to live with Peter's family. What he's not happy about is the fact that his grandfather will be moving into Peter's room, and Peter will be moving upstairs to a dingy room in the attic. When his grandfather arrives, Peter declares war on him and keeps up a series of playful "attacks" in an attempt to get his grandfather to surrender the room. Along the way, Peter learns that his grandfather is a good sport, that war is not a game, and that talking rather than fighting is a better way to handle problems.

Basic Book Information

The War with Grandpa has 140 pages divided into 37 very short chapters. There is a table of contents. The chapter titles are catchy and give an inkling of what a reader can expect. The cover drawing is more interesting than any of the interior illustrations. *The War with Grandpa* is the winner of ten state reading awards.

Noteworthy Features

Peter "writes" this story as he narrates it. "This is the true and real story of what happened when Grandpa came to live with us.... I am typing it out on paper without lines...." As he is writing his story, Peter talks about some writing techniques, such as the advantage of using short sentences. Several of the chapters open with Peter telling what the chapter is going to be about. This alerts the reader to the main idea of the chapter. That Peter is writing the story is a clever and effective device, but it's possible that a few students may be confused as to the role of the author, if it is Peter who is writing this book. It might be worth asking students: Who is Robert Kimmel Smith and what did he have to do with the book if Peter is the one writing it? A discussion about the distinction between narrators and authors could ensue; students could talk about the author's prerogative to pretend to be someone else while he or she writes. This, in turn could lead to a discussion of voice.

Important issues regarding the elderly-depression, illness, pain and loss-are raised in this book. These provide opportunities for students to discuss the discomforts many older people must struggle with, and to consider ways in which they may be made more comfortable.

Since Peter declared "war" on his grandfather, several references to real wars are brought up in the book. Peter's friends help him to strategize by recalling what they know about the Revolutionary War and WWII. The boys give clear explanations for all the terms they use: tyranny, Minuteman, Redcoats, Pearl Harbor. Teachers may want to make sure students understand the meanings or expand on the meanings. Also, one boy makes

Illustrator
Richard Lauter

Publisher
Yearling/Bantam Doubleday Dell, 1984

ISBN
0440492769

TC Level
10

A Field Guide to the Classroom Library, Lucy Calkins and the Teachers College Reading and Writing Project, Heinemann, ©2002 Teachers College, Columbia University; http://www.heinemann.com/fieldguides

reference to Machiavelli. Though his explanation of who Machiavelli is will be sufficient for some readers, the teacher should be prepared for questions. What is noteworthy about these sections is that this knowledge of history is taken for granted. It is not just the smartest boy who knows about the American Revolution, etc.; all the boys clearly have an interest in history.

Teaching Ideas

The story should be read in just a few sittings. Momentum builds from chapter to chapter, and if the student reads only a two-page chapter a night on her or his own, that momentum will be lost. Weaker readers could also be paired with stronger readers to help them keep pace.

In Chapter 22, Grandpa tries to discourage Peter from his war. But Peter is adamant, claiming that war is just like the game of Risk and when a person's territory is taken, that person must retaliate. Grandpa gets very upset and slaps Peter. Students could be asked why they think Grandpa got so upset. They could also be encouraged to infer that Grandpa has actually been in a war and so knows that it's not a game. Students could discuss what they know of war and what any of their relatives have experienced of it.

Students can be asked if they feel Peter went too far when he stole Grandpa's false teeth. How do they think Grandpa felt? Why was Peter ashamed? How do they feel they treat their own grandparents? How do their grandparents treat them? Has the book helped them to understand their grandparents any better? This building of personal connections with a text can inform and change not only a reader's understanding of a book but of the real world.

Genre
Chapter Book

Teaching Uses
Independent Reading; Read Aloud; Critique; Character Study

A Field Guide to the Classroom Library, Lucy Calkins and the Teachers College Reading and Writing Project, Heinemann, ©2002 Teachers College, Columbia University; http://www.heinemann.com/fieldguides

The Wildlife Detectives: How Forensic Scientists Fight Crimes Against Nature

Donna M Jackson

Book Summary

The Wildlife Detectives can be used in several ways because it is formatted in 2 different ways. There is a story being told and that appears on light blue pages, often with captioned photos. These pages, the narrative or the story of the case study, are interspersed with "files" pages (A case study is an example of how the work goes. Case studies are used to understand not only the content of the work, but also the process.). These pages give more detailed explanations and background information to the reader. The book could be read as a whole, straight through, or read for the case study alone, or the "files" alone. Either way, it would make a valuable read.

Basic Book Information

The Wildlife Detectives is 47 pages with an index at the end. There is a table of contents that serves as an outline, but it gives no page numbers. Between episodes of the case study, on the killing of Charger the elk in Yellow Stone, are "files" of background information. These files have a different format, appearing on manila file folders with a tab on the side. This text is expository and packed with facts and detailed vocabulary. The print on these pages is small (smaller than the text in other pages), with medium spacing between lines and words. The style of the text is narrative. It is the story of the discovery of Charger the elk's body and the resulting investigation. The print on these pages is medium with medium spacing between words and large (double) spacing between lines. All narrative pages present the text on light blue background that is contrasted around its edges by the white of the page. Full-color photographs appear on almost every page and have captions explaining the photo.

Noteworthy Features

The formatting or structure of this book is versatile and will accommodate the different purposes of nonfiction readers. Some will read straight through, going from the ride or journey. Some will read and use the case study in order to make wildlife detection concrete, and others will use the files to give background information from the case study or alone as a source to consult for information on endangered species and their protective laws in general. There is a lot of information here but it is chalked by the episodes, the "files." The print is not dense and where it is a full-page

Publisher
Houghton Mifflin, 2000

ISBN
0395869765

TC Level
12; 13; 14

A Field Guide to the Classroom Library, Lucy Calkins and the Teachers College Reading and Writing Project, Heinemann, ©2002 Teachers College, Columbia University; http://www.heinemann.com/fieldguides

(pages 19 and 23) dialogue is usually embedded in the text that gives context to the meaning. However, the vocabulary is also in a glossary at the end of the book that is very useful.

Page numbers are not given in the table of contents and the reader won't know there is a glossary unless he turns to the end of the book. This is a good book to thumb through because then the reader can understand the structure and decide how to read or use this book.

Teaching Ideas

Because of the juxtaposition of narrative and expository text, this is an excellent book to use to show the differences and similarities. The narrative story (and so too the entire book) begins, "It was the last straw." This is a well-chosen lead because it is a familiar saying to children and adults to show a history with a turn of events. It points to frame and sucks the reader in immediately. Then, through the narrative, facts are woven into the story by way of quotes, titles of people's positions, descriptions of land areas, animals, and job descriptions.

By contrasting the narrative and the facts file, students can learn how to use both for different reasons and at different times. This structure can become easily recognized and will aid all students in nonfiction reading.

Point of view can also be studied in this book. The use of adjectives and adverbs is interesting and can show prejudice (i.e., "thoughtless people" (p. 5), and "steal shamelessly" (p. 5). It is good to check where these emotional terms occur and where they do not. The reader can collect these in order to critique the values from which the book was written.

Genre
Nonfiction; Mystery

Teaching Uses
Reading and Writing Nonfiction; Content Area Study; Independent Reading; Critique

The Witch of Blackbird Pond

Elizabeth George Speare

Book Summary

After the death of her grandfather, Kit Tyler leaves her home in Barbados to live with an aunt and family in the Connecticut Colony. Almost immediately, she distinguishes herself as different by jumping into the water to retrieve a doll for an anguished child. She soon realizes that this action was unusual and, as such, unacceptable to her neighbors. Kit's differences are not welcome and are, in fact, looked upon suspiciously by the strict-minded Puritans of the colony.

Kit settles into life with her aunt, uncle, and two cousins. But it is not the carefree existence she had known with her grandfather. Instead, her daily routine consists of constant, grueling work with few intermissions. Kit finds this Spartan way of life suffocating. Her only release is in the visits she makes to the meadow and to the old woman in a nearby cottage, known as the Witch of Blackbird Pond to her neighbors. When this innocent friendship is discovered, however, it casts a greater shadow of suspicion over Kit and she is accused of witchcraft.

Basic Book Information

This book is 249 pages long, divided into 21 chapters, and is not illustrated. The author is a noted writer of historical fiction. *The Witch of Blackbird Pond* received one of the two Newbery Medals awarded to Ms. Speare.

Noteworthy Features

This book should be read for the sheer power of its story. The characters are admirable, and Kit and the Witch of Blackbird Pond exemplify strong, smart, brave characters.

Some students may wonder the extent to which this historical fiction story is true. One way to explore this would be to study an excerpt from a similar text, such as Gary Bowen's *Stranded in Plimouth Plantation*.

Readers will notice that characters use the language of the time. Additionally, the book includes excerpts from a primer reader, a posted notice at the meeting hall, and a poem of a colonial poet. All of these forms of written expression provide ample insight into the mindset of the time, all with reference to the Puritan ethics readily portrayed elsewhere in the book.

Teaching Ideas

This is a coming of age story-the story of a young woman who is compelled to make decisions that will color the complexion of the remainder of her life, choices from which her future will be determined.

There are a number of other themes that are prevalent in *The Witch of*

Publisher
Bantam Doubleday Dell Books

ISBN
0440495962

TC Level
13

A Field Guide to the Classroom Library, Lucy Calkins and the Teachers College Reading and Writing Project, Heinemann, ©2002 Teachers College, Columbia University; http://www.heinemann.com/fieldguides

Blackbird Pond. These include, but are not limited to, the conflict between the individual and the community (self versus society), the role of religion in the colonization of America (tyranny versus tolerance), the nature of prejudice (fear of the unknown), and the personal choices one makes because of, or in spite of, these varied circumstances.

This book lends itself particularly well to an in-depth study of character, specifically the growth of Kit Tyler throughout the developing plot. Additionally, the changes in Kit can be compared and contrasted to some of the other characters-such as the ever-constant Mercy, or the faithful John Holbrook.

An interesting extension of this character study could be the study of author's craft as it pertains to characterization. This line of inquiry could begin with questions. How does the author play characters off one another (e.g, William Ashby vs. Nat Easton)? Are there parallels between characters or the actions of characters (e.g., Kit's decision to give up William Ashby, John Holbrook's decision to marry Mercy instead of Judith)? Do characters symbolize ideas relative to the major themes within the text (e.g., Uncle Matthew, patriot vs. Reverend Gersholm, royalist; Goodwife Cuff, religious intolerant vs. Hannah Tupper, religious tolerant; Nat Easton, independent vs. William Ashby, society's child)? How do the actions of characters signify the changes in characters (e.g., Kit's abandonment of William Ashby and acceptance of Nat Easton; Kit's decision to help Hannah Tupper)?

Book Connections

Stranded in Plimouth Plantation by Gary Bowen is another example of historical fiction that takes place during the same era as *The Witch of Blackbird Pond*. It is written in journal format by a visitor to the colony and is rife with factual information pertaining to the time period.

The Crucible by Arthur Miller is a play depicting the witch hunts that took place in Salem, Massachusetts in 1692. There are many parallels between themes and characters within this play and *The Witch of Blackbird Pond*.

Genre
Historical Fiction; Chapter Book

Teaching Uses
Independent Reading; Character Study; Interpretation

A Field Guide to the Classroom Library, Lucy Calkins and the Teachers College Reading and Writing Project, Heinemann, ©2002 Teachers College, Columbia University; http://www.heinemann.com/fieldguides

The World According to Horses, How They Run, See and Think

Stephen Budiansky

Book Summary

This book came about as a result of the author's own study of horses. He had many questions and researched to find the answers. This book represents the information that he gathered in response to his inquiries. The chapter titles highlight the focus or main ideas presented in the chapter (e.g., The Cult of the Horses and The Horse Society). Basically, the author shares all that he learned about how horses live and how they came to live the way they do. Each chapter not only provides information, it also answers a stated question, "How do we know?" The question and answer format is prevalent throughout the book.

Basic Book Information

This 100-page chapter book presents information about horses.

Noteworthy Features

Some of the sentence structures are complex and the vocabulary is rich. The ideas presented within a paragraph are dense at times throughout the book. The structure of the text is explained in the introduction. The chapter title sets up the reader for the information that is being presented; the subtitle is in the form of a question that presents a different slant-specifically how the information that was just presented was learned. Each chapter presents here's what we know and here's how we know it. This consistent structure supports the learning process. Charts, pictures, and diagrams also support the text.

Teaching Ideas

This book is a good example of an inquiry. Teachers could use it to demonstrate to students how inquiry is question driven. It could be used to show how an interest in something can lead a person to study, research, and gather information just as the writer did. The writer also chose to present the gathered information to readers and invite the reader along on the inquiry with him.

The book is probably best read straight through, however the table of contents and the index allows a person looking for specific information about this subject to use it as a reference tool. This book may also be included in independent reading libraries for about the fourth grade level and beyond.

Publisher
Henry Holt and Co., 2000

ISBN
0805060545

TC Level
12; 13; 14

Book Connections

The Snake Scientist by Sy Montgomery might interest readers of this book.

Teaching Uses

Reading and Writing Nonfiction; Independent Reading

There's an Owl in the Shower

Jean Craighead George

Book Summary

There's an Owl in the Shower is a story about learning to respect and protect the environment. In a small town in California, tree-fellers have lost their work in response to local environmental concerns. The boy, Bordon Watson, imagines shooting an endangered spotted owl so that his father can go back to work. In one of his forest expeditions, Bordon discovers a small abandoned owlet and brings him home to nurse him, thinking he is not one of the endangered spotted owls. Before long Bordon's father, Leon, grows attached to the owl too. In the ensuing story, the bonding between Leon and Bardy becomes a focal point for the resolution of the conflict between man and nature. Ultimately, the source of their troubles, nature, also becomes the source of their growth.

The animosity in the town is clear: those that seek to protect the owl-the environmentalists, and those who have long worked in the forests-the loggers. The fact that Bordon, the son of a logger, is raising an owl is something that must be kept secret from the community. In the absence of work, father and son take long excursions into the hillsides to trap mice for Bardy. During this time they share each other's thoughts and feelings about the environment and each other. We come to understand that Leon and the other loggers care deeply for the forest. They take pride in their ability to fell trees carefully.

Bardy's development from owlet to owl is a central part of the story. We learn how an owl imprints his "mother" (or mother-figure) and develops a permanent bond with this figure. The story intertwines the increasing attachment of Bardy and Leon with a pending court case over a fist-fight between Leon and Paul James over the owls. Leon camouflages his true feelings for Bardy by saying that he is only going through this effort to raise Bardy so that the judge will see that he doesn't really hate owls and will therefore let him off of the pending fine.

Leon and Bordon struggle to make sense of the owl's needs so they frequently, though surreptitiously, probe another character, Paul James for his advice on the "how's and what's of owls." They learn how to feed an owl (p. 39), how an owl gets juvenile feathers that are different from both baby and adult feathers (p. 66), that an owlet "imprints" the face of the person nurturing them and follows them everywhere (p. 71), about hunger streaks on the feathers that indicate poor feeding (p. 78), and that the last thing a little bird does before it is about to fly is bathe (p. 86). Later on they will have to graft a feather (p. 100) because of weakness.

Within a week of the court case we suddenly discover that Bardy is in fact a Spotted Owl. With this news Leon and Bordon decide to take Bardy back to the forest and let him return to his natural environment. They take Bardy to an old nobleman, Enrique, whom Leon knows from his work in the forest. And there he resumes his life in the wild.

Illustrator
Christine Herman Merill

Publisher
Harper Collins, 1995

ISBN
0064406822

TC Level
11

A Field Guide to the Classroom Library, Lucy Calkins and the Teachers College Reading and Writing Project, Heinemann, ©2002 Teachers College, Columbia University; http://www.heinemann.com/fieldguides

Throughout the story the strength of fathers has been evident. It becomes all the more poignant when Bardy joins Enrique rather than a female owl.

Basic Book Information

The book is 134 pages and is divided into 17 chapters. The chapters are titled. There are illustrations by Christine Herman Merill that discreetly guide the story. The story is told in the first person narrative, though the points of view vary between the boy, Bordon, the father, Leon, and occasionally the owlet, Bardy.

The boy and the father are the central characters. Supporting characters include Paul James, the environmental high school teacher, Sally, the sister, and Cindy, the Mother.

Noteworthy Features

The book uses descriptive phrases such as "cool green silence," "needle carpeted ground," "soundless distance," and "ankle deep in ferns and wildflowers." This may be a useful touchstone text for a student looking to develop descriptive writing techniques.

Leon ultimately becomes the father figure for Bardy. Even in the home life of the family it is Leon who prepares the food for the family meal in the evening. The strength of the father figure as a compassionate and present family figure is evident.

There is an abundance of nature references throughout the book. The following animals and flora/fauna are referenced, and it may be fun to go back to science after a full reading of the text in the reading workshop: golden-crowned kinglet (p. 10), black-tailed deer (pp. 10, 28), rhododendron (pp. 10, 125), Douglas fir (p. 10), redwood (p. 10), owlets (p. 16), barred owl (p. 17), chipmunk (p. 29), coyote (p. 29), ancient oak (p. 29), Stellar's jay (p. 29), pine siskin (p. 30), vibrissae (p. 32), salmon (p. 32), pine marten (p. 34), red-tailed hawk (p. 45), black-shouldered hawk (p. 45), northern harrier hawk (p. 45), swallow (p. 47), wood rat (p. 56), grassland lark (p. 76), pollywogs (p. 122), big-leaf maple (p. 126), incense cedar (p. 128), prime Western hemlock (p. 128).

Teaching Ideas

This book could be used as part of a nonfiction study. Students would research one or more of the following: birds, animals, fauna, and tie-in references from the text, to an analytical description of the particular reference. In doing so they would draw connections from their reading to the world around them, through investigative probing of the text.

Students could also use this as a launching pad for learning about endangered species in their local environment, and exploring possible causes for the endangerment (pollution, development, loss of food source, changing weather patterns, etc.) and what is being done about the problem and the organizations active in preservation efforts.

This book could be a touchstone text for descriptive writing techniques. Students could re-visit former journal entries or published pieces with the sound of this text in mind, and try some revision strategies.

A Field Guide to the Classroom Library, Lucy Calkins and the Teachers College Reading and Writing Project, Heinemann, ©2002 Teachers College, Columbia University; http://www.heinemann.com/fieldguides

This book might be good for a character study. Leon undergoes a transformation in the book from being an angry and ardent owl hater to being filled with love for a little owlet that he raises and then must let go. Exploring the symbolism in the book is another way of inquiring and gaining insight into how we learn about the characters.

The book can be used to consider tolerance, understanding, family ties, and the nature of unexpected situations in our lives. Each of these themes are found within the book and could be used to launch individual inquiry which may then lead to memoir or poetry writing.

Book Connections

Books that speak heavily to nature follow the theme of fostering respect for our environment. *There's an Owl in the Shower* realizes the fact that there is a deep concern that we have a responsibility to nature. Creatures, small and large, depend on our ability to make intelligent decisions about our actions. *There's an Owl in the Shower* assumes that man is capable of making the correct decisions, if he is properly informed.

Genre
Chapter Book

Teaching Uses
Book Clubs; Teaching Writing

A Field Guide to the Classroom Library, Lucy Calkins and the Teachers College Reading and Writing Project, Heinemann, ©2002 Teachers College, Columbia University; http://www.heinemann.com/fieldguides

Through My Eyes

Ruby Bridges

Book Summary

As a six-year-old girl, Ruby Bridges was the first Black child to enter an all-White school in New Orleans. She was escorted to school by U.S. Marshals, who protected her from the violent, taunting crowd that opposed her attendance. This book tells of her life before that pivotal year, witnessed by the rest of the country; the experience of walking past those jeering crowds every day, and her time inside the school, learning alone with her first-grade teacher. The text also offers the story of what happened to her as she grew into an adult.

Noteworthy Features

This autobiographical picture book/chapter book is about 60 pages long. It is about two-thirds text and one-third photographs. There is no table of contents or index. The text is structured as a chronological narrative, with a focus on the details of Ruby's life that tell also of the times, and then of her year in first grade. It is divided into sections of about two pages each, with headings that clearly indicate what each section is about. The last page of the book presents the lyrics to a song about Ruby. Sidebars to the text offer quotations from civic leaders, writers and newspapers of the day describing the same events Ruby describes, but from an outsider's point of view.

Teaching Ideas

This book can be read aloud in grades two, three, and up. Many readers prefer fiction reading to nonfiction reading. It's important that all readers have a balanced reading life however, one that includes information books. This book, then, could simply be one among many on the library shelf.

If a teacher sees that the class as a whole tends to select fiction books only during independent reading, the teacher may institute some rituals that steer children towards nonfiction. The least intrusive would simply be to do promotional book-talks in which one "sells" nonfiction books. The teacher could go a step further and talk to children about the importance of having a balanced reading life. She could ask the students to make sure that if they have a personal book bin full of four to five books they're reading or planning to read, that at least one of these is nonfiction. Finally, it's possible to go a step further and to suggest that, for a time, all children need to read only nonfiction texts during independent reading.

Teachers may want to do mini-lessons on the strategies for skilled nonfiction reading. They could tell children that nonfiction readers sometimes read like magnets, looking for intriguing details that they pull from a text. One teacher told her students that highly literate people then fact-drop these little bits of information into conversations, sharing in

A Field Guide to the Classroom Library, Lucy Calkins and the Teachers College Reading and Writing Project, Heinemann, ©2002 Teachers College, Columbia University; http://www.heinemann.com/fieldguides

Publisher
Scholastic Press, 1999

ISBN
0590189239

TC Level
10; 11; 12

passing whatever they've been learning. The reader of this book would be full of such facts.

Another mini-lesson might show children that if a person read this book and loved it, the logical thing to do would be to collect other texts on the same topic. Information from one text and then another cumulates; some of the information overlaps and some of it may be contradictory. Depending on the students and the grade level, the teacher would determine the length of time and frequency of discussion necessary to support comprehension. The ability to sustain a conversation on a topic will support comprehension as well.

This is a great book to engage students in conversation about civil rights, life in southern states in the 1950s-1960s, and how one person, a child, was affected. This text could support a number of units of study in the social studies curriculum. It could also be used in an interpretation unit of study in grades four and above. The setting (place and time) plays a major role in the way the events in the story unfold and is crucial to deep comprehension. Students can do further research about the time period and use it to support an interpretation. This could lead to developing an awareness of social action.

It is recommended that this text be included in the independent reading library in grades three and up. It could be chosen for a variety of reasons and purposes that would be determined by the reader. The teacher can support the book choice process by giving an orientation to the text as part of a mini-lesson. The teacher could show the students how to negotiate the text as well.

Through My Eyes is an example of narrative nonfiction. Therefore some reinforcement of the story elements would help students make meaning of the text. This book also contains many nonfiction text features (captions, subtitles, sidebars, graphs, diagrams, etc.) that make this genre seem dense.

Many teachers who have used this book have helped make it more accessible by doing mini-lessons on "how to navigate one's way through nonfiction." Students can use Post-its or other indicators to mark the many sections where news articles or quotes appear, and then in pairs help each other insert this information into the main text.

As a touchstone text in a writing workshop, sections can be pulled out as examples of personal narrative. The voice is clear and the language is simple enough for all students to try.

Ruby Bridges is an important historical figure. In the class's collection of books about important people, *Through My Eyes* will help introduce one of the many little-known heroes worth learning about.

Book Connections

This book goes well with *Walking For Freedom: The Montgomery Bus Boycott* edited by Richard Kelso.

Genre

Memoir; Picture Book; Chapter Book; Biography

A Field Guide to the Classroom Library, Lucy Calkins and the Teachers College Reading and Writing Project, Heinemann, ©2002 Teachers College, Columbia University; http://www.heinemann.com/fieldguides

Teaching Uses
Book Clubs; Read Aloud; Partnerships

Tulip Sees America

Cynthia Rylant

Book Summary

Tulip Sees America tells the story of a young man's journey across the United States. The young man has not yet explored outside of Ohio. When is he grown up, he gets a car, packs his belongings, takes his dog, Tulip, and drives west to make a home for himself in Oregon. The story begins by explaining how the young man's mother and father enjoyed being home in Ohio. The young man knows he is different from them and wants to explore the country. The story describes the scenery throughout Iowa, Nebraska, Wyoming, Colorado, Nevada, and Oregon. The story ends, "And this is where we stayed." with the young man painting a portrait of Tulip in Oregon by the ocean on the beach.

Basic Book Information

Cynthia Rylant has written more than sixty books for children. She has been honored with the Newbery Medal and the Boston Globe-Horn Award. Other picture books she has written include *Appalachia, When the Relatives Came, All I See,* and *Bookshop Dog.* Some of the chapter books she has written are *Missing May, A Fine White Dust,* and *The Islander.* Cynthia Rylant drove with her son and two dogs from Ohio to make a home in Oregon. This was the first time they had ever seen the places they drove through and their wonderful trip was inspiration for the book. Cynthia Rylant lives in a green cottage in Oregon with her son and many pets.

Lisa Desimini is known for her innovative style. She has created artwork for seventeen books and many book jackets. For this book, Desimini created layered oil paintings and scanned them in a computer where they were completed. Her last book for The Blue Sky Press, Arnold Adoff's *Love Letters,* received great reviews in School Library Journal and Booklist. Lisa Desimini lives in New York City.

This picture book is thirty pages. Each place visited is described over four pages. The story is told in the first person narrative from the young man's point of view. The illustrations are brightly colored and truly bring meaning to the text with great attention to detail.

Noteworthy Features

This book provides students with a beautiful example of one person's experience and how it inspired her to write, using descriptive language, and based on her observations. The curved print of the sentences on some of the pages creates movement. The multicolored print is shown in the bright illustrations. This book celebrates the uniqueness of each state visited with

Illustrator
Lisa Desimini

Publisher
The Blue Sky Press, 1998

ISBN
0590847449

TC Level
5

A Field Guide to the Classroom Library, Lucy Calkins and the Teachers College Reading and Writing Project, Heinemann, ©2002 Teachers College, Columbia University; http://www.heinemann.com/fieldguides

detailed descriptions of the particular differences. For example, "There is no ocean like Oregon's." displays that each coastline is special. It also shares the brave and courageous journey of a young man leaving home and taking in his surroundings. Cynthia Rylant lives with and loves her many pets. Pets are characters in many of her books. Cynthia Rylant dedicates the book to Leia and Martha Jane "for being such good dogs on our trip."

Teaching Ideas

The book provides many opportunities for reader response and can be used as a touchstone text. The book starts out with a young man about to embark on a journey. In comparison to his parents who are "homebodies" he says, "But when I grew up, I knew I was different. I wanted to see America." Students can talk about what they know about the character and how they know it based on his actions, feelings, words, and thoughts. The students can begin to predict by asking questions before, during, and after based on the title, author, illustrator, blurb, and reviews. What does he do? What does he see?

This book provides an excellent example of setting. It is also a great example of the genre of memoir and a linear story. Throughout the book, the young man describes what he sees. The descriptions are not told in complete sentences in some of the scenes. Students can discuss why a writer may use poetic language, a significant word, or list of words that can stand alone (for example, "The farms in Iowa. They are pictures: white houses. Red roofs."). A teacher can explain how a writer can use punctuation to make it easier for a reader to understand these lists.

This is a great mentor text to use when writing personal narrative. The story describes the young man's journey in sequential order. It could be used to show how a story is written in order with a connecting theme. Repetition is used in a simple and purposeful way. Students could use the style and structure of the writing in their own writing to connect the text to a central theme and for emphasis.

This book would serve as a good example for students struggling with endless stories and stories with heaps of extraneous details. *Tulip Sees America* has a definite time frame, and a simple way of showing movement through time-the passage from one state to another. There is a short amount of very specific information about each part of the author's journey. The text is balanced.

Book Connections

In *All I See* by Cynthia Rylant a boy is inspired by an artist's observations of his surroundings. In *When the Relatives Came* by Cynthia Rylant, the people travel by car to visit family. In *The Islander* by Cynthia Rylant, the ocean is an integral and significant piece of the story.

Genre
Picture Book

Teaching Uses
Author Study; Character Study; Teaching Writing; Language Conventions

Verdi

Janell Cannon

Book Summary

Verdi the snake is yellow and energetic. The older snakes he sees that have already turned green, just lie around and look at things. Verdi thinks they are boring and slithers off into the jungle to catapult himself into the sky using elastic vines. One day he realizes he has a green streak on his back! He tries to scrub it off and in the process almost gets eaten by a fish. Then he coats himself with brown mud to keep the green away, but the mud dries and flakes off. Full of zest and anxiety about turning old and green, Verdi shoots himself higher into the sky than ever before. He lands on a hard log and injures himself so much that he can't move. The old green snakes bind him to a log to mend, and he hears stories of their wild adventures when they were young. When he is healed he finds himself happy to rest and watch the world while his green skin provides natural camouflage. Some little yellow snakes turn away from him in disgust, but he surprises them by offering to play figure eight games. After all, he may be green but he is still himself.

Basic Book Information

This large-format picture book is striking in its clean, bold illustrations.

Noteworthy Features

The surreal and realistic illustrations in this book, with their bold and bright colors, usually attract readers. Children who liked *Stellaluna*, by the same author, have yet another reason to pick it up. The book usually needs no introduction or list of selling points to keep it in circulation.

The vocabulary in this book does not baby the readers. Words at the frequency and complexity level of "ventured," "dawdled," and "cruising" are sprinkled throughout. In most cases, the tougher words have enough context and easier text between them that they don't leave holes in the story. Kids can either figure out roughly what they mean or leave the words behind without a problem.

Early in the story, several new characters are introduced all at once. Suddenly, a conversation is going on between four snakes, three of whom the reader has never met before. It will be the unusual reader who doesn't stumble a bit here, mentally or literally, in keeping the snakes straight. Actually, for the sake of the story, it is not at all necessary that the reader keep the snakes straight from each other. They are all adults, and they all share a common attitude toward Verdi and a common lifestyle preference in their later years that is different from Verdi's. That is the key thing to know, and ponderously trying to separate the individual adult snakes really doesn't add much depth or meaning to the story. Readers who do get bogged down

Illustrator
Janell Cannon

Publisher
Harcourt, Brace & Company, 1997

ISBN
0152010289

TC Level
9

in tracing the characters might ask themselves why the writer is letting them get bogged down. Some will decide that the writer made the differentiation of the adult snakes less than easy because that is the way that Verdi sees them, lumped together as one kind of adult-unadventurous and boring.

Teaching Ideas

Verdi is often a good choice for children who are working on interpretations. While the book's interpretations aren't necessarily spelled out one hundred percent, they aren't buried so deeply within the text that kids get frustrated before they get ideas. It is also true that one of the most obvious themes, that you are yourself no matter what you look like, is the kind of message that comes up again and again in literature so that children who have been interpreting books for a long time may hone right in on it. Because it is the kind of message that comes up again and again, it is helpful to make sure children understand. This message can join their list of possible interpretations to look for in books, and may make the job of interpreting the next book easier.

Of course, as always, there are many other interpretations possible in this story. Children may decide that the most powerful message of the book is that you can't stay the same all the time, that everybody changes and no one can stop that. Some children think that the main idea is that people always act the way they do for a reason, and you can't judge them because you've never been in their position. Some say the message is that we are all more similar than we know, and if we take the time to go deeper into what people are and what we are, we will find we aren't as different as we think. The real reading skill development comes in building a case for any one of these or other interpretations. That is where children strengthen their grasp of both the whole of the story and all its parts; that is where they weigh incidents and conversations in the story and decide how much weight and interpretation they deserve. Those are reading skills, indeed, life skills, that can serve us all long and well.

Book Connections

Janell Cannon is also the author of the well-loved book about the bat, *Stellaluna*.

Genre
Picture Book

Teaching Uses
Independent Reading; Read Aloud; Interpretation

A Field Guide to the Classroom Library, Lucy Calkins and the Teachers College Reading and Writing Project, Heinemann, ©2002 Teachers College, Columbia University; http://www.heinemann.com/fieldguides

Waiting to Sing

Howard Kaplan

Book Summary

Waiting to Sing has the feel of a memoir. The narrator tells of the importance piano music has always had in his life, and even of the importance of the piano itself. As a boy he watched his father play and sing while his mother and their friends would laugh and enjoy the music. His sister would play and he too would put his hands over his father's and learn to navigate the keys. Then, his mother passes away, and the piano is silent for many months while the family grieves. Then, one day, his father began to play his mother's favorite piece, Beethoven's "Fur Elise." The boy began to practice again, and when he finally has his recital, there is an empty seat between his father and his sister.

Basic Book Information

This is a picture book with text. There are illustrations on every page.

Noteworthy Features

The first sentence of the book, though it contains a lovely image, is a bit awkwardly constructed, with a bit too much information in it to easily digest. Readers who choose books by reading the first sentence may put this one down as its first sentence requires two readings to make sense. The rest of the story is smoother to read, so kids might need to be encouraged to read beyond the first page before they decide whether or not to read it.

Teaching Ideas

As a memoir, *Waiting to Sing* has many qualities that children may find helpful to model in their own memoir writing. For older children, the book is an illustration of looking at a part of one's life from a specific perspective. For example, the book is not just about the death of the boy's mother, it is about the death of the boy's mother told through the angle of the piano music in the boy's life. This can serve as a model for children choosing their own lens through which to relive particular large or important memories or themes from their own lives.

A teacher might make sure that this book is not weighed too heavily as an example, because many children believe that their memoirs have to be focused on an important event in their lives, such as the death of a parent. Since not every budding writer has experienced something like this, and since the biggest topic does not always make for the best writing, the example presented in this book can overshadow their own possibilities or put them out of their mind.

Within the text too, of course, there are aspects of the writing that can

Illustrator
Herve Blondon

Publisher
Dorling Kindersley, Inc., 2000

ISBN
0789426153

TC Level
9

inspire and instruct young writers. When working with children using writing notebooks, many teachers help children with a phase of writing that involves collecting more information around a topic. The writer of this book has apparently done this, and it shows. Teachers can use parts of the text as examples of this phase. The writer was thinking of the significance of the piano in his life, so the piano was connected to his every thought and every action. In his mind or at least in his writing, even sorting the laundry was connected to playing the piano because of the lights and darks!

Some of the phrases in the book may inspire playful, metaphoric language in children's writing. The book is full of phrases like "[The music] covered me gently, like the whisper of an August blanket," or "In her flowery dress she looked like summer," or "The notes looked like a thousand birds had landed in front of us." Reading some of these aloud with particular attention and reverence can inspire children to try their own kinds of figurative language. Even if children don't take these bits of language as examples and inspiration to try their own hand at it, they will probably learn to relish and savor them as many experienced readers do.

Older writers might appreciate this writer's way of using metaphors from his own memories to depict what is happening in the story. In this memoir, the boy remembers a trip to the beach that he took with his mother. While there, he dug for clams. If the clams were small enough to pass through a ring they had to be thrown back. Later, he writes that his mother passed through the ring of the world. This kind of self-made metaphor is easy to understand and interesting for writers to try.

Readers who are not reading the book from a writing perspective will most likely focus on other aspects of the book. Some may wonder at how little good is said about the boy's mother. They may notice that all the references to his mother before she dies are of her correcting him or fixing his hair. She isn't the one who kisses him goodnight or plays piano with him. These readers may wonder whether the narrator was very close to his mother, or if he doesn't remember her very well.

Genre
Memoir; Picture Book

Teaching Uses
Teaching Writing; Independent Reading

Walk Two Moons

Sharon Creech

Book Summary

In this story within a story, Salamanca Tree Hiddle travels west with her warm and perhaps dotty (half-witted) grandparents and relates the mysterious story of her classmate Phoebe Winterbottom and Phoebe's missing mother. In between installments of Phoebe's story, Sal (as she is called) considers the circumstances surrounding her own mother's disappearance from their home in Kentucky. With humor, bravery, and honesty, Sal confronts difficult truths about family and growing up.

Basic Book Information

The book begins with a quotation, "Don't judge a man until you've walked two moons in his moccasins." *Walk Two Moons* is winner of the 1997 Heartland Award for Excellence in Young Adult Literature, winner of the 1995 Newbery Medal, 1995 ALA Notable Children's Book, School Library Journal Best Book of 1994, winner of a 1994 Bulletin Blue Ribbon, and A Notable Children's Trade Book in the Language Arts (NCTE). Though not the focus of *Walk Two Moons*, American Indian themes are raised in the novel to describe Salamanca Tree Hiddle's ancestry.

The first-person narration depicts a girl who is extremely thoughtful, objective, literary, funny, and warm. While she sounds older than thirteen in many ways, her experience of the more typical parts of adolescence (a crush and a kiss) sound genuine. Settings switch between rural Kentucky and suburban Ohio, with scenes from the drive west. *Walk Two Moons* shares locations and characters with those of other stories by Sharon Creech (including *Absolutely Normal Chaos*), but each book stands alone.

Noteworthy Features

Walk Two Moons presents complex themes, rich characters, and an eventful plot in an understandable package. There are over fifteen important characters and frequent changes in time and location, but the narration prepares readers for these transitions. Readers' ability to handle the shifts will, of course, vary.

Walk Two Moons is true to the adolescent experiences of students. Boys and girls squirm in their seats as the teacher, Mr. Birkway, reads private journal entries out loud to the class. Interest in the opposite sex starts budding and classmates start dating. Sal and Phoebe's imaginations go wild as they fear a lunatic stalker is chasing them, and they concoct visions of Mrs. Cadaver axing her husband to pieces. Some students will connect with this book on many of the complicated, confusing, exciting, and fearful levels of adolescence.

The significance of the initial quote carries through the novel in many of

A Field Guide to the Classroom Library, Lucy Calkins and the Teachers College Reading and Writing Project, Heinemann, ©2002 Teachers College, Columbia University; http://www.heinemann.com/fieldguides

Publisher
Harper Collins, 1994

ISBN
0590674099

TC Level
13

the characters' misunderstood lives. Subsequent quotes/notes mysteriously appear on Phoebe's doorstep one after another: "Everyone has his own agenda."; "In the course of a lifetime, what does it matter?"; "You can't keep the birds of sadness from flying over your head, but you can keep them from nesting in your hair."

Like the characters in the story, students may not be able to discern the quotes' significance until the end of the book. The quotes are part of Sal's changing emotional states throughout the novel; they are part of her emotional and mental development as an adolescent girl full of confusion and anger over why her mother would choose to leave home, and forget all about Sal and Sal's loving father. It is only when Sal discovers and comes to terms with the reality of her mother's death that she truly comprehends each quote's significance and can mirror herself in them. Readers undergo these revelations along with Sal.

In the first chapter, the speaker (Sal) establishes not only a theme of the book, but the book's structure: "The reason that Phoebe's story reminds me of that plaster wall and the hidden fireplace is that beneath Phoebe's story was another one. Mine." *Many* stories lie hidden behind Phoebe's: Phoebe's mother's, Sal's, Sal's mother's, Mrs. Cadaver's (a neighbor), the grandparents', Sal's father's, and Sal's friend Ben's.

A wide range of topics will help to attract a variety of readers. Some of the topics are light; Sal kisses a boy for the first time and deals with a demanding but interesting English teacher. Phoebe's mother's disappearance is treated as a mystery, with strange written clues dropped on the doorstep. A neighbor with unruly hair may or may not be a murderer. Some characters like Phoebe's sister Prudence and Sal's grandparents, add humor. Then there are some very serious and more adult topics, such as a mother's wishes for something beyond her family, and the deaths of a newborn, a mother, and a grandparent.

Teaching Ideas

Readers can use the opening metaphor of the fireplace hidden behind the wall to discuss how Creech "hides" one story behind another. How many stories can they find? Does *every* character turn out to have a story? What does this say about real life? By doing this, students can learn to take metaphors from stories and use them to help understand the stories they come from.

Readers may want to discuss how Sal's and Phoebe's stories parallel each other. Both of the girls' mothers left them, and neither girl understands why. Does Sal learn more about her own mother by telling Phoebe's story? As readers do this, they will be learning to study how characters in a book interrelate. They will need to learn tools to help them with this study-perhaps a notebook divided into three columns would help. Students can fill one column with details about one character, the next column for related details about another character, and the third column with thoughts about how the two relate.

As students re-read the book, they can go on a metaphor and symbol hunt. Sal uses metaphors and similes constantly: Megan and Christy jump up and down "like parched peas"; Sal's friend's hair is "yellow as a crow's foot." Certain recurring metaphors are tied to themes. Sal's "fishing in the air" shows both that she seeks the impossible and that she is imaginative. A blackberry image repeats, as does a line about the grandparents' marriage bed. Readers can see where these images crop up, and discuss what their significance might be.

This touching novel is sure to evoke heartfelt responses from all children. *Walk Two Moons* will particularly grasp children who have experienced the anger, pain, and hurt of losing someone close to them. Students living in single-parent homes, or whose parents are divorced or separated will also profoundly understand Sal and Phoebe. For these particular children, the book can serve as a springboard that allows them to articulate their emotions with empathetic classmates. In the process, such students can begin to heal.

A number of important minilessons may be implemented throughout the book. Students should note how the main character Sal changes throughout the book and mark evidence to refer back to. Reading partners can discuss Sal's changing emotional maturity throughout the book, and even plot their views of Sal's maturity. Along with this idea, students can stick post-it notes on pages where new quotes are introduced. As mentioned earlier, students will not fully understand these quotes until the conclusion of the book. They can then flip back to the quotes, and write text-to-text, text-to-self, and text-to-world connections about each one. Characters' understandings of the "Don't judge a man until you've walked two moons in his moccasins" quote occurs predominantly in the last chapter when Gramps and Sal take turns pretending they are walking in someone else's moccasins. Gramps says, "If I were walking in Peeby's moccasins, I would be jealous of a new brother dropping out of the sky." Sal responds, "If I were in Gram's moccasins right this minute, I would want to cool my feet in that river over there," to which Gramps adds, "If I were walking in Ben's moccasins, I would miss Salamanca Hiddle."

Similarly, much of Sal's understanding and acceptance of reality occurs toward the end of the book. Students could mark evidence of her coming to terms with her mother's death.: "We walk in everybody's moccasins, and we have discovered some interesting things that way. One day I realized that our whole trip to Lewiston had been a gift from Gram and Gramps to me. They were giving me a chance to walk in my mother's moccasins-to see what she had seen and feel what she might have felt on her last trip."

Sal understands, accepts, and empathizes with her father when she says, "I also realized that there were good reasons why my father didn't take me to Idaho when he got news of her death. He was too grief-stricken, and he was trying to spare me. Only later did he understand that I had to go and see for myself."

Likewise, students can discuss point of view in terms of emotional maturity. An example is when Sal says, "If I were walking in Phoebe's moccasins, I would have to believe in a lunatic and an axe-wielding Mrs. Cadaver to explain my mother's disappearance," as she reflects upon Phoebe and her then-unknown brother. Moreover, the dense layers of the text can be peeled back when Sal remarks, "Phoebe's tales were like my fishing in the air: for a while I needed to believe that my mother was not dead and that she would come back."

A Field Guide to the Classroom Library, Lucy Calkins and the Teachers College Reading and Writing Project, Heinemann, ©2002 Teachers College, Columbia University; http://www.heinemann.com/fieldguides

Book Connections

Sharon Creech's books tend to explore common themes of adolescent growth and emotional maturity, so reading *Walk Two Moons* and another one of Creech's novels can provide nice comparisons. For example, the characters Sal and Dinnie in *Walk Two Moons* and *Bloomability* respectively, face similar life issues of being uprooted, dealing with new environments, and facing hardships in their lives. Creech is also the author of *Absolutely Normal Chaos*, a companion novel to *Walk Two Moons* .

Genre
Chapter Book

Teaching Uses
Partnerships; Language Conventions; Character Study

What Jamie Saw

Carolyn Coman

Book Summary

This book poignantly chronicles the aftermath of abuse. Jamie, his mother Patty, and baby Nin move to a tiny trailer in the hills after Patty's boyfriend Van throws the baby across the room. Jamie and his mother are scared, hiding in the hills, living in fear of Van. Jamie's mother takes him to the Grovetown Christmas Carnival and Fair where he eats and drinks and races from game to game. But just before they go to leave, his mother grabs him and yanks him to the side of the duck-shooting stand. "At first he couldn't find anything at all, but then he did see: Van-his back, walking along the bleachers. . . . They watched him like a scary movie as he walked...to where they'd just been, and then watched as he turned and looked back in their direction. . . . It wasn't Van."

Then while Jamie's mother is out, Van comes to the trailer to wait for her: "He was there-where he didn't belong-but he was just there." When she gets there, "she burst inside, wild. Just the sight of her, her enraged and terrified face, so terribly, totally there, scared Jamie. . . . " Finally she tells Van not to come around, and after he leaves, Jamie cries. "His crying was way beyond being a baby and way beyond being dangerous-the only two things he'd known about crying up until that moment." And his mother comforts him. Then they know that everything is going to be okay.

Basic Book Information

This Newbery Honor book is 126 pages. It is divided into 10 chapters, which are numbered. There are no illustrations in the book; however the vivid, descriptive language designs pictures in the reader's mind. Coman draws readers in and surrounds them with beautiful prose that describes feelings and ideas. *What Jamie Saw* was also a National Book Award Finalist.

Noteworthy Features

Coman creates an unforgettable story about the aftermath of abuse. Jamie and his mother are scared, every day. They try to shut it out, Jamie stays home from school, and his mother stays home from work, hibernating in their cocoon to avoid the fear but it doesn't last. "Oh God, Jamie, we're afraid-just sick with fear. And it's so settled inside us that we don't even know what living feels like without it. That must be the thing about fear, the trick of it-you forget that that's what it is because it just starts to feel like your life. We're afraid, Jamie."

The language in this text is like poetry, weaving in and out around the plot, tangibles becoming intangibles and vice versa for Jamie and his mother. The reader starts to feel and understand the fear, internalizing, like Jamie tries to, the reactions and confusions of what he is going through.

A Field Guide to the Classroom Library, Lucy Calkins and the Teachers College Reading and Writing Project, Heinemann, ©2002 Teachers College, Columbia University; http://www.heinemann.com/fieldguides

Publisher
Front Street, 1995

ISBN
1886910022

TC Level
13

265

When Jamie breaks down and lets it all out the reader sighs with relief, and when his mother clings to her son the reader can feel the pain she is feeling, the hope that her son will be okay, not just on the outside but inside as well.

Teaching Ideas

Readers will need to talk with someone about the content of the book. If the book is used as a read aloud, the whole class can talk together. Otherwise, students could talk in partnerships or book clubs. This is not the kind of book that a reader can put down and turn off-the ideas need to be processed, and the images shared and talked over. This may even be a book that prompts readers to take social action. Teachers can be there to support this response.

After children have had time to process this book, it could be a good model for teaching descriptive writing. Students could mark places in the text where the description creates a clear picture in the reader's mind. They could then discuss which words help to draw readers in so that they own and understand the text. When Jamie first sees the trailer that he and his mother and sister will be living in he says that it "made him think of a big silver toaster." When they are inside of the trailer for the first time he says, "No matter where he stood in the trailer, he was always near somebody else-his mother, or Nin, or Earl." Does Jamie like the trailer? Does it make him feel safe? Which description tells us this?

Jamie and his mother grow very close. At many points, they "read" each other's body language. How does the reader know this? Is it dialogue that shows their closeness most or something else? What kinds of language are the most powerful in this story? When Jamie gets sick after the carnival and his mother comes to him, it is "the sound of her voice that he heard more than the words-it was her real voice." Also, there are many places in the book where actions speak louder than words. While reading, students can mark sections (with Post-it Notes) that speak to these questions, and then share their discoveries.

Metaphor would also be a good discussion topic. Every word, fragment, or group of sentences brings to the reader characters that can almost be touched. When Jamie is describing Van after he throws Nin, he says of Van, "Everything about him was hanging: his shoulders hung and his arms hung from his shoulders, and his big hands hung off his arms. Hanging, drained. A big, dumb, drained bathtub." Through this metaphor, of Van being a bathtub-drained, now useless and dumb-we can see that Van himself is indeed feeling drained, tired, and useless.

Another focal point for studying *What Jamie Saw* could be the role of magic. Each student could mark (with Post-it Notes) the sections of the book where magic is referred to (or is taking place). After a chance to share their results in pairs, students could talk through their questions and ideas based on this set of information about the text, making reference to the pages they have marked.

Genre
Chapter Book

A Field Guide to the Classroom Library, Lucy Calkins and the Teachers College Reading and Writing Project, Heinemann, ©2002 Teachers College, Columbia University; http://www.heinemann.com/fieldguides

Teaching Uses
Independent Reading; Teaching Writing; Language Conventions

A Field Guide to the Classroom Library, Lucy Calkins and the Teachers College Reading and Writing Project, Heinemann, ©2002 Teachers College, Columbia University; http://www.heinemann.com/fieldguides

Where was Patrick Henry on the 29th of May?

Jean Fritz

Book Summary

This slim book offers a biography of Patrick Henry, whose speeches and famous words, "Give me liberty or give me death," rallied the early American colonists to rise up against British rule. The bulk of the book is devoted to Patrick Henry's childhood and his early career, neither of which promised that he'd go down in the ranks of history as a great leader. Instead of portraying a gradual evolution from Patrick Henry's carefree and lighthearted childhood (where he did not have any obvious talents) to a committed man with a passionate voice, it instead shows a sudden transformation. In the midst of one law case, Patrick Henry suddenly and almost magically transforms himself from a bungling, awkward speaker to a powerful orator.

Basic Book Information

Where was Patrick Henry on the 29th of May? is one of a series of historic biographies written by the award-winning author Jean Fritz. She has received the Regina Medal by the Catholic Library Association, the Laura Ingalls Wilder Award by the American Library Association, and the Knickerbocker Award for Juvenile Literature. Along with this biography of Patrick Henry, she has similar books about Paul Revere, George Washington, Abraham Lincoln and others including *The Double Life of Pocahontas,* an 85-page, five chapter book which does not have the picture support of *Where was Patrick Henry on the 29th of May?*. Jean Fritz is also the author of a very special memoir, *Homesick.*

Where was Patrick Henry on the 29th of May? is a small, 47-page book containing no chapters, table of contents, or index. Jean Fritz includes a few notes at the end of the book pointing readers toward additional information.

Noteworthy Features

The biography is told chronologically, beginning on May 29, 1736 when Patrick Henry was born. The date, May 29th, resurfaces periodically throughout the book, subtly dividing the continuing narrative into sections. On May 29, 1752 Patrick is sixteen (and this commences a section about his early struggles to find a career as a shopkeeper and a lawyer). On May 29, 1765 Patrick is now 29 and Fritz again asks the recurring question, "What was he doing?" On Friday, May 24, 1777, Patrick is 41 years old. Fritz links the story's end back to its start. As a child, Patrick heard the redbird call... as

A Field Guide to the Classroom Library, Lucy Calkins and the Teachers College Reading and Writing Project, Heinemann, ©2002 Teachers College, Columbia University; http://www.heinemann.com/fieldguides

Series
Jean Fritz's biography series

Illustrator
Margot Tomes

Publisher
Scholastic Inc., 1975

ISBN
059041206X

TC Level
11

a 41-year-old man, he was so busy that "if a nice spring day came along, he wouldn't even have heard a redbird call" (p. 39).

Although the book itself is brief and has illustrations, it is not as accessible to readers as one might think. Fritz writes in lively, varied sentences and fragments, which often require that the reader take in paragraphs, rather than sentences of thought, in order to comprehend the text. For example, "Patrick had other listening pleasures. The sound of rain on the roof was one. The long, low, lonesome far-away echo of his father's foxhorn. The bulging of the dogs on the trail. The sweet music of fiddles and flutes. (He taught himself to play the flute when he had to stay indoors with a broken collar bone.) The voice of his Uncle Langloo Winston when he made a speech. On Election Day, it was said, Langloo Winston would roll his rich words into a crowd until he had the hair standing up on people's heads" (pp. 10-11).

Fritz has written and spoken often about the process of trying to write lively prose that nevertheless has historical integrity. She is well known for the historically accurate and intriguing details and especially the numbers which add life to her text. For example, Patrick and his wife Sarah tried to be shopkeepers but "when they had only 26 customers in six months, they quit" (p. 20), and "When the courts were in session, every bed in the tavern would be taken. (It cost 75 cents a night for a bed with clean sheets.)" (p. 21)

Fritz is careful not to put words in her characters' mouths or heads. She will, however, say that "Come a nice spring day with redbirds calling, Patrick would be off to the nearest creek." Is it research or imagination that supplies the color of the bird? Where does she draw the lines between historical accuracy and historical fiction? Fritz is a master at this genre and students may want to study her decisions with care.

Teaching Ideas

Students will turn to this book to learn about early American history through the lens of one man's story, and they'll turn to it also to read historic biography written by someone who is considered an expert at the genre. The book is also an interesting and surprising story of one person's journey to greatness.

Readers who plan to use Post-It Notes or otherwise mark "cool things they're dying to talk about" will have a lot to notice and discuss. But how do we tell the forest from the trees, when we're marking all the trees? How do we focus on the book as a whole while talking about the individual pages? What is the significance of the each interesting detail (e.g., the hotel room costing 75 cents)? There are tiny details that do more than engage the reader. They speak to the broader themes in the book. Teachers may encourage readers to look at these details to see if they build a theme in some way. Or, they may ask specific questions like, what details does Fritz use to show the economy of the times? The educational system? The average family?

It can be helpful for young readers to learn that when reading all literature (and especially nonfiction), it is beneficial to read a cluster of related books and to think, talk, and write among those books. Readers may want to set this biography of Patrick Henry alongside others, and to think about it and Fritz's biographies of Paul Revere and George Washington or

A Field Guide to the Classroom Library, Lucy Calkins and the Teachers College Reading and Writing Project, Heinemann, ©2002 Teachers College, Columbia University; http://www.heinemann.com/fieldguides

to read other less literary biographies of these same people.

The rich complex sentences, full of subordinate clauses, make this book a good challenge for readers who are trying to read more difficult texts with fluency and phrasing. It is a good text for practicing reading aloud to one other.

Book Connections

Where was Patrick Henry on the 29th of May? is one of a series of historic biographies written by the award-winning author Jean Fritz.

Genre

Biography; Nonfiction

Teaching Uses

Reading and Writing Nonfiction; Content Area Study; Independent Reading

Yolanda's Genius

Carol Fenner

Book Summary

Yolanda's family has moved from urban Chicago to suburban Michigan to be rid of violence and drugs. As Yolanda struggles to find friends, Andrew, Yolanda's baby brother, plays his harmonica and gets into trouble with the "Dudes," a gang that sells drugs to the suburban kids. Andrew's harmonica is his way of communicating with the world and after the Dudes break it he retreats into silence. Yolanda, who knows what a genius Andrew really is, defends his lack of progress in school and determines to show the world Andrew's genius. Through Yolanda's own genius, she gets her brother to meet and then play on stage with a famous blues artist at the Chicago Blues Festival. The family heads back to their new home in Michigan, Andrew set with a music teacher for geniuses, Mother with renewed hope for her children, and Yolanda with a sense of dignity and self-worth.

Basic Book Information

Yolanda's Genius won the Newbery Honor in 1997 as well as being selected as the ALA's Notable Children's Book of the year. It is a 208-page realistic fiction novel with eighteen chapters, which portrays urban and suburban life for adolescents with candor and sensitivity. There is plenty of street talk and some suggested profanity as one boy says, "Get off my effin' foot," to Yolanda. Fenner doesn't sugarcoat her characters or their language and behavior and this is just what makes this book so strong, but may be worrisome to some adults. The story is told in the third-person narrative, with Yolanda as the point of view. This helps to moderate any potential negative messages, as Yolanda is a strong character: bright, responsible, and motivated to protect her family from harm.

Noteworthy Features

Part of what makes this story so real is the true-to-life speech patterns used by the characters, and especially Yolanda's thoughts. However, for readers not familiar with city street talk this may be confusing, and some introduction to this language will be helpful. The strong character of Yolanda will be an aid to many readers. She is a bright student who gets straight As and is sometimes referred to as the Teacher's Pet. Her command of language is immense and she acts as interpreter for much of the vernacular used.

The story line is very involved, swirling from school to home, from Shirley (Yolanda's new friend), to Aunt Tiny from Chicago. Again, the strong character of Yolanda can mediate some of this difficulty. A character study of Yolanda would enhance a struggling reader's attachment to Yolanda, thereby helping the story to hold together better.

Publisher
Aladdin Paperbacks, 1997

ISBN
0689813279

TC Level
12

Teaching Ideas

This is a great read aloud for fifth and sixth grade classes. *Yolanda's Genius* brings many issues to the front, like drugs, self-esteem, racism, suburban prejudice, violence, and special education. Fenner does a great job bringing Yolanda to life, making it possible to consider and talk about real life issues.

Yolanda's Genius is a book full of issues and interwoven with many stories. It is the plot structure that can make it difficult for many readers. Upper grade teachers like to use this book as a read aloud in order to identify the plot structure and to teach some supportive strategies for handling it. A sixth grade teacher decided to use *Yolanda's Genius* as a read aloud because it had a similar plot structure to many of the advanced chapter books that her students were reading. The students were having difficulty staying on top of all the stories going on within the book. "*Yolanda's Genius* is our read aloud and I've chosen it to help us all know and deal with books that have complicated plots. *Yolanda's Genius* has a plot that is sort of like a big rug, it has many threads that go through the whole rug, sometimes mixing with the other threads. [Here she held up a colorful rag rug that the class used to sit on during independent reading time.] There is the story of Yolanda. She is the main character or protagonist of the story, and she narrates the story. The story is of a time in her life when she moved to a new town. Yolanda's story is in the present, but like all of us, she has lots of memories. These memories come back and get woven into the present story to help us understand Yolanda's overall story."

The teacher and the class went on to use this picture of the story lines to help define all that was going on in the book. They called this plot structure the "rug plot," using this to help them identify and understand similar plots in other books.

Genre
Chapter Book

Teaching Uses
Independent Reading; Read Aloud

Your Mother Was a Neanderthal

Jon Scieszka

Book Summary

Joe, Fred, and Sam, The Time Warp Trio, use a magical book to transport themselves through time. By simply turning to a particular page in *The Book,* they can visit that place. And as long as they bring *The Book* with them, they can travel back to their own time whenever they're ready.

On this afternoon, bored by their math homework, the trio decides to travel back to the time of cave people. *The Book* sends up a green mist which envelopes the group, and they begin their journey. When they arrive in 40,000 B.C., they discover that they are naked, and that *The Book* somehow didn't make it through the transport. After arranging some large leaves around themselves for pants, they must face the larger challenge of finding a way back to their own time. In their search for a way home, the trio faces many problems: a volcano, a strange clan of cave women which seems to be led by someone who looks just like Joe's mother, a stranger clan of cave men, a saber-toothed tiger, a wooly mammoth, and an earthquake. Eventually they find a way home in time to finish their math homework.

Basic Book Information

Your Mother Was a Neanderthal has 76 pages divided into 13 short chapters. There is no contents page; the chapters are numbered but not titled. A "pop quiz" appears at the end of the book.

Noteworthy Features

In *Your Mother Was a Neanderthal,* Sam, Joe, and Fred tease each other, and often answer with sarcastic remarks. Students will likely find this dialogue realistic and amusing. The "pop quiz" at the end of the book is in the same irreverent tone. Question 2 asks: Given a fulcrum, a long enough lever, and a place to stand, a person could theoretically move: a) the world, b) to Alaska, c) I don't know, d) I don't care, e) I can't tell you because I've just been run over by a wooly mammoth. The correct answers are provided and students should be urged to find the correct answer, but they will also enjoy reading the silly choices.

The chapters are interrelated and build on one another. Though a specific action takes place in each chapter, the chapters often end on a note of slight suspense or comedy, and urge the reader to go onto the following chapter to discover what happens next.

Fred and Joe call Sam "Brainpower" because he is smart and likes to see things in terms of math problems (word problems). Students can be encouraged to see how often math and critical thinking are called on to solve problems. Sam also introduces the readers to Archimedes, the Greek mathematician, and to the concept of the lever and fulcrum. Enough of an

Series
The Time Warp Trio

Illustrator
Lane Smith

Publisher
Scholastic, Inc., 1993

ISBN
0590981382

TC Level
10

explanation for who Archimedes was and how a fulcrum works is provided in the book so that students should be able to read on without feeling lost. An illustration of a fulcrum and lever is also provided.

For the most part, the illustrations add to the comedy of the book, but in some cases, such as the fulcrum and lever and the wooly mammoth, they do provide an image to aid in comprehension.

Though students might find the dialogue amusing, teachers should be aware that it is easy to confuse Joe, Sam, and Fred with one another. It is not always clear who is talking. The book is told in first person by Joe. He refers to himself as "I." Since his name is so rarely mentioned, students may have a little difficulty recognizing him when he is spoken of as "Joe" instead of "I."

The idea of *The Book* can also be somewhat confusing to readers. The story opens with the boys discovering that they have landed, naked, in some prehistoric time. They then begin to fret over the fact that *The Book* has apparently been lost. At this point, the readers will not know what *The Book* is. They may feel that they have missed something or that some information about *The Book* was provided in a previous *Time Warp* story. In fact, the second chapter goes back and explains how the boys got into their predicament and what *The Book* (though the explanation is still vague) is-a book that allows them to travel through time. Some students may need to be guided through the first two chapters so that they don't become confused. A satisfactory explanation for *The Book* is not provided until the final chapter, and students may find this lack of information distracting. They may want to know what this mysterious book is, and without giving away anything at the end (the fact that Joe's mother was the original owner of *The Book* and probably a time traveler), a teacher can explain that it is a magic book given to Joe by his uncle. If students are interested in reading the entire series of The Time Warp Trio, it might be a good idea to start with *Knights of the Kitchen Table,* as it explains how Joe was given *The Book.*

Teaching Ideas

This book can be read by the class as a whole, or individually. Since there is so much dialogue, students may enjoy taking the parts of Fred, Sam, or Joe and reading them aloud.

Your Mother Was a Neanderthal is part of *The Time Warp Trio* series; students can read the entire series or can choose to read just one book. If they choose to read the series, the format of the books will become familiar to the readers: the first chapter drops The Time Warp Trio somewhere in a time other than their own; the second chapter explains how they got there. Students reading the entire series will learn bits of information about *The Book* that students reading just one book won't. Nevertheless, each book can stand on its own.

The adventures of The Time Warp Trio while they are in 40,000 B.C. can be summed up rather simply: they land, naked; they are met by a clan of women, and so on. Students may want to retell and may even challenge themselves to do so chronologically.

Since the chapters are untitled, students might discuss with their partner or group an appropriate title after each chapter has been read. This will allow students to focus on the main idea of the chapter. The tone of the book can also be spoken about. It can be mentioned that the book is told in

A Field Guide to the Classroom Library, Lucy Calkins and the Teachers College Reading and Writing Project, Heinemann, ©2002 Teachers College, Columbia University; http://www.heinemann.com/fieldguides

a humorous tone as opposed to a serious tone. (The teacher may want to make a comparison with a book the class has read, perhaps an historical book, a biography, or some drama.) Students can be asked to recall other humorous books they have read. Once they have established an understanding of the tone, they can be asked to revise their chapter titles to reflect the humor.

Since it is sometimes difficult to distinguish the characters from each other, the readers may want to begin a character sketch of each of the boys. They can go back through the book and list as much information about each boy as possible. For example, Sam likes math problems; Fred seems to make the funniest remarks. Students in partnerships and book clubs can share information about the characters and build on their sketches together.

The cave men and cave women live apart from each other. The cave women are more advanced than the cave men. Students may want to discuss both issues, or teachers may want to point it out and ask children to critique these details.

Book Connections

The Time Warp Trio series includes: *Knights of the Kitchen Table; The Not So-Jolly Roger; The Good, the Bad, and the Goofy; 2095;* and *Tut, Tut.* Other connections outside of the series: *A Wrinkle in Time, The Time Machine.*

Genre
Short Chapter Book

Teaching Uses
Critique; Independent Reading; Book Clubs; Partnerships

Zlata's Diary

Zlata Filipovic (Translated by Christina Pribichevich-Zoric)

Book Summary

This book is the actual diary of an eleven-year-old girl-Zlata Filipovic-during the conflict in Sarajevo. It spans a period of two years until her family is allowed to leave Sarajevo for Paris. In her diary, she records the daily events in her life-both the typical concerns of a pre-teenager and the horrors of the war around her.

Basic Book Information

The 200-page diary is left in its original chronological order (eleven to thirteen-year-old Zlata). Sometimes Zlata writes every day; often she will skip an entire week.

Noteworthy Features

This remarkable first-hand account of the war is very poetic for a young girl. Her diary gives insight into the typical child's mindset in Sarajevo, before and during the war. However, because the writing was not originally intended for an audience, there are parts that may seem static and repetitive. There will also be references that we may not understand. Nevertheless, it is interesting and personal, and will be a good first step toward nonfiction for students who are reluctant to venture away from novels. Also, *Zlata's Diary* can reinforce the idea that our journals can constitute literature. It can serve as a mentor text encouraging students to be more thoughtful and descriptive in their own notebooks.

Teaching Ideas

Some teachers may decide to introduce this book by telling students about its author and form. Because the book contains many names of friends, family, and locations which will be unfamiliar to American students, teachers may also overview some of the most important of these. It might be important to allow readers to be free to focus on the heart of the story-Zlata's experience of war. Although Zlata herself writes that she is not fully aware of the global information about what is happening, students may benefit from at least an overview of the conflict in Bosnia so they can better understand the references Zlata makes. The list of characters at the beginning of the diary can serve as a reference to help readers recall the various people and relationships in Zlata's life.

Zlata's world turns upside down in a relatively short period of time. Students in partnerships or book clubs may mark events with Post-Its and discuss those that indicate Zlata's situation is worsening. Also, students may want to compare how Zlata lived prior to the acceleration of the conflict to

Publisher
Penguin Books, 1995

ISBN
0140242058

TC Level
13; 14; 15

her daily activities during the worst of the fighting. They may also want to embark on a character study: Does Zlata change in this time period? If so, how?

Students who are interested in this war may want to conduct more research using the school library.

Book Connections

Students who enjoy this book may wish to also read *The Diary of Anne Frank*, although it is a more difficult text.

Genre
Nonfiction; Chapter Book

Teaching Uses
Reading and Writing Nonfiction; Book Clubs; Content Area Study; Partnerships

A Field Guide to the Classroom Library, Lucy Calkins and the Teachers College Reading and Writing Project, Heinemann, ©2002 Teachers College, Columbia University; http://www.heinemann.com/fieldguides

Index